The Queen's Dumbshows

THE MIDDLE AGES SERIES

Ruth Mazo Karras, Series Editor
Edward Peters, Founding Editor

A complete list of books in the series
is available from the publisher.

The
Queen's Dumbshows

John Lydgate and the Making of Early Theater

Claire Sponsler

PENN

UNIVERSITY OF PENNSYLVANIA PRESS

PHILADELPHIA

Published by
University of Pennsylvania Press
Philadelphia, Pennsylvania 19104-4112
www.upenn.edu/pennpress

Printed in the United States of America on acid-free paper
10 9 8 7 6 5 4 3 2 1

Library of Congress Cataloging-in-Publication Data
Sponsler, Claire.
The queen's dumbshows : John Lydgate and the making
of early theater / Claire Sponsler. — 1st ed.
    p. cm. — (Middle Ages series)
Includes bibliographical references and index.
ISBN 978-0-8122-4595-0 (hardcover : alk. paper)
    1. Lydgate, John, 1370?–1451?—Criticism and
interpretation. 2. Theater—England—History—Medieval,
500–1500. 3. English drama—To 1500—History and
criticism. 4. English literature—Middle English, 1100–1500—
History and criticism. I. Title. II. Series: Middle Ages series.
PR2037.S73 2014
821'.2—dc23
                                        2013038739

CONTENTS

ABBREVIATIONS

CCMET   *Cambridge Companion to Medieval English Theatre*, ed. Beadle

CHMEL   *The Cambridge History of Medieval English Literature*, ed. Wallace

DTR   *Dramatic Texts and Records of Britain*, ed. Lancashire

EETS   Early English Text Society

e.s.   extra series

JMEMS   *Journal of Medieval and Early Modern Studies*

LALME   *A Linguistic Atlas of Late Mediaeval England*, ed. McIntosh et al.

MED   *Middle English Dictionary*

MPJL   *The Minor Poems of John Lydgate*, ed. MacCracken

OED   *Oxford English Dictionary*

o.s.   original series

PMLA   *Publications of the Modern Language Association*

PPC   *Proceedings and Ordinances of the Privy Council of England*, ed. Nicholas

PROME   *The Parliament Rolls of Medieval England*

REED   Records of Early English Drama

RP   *Rotuli Parliamentorum*

s.s.   supplementary series

Theater History as a Challenge to Literary History

The standard history of medieval English literature is one in which a queen's dumbshows would not readily find a place. That history enshrines a written (in verse) canon fashioned in the fifteenth century around the works of a group of (male) London writers who followed in Chaucer's footsteps. According to this account, the formation of that canon began with the inner circle of Chaucer's fellow civil servants and writers and was given a boost by the promotional efforts of England's Lancastrian rulers and London elites, who were interested (for not entirely identical reasons) in the establishment of English as a prestige language in the years after Chaucer's death. The works that resulted were disseminated through William Caxton's press and put to use by the Tudors for their program of nationalist propaganda, going on to shape the contours of early English literary history in the sixteenth and seventeenth centuries.[1]

In calling this book *The Queen's Dumbshows*, I aim to underscore the fact that durable though this history has proven, it tells only part of the story of literature and culture in the years before and around the invention of the printing press. As recent work has begun to show and as evidence from the period demonstrates, this literary history rests on a blinkered view of the generic, regional, and thematic scope of imaginative writings in Middle English. From within a modern classification scheme that defines the literary as written poetic texts, many Middle English texts look distinctly nonliterary: that is, they took the form of collaboratively produced performances, visual representations, or mixed-media productions, rather than single-authored poems. Additionally, because their audiences and, in some instances, authors included women or males who were not elite, they were not always noted by those with the power to record and transmit literary works; when they entered the written record, they often did so in a scattered and fragmentary fashion. Their circulation in provincial communities in northern and southeastern England also often put many texts in Middle English beyond the purview of scribes and book-sellers in the metropolis. Finally, since their themes were often religious rather than secular, many of these works, including a great deal of Lollard writings, did not mesh with postmedieval understandings of literariness and thus were excluded from the literary history of the period.[2]

Chief among the excluded texts are the dramatic performances that were part of the seasonal calendar of religious and governmental ritual, performances that included unscripted entertainments such as mimed and improvised dumbshows and mummings that were created and performed on the periphery of London-centric poetic literary production. Often anonymous, nearly always ephemeral, and typically collaborative, those performances— and especially play-texts related to them—have survived only haphazardly and in numbers that belie their popularity. We know of those performances chiefly through brief mentions in various kinds of public records, including chronicles, legislation against disturbances associated with them, and expenditure accounts by guilds and households. Those records offer tantalizing glimpses of a wider world of public and private ceremonies, plays, and dramatic enactments beyond that revealed in the handful of surviving scripts (such as those of the biblical cycle plays) or the few examples of morality and miracle plays (including the Croxton *Play of the Sacrament*, the Digby *Mary Magdalene*, and *Mankind*).

Acquiring access to that wider world while grappling with the theoretical and practical complexities posed by the spotty archive of medieval performances has motivated some of the best recent work in early theater studies. As a result of such archival projects as the Records of Early English Drama (REED), which was begun in the 1970s at the University of Toronto, scholars of early drama now have at their fingertips detailed information about performances that never took, or did not survive in, the form of a play-script. With help from REED and similar archival work in European countries, we can now balance the paucity of surviving scripts of plays with the abundance of records documenting public and private, indoor and outdoor, performances on a variety of occasions and for a range of audiences throughout the year. Even if most of those records (with the exception of records from England) are still unpublished, scholars increasingly turn to local and other archives for the traces of dramatic activity that can be found in legal documents, account books, chronicles, and other similar sources.[3] Thanks to such archival work, we know, for instance, that a confraternity in the Hanseatic town of Lübeck put on a carnival play that enacted a recent incendiary political event, the rout by Frisian farmers in February 1500 of a band of mercenaries hired by King Johan of Denmark to subdue the rebellious farmers.[4] No text of the Lübeck play exists today, but accounts kept by the confraternity record the performance. Similarly, we know that a passion play was performed at Chelles, outside Paris, in May 1395, not because a play-text survives but because a legal document was issued by King Charles IV three months later granting clemency to the assailant in a crime committed following the play.[5] If we were going strictly by texts of plays, we would never know about the existence of these and any number of other scriptless early performances.

Although painstaking archival recovery work over several decades has greatly expanded information about early performances, its implications for theater and literary studies have not yet been fully digested. As Carol Symes has noted, as evidence for actual performances, much of the written record for early drama is problematic: not all performances were recorded, those that were may not have hewed closely to written scripts, and some texts were made after (sometimes long after) the performances they commemorate.[6] The survival rate for texts of medieval plays is low, given their often ephemeral nature as prompt sheets or players' texts, even lower than for other medieval manuscripts. Moreover, it is not always certain that a surviving script for a play represents the record of an actual performance. At the same time, references to performances in legal records and other such documents do not always provide enough information to indicate what sort of performance is being described, much less what dialogue or action it included, how long it was, what its costuming and stage properties were, who created and performed it, who watched, and what those watching thought about it.[7]

The written record of medieval performances may pose difficulties of interpretation, but many theater scholars nonetheless recognize the need to wrestle with its evidentiary complexities and have begun to do just that. At a minimum, most historians of drama are now aware that surviving play-texts represent only a small portion of the rich performance cultures of late medieval England and Europe. Among literary scholars, however, that same written record of performances—beyond the handful of well-known play-texts such as the biblical cycle plays and a few famous noncycle dramas—remains for the most part unrecognized and unexplored. That situation is, in my view, unfortunate and works to the detriment of the discipline, whose field of inquiry is too narrowly corralled by the shutting out of the full range of evidence that might be drawn on to construct a genuinely representative textual history.

Hans-Robert Jauss famously offered literary history as a challenge to literary theory, and it is my claim in this book that theater history provides a similar provocation to literary history.[8] It does so, first and foremost, by calling attention to the large number of texts that have been excluded from the London-based, secular, and Chaucer-centered canon of medieval English literature that most modern readers almost exclusively associate with the literary activity of the period. As theater history shows, those texts represent only a slim segment of the corpus of imaginative writings in Middle English. Beyond them lie many other works that were widely heard and seen—in mimetic performances, viva voce recitations, processional tableaux, wall hangings, or on the page of manuscript books. Ralph Hanna III's assertion that within the "prenational literary culture" of late medieval England there were "plural literary canons," dependent on many variables, such as geography, gender, and political affiliation, has not received enough attention, but its accuracy is affirmed by the example of vernacular dramas.[9] In the variety of their venues, audience, and forms, performative works offer an important corrective to a view of medieval literature that has been shaped more by modern categories and preferences than by the tastes and expectations of those who actually created and encountered it.

While canon broadening is one salutary outcome of integrating drama into medieval literary history, attending to theater history also has conceptual and theoretical benefits, particularly in its call for a rethinking of the development of vernacular literature in England. Debates about vernacular culture and its contestation have made us aware of the effects of the rapid rise of vernacular literatures across medieval Europe, which brought with it new subject matters, new styles, and new genres, even as Latin continued as the touchstone language of the learned and, despite its qualified embrace of mother tongues as a means of reaching the laity, the church. Literary scholars have charted the uneven impacts of vernacularity across Europe and the corresponding erosion of Latin as a spoken and written language, demonstrating the ways it brought greater freedom of expression, reached broader audiences, and intersected with growing literacy.[10]

For England, such work has been essential in mapping the contours of medieval Anglophone literary history and especially in charting the increasing dominance of English poetry in the later medieval period. What theater history can add to the discussion is the recognition that English poetry's rise to prominence was less an inevitable outcome and more the result of successful competition between different cultural forms vying for position. That competition was between Latin and English but also, and perhaps more important, between poetry and drama. This point has been convincingly made by Seth Lerer in regard to Chaucer's antitheatricality, which Lerer argues is the necessary stance of a vernacular poet attempting to achieve for his writings the same prestige that accrued to theatrical and ceremonial culture in fourteenth-century England.[11] While focused just on Chaucer, Lerer's claim fits within other important discussions of English vernacular public culture by Anne Middleton and David Lawton, among others, which I consider more fully later in this book, particularly in terms of what such scholars say about the conflict between poetry and performance as forms of cultural prestige in late medieval England.[12]

At some level, the contest was between writing and speaking, a contest that theater history can be helpful in examining. That is because poetry and even other genres such as chronicles that at first glance would seem confined to the written page and to silent reading could be and were publicly performed. As scholars of textuality and orality have noted, reading and performing overlapped to a large degree. "Hearing the text aloud in a performance—even if the sole performer was the reader himself—was therefore the rule rather than the exception," and thus medieval writing "was understood to represent sounds needing hearing," Michael Clanchy observes.[13] Material philology's notion of *orature*, a recent coinage that links features of the oral tradition with literary forms, offers an opening for theater history and its analysis of precisely that intersection.[14] Active listening, the aurality of literature, and performative reading are topics to which theater history, with its concentration on live performance and mimetic action, can make valuable contributions, as scholars such as Joyce Coleman, Jessica Brantley, and Robert Clark and Pamela Sheingorn have shown.[15] In particular, the dramatic record makes clear that a poetic text could reach its publics by many routes, that it probably varied on each performance occasion, and that it could exist simultaneously in different media—as image, written text, mimetic enactment, and so on.

Another useful feature of theater history is that it also points to the important impact of religion and, in so doing, undermines the tendency to construct a medieval literary history composed almost exclusively of secular texts. In a study of the dispersion of stories about Mary Magdalene across diverse genres and media, Theresa Coletti uses the Digby *Mary Magdalene*, the extraordinary East Anglian play on the life of that saint, to argue for the importance of religious texts to medieval literary history.[16] A similar claim has been made by scholars of Lollardy, who have pointed to the proliferation of Middle English religious writings and the Lollard emphasis on lay literacy as formative features of late medieval literary culture.[17] In a broader sweep, Nicholas Watson's examination of vernacular theology and the church's long compromise with the mother tongue provides a backdrop for the aesthetic impact of religious writings on Middle English literature and makes a case for their inclusion in the literary canon.[18] Religious texts were written by women and, more frequently, read by them; expanding the literary canon to include those texts reshapes the standard male-centered literary history and more accurately recognizes what was being written and read, and by whom, in the late medieval period. Because many Middle English religious plays, such as the Digby *Mary Magdalene* and the biblical cycle plays, were performed outside London, they expand the canon geographically as well, by taking in regional literary and performance cultures, and thus better embrace the entirety of writings produced in late medieval England.[19]

In these and other ways, theater history can be a provocation to literary history, if we allow it to. Although disciplinary divisions too often erect barriers between those who study medieval literature and those who study drama, I believe that there is much to gain from stepping over those obstacles. Among other advantages, paying attention to the history of medieval drama constructively places emphasis on the overlap between the private reading of written texts and the public viewing of spectacles and performances. It also makes it harder to ignore the role of women and those who were not elite as patrons and audiences for literary works. And it urges the adoption of a methodological model of intertwined performance and textuality attuned to the persistent blurring of genres that characterizes so many of the cultural products of premodern England and Europe.

Last, theater history points to the advantages of a methodological approach to the study of medieval literature that embraces a material philology. As Stephen Nichols and Siegfried Wenzel observe, manuscripts "furnish material contexts" that can yield information about "the text's audience, its purpose, and even the intention an individual scribe may have had in producing" a particular copy.[20] While the materiality of the text has by no means been ignored by literary scholarship and is particularly evident in studies that engage with book history, scholars of medieval drama have embraced materiality more energetically and with potentially wider-ranging consequences. Coming as perhaps a logical next step after the last decades' turn to the archives and the search for traces of dramatic activity in account books, legal documents, and other records, inquiry has increasingly focused on the manuscript environments of early plays, as scholars have looked at the physical evidence provided by the codices into which dramatic texts were copied. For Middle English drama, this work has led to reassessments of the dates and performance histories of the extant play-texts and has shown under what circumstances the manuscripts in which they appear were created.[21] Examining the manuscript environments of early plays has also brought a heightened awareness of the complex relations between live performance and written script, including that audiences of dramatic enactments were also readers of play-texts and that literature gained an audience precisely through performances that brought it to the eyes and ears of readers.[22]

It would be possible to use any number of medieval dramatic works from across Europe to illustrate this challenge to literary history, including the great biblical cycle plays, saints' dramas, and miracle and conversion plays, but fifteenth-century England's best-known and most prolific writer offers a particularly apt example.

John Lydgate, remembered today for such magisterial narrative poems as the *Fall of Princes*, the *Troy Book*, and the *Siege of Thebes*, not only helped create the conventional history of English literature grounded in Chaucer but also has long claimed a privileged place within it. Lydgate praised Chaucer as a poetic master and deliberately shaped his own writing in imitation of Chaucerian texts, adopting Chaucerian themes and even imagining himself as a participant in the Canterbury pilgrimage. His voluminous writings, with their distinctively elaborate—and, to modern readers, often off-putting—and syntactically convoluted aureate style, earned Lydgate his status as the favorite writer of court, monastery, and city.

Less frequently noticed is that Lydgate was also the author of a wide range of dramatic entertainments that were no less influential in shaping theater history. The mummings and other performance pieces he wrote in a flush of activity in the late 1420s and early 1430s form possibly the most important body of dramatic work by a known author in English before the sixteenth century. Yet Lydgate is largely absent from accounts of early performance. He makes virtually no appearance in anthologies of medieval drama, much less in anthologies of major plays from the Greeks to the present. Histories of the theater ignore his dramatic works and, until recently, there have been no editions, no modern performances, and relatively few critical studies devoted to them.[23]

One reason for this neglect is that Lydgate's performance pieces do not look particularly dramatic, at least to modern eyes, and they cannot be readily classified as plays. Henry Noble MacCracken, for instance, printed a number of Lydgate's dramatic pieces but treated them as poetic works included in his two-volume edition of Lydgate's minor poems, not as plays. Lawrence Clopper speaks for many drama specialists when he judges Lydgate's mummings and disguisings to have been presentational rather than mimetic, and Seth Lerer similarly argues that Lydgate's poetic preference is for works that favor philosophical monologue and thus move away from "forensic, dramatic, and dialectical forms of expression." When subjected to scholarly analysis, Lydgate's performance pieces have typically been examined from the perspective of literary rather than theatrical history.[24] John Shirley, the fifteenth-century scribe who copied and preserved many of Lydgate's performance pieces, uses a variety of terms to describe them but never once calls them plays. The difficulty of nomenclature is echoed in modern criticism, which offers no term fully adequate for capturing the nature of the works in question.

The apparent lack of theatricality in Lydgate's dramatic works is compounded by the typical ways in which early drama was transmitted scribally. As was the case for music, a system of recording that could capture features of performance was slow to develop in medieval Europe, and plays did not always retain markers of performance, such as speech tags and stage directions, when they were copied into manuscripts.[25] This is especially the situation with texts associated with public spectacles and ceremonies, which were usually occasional and ephemeral in nature: they often entered the written record as eyewitness accounts or commemorative texts (for example, in chronicles), not in the form of play-texts.

It may be that the impulse to downplay the dramatic aspects of Lydgate's performance pieces and to merge them with his nondramatic poetry is correct. Yet doing so overlooks what their seeming insufficiencies reveal about our historical narratives for medieval English theater and, to return to my opening point, obscures how theater history encourages a rethinking of literary history. If early English literary history has been too narrowly constructed, early theater history has suffered the opposite fate of being unable to identify and corral the performances that form its corpus. A browser in any research library can readily find the standard texts of Middle English literature, tidily arranged side by side on a compact number of bookshelves, but locating medieval theatrical works calls for a more determined and inquisitive bush-whacking through the stacks.

The first attempts to describe a body of texts that could be identified as medieval plays began as early as the surviving manuscripts of what are taken as the quintessential examples of English medieval plays—the cycle plays in the York, Chester, Towneley, and N-Town manuscripts—manuscripts that for the most part are Tudor, not medieval, artifacts. Compiled for a variety of reasons, what is perhaps most remarkable about the cycle collections is that they survived the Reformation's dismantling of the traditional religious culture of which the cycles were a prominent example. While deliberate destruction took place, as Eamon Duffy and other scholars have shown, records and artifacts of medieval performances may also have fallen victim to neglect, carelessness, and changing tastes, as much as to ideological and political forces.[26] Well before Shakespeare's time, medieval performances were already disappearing or going underground, becoming faint memories of old practices. With demise came the impulse to categorize what in its heyday had been a rich variety of performances that shaded into other cultural forms, including music, dance, and poetry. Joseph Dodson's collection of *Old Plays* had an early and formative role in the classifying of pre-Shakespearean drama as a genre, and by the nineteenth century, scholars had identified bodies of premodern dramatic texts from all the European countries, as part of an attempt to construct national histories based on distinctive past folkloric practices; by that point, medieval drama scholarship had also been established as a specific disciplinary field.[27] The result of this disciplinary legacy is that medieval drama has long been subordinated to literary history, its texts usually deemed deficient, especially from the perspective of formalist criticism. Any attempt to examine Lydgate's performance pieces is inevitably haunted by those inherited assumptions about medieval drama.

The marginalization of medieval drama within English literary history is in many ways the result of a contest between literary and theatrical cultures during the fourteenth and fifteenth centuries, a contest that was won by the upstart genre of vernacular poetry. As Lerer has argued in regard to Chaucer's self-identification as a poet and as Robert Epstein has observed about aristocratic resistance to drama, Middle English literature was shaped in opposition to drama.[28] What Lerer and Epstein describe is competition between forms of cultural production, a battle that, thanks to the growing dominance of writing and printing, would be won by literature. Vernacular literature's ascendance in England did not come about easily or inevitably; it was instead produced by a struggle against the period's most popular cultural form, drama.

Chaucer may have defined himself against theatrical culture, even as he smuggled its features into his poetry, but Lydgate joined traditions of performance with an emerging literary culture.[29] His long poems and his short mummings and entertainments share a similar style and content and speak to the same concerns. They also address a similar audience, having been commissioned largely by elites from the overlapping spheres of city, court, and monastery. In Lydgate, the cultures of ceremony and writing meet. His willingness to produce works for both silent reading and public performance, his tendency to employ a common style for both, and his penchant for drawing on the same sources and themes in his literary and dramatic texts all point to a convergence between drama and literature not just in his writings but in late medieval culture more broadly. In so doing, it moves drama to a more central position in relation to English literary history, a position where, as Coletti has noted in a discussion of Middle English dramatic texts as a form of vernacular theological writing, drama's "material and discursive intersections with other late medieval cultural texts and practices" become evident.[30]

The chapters that follow explore the importance of Lydgate's dramas to literary and theater history alike. They do so by bringing Lydgate's performance poetry into dialogue with late medieval English literary culture, considering its intersections with vernacularity, the materiality of its textual production and consumption, and its competition with other cultural forms. They also consider what Lydgate's performance pieces reveal about early drama, particularly the forms they took, how they were commissioned and performed, and where and why they were recorded and preserved in written documents.

In pursuing such subjects, this book joins ongoing discussions of the relation between surviving evidence and live performances or, as theater historians would describe it, between the archive and the repertoire. Medieval performances themselves have vanished, leaving our only access to them the relatively few documentary and material remains of medieval dramatic culture that have survived (a handful of play-texts, a much larger body of references to performances, and the occasional account, material object, or visual image). To treat any of this evidence as a window onto early performances or to regard it as a straightforward and factual account of what actually was enacted would be to misunderstand both early performances and the archival traces through which they survive. Dominick LaCapra's admonition that we not fall for "archival fetishism" and instead remember that written documents are never neutral or unmotivated and, as a consequence, have to be read critically is particularly germane to considerations of the relation of documents to practices.[31] The archive is always political, in the broadest sense of that term, with its own agendas, strategies, and biases that shape what is recorded, how, and for which purposes.

Recent trends in theater history have highlighted the documentary practices through which dramatic texts have been preserved and disseminated, while also stressing the need to grapple with the cultural meanings of performances. In the case of Lydgate, such trends ask for a rethinking of what constitutes "drama" in late medieval England, what role it played in public life, and how it intersected with other cultural activity, including politics, commerce, religion, and literature. Drawing on a broad array of critical work on public culture, performance, and textuality, this book pursues a cultural history of early English theater that situates theatricality at the hub of public culture. The relationship between overtly public forms of political theater, such as royal entries and processions, and more private ones, such as household banquets and mummings, is one of my concerns. Another is the intersection of performance with other kinds of representation, such as feasts, pictorial displays, and tableaux. I also consider the neglected role of women within ceremonials, the social and ideological uses to which performances could be put, and, finally, what Lydgate can teach us about how early plays came to be preserved in manuscript form. The intersection of the primarily visual and aural modes of performance with the reading of literary texts written on paper or parchment forms another strain in my study.

Unlike the so-called Carthusian Miscellany, whose scribe(s) used a variety of visual tactics to create a performative context for its written texts, as Jessica Brantley has shown, the scribes and compilers who copied Lydgate's performance pieces seldom sought to preserve or invoke recollection of the original performative or ceremonial context, instead converting spectacle into poetry.[32] Their efforts were aided by the nature of Lydgate's texts, which were, as Maura Nolan has argued, consciously poetic; that is, one of Lydgate's goals was to elevate public spectacle and private ceremony into literary art. His performance pieces "exist at the intersection of genres and of media—not quite 'poetry' nor yet 'drama.' "[33] Those patrons who commissioned his works for performance were hiring him to do just that, to add new poetic scope to what had in many cases been performances shaped chiefly by gesture or visual appeal or aurality, but which now began to incorporate written texts of increasing length and elaborateness.

The scribal tendency to turn theatrical texts into literary ones has two implications. On one hand, it tells us something important about relations between performance and written text in the fifteenth century at a key moment in both literary and theatrical history, suggesting a relative valuation of the two (with poetry coming out on top). On the other hand, for scholars whose chief access to performances that were by nature fleeting is through written texts, it offers a cautionary reminder about the difficulties of identifying a play from its written artifacts. Both of these implications are woven through this book's examination of how drama and literature both fed and competed with each other, while spilling over into other visual and verbal arts of the period.

My decision to concentrate on one writer from late medieval England reflects my own perspective as a scholar who works primarily in the area of Middle English literature and culture, but the topics I take up in this book could be profitably explored through an examination of other medieval writers of plays—in some cases, earlier and non–English speaking—such as Hrotsvit of Gandersheim and Jean Bodel, about whom we know enough to situate their works within the cultural milieu in which they wrote and to understand how the plays they created were performed and entered the written record.[34]

Lydgate is particularly useful for this investigation, in which I aim to contribute broadly to knowledge about the literary and theatrical cultures of the medieval period and, more pointedly, to English literary and theatrical history. His particular appeal for my inquiry comes from the extraordinary fact—rarely encountered within the corpus of medieval literature or drama— that most of his shorter poems and performance pieces have been preserved by a scribe whose identity we know. Chapter 1 of this book, "Shirley's Hand," investigates the evidence offered by the surviving copies of Lydgate's dramatic works. Nearly all of Lydgate's performance pieces are available to us today thanks to John Shirley, who included them in three anthologies he compiled between the late 1420s and the late 1440s. Shirley's copies point to the complex processes that a visual and aural form like medieval drama underwent as it entered the written record and pose questions about the nature of the textual evidence for drama before print: what do manuscripts tell us about early performances; should the canon of early theater be expanded to include texts that do not look like plays but may have been part of some sort of public performance; and how did drama merge—both in practice and in the documents that record that practice—with the large repertoire of creative activities produced within a broadly performative culture?

Subsequent chapters explore the place, form, and functions of drama as evidenced by Lydgate's writings, taking up such topics as the cultural meanings of performances, the tendency toward genre and media blurring, the effect of visual display and spectacle, the relation of commemorative poems to the performances they record and the larger issue of performative reading, the ephemeral quality of performance texts, gender and drama, and the question of authorship and attribution of medieval plays. Chapter 2 examines the mummings Lydgate wrote for the entertainment of London guildsmen during their holiday revels, considering especially how in them Lydgate creates a kind of vernacular cosmopolitanism. Chapter 3 turns to the poems Lydgate wrote for visual display, poems that confront us with an insistent blurring of representational forms that leaves us wondering what difference, if any, it made that a story was read from a manuscript page, viewed on a wall hanging, or listened to in a performance. Chapter 4 focuses on a rare example of a Corpus Christi performance in London, while Chapter 5 examines the poem Lydgate was commissioned to write to commemorate Henry VI's royal entry into London on 21 February 1432. Chapter 6 explores the verses Lydgate wrote to accompany the subtleties for Henry VI's coronation banquet, and Chapter 7, from which this book takes its name, "The Queen's Dumbshows," looks at the three mummings Lydgate wrote in the 1420s for Catherine and her son, the child who would become Henry VI.

The final chapter turns to an anonymous Christmas mumming as a way of giving prominence to the issues of auspice, provenance, performance practice, inscription, and authorship that are fundamental to the study of medieval performances. There is no definitive evidence that Lydgate wrote this mumming and no definitive evidence that that is what it was. But to make the case for his authorship and for possible performance before Henry VI throws into relief key questions about the relationship of the archive to the repertoire of medieval dramas. How were dramatic texts transmitted? How did the material conditions of textual dissemination—the copying and circulation of texts in manuscript form—shape literary and theatrical history? What features of a text matter in deciding whether it should be called a play or a poem?

In taking up these and other questions, my study joins and expands on other recent reassessments of Lydgate's contributions to English literature.

Within the last decade, there has been a surge of interest in Lydgate, which has built on often strong but too often sparse earlier work on his poetry and career, such as the valuable studies by Lois Ebin, Alain Renoir, and, most thoroughly, Derek Pearsall.[35] Gathering momentum in a series of compelling articles by scholars of fourteenth- and fifteenth-century Middle English poetry, this renewed interest in Lydgate built to a 2005 monograph by Maura Nolan, a collection of essays edited by Larry Scanlon and James Simpson in 2006, a 2007 study by Robert Meyer-Lee assessing Lydgate's place in early English literature, and another collection edited by Lisa Cooper and Andrea Denny-Brown a year later.[36] Much of this new scholarship has been deliberately revisionist in nature and has had as its explicit and salutary goal the reassessment of the quality of Lydgate's writing as well as its significance.

The story I tell in the following chapters often develops from and meshes with the work of these revisionist scholars, but it also takes a somewhat different approach, coming to different conclusions. I share the perspective that runs through the essays in Scanlon and Simpson's collection, a perspective that takes a fresh look at Lydgate's writings with the aim of moving beyond the prevalent understanding of Lydgate as a derivative, aesthetically deficient, and thus insignificant writer despite the volume of his output. The insistence of the scholars in Scanlon and Simpson's collection on viewing Lydgate as a major writer who wrote "within and across different literary systems" and "from very different historical situations" informs my own understanding of his work.[37] Meyer-Lee offers a similar reassessment of Lydgate's aureate poetics and, by extension, the value of fifteenth-century poetry, insisting that to understand fifteenth-century poetry, we need to understand Lydgate's influence, a perspective I extend to fifteenth-century performance. I also share the emphasis found in Cooper and Denny-Brown's collection on the importance of connections between material culture and literary discourses; as they note in their introduction, Lydgate's own alertness to the material world has often played a role in his marginalization as a writer, and critical assessments of his work, even in recent years, have tended not to consider the place of materiality in his work, addressing instead "the politics and public sensibility of his poetics."[38] Finally, along with Nolan, I look most closely at Lydgate's public poetry, examining his engagement with ceremonial culture. Indebted though I am to many of its findings, where I differ from all of this scholarship is in stressing physical forms and their locations, as well actual impacts and effects on audiences and readers. Whereas Nolan, for example, focuses on the literary and the symbolic in her analysis of the works Lydgate wrote for public

consumption, I point up the materiality of both performances and their written residue and consider how those performances and written texts acquired
meaning for those who watched or read them. My contribution, broadly
construed, is thus to attend to what we might call situatedness—whether
that situatedness is understood as a text's positioning between poets and artisans who together create a drama, its location in an actual performance space
such as a city street, its emplacement on a tableau or painted cloth, or its inscription into a chronicle—and to put the lens on audiences and readers as
much as on authors and texts. That means readers of this book will not find
lengthy discussions of Lydgate as a writer or extensive close readings of his
poetic texts, but instead analysis of the processes by which his work was embodied in particular performances and then circulated in various media, including
as verses written in manuscripts. In taking that approach, my analysis shows
itself to be materially grounded, and the arguments in this book have benefited from the on-the-ground archival work and manuscript research that
went into my edition of Lydgate's mummings and entertainments, as well as a
series of essays in which some of the ideas in this book had their first airing.[39]

That Lydgate was involved in making dumbshows for the queen of
England is, I argue in this book, an astonishing fact—at least as viewed from
within the standard literary history—that ought to realign our understanding not just of his writings but also of the interdependence of poetry and
performance, of reading and spectating, of textuality and orality, and of
permanence and ephemerality. It is astonishing—just try to imagine Chaucer doing the same—that between the time when Lydgate wrote his monumental poems, *Troy Book* and *Fall of Princes*, for Henry V and the duke of
Humphrey, he also participated in the creation of fleeting holiday entertainments for Queen Catherine of Valois, by that time the widowed mother of
the boy who would soon become Henry VI. When Lydgate turned his hand
to verses for mummings and a disguising for her pleasure (and perhaps in at
least one case, and quite pointedly, her edification), he extended the service
he had long offered to the ruling men of England to a woman, thus remind-
ing us that women could be patrons and recipients of poetry and performance alike. He also made clear that a poet's work in Lancastrian England
could encompass the craft of play-designing and that the aureate style and
classical content of his major poetic works could be readily translated into
brief, live performances.

Lydgate's dramatic writings may seem, and indeed are, sparse and spotty
in comparison with the bulk of his corpus, but they are just as important for

literary history as his longer, better-studied works are. They tell us about patronage and the commissioning of performances, about tastes and values, about how word and sound and image interacted, about collaborations between writers and artists, about the mixing of genres and media, and about the evidence offered and concealed by scribes and manuscripts. They tell us, in short, about late medieval culture and the central role of performance in it and, in so doing, expand and complicate our understanding of premodern literary and theatrical history.

By looking at the queen's dumbshows and other short poetic texts that Lydgate wrote for public or private performance, we can also better see Lydgate's contributions to literary history. Those contributions include not just the fulfillment of a Chaucer-inspired "Lancastrian project of promoting an English vernacular tradition of high literary status," as Scanlon and Simpson describe it, but also the embrace of poetic forms, material contexts, and mixed audiences that create and reveal the intersection of—to use, for the sake of convenience, two words that in the fourteenth and fifteenth centuries refuse to stay separate—literature and theater.[40] Written in some sort of uneasy relation to mostly elite patrons;, inserted into collaboratively assembled live performances and written documents;, and looked at, listened to, and read by audiences both intended and not, Lydgate's dumbshows and the other performance pieces discussed in the following pages shed light on the complex ways in which late medieval poetry and performance fueled each other and, in so doing, ask us to rethink how we understand both of them.

CHAPTER I

Shirley's Hand

Unlike other fifteenth-century writers of short poems, Lydgate appears not to have kept a portfolio of his shorter verses, including those for performance, or to have supervised its circulation in authorized collections.[1] In fact, the survival of Lydgate's dramatic texts is due almost entirely to John Shirley, who included them in three anthologies he compiled between the late 1420s and the late 1440s. Whether or not Lydgate played any role in Shirley's compilations, and there is no evidence that he did, in copying Lydgate's performance pieces, Shirley provided crucial information about the circumstances of their original performance as well as their afterlife. The decisions Shirley made about what to copy and how to present it on the manuscript page say a good deal about what happened when a visual and aural form such as drama entered the written record. His copies also include information that helps piece together the circumstances of their original performance and written afterlife. Shirley's copies also help answer questions about the nature of the textual evidence for drama before print. What do manuscripts tell us about early performances? Should the canon of early theater be expanded to include texts that do not look like plays but may have been performed? How does the archive of written scripts and references to performances relate to the plays people in medieval England put on and watched? How do we know what was a play and what was not?

The place to which scholars have usually turned in trying to answer these questions has not been Shirley's compilations but rather the Toronto-based Records of Early English Drama (REED) project, whose goal since its inception in the 1970s has been to identify and publish all extant external references to early drama in Britain.[2] It is no exaggeration to say that REED's findings have radically revised scholarly assumptions about medieval drama. REED has shown, for instance, that the so-called Corpus Christi cycles were in most cases loosely put-together, episodic biblical dramas that could be performed on Corpus Christi but also at Whitsun; that folk dramas, such as Robin Hood plays, were the most frequent kinds of performances; that folk and other secular plays often took place on holy days and in religious settings; that the distinction between "medieval" and "renaissance" drama is hard to maintain (with a roughly 200-year performance span, the biblical plays of Coventry, Chester, and York lasted until 1575 or longer, while the manuscripts in which the biblical plays survive are chiefly Tudor documents, and "medieval" morality plays flourished alongside sixteenth-century school plays); and that the commercial theater, in the form of companies of traveling players, existed well before the age of Shakespeare.[3] REED has also shown that surviving play-texts do not accurately reflect the kinds and amounts of early drama: the large-scale biblical cycle plays such as York's, for instance, which have long been taken as the quintessential form of medieval drama, in actuality represent only a small fraction of extant performance records (David Bevington estimates it at 16 percent), and morality plays were even rarer.[4]

In the midst of all these surprises, perhaps the most unexpected finding is what REED has not discovered: new texts of plays. After years of diligent archival work, the corpus of Middle English drama still consists of the same long-known handful of texts from northern and southeastern England, as well as Cornwall. That handful includes four extant collections of biblical-history plays from the north: the York Register, which contains forty-seven pageants (1460s to 1470s through the mid-sixteenth century), the Towneley manuscript (mid-sixteenth century), two pageants from Coventry (both of them revisions by Robert Croo dated 1534), and five manuscripts of the Chester cycle (1591–1607).[5] The plays from the southeast, while more diverse than those from the north, are for the most part contained in three manuscripts. They are the Digby plays (*Mary Magdalene*, dating to the end of the fifteenth century; *The Killing of the Children*, ca. 1512, a farcical *Slaughter of the Innocents*; *The Conversion of Saint Paul*, 1500–1525; and a fragment of *Wisdom*, ca. 1470–75, all in Oxford, Bodleian Library MS Digby 133, owned in the mid-sixteenth century by Myles Blomefeld, a collector of books), the Macro plays (*Castle of Perseverance*, 1400–1425; *Mankind*, 1474–79; a complete version of *Wisdom*, all in Washington, D.C., Folger Shakespeare Library MS V.a.354, which was owned at some point by a monk named Hyngham of Bury St. Edmunds), and the N-Town plays (a compilation of plays originally of separate and earlier origin brought together by a scribe-compiler in or after the last decade of the fifteenth century, contained in London, British Library MS Cotton Vespasian D.8; the N-Town plays are also sometimes, confusingly, referred to as the *Ludus Coventriae* because of a flyleaf note giving them that name and are also sometimes called "the Hegge manuscript" based on the name of a family that once owned the manuscript).[6] Along with a few other fragments and single-pageant manuscripts, these constitute for the most part the same body of medieval plays in English identified by nineteenth-century scholars and antiquarians.

What these manuscripts suggest is that in most cases, the scripts of Middle English plays survived only under unusual circumstances, often involving antiquarian or recusant interests, and that they were recorded in the form in which they were preserved for posterity after—sometimes long after—they had been performed. Before the end of the fourteenth century, as Alexandra Johnston has noted, and indeed for much of the fifteenth century as well, nearly all of the evidence for the existence of theater in England is incidental, and that evidence for the most part does not include scripts of plays.[7]

One reason for the lack of surviving scripts is that many early plays probably originally existed in forms that were bad candidates for preservation, such as part sheets, roles, or performance copies not often of a status deemed worth preserving.[8] Dramatic texts may have been treated as ephemera, to be disposed of once the performance was over, no matter how elaborate or expensive that performance had been. That might explain why we find incidental mention of performances in account books, chronicles, and other public and private records but infrequent copying of the spoken lines. Another reason for the lack of surviving play-texts might be that mimetic dramas featuring spoken lines may have been relatively rare; miming, dumbshows, tableaux vivants, and other types of visual spectacle, perhaps accompanied by music, may have been the predominant forms of performance for most of the medieval period, rather than what we would now identify as plays structured around dialogue.

It is also possible, however, that more plays have survived than we suspect and that they lie hidden within manuscripts that conceal their distinctively performative features. At least since the time of Karl Young, who in his monumental *Drama of the Medieval Church* considered as dramas only those texts that contained rubrics explicitly describing costume and action, scholars have relied on overt signs of staging to identify early plays.[9] But agreeing on what constitutes signs of a performance has proven hard. Lawrence Clopper, for instance, has raised questions about references to saints' *ludi* that are often taken to signal plays but that in his view point to games, processions, or other nondramatic activities associated with the saint's day rather than plays proper.[10] If terminology and genre definitions are a problem for the identification of medieval dramas, as Clopper suggests, so too are scribal techniques that do not always differentiate speaking parts or include stage directions, much less descriptions of costumes or stage properties, with the result that plays do not always look distinctively like plays. The upshot, as Ian Lancashire has said, is that at times "what is and what is not dramatic is not obvious."[11]

The case of Lydgate is instructive in thinking about what is and is not a play. When Shirley made his copies of Lydgate's mummings and entertainments, he often included rubrics describing them as specific kinds of performances and mentioning the occasions and audiences for which they were designed. This information is crucial, since while internal evidence sometimes allows us to guess at some sort of performance context, without Shirley's rubrics, few of these texts would today be identified as performances of any kind. Take away Shirley, and we would have little reason for thinking that Lydgate had ever turned his hand to writing verses for theatrical events.[12] Shirley's copies of Lydgate's short performance pieces serve, then, as crucial documents of performance that provide us with our best sense of how, why, where, and for whom Lydgate wrote his verses for ceremonies and entertainments. They also serve as good support for David Scott Kastan's assertion that "the material form and *location* in which we encounter the written word are active contributors to the meaning of what is read."[13]

Despite identifying them in his headnotes as having been performed at specific times and places and before specific audiences, Shirley does not generally preserve markers of performance in his copies of Lydgate's mummings and other dramatic works. That his copies do not appear to present dramas reflects Carol Symes's observation that in most cases, "the formats of plays were as flexible as those of other texts, which were routinely tailored to conform to the overall presentation of the parent codex." Shirley's anthologies show such tailoring, a tailoring that was shaped by his aims in compiling them. The layout, rubrication, and extra-textual material in Shirley's copies of Lydgate's play-texts also support Symes's broader claim that such features "indicate that the generic definition of a play as such was in flux for most of the Middle Ages."[14] Shirley's copies reveal how the fluid relations that drama had with other cultural forms—such as liturgy, literature, and games—were transferred to the physical appearance of performance pieces when they were copied into manuscripts. His copies also demonstrate how the aims of individual scribes and the intended uses of specific codices could influence the look of dramatic works copied into them.

The manuscript matrix of Lydgate's performance pieces, with their *mise-en-page* at Shirley's hand, offers another instance where manuscript contexts have been inadequately examined or misunderstood. As Jessica Brantley has shown in her perceptive analysis of the meditative dramas in British Library MS Additional 37049, careful scrutiny of page layouts and the interplay of various features of the text and illustrations can help us envision how various forms of religious and secular writing were used by their readers.[15] Similarly, recent studies of the English dramatic manuscripts copied by Tudor and Stuart antiquarians and recusants, including the Towneley family and the scholars who made the five copies of the Chester plays, have drawn attention to peculiarities in those manuscripts and have reshaped knowledge about the processes of revision and transmission that gave us the surviving texts of medieval biblical plays in England.[16] Painstaking examination by Peter Happé, Barbara Palmer, and Malcolm Parkes of the "idiosyncratic assemblage of material from a variety of sources" that constitutes the Towneley manuscript has shown, for example, that the manuscript is not the scripts from a medieval cycle play from Wakefield but a Tudor dramatic anthology from Lancashire and Yorkshire. Similarly, the textual analyses of R. M. Lumiansky, David Mills, and Lawrence Clopper have revealed the strong desire to preserve and recuperate the city's past that animates the Chester plays.[17] As this and other work on manuscript formats and contexts has demonstrated, how we identify medieval texts and how we reckon with how they were received often hinge on how well we interpret the evidence left on the manuscript page.

Shirley as Copyist

Shirley's importance as a preserver and disseminator of English literary texts is well established. A number of Middle English poems are known only from his manuscripts, and attributions and contexts are available for other texts only on the basis of information contained in his headings and marginal glosses. Shirley is especially crucial for establishing the Lydgate canon and is the sole authority for a number of Lydgate's minor poems, including nearly all of his dramatic texts (among the few that do not survive in Shirlean manuscripts are the 1432 entry of Henry VI into London, the subtleties for Henry's 1429 coronation banquet, and the *Pageant of Knowledge*).[18]

Although there is agreement about Shirley's crucial role as a disseminator of texts, the precise nature of his scribal activities has been a matter of debate; some scholars view him as a commercial publisher with a London scriptorium, while others see him as an antiquarian who copied books chiefly for his own pleasure.[19] Margaret Connolly has convincingly argued, however, that Shirley was neither a commercial publisher nor an antiquarian book lover but instead a compiler working within a context formed by the "culture of service" that shaped his long career in the household of Richard Beauchamp, the earl of Warwick.[20] It was from inside this culture of service that Shirley compiled his anthologies, with the assumption that they would be read by "bothe the gret and the commune" of Beauchamp's household, as Shirley states in the preface to the first of the anthologies.

Shirley's goal of producing compilations that would appeal to members of Beauchamp's household is evident in his choice of texts for inclusion in them. It is apparent from their contents that, far from being an antiquarian collector of authors from the past, Shirley was interested in copying the writings of contemporaries and especially the work of Lydgate. All three of Shirley's anthologies contain a substantial number of poems by Lydgate, along with other items of verse and prose in French, English, and Latin. The earliest (London, British Library MS Additional 16165, compiled in the late 1420s) contains fourteen poems by Lydgate, none of them apparently designed for performance, as well as some forty-five texts that encompass works by John Trevisa; Chaucer; Edward of Norwich, duke of York; and Beauchamp. Shirley's second anthology (Cambridge, Trinity College Library MS R.3.20) was compiled in the early 1430s and contains twenty-six pieces by Lydgate out of some seventy-five texts, among them six of Lydgate's mummings along with the *Procession of Corpus Christi*, the *Legend of St. George*, and *Bycorne and Chychevache*. The actual proportion of work by Lydgate included in this anthology is even larger than these numbers suggest, since twenty-seven of the non-Lydgatean pieces are short, anonymous poems in French; the other named authors in the anthology include Chaucer; William de la Pole, earl of Suffolk; Thomas Hoccleve; and Thomas Brampton. Shirley's last anthology (Oxford, Bodleian Library MS Ashmole 59), compiled in the late 1440s, contains thirty-five pieces by Lydgate, including the *Mumming at Bishopswood*, out of around eighty texts, among them works by John Gower, Henry Scogan, and Chaucer.[21]

The contents of these three anthologies hint at Shirley's motives in compiling them and at his reasons for including poems by Lydgate. With the exception of the *Temple of Glas* (which appears in BL MS Add. 16165), all of the works by Lydgate in the three anthologies are short—deliberately so, it seems, as suggested by the fact that Shirley copies, for example, extracts from the *Fall of Princes* but not the entire poem. Additionally, almost all of the Lydgate poems appear only once and are not recopied in Shirley's other anthologies. Combined with this lack of duplication, the emphasis on short pieces suggests that Shirley's aim was to collect and preserve Lydgate's shorter works, including those like the mummings that were occasional in nature and might otherwise have disappeared; having once done so, Shirley apparently had no reason to recopy the same poems again elsewhere. While there is some evidence that Shirley loaned out his anthologies, thus implicitly making Lydgate's works available for others to copy should they wish, there is no hint that Shirley himself was engaged in making multiple copies of Lydgate's poetry for commercial gain or circulation among readers. The choice of texts, while apparently designed to gather and save Lydgate's short, ephemeral texts from oblivion, seems also to have been motivated by the tastes of Shirley's intended audience—particularly so in the case of Trinity MS R.3.20—that is, readers within the Beauchamp household who formed the milieu for Shirley's efforts when, in the 1420s, he first turned his hand to copying literary texts.[22]

Why did Shirley copy so many poems by Lydgate? Connections and acquaintance presumably played a part. There is no direct evidence that Shirley knew Lydgate, but because both men moved in the same aristocratic and civic circles, it is likely that they were acquainted. Shirley (ca. 1366–1456) was roughly the same age as Lydgate (ca. 1370–1450) and, like Lydgate, had close ties to the Lancastrian affinity, through his attachment to the household of Beauchamp, who was appointed tutor to Henry VI in 1428. Beauchamp was Shirley's employer and one of Lydgate's patrons: records show that Shirley was in Beauchamp's retinue in France and England from 1403 until the late 1420s, and London, British Library MS Harley 7333, folio 31, points to Lydgate's connection to the earl.[23] Some degree of acquaintance between the two can be inferred from John Stow's copy of what was presumably Shirley's preface (now missing) to his second anthology, which suggests that Shirley had an interest in promoting Lydgate. The preface praises the poet and includes a plea that he be rewarded financially for his poetic efforts.[24] It also locates Lydgate within an imagined aristocratic/gentle social milieu, calling him a purveyor of "morall mater and holynesse / of salmes and of ympnes

expresse / of loue and lawe and of pleyinges / of lordes of ladies of qwenes
of kynges," precisely the kind of instructive yet pleasing courtly poetry that
could be expected to suit the tastes of readers associated with the Beauchamp
household.

It is unlikely that Shirley was to Lydgate what Adam Pinkhurst was to
Chaucer, a scribe who turned Lydgate's "foul papers" or wax drafting tablets
into fair copies of his work, but the example of other poets indicates that such
collaboration, had it happened, would not have been unusual. Signs of super-
visory direction in some copies of the *Confessio Amantis*, for example, imply
that Gower may have supervised his own scriptorium in Southwark at the
Priory of St. Mary Overy, where he lived at the end of his life. While Hoccleve wrote out copies of his works in his own hand (because he was too poor
for a scribe or perhaps did not trust one), John Capgrave both wrote some
copies in his own hand and supervised others at the scriptorium of his friary
in Lynn.[25] Some scribes apparently specialized in the texts of one author,
such as Pinkhurst, who worked for Chaucer; the Beryn scribe, who made five
copies of the *Brut* as well as copies of Chaucer and Lydgate's *Life of Our Lady*;
and the scribe working in the region near Bury St. Edmunds, who specialized
in copying Lydgate.[26] The tendency of scribes to specialize in one author may
imply that authorial employment or supervision was an accepted practice.

Whether he worked closely with Lydgate or not, Shirley evidently copied
the performance pieces out of a desire to preserve Lydgate's short texts and to
please a coterie audience of readers, some of whom might have seen Lydgate's
entertainments when they were first performed. Although Shirley took pains
to note the original performance context, he apparently had little interest in
conveying details about the performance itself. With only a few exceptions,
Shirley gives no indication of the costumes, special effects, gestures, actions,
vocalizations, or musical accompaniments that would have featured in the
staging of these performances. The result is that in Shirley's hands, Lydgate's
dramatic pieces do not look much like plays.

Perhaps Shirley omits details of the productions because he did not
witness or have access to full information about them, although given Beauchamp's close ties to the court, Shirley might well have been present for at
least some of the entertainments, especially the royal mummings.[27] Or
perhaps the omission reflects the fact that, as Gordon Kipling has argued,
Lydgate's role was often that of a "deviser" who was responsible merely for
the written text or "device" (i.e., the design instructions) for the performance,
which is what we find recorded in Shirley's manuscripts.[28] Or perhaps Lydgate

was, as Clopper has argued, "a presenter not a playwright," whose art "is presentational rather than representational" with characters who seldom speak in their own voices, little interaction between characters, and a predisposition toward "reading" rather than performing; in other words, the mummings and other entertainments may be literature, not theater.[29] Or perhaps the lack of detail about the original performances derives from the difficulties of recording aural and gestural material within the medium of writing.[30] Or, finally, perhaps the nondramatic appearance of so many copies of Lydgate's performance pieces may result from Shirley's intent to create codices for readers, an intent that led him to erase signs of live performance.

Many of these uncertainties about authorial agency, dramatic terminology, modes of presentation, and scribal habits that are aspects of the preservation of Lydgate's performance pieces in Shirley's manuscripts are shared by other medieval and early modern dramatic works and have been addressed by scholars alert to the difficulties involved in studying an ephemeral and embodied art form. Work on the aural, the gestural, and other sensual or phenomenological features of early performances has attempted to reintroduce what audiences would have heard, seen, felt, smelled, or even touched in the course of watching a performance.[31] The findings of this scholarly work have usefully reminded us of what the manuscript page does not do a good job of capturing: the experience of being in the audience at a performance. While I draw on this work in subsequent chapters, I also agree with Sheila Lindenbaum that despite the widespread assumption in medieval drama studies that "plays become fully accessible only in the moment of performance," the "privileging of performance over text" does not have to be "the inevitable corollary of drama study." It would be unreasonably blinkered to ignore performance, but especially in this chapter, I share Lindenbaum's perspective that "a play belongs first and foremost to its material manuscript and manuscript context."[32]

From Performance to Codex

The ease with which Shirley could reshape live performances as poems to be read underscores Symes's point about the flexibility of texts in this period, a flexibility that is evident in the terms Shirley uses in his headnotes to describe the nature of Lydgate's role. The phrase Shirley most often uses in headnotes to the mummings and other entertainments to describe Lydgate's creative activities is "made by," although he also twice uses "devysed" (*Disguising at Hertford* and *Bycorne and Chychevache*) and once "ymagyned by . . . and made" (*Legend of St. George*). Other fifteenth-century documents use variations on *make* to refer to orchestrators or organizers of mummings, but Shirley's headnotes do not make clear whether he is similarly referring to Lydgate as the mastermind behind the whole performance or more restrictedly designating him as just the author of an accompanying text.[33] The word *devise* had a range of meanings, of which the most relevant for Shirley's usage include the acts of designing, constructing, or composing. Used technically, *devise* referred to the drawing up of the specifications for the visual and verbal subject matter (the "device") for a painting, pageant, or sculpture. Yet the technical and general senses of "devising" were not mutually exclusive, as suggested by Shirley's headnote to the *Legend of St. George*, which describes the verses as the "devyse of a steyned halle . . . ymagined by Daun Johan . . . and made with the balades" at the request of the armorers of London. In the same way, *making* and *devising* were not necessarily unrelated activities, as implied by Chaucer's description in the "Knight's Tale" of Theseus's employment of every available craftsman "to maken and deuyse" the tournament.[34]

While *making* could be used, as these examples show, to describe the work of mounting a performance, it could also apply to the labor of crafting a written text. "Made by" is the phrase Shirley most often employs to describe Lydgate's authorial activities in relation not just to his dramatic verses but to his nondramatic poems as well. Just once does Shirley say that Lydgate "wrote" the following verses, although in another instance he combines the acts of writing and making, saying that Lydgate "wrote & made" a poem for Queen Catherine.[35] Shirley seems to have thought of *making* as an act of original composition, since he tends not to use *made by* when describing verses that Lydgate translated.[36]

Whether referring to performances or texts composed for reading, when he designated Lydgate a "maker" of verses, it is probable that Shirley was reflecting the notion of courtly *makyng* that informed understandings of late medieval literary activity. Courtly *makyng*, as Anne Middleton notes, involved the creation of work that was "conceived as a performance in the current scene of polite amusement and secular ritual."[37] Deliberately re-creative and highly aestheticized, courtly *makyng* produced texts that served the ideological needs of and socially reproduced the late medieval aristocracy. As Lee Patterson has observed, the courtly "maker" "offered a ritualistic rehearsal, with minute variation, of familiar tropes of socially valuable modes of speaking and feeling" that "played an important role in the project of aristocratic self-legitimization."[38] What is perhaps most important in regard to Shirley and Lydgate is that courtly *makyng* implied that the texts thereby created were public and meant in some way to be performed. When Shirley used the phrase "made by" to express Lydgate's authorial role, he was presumably signaling that the accompanying poem, like courtly poetry in general, was designed for public airing, whether in the form of verses offered as a gift (as appears to have been the case for the "Ballade on a New Year's Gift of an Eagle," which Shirley says was "gyven vn to" Henry VI and his mother Queen Catherine and was perhaps read aloud on that occasion), a pictorial display (such as the "Ballade on the Image of Our Lady," which contains internal clues suggesting it accompanied a painting), or a mumming or disguising.[39]

In any case, Lydgate's *makyng* of verses for performance was complicated by its location within the collaborative process, common then and now, of putting on a play. Although terms such as *play-maker* or *playwright* or even *poet* may obscure the degree to which a performance text was stitched together and into the creative activities involved in mounting a show, the fact of collaboration was widely recognized. As Tiffany Stern has shown, authors of early modern English plays were often called *play-patchers*, a term that acknowledged the shared and often piecemeal work of the theater.[40] Although that phrase was not current in fifteenth-century England, what it describes was far from nonexistent.

Like the terms Shirley uses to describe Lydgate's authorial efforts, the labels he applies to Lydgate's verses designed for entertainments suggest a porosity of representational borders. In various headnotes, Shirley calls them variously *ballades*, *letters*, *bills*, *ordinances*, and *devices*. While these terms are performance charged, they also call attention to the way that these verses, in Kipling's words, "represent themselves self-consciously as texts." Kipling reads this textual self-consciousness as evidence of Lydgate's limited role in creating dramatic performances, believing that Lydgate was asked to provide texts that served as "actual documents used in performance."[41] But since the choice of labels is Shirley's, this textual self-consciousness can also be seen as a part of his efforts to convert Lydgate's publicly performed works into texts meant to be read privately, especially by members of Beauchamp's household.

When we turn from Shirley's headnotes to the texts they introduce, we can see the same genre blurring combined with the act of adapting texts to private reading. Several of the performance pieces contain rubrics or glosses that point to dramatic actions. The *Disguising at Hertford*, for instance, introduces the reply of the wives to their husbands' complaint with the line "Takeþe heed of þaunswer of þe wyves." And marginal glosses in Latin and English in the same text (e.g., "i. demonstrando vj. rusticos," "demonstrando þe Tynker," "distaves") seem to indicate the appearance of the various actors who performed it. The *Disguising at London* contains similar notations, such as "Nowe komeþe [or "sheweþe"] here," followed by the name of the character. More frequently, however, the text and marginalia stress reading over performance, while also underscoring Bernard Cerquiglini's assertion that the medieval vernacular text was always unstable: "open and as good as unfinished," the handwritten text "invited intervention, annotation, and commentary."[42] In the *Mumming for the Mercers*, for example, extensive glosses in English and Latin explain the various classical gods mentioned in the text (e.g., "Mars is god of batayle"). The *Disguising at London* and the *Mumming for the Goldsmiths* also include explanatory glosses that appear to be in Shirley's hand, such as a comment describing Julius Caesar as "a bakars seon" (*Disguising at London*, at l. 67). Presumably, Shirley copied these glosses from his exemplars, although he might have supplied at least some of them himself.[43] Whether originating with Shirley or not, the glosses provide information that aids understanding of the written text rather than imaginative re-creation of the performance; they are notes intended to explain references and allusions in Lydgate's poetry and, as such, enhance the reading experience rather than (in most instances) conjuring up the performances for which the verses were written.

Within each of Shirley's anthologies, the *mise-en-page* of Lydgate's performance pieces is virtually indistinguishable from that of the rest of the manuscript's contents. In Trinity MS R.3.20, for instance, they resemble the other poems in size, ink, and position on the page, blending into them without any use of features that would set them apart. As in the example on page 40 from that manuscript—which contains the ending of the *Mumming at Eltham*, with its "Lenvoie," and, immediately afterward, the start of the *Disguising at Hertford*—headers appear in bolder script in spaces left for them between the texts (see Figure 1). Running titles were added by Shirley in blacker ink, preceded by what appears to be an *n* for *nota*. Shirley began individual texts with three-line black-ink initials that feature his distinctive style of decoration, including lozenges, foliage or geometric patterns, wide otiose strokes, long descenders, and occasional crosshatching.[44] Most of the texts in the Trinity manuscript are in single columns, centered on the page. Lydgate's performance pieces are interspersed among other short poems in

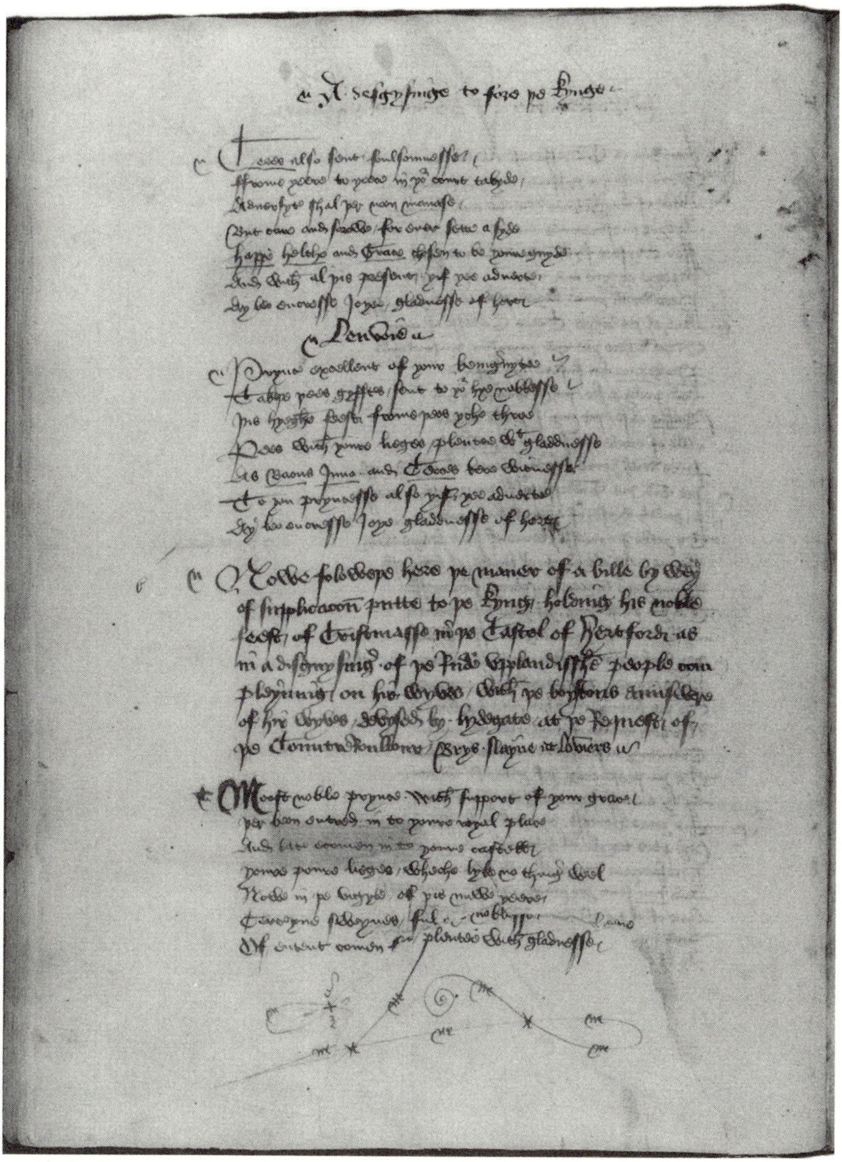

Figure 1. Example of Shirley's hand. *Mumming at Eltham* (last two stanzas) and *Disguising at Hertford* (headnote and first stanza). Cambridge, Trinity College Library MS R.3.20, p. 40. By permission of the library.

French and English and are in no way visually differentiated by format or rubrication, and they include few or no stage directions, speech tags, or other signs of the performance for which they were originally made.[45]

This intermixing can be seen in the second and third quires of the Trinity manuscript, which contain seven short French poems, as well as five poems by Lydgate, among them the mummings at Eltham and Hertford, as well as the brief "Balade de bone counseyle," which is also thought to be by Lydgate. The fourth quire is made up of poems by Lydgate, including the mumming at London, and three French lyrics. It is not certain where Shirley acquired his exemplars for the French poems in the Trinity manuscript, and Margaret Connolly and Yolanda Plumley suggest that Shirley himself was the conduit through which these poems reached England, either through his travels to France or, indirectly, through Warwick's household.[46] Connolly and Plumley observe that a number of the French lyrics Shirley copies were song-texts, but it is impossible to tell whether Shirley knew them as songs and perhaps transcribed them from aural memory since there is little "which might be construed as evidence of aural transmission."[47] As with Lydgate's mummings, these lyrics lose their musical markers when Shirley copies them, although their connection with the musical repertoire can be established from their presence in musical manuscripts as well as textual ones, such as Trinity MS R.3.20.[48]

What, then, do Shirley's copies of Lydgate's performance pieces tell us? First, they demonstrate that dramatic texts, when copied into textual manuscripts, do not always signal that they were meant for performance. Without Shirley's headnotes, there would be little to suggest that Lydgate's performance pieces were anything other than nondramatic poems. This lack of visible difference between poetic and dramatic texts is by no means unique to Shirley's manuscripts and, as Symes has argued, the appearance of a text in a manuscript context "may have little to do with whether or not it was performed or regarded as a play."[49] The same is true for songs, which can appear as lyrics in textual manuscripts or with notation in musical ones. Particularly before 1300, formats of plays were fluid and altered to suit the pattern of the whole codex; different versions of pieces suggest they could be changed to suit different textual contexts or the needs of different readers.

Moreover, layout and rubrication indicate that the generic definition of a play was in flux throughout the premodern period. Since plays were recorded through scribal techniques borrowed from other sources—musical, didactic, scholastic, and poetic—many do not look like plays when viewed in their manuscript contexts. Somewhat disconcertingly, especially for attempts to decide on a corpus of medieval drama, texts now regarded as plays are not always accompanied by a dramatic apparatus in their manuscript contexts, while texts not currently viewed as plays are laid out and rubricated in the same way, and those seemingly nondramatic texts are also often juxtaposed with identified plays, thus suggesting that they might have been performed.[50] That generic definitions were in flux can be linked to a similarly fluid continuum of performance practices, in which mumming blends into disguising into tableaux or other visual spectacle and beyond. In other words, the fluidity of terms that were used to describe performances corresponds with an analogous mutability of kinds of performances, as the range of ceremonies and entertainments to which Lydgate contributed so clearly shows.

Shirley may have seldom recorded features of performance, such as stage directions or details about costumes, for the same reasons he does not include musical notation for the French songs he copied: lack of knowledge of a standard method of transcription of performance texts as well as a desire to create a manuscript for use by readers, rather than practitioners of the performance arts. Shirley does, however, take pains to situate Lydgate's dramatic works in their social milieu, telling us for which powerful patron and on what ceremonial occasion they were performed.[51] That Shirley noted these details of provenance is understandable given his apparent interest in promoting Lydgate's writings, since they associate the poet with influential patrons and important ceremonial occasions.

Whether deliberately or not, Shirley's scribal practices tended to emphasize the literariness of Lydgate's dramatic works, not their theatricality, and thus represent a move away from the earlier situation identified by Michael Clanchy in which literary works, especially vernacular ones, "were frequently explicitly addressed by the author to an audience, rather than to readers as such."[52] As with the French songs he copied, Shirley adapted them to a specifically literary—that is, a writerly and readerly—aesthetic. In doing so, Shirley followed the pattern that Seth Lerer has argued defined Chaucer's writings, as Chaucer attempted to stake out a place for his new kind of poetry against the then dominant cultural forms of courtly spectacle and civic religious drama.[53] Chaucer's search for authorial autonomy, in Lerer's view, takes him away from public theatrics toward a place where spectators become solitary, private readers and performances become fictions. Unlike Chaucer, however, Lydgate did not define himself as a poet in opposition to theater and spectacle and in fact appears to have embraced them, judging by the frequency with which he turned his hand to the crafting of pieces designed for public ceremonies. Lydgate's career was founded on the production of a courtly and civic poetry that enthusiastically included spectacle and ceremony.

It is certainly possible that Shirley's omission of markers of drama was inadvertent, the result of a lack of scribal conventions needed to replicate qualities of performance on the manuscript page. It is also possible that he did not know enough about the original performances to reproduce them and was working from exemplars that contained only the written text. But the omission is also consistent with Shirley's larger purposes in his anthologies, especially in the Trinity manuscript, to preserve Lydgate's performance pieces for literary culture. Shirley takes what were originally courtly or civic ephemera—entertainments designed for a one-off performance on a specific occasion and not expected to have much afterlife—and converts them into enduring poetry that will be continually accessible through the act of reading. It was presumably a similar impulse that prompted Robert Reynes, a churchwarden from the village of Acle in Norfolk, to copy play extracts into his commonplace book in the late fifteenth century as a way of remembering, as well as making available for repeated reading, performances that would otherwise be fleeting, and the same may be true of some copies of other medieval plays.[54] If Shirley is to be credited with preserving knowledge of Lydgate's involvement in the production of dramas, he is also answerable for obscuring details of the live enactment, including their visual, mimetic, and aural aspects.[55] It is in this regard understandable that scholars might view Lydgate's performance pieces—at least in the form in which they have come down to us—as nondramatic, because that is what Shirley made them.

Preservation and Dissemination

Even though they were written for a coterie audience within Beauchamp's household, Shirley's three surviving miscellanies owe their survival, as Linne Mooney notes, "to their usefulness as exemplars for the book trade in London and their intrinsic interest to bibliophilic antiquarians in London in the century when many paper manuscripts were being discarded for the more 'modern' printed copies of the same texts."[56]

A noteworthy path of dissemination leads through John Vale, to whom Shirley was linked through family and other connections. Shirley's second wife, Margaret, was the sister of the wife of Avery Cornburgh, who owned the manor of Gooshayes in Havering, Essex, and was thus a neighbor of Thomas Cook (the younger), whose secretary was John Vale. We know that Shirley knew Cornburgh, since in one of the manuscripts he copied, Shirley wrote, "Iste liber constat Aluredo Corneburgh de Camera Regis." Cook was a prosperous draper and influential former mayor of London who had literary ties: Robert Fabian, the future chronicler, was Cook's apprentice at the time of Cook's arrest for treason in 1468. Cook also had lands at Bury St. Edmunds and, at some point in the 1460s, moved to a large house adjoining the Austin friars, in the parish of St. Peter the Poor. [57] Shirley, too, may have had connections with Austin friars after he moved to the close of St. Bartholomew's Priory; Estelle Stubbes notes that Shirley is associated with a number of manuscripts of the *Canterbury Tales* and that BL MS Harley 7333, which seems to depend on Shirley-influenced exemplars for some texts, was mainly produced at a house of Augustinian friars in Leicester.[58] The Austin friar John Lowe was confessor to the young Henry VI and part of the royal household when Warwick, with Shirley along, was tutor to the king; Lowe was a friend and colleague of Capgrave.

Vale had other connections to Shirley and possibly Lydgate as well. He knew John Baret, the wealthy clothier from Bury and close associate of Lydgate, whose will of 1463 included a reference to payment of a monetary "recompence" to Vale, apparently for a piece of cloth (or possibly plate); Vale's father Thomas was a dyer who owned property in Bury, where Vale may have been educated.[59] Three of the manuscripts written by the copyist known as the Hammond scribe contain a monogram of John de Vale, including the Shirley-derived miscellany, London, British Library MS Harley 2251. The London stationer John Multon, from whom Vale purchased Harley 2251, may be identical with the Hammond scribe, which would give Vale a personal connection with Shirley and an interest in Lydgate. Vale was probably an important intermediary between Shirley's books and the sixteenth-century antiquarian Stow.[60]

In the case of many of Lydgate's performance pieces, the conduit leading from Shirley to Vale and then to Stow was especially important. Six of the mummings exist only in copies made by Shirley and Stow. *Bycorne and Chychevache* survives in Shirley's Trinity MS R.3.20, as well as in Trinity MS R.3.19, BL MS Harley 2251 (owned by Vale), and Stow's London, British Library, MS Additional 29729; the *Procession of Corpus Christi* and the *Sodein Fal* survive in Trinity MS R.3.20, BL Harley 2251, and Stow's copy; and the pattern is repeated for a number of Lydgate's other entertainments. Unlike the household members Shirley envisioned as the audience for MS R.3.20, Vale and readers were far removed from the original performances that Shirley copied into that manuscript, and their interest in them would have had little to do with recollection of a once watched entertainment.

Not all of Lydgate's poems for public ceremonies and entertainments were transmitted through Shirley (most notably, those poems associated with civic-royal events such as the coronation and entry of Henry VI into London, which were copied into London chronicles). But those that were survive in forms shaped first by Shirley and later by the London book circles through which they subsequently passed. That history of copying and transmission left marks on Lydgate's dramas that color any attempt to envision how they had been performed.

Shirley's hand, then, not only helped preserve a record of Lydgate's mummings and entertainments but also fashioned them into forms that partake of and reveal the complicated relationship that existed in late medieval England between play-texts and enactment. "Everything about medieval literary inscription," Cerquiglini has written, "seems to elude the modern conception of the text."[61] Although Cerquiglini is thinking about spelling and punctuation in particular, his comment nonetheless calls attention to the larger sense of alterity that exists between the handwritten codex and the printed book. It is by looking at the medieval paratext or formatting decisions and conventions involved when a scribe puts spoken words into the space of writing that we can discover the nature of medieval textuality and recognize that "the written word is not simply a deposit of knowledge; it is above all an incomparable means of classifying and retrieving it."[62] While less ephemeral than the performances they record, Shirley's copies of Lydgate's entertainments and ceremonies remind us that the act of inscription, whereby performances become written texts, involves choices and omissions. Thanks to Shirley, we can glimpse something of the ceremonies for which Lydgate created texts, even if in the act of preserving them Shirley erased most of the details that would offer a full sense of what they were like as live entertainments.

CHAPTER 2

Vernacular Cosmopolitanism: London Mummings and Disguisings

Only recently has Lydgate begun to be thought of as a London writer, as scholars have acknowledged the time he spent in the city, the connections he had with its residents, and the number of texts he wrote for or about it, including four mummings and disguisings apparently intended for performance in the city.[1] According to John Shirley, the *Mumming for the Mercers* was performed on Twelfth Night (i.e., 6 January), to entertain William Estfeld, mayor of London, who was a member of the Mercers' Company. In it, a presenter disguised as a herald from Jupiter recounts a journey across Africa and Europe to the Thames, then ushers into the hall three ships from which mummers dressed as oriental merchants bearing gifts of silk descend to greet the mayor. The *Mumming for the Goldsmiths* was performed on Candlemas Eve (i.e., 2 February), Shirley also says, once again for the mayor. It features Fortune, who brings a letter with news that David and the twelve tribes of Israel have come with the Ark of the Covenant to visit the mayor and present gifts. Estfeld was mayor of London in 1429–30 and 1437–38, but the latter can be ruled out as the date of the performance of these two mummings given that Trinity MS R.3.20 was composed in 1430–32.[2] The *Mumming at Bishopswood* was written for May Day for London's sheriffs, Shirley claims, possibly in the same year, although he gives no date; it introduces Flora, who ushers in springtime to drive away winter's discords. The date and occasion of the *Disguising at London* are unknown, but its theme of good governance, which is seen as a remedy for Fortune's dangerous instability, would have been well suited for the opening of parliament, as suggested by Shirley's remark that it was performed "afore the gret estates of the lond," in

the long Christmas season of any year at the end of the 1420s or beginning of
the 1430s.[3]

During Lydgate's career—as in the century before, as well as that
following—writing in English was a complicated sociopolitical activity that
touched on questions of national and cultural identity, across status and gender divisions. Those questions, as Nicholas Watson observes, were mirrored
"in every feature of the vernacular literature of the period, including a writer's choice of genre, length, vocabulary, syntax, and poetic or prose style." By
the 1420s, relations among the trilingual literary cultures of England had
shifted as texts written in English appeared in increasing numbers and as "a
new sense of their importance" gave Middle English for the first time a status
"closer to that of French or Latin."[4]

Interest in that shift has made vernacular politics an important topic of
scholarly investigation in recent years, particularly in analyses of the Lancastrian turn to English as a national language and the marketing of Chaucer as
a key figure in attempts to make English a prestige language. In the second
half of the fourteenth century, English began to be taught in schools, became
the official language of the courts and parliament, spread dissent through
Wycliffite treatises and bibles, was championed by Henry IV and Henry V
for political purposes, and spawned a large body of literary works. In these
historical processes, Lydgate's position is one of cultivated dependence on
Chaucer as "a poet worth citing and imitating," as Watson observes, a dependence that signals "the arrival of English as a vernacular of a value compara-
ble to that of French or Italian.[5] Lydgate was, in the memorable phrasing of
Larry Scanlon and James Simpson, "Chaucer's first great impresario and com-
petitor," both relying on and battling a Chaucerian poetics. As a skilled user of
the vernacular to suit Lancastrian and other—sometimes oppositional, or at
least not fully equivalent with—interests, Lydgate moved beyond a Chaucerian
poetics in various ways, including the creation of an ornate style intended to
signal an orthodox form of writing in the native tongue as distinct from the
heterodox threat posed by the Lollard use of English.[6]

Lydgate's mummings and disguising for mayor, sheriffs, and parliament
complicate this view in two ways: they use English—and, more specifically,
specific genres of written English—in live performances, and they use the
vernacular not as propaganda for court or church but to create a specific image of London. Making an argument against too easy slippage of the "idea"
of the vernacular to the "ideal" and hence a valorization of vernacularity
as the triumph of democratic freedoms over the oppressions of Latin and

French, Sarah Stanbury notes that a vernacular language "exists only in relation to that which is standard, official, monological, or even imperial." While
Stanbury's claim is part of her cautionary reading against assigning Middle
English "heroic stature," it stands as a useful reminder of the competition of
languages, including multiple forms of the vernacular, that is part of the historical process of language change.[7] It is within this context of linguistic
competition and growing prominence of English that we can place Lydgate's
stylistic habits, such as his importing of Latin nouns and adjectives into Middle
English, chiefly from liturgical or Vulgate Latin, to create what John Norton-
Smith has described as the "word or phrase 'calques'" that are such a notable
feature of Lydgate's verses, including the mummings and disguising he made
for Londoners.[8]

Issues of genre and place are one of the first things that have to be reck-
oned with when considering the style and impact of Lydgate's mummings
and disguising for Londoners. Genres (or media) are at the center of Maura
Nolan's forceful analysis of the historical and literary situatedness of what she
describes as Lydgate's "public" works, a group that includes the *Serpent of
Division*, several of his mummings, the disguisings at Hertford and London,
and the verses associated with Henry VI's 1432 entry into London. Nolan's
analysis of these texts hinges on the claim that in them Lydgate translated
"the poetic and literary techniques he had learned from Chaucer into new
media, especially spectacle," thereby "remaking the forms of public culture
available to him." In transferring poetry to the realm of performance, Lydgate
"creates uniquely hybrid texts, part reassuring moralisms or praise, part literary works in search of educated and savvy readers." These texts are "public," in Nolan's view, both because they were designed to commemorate
public occasions and because they constructed and spoke to an imaginary
public; whether performed or not, these texts are conscious of their public
status, and they imagine their audience as a public rather than an inchoate
group. But unlike the "public poetry" of the late fourteenth century described by Anne Middleton, which was based on notions of "common profit,"
Lydgate in Nolan's view attempts to assert the sovereignty of the king, creating a shift from the Chaucerian sense of social whole as diverse and inclusive
to a notion of it as hierarchical and exclusive.[9]

While the reading of Lydgate's mummings and disguisings for Londoners that follows in this chapter intersects with Nolan's understanding of the
cultural work of those texts, it also diverges in a number of ways, especially in
relation to place. The specifically London—and even more localized (e.g., in

a guildhall)—location of the performances this chapter takes up is, I hope
to show, central to their design and achievement, as is their later location in
specific manuscripts, from which they reached an audience beyond their
original spectators. Through the workings of what might be called vernacular
cosmopolitanism—that is, the creation of an English poetics that relies on
borrowings and assimilations—Lydgate's London performances help imagine a particular version of the city. Lydgate may have channeled "the official,
public voice of London," in C. David Benson's words, but he also found ways
to deny that official voice, in works such as these that show London less as it
is than "as it ought to be."[10]

The Porous City

Unlike the biblical cycle plays from York and other provincial cities, Lydgate's
London mummings and disguising were performed not in the streets but
within the relative privacy of halls and households. While less obviously public than many other civic performances, their in-house performance venues
make them no less crucial in shaping opinion, working out cultural conflicts,
and apportioning power, in this case, with an urban and mercantile rather
than royal inflection, as a close reading of the texts and their audiences shows.
That effect can be seen on both their primary audiences (those who commissioned and watched the performances) and their secondary audiences (those
who read Lydgate's verses for the performances when they circulated in manuscripts).[11]

Most likely performed at the height of nationalist fervor in the midst of
the English-French military campaigns of the late 1420s, as the young Henry
VI was being crowned king of England and France, these four mummings
offer an image of London as cosmopolis, its prestige enhanced by the gloss of
poetry, poetry in the native tongue. The mummings for the Mercers and
Goldsmiths rework the threat of invasion as invited visit, thus refashioning
enemies into guests. They similarly reimagine the problem of alien merchants
and tradesmen, which for much of the fifteenth century was a pressing concern for London guilds, by turning unwelcome competitors into beneficent
gift givers and supporters, not underminers, of the mayor's authority, supporters whose fealty is secured through vernacular eloquence. The mumming
that took place at Bishopswood and the disguising for parliament accomplish
some of the same integrative work as they draw various groups of officials

together, aligning sheriffs, who were agents of the king, not the city, with the interests of the civic government and making the concerns of a nationally focused Parliament mesh with those of the city.

In contrast with Chaucer, whose inability or unwillingness to represent London has been noted by scholars, Lydgate provides a clear image of the city in his verses for these groups.[12] In these four entertainments, Lydgate achieves a literary merging of native and foreign, urban and courtly, civic and national relations within a city that was polyglot, ethnically diverse, socially divisive, and economically competitive. By inscribing foreign merchants and representatives of king and country into the space of London trading relations, even if only temporarily and under the guise of holiday gift giving and entertainment; by stressing the power of English poetry; and by emphasizing the importance of good governance, these performances bring together various fractured publics, shaping them into what Benedict Anderson has taught us to think of as an imagined community, a cultural artifact created and kept alive by specific historical forces.[13]

Recent literary scholarship has tended to characterize late medieval London as a place of diversity and multiplicity, with blurred boundaries between fragmented groups and oriented toward conflict.[14] Statistics gathered by historians suggest that in the early fifteenth century, London was a cosmopolitan city whose 50,000 or so residents were linguistically and ethnically varied.[15] Unique among English cities, London recruited its residents from every region of England as it expanded its population each year. To give a sense of the numbers involved, in the years from 1404 to 1442, some 578 apprentices were admitted to the Goldsmiths' Company, an average of seventeen per year. Where they came from is not known, but of the fourteen admitted in 1407, the only year in which full details are given, only one was from London; the rest were from other parts of the country.[16] In addition to the constant influx of new residents from the surrounding countryside and farther afield in England, individuals and even communities from various countries on the continent also lived in the city or its suburbs, especially in Westminster and Southwark. Colonies of foreign merchants had long been established in London, at least from the early fourteenth century on. Most of them came from the Low Countries, the Rhineland, and the ports of the Baltic coast, with a few from central Germany and France, as well as Italy, Spain, and Greece.[17] Lombard Street had an Italian community of long standing, and the Hanseatic merchants even had a guildhall in London in Thames Street next to the Steelyard allotted the merchants of Cologne. Some of these foreigners, like the Hansards, had well-established rights and immunities—including the right to hold property and sell retail—while others depended more tenuously on royal or civic tolerance and made easy scapegoats when times turned bad.[18]

This diversity did not preclude segmentation among London's various residents, especially as they were variously slotted into the broad categories of citizens, foreigners, and aliens. The term *foreigners* was used for the English-born unenfranchised, that is, those who were not "citizens" but had sworn loyalty to the city government and promised to bear their share of taxation and civic duty; local birth was no assurance of citizenship since even people native to London might be called foreigners if they were not enfranchised. Those born oversees were referred to as "aliens" or sometimes "strangers" or "Dutchmen." Citizenship had distinct advantages, as well as a few liabilities. Only citizens were legally entitled to buy in the city with the intent to resell and to keep shops for the purpose of retailing merchandise.[19] Thus, to citizens alone went the full rights and privileges of enfranchisement. But citizens also bore the burden of taxation and were subject to trade regulations and various civic responsibilities that noncitizens could escape.

Given the perception of their unfair edge over citizens, by virtue of this ability to evade regulations, aliens were not always welcomed into the city and could be frequent targets at moments of social, economic, religious, or political discontent, as the Flemish merchants murdered in the riots of 1381 attest.[20] Steven Justice has argued that it was not just the economic success of Flemings in London that led to their murder but also their difference, especially their linguistic difference, which made them seem to be "figures of domination distinguished by a language the English artisan or rural worker could not understand." As Justice also points out, the rebellion has a direct relationship to dramatic performance, given its occurrence just after the annual feast of Corpus Christi, a ceremony of communal identity, which "has some claim to be thought not only the occasion of the rising, but also a source of its public idiom."[21]

Jews offer the best-known example of a xenophobia in which ethnic and religious outsiders were purged from England, but other groups, while allowed temporary residence within the country, were also on occasion vilified and physically attacked as well. Sylvia Thrupp's assessment that parliament had been an "outlet for xenophobia" for years, with group after group being expelled, is borne out by the evidence of repeated expulsions from 1345 onward.[22] Particularly as English nationalism grew in the fifteenth century, foreigners faced increased antagonism. In a flare-up of sentiments against foreigners in 1406, for instance, parliament ordered many aliens to leave England; seven were goldsmiths in London who paid the exchequer for the right to stay.[23] The insular hostility expressed in the *Libelle of English Polycye* of 1436 and in various protectionist trade and sumptuary statutes was echoed in the riots of 1456 and 1457 against the presence of aliens in London, especially Italian and Lombard merchants.[24] Closer to the time when Lydgate's mummings were being performed, in a widely reported incident in 1429, a Breton servant and alleged spy, who had been accused of murdering a widow, was being escorted into exile by parish constables when he was overtaken by a crowd of women who snatched him away and stoned him to death; presumably his nationality was part of what incited this episode of women's justice.[25] This antipathy toward outsiders was mirrored in the London guild system, which tended to exclude aliens, as well as "foreigners" from the countryside, in most cases forbidding them to be enrolled as apprentices or to set up shop.[26]

Despite these attempts at exclusion, the economic advantages of working and trading in London were such that aliens persisted in finding ways of infiltrating the city's commercial system; as a result, for most of the fifteenth century, London's companies grappled with the problem of alien merchants who openly or covertly sought work in the city or its suburbs. Guild records reveal an oscillation between tolerance and hostility toward aliens, with an increasing hardening of attitudes against the presence of alien merchants by mid-century. The Goldsmiths' accounts from the 1420s and 1430s, for example, authorized wardens and officers to conduct searches to hunt down alien goldsmiths, especially in Foster Lane and Lombard Street, which housed most of the craft; the wardens seem also to have searched Southwark—a favorite locale of alien goldsmiths—for "false boys" (i.e., foreign or alien apprentices) or "untrue workers," often pursuing their quarry with vigor, to judge by the fines levied. In 1424, for instance, ten "Dutchmen" were fined for "misworking," and in 1434, the "Ordinance of Dutchmen" forbade the employment of aliens.[27] This rhetoric of truth and falsehood, of right and wrong persons and labor, deserves fuller analysis, but for the purposes of my argument here, it is perhaps sufficient to note that one of its effects is to bring to the question of national identity the value-laden language of moral imperative: to be an alien is to be false or wrong.

No matter the results of these attempts to root aliens out, or—more accurately, given that they were more often fined than expelled—to make them less of a competitive threat to citizens, many aliens found admission to London's guilds. To cite just two examples, in 1428, the alien goldsmith John Coster paid ten marks for a license to work in his chamber for life and swore to keep the craft's secrets, and in 1434, a Parisian goldsmith named Raymond Wachter paid twenty marks for a license to work with his four servants and later that year paid forty pounds to be admitted as a freeman of the Gold-smiths' Company.[28] The statute of 1477–78 reiterated that alien and stranger goldsmiths within the city and within two miles outside were to be subject to the wardens of the Goldsmiths' Company; at first, the company granted these aliens licenses to work, and most were established around Lombard Street, removed from the center of goldsmith activity at the west end of Cheapside, although many were settling in Southwark and Westminster beyond the city limits.[29] There were apparently enough alien goldsmiths living in London that they had a fraternity of St. Eloi, named after the goldsmith who in the seventh century became bishop of Noyon and was adopted as the patron saint of goldsmiths in many European countries. The extent to which aliens had infiltrated guilds is suggested by records for the Goldsmiths' Company indicating that in 1444, the total full plus pensioned members were approxi-mately 140, which probably included proportions similar to those in 1477 when the members included fifty-seven wardens, assistants, and liveried members; sixty-two young men; nineteen pensioners; and twenty-three aliens living in the city and eighteen in Westminster and Southwark. Indeed, some aliens seem to have spent their entire adult lives under the aegis of the guilds, such as the "Dutchman" Gerard Haverbeke, who had paid for full member-ship in the Goldsmiths' Company and, on his retirement in 1476, was granted 1s. 2d. per week for the rest of his life.[30] Lydgate himself describes assimilated aliens in his account of the 1432 welcome of Henry VI into London, in which richly attired "Esterlinges" rode in procession in a privileged position behind the mayor.[31]

Whatever degree of success individual aliens had in becoming members of London's companies—usually by buying their admittance—nativist ani-mosities lingered. Part of the hostility toward alien practitioners of the crafts had to do with the desire to maintain standards, to regulate prices, and to lessen competition. But another part arose out of nativist biases against out-siders. These attitudes are crystallized in a wager that took place at the Pope's Head Tavern in Cornhill in 1466. The wager involved a test of skill between one Oliver Davy, a citizen and goldsmith of London, and a Spanish gold-smith of the same city and was designed to ascertain whether native or foreign goldsmiths were more adept at their craft, based on how well each man worked a small gold cup. Perhaps not surprisingly, the wager was judged in favor of the English goldsmith, stamping English craftsmanship as superior to that of strangers.[32]

London was porous in other ways as well, including the spatial and the political. Although often self-identified with the area within its walls, the city sprawled beyond those limits into suburbs and the surrounding countryside, into areas such as Southwark and Westminster. Bishops Wood lay outside London proper, in the parish of Stebunheath (present-day Stepney) near Bethnal Green. As the name suggests, these lands belonged to the bishop of London and thus were not under the control of the city, although Caroline Barron notes that Londoners claimed their principal hunting rights on the bishop's lands.[33] London was the seat of national government and the "king's chamber," as Lydgate styled it in his verses commemorating Henry VI's royal entry in 1432, and its civic affairs overlapped with royal and national interests. Westminster, where the *Disguising at London* would have been performed if written for the opening of parliament, was also outside the city and, as the royal capital, was a courtly, not civic, domain, with its own economy and identity.[34] Yet, Westminster was linked to London by proximity, trade, and ceremony, including such enactments as royal entries that ended at Westminster after traversing London and ridings to Westminster to obtain the king's approval of mayoral elections, both of which used their processional routes to create a symbolic link between city and crown. Parliament drew men from the various regions of England to London, outsiders who nonetheless had connections in the city if only by virtue of their residence in town during parliamentary sessions. The city itself was often involved in affairs of parliament, as it sought to represent its own interests. The king's presence at parliament, along with members of the royal court, nonetheless made visible the city's subordinate position in relation to the central government. On a smaller scale, sheriffs did the same, since they were technically agents of the king, charged with keeping order in his name. Fines levied by them went to the king's, not the city's, coffers, and their first loyalty was to the crown, not the city. Nevertheless, because they were important officials, sheriffs were inevitably linked to the civic government, as Stow suggests when he claims that not just bishops but aldermen and other commoners were in attendance at the May Day festivities of which the *Mumming at Bishopswood* was part.[35] In this and other ways, whatever its insistence on its own prerogatives and rights, London tended toward an openness and inclusivity that allowed it to absorb, at least temporarily, a wide range of people whose interests may not

have entirely meshed with those of the city's government or the citizens that
government at least nominally represented.

Domesticating Poetry: The Mummings
for the Mercers and Goldsmiths

Lydgate's entertainments for the Mercers and Goldsmiths can be seen as festive interventions into this complex set of relations between London and the
continent. In both performances, alien merchants are freely admitted into
the fellowship, in the guise of Jewish or Eastern merchants who sail from afar
to the port of London. Antiforeigner sentiments, which animated the polemics
of the late 1420s, are submerged in these performances under a glowing pa-
tina of openness, amiability, and generosity—virtues in short supply on the
streets of London outside the Mercers' and Goldsmiths' halls. But if in these
mummings foreign merchants are welcomed into London's guilds, they are at
the same time placed in a clearly subordinate position of submission, as gift
bearers come to pay tribute to the mayor, the crowning symbol of London's
civic might.[36] What underscores civic power is the mummings' emphasis on
the literary; Lydgate's verses not only present an example of the poetic arts
but also serve to instruct Londoners in a literary aesthetics grounded in a
specific use of written English. In so doing, the mummings create a vision of
cosmopolitan vernacularity in which foreign culture is made native.

The occasion of the *Mumming for the Mercers*, as well as its content and
performative features, plays into that vision. The liturgy associated with the
Feast of the Epiphany, for which Shirley claims the mumming was performed,
commemorated Christ's birth and baptism as well as the visit of the Magi,
muted echoes of which can be found in the mumming. The 105 lines that
Lydgate wrote apparently to assist the Mercers in entertaining the newly
elected mayor, who was himself a mercer, take the form of a long introductory
speech that was probably spoken by a presenter (a "poursuyaunt") and seems
designed to usher into the hall three ships, possibly carrying mummers disguised as merchants from the Far East. As Glynne Wickham notes, Lydgate
allegorizes this visual spectacle by combining the idea of the Magi with the
miraculous draught of fishes to enhance the presentation of gifts to Estfeld.[37]
The text is a kind of geographic, mythological, and literary grand tour that
describes how Jupiter's messenger travels from the Euphrates to the Thames,

passing various mythic sites, including those important for the origins of poetry, and encountering along the way three ships with slogans on their sides.
The messenger finally reaches London, coming ashore where the Mercers have
gathered to honor the mayor. The actual performance, which probably followed the reading aloud of the letter and which the running titles in the
manuscript in which it survives refer to as a disguising, seems to have been as
elaborate as Shirley's comment that it was "ordeyned ryallych" (i.e., royally
arranged) suggests: the verses imply that three pageant ships, costumed actors,
music, dancing, action in which the ships cast their nets, and gift giving were
part of the entertainment.

As first in precedence among London's companies, with many members
becoming mayor or sheriff, the Mercers possessed the means for a mumming
as elaborate as this one. By the fifteenth century, the mercers had a hall, a chapel, and at least one other room (as well as a chest for keeping records) in the
church of St. Thomas of Acre in Cheapside, near the birthplace of Thomas à
Becket in an area once occupied by prosperous Jews.[38] While their hall would
have been suitable for feasts and entertainments, the mumming Lydgate
wrote may have been performed in the mayor's own hall, as the last stanza
implies in mentioning that the mummers have come to visit the mayor and
await his permission to enter. Estfeld was an especially illustrious mercer,
serving as alderman, sheriff, mayor, and member of parliament for the city.
He built the conduits at Aldermanbury and at the Standard in Fleet and was
a benefactor of St. Mary Aldermanbury, where he was buried.[39] In November
1429, he attended the coronation of Henry VI and received the gold cup used
in the coronation ceremony, which he kept until his death in 1445.[40] He appears to have been knighted in the 1430s.[41] While an exceptional figure,
Estfeld suggests the wealth and standing mercers could attain and the resources they could command for entertainments. Unfortunately, although
the mercers' accounts show payments toward royal mummings in the 1390s
and in 1400–1401 and although the mercers seem to have had an interest in
the short-lived London *puy*, as records from 1304 show, there is no extant account of this performance beyond the verses Shirley copied.[42]

The mumming makes reference to contemporary events, perhaps including commercial transactions involving Mayor Estfeld, but it more broadly
functions as a form of cultural capital.[43] With its extensive classical allusions,
its conceit of Jupiter's herald being sent as an envoy to the mayor, and its mixing of real and mythic geographies, the mumming constructs an image of

London as the center of the trading universe—the mercantile hub of the commercial world. Its fifteen stanzas sketch an expansive geographic panopticon, beginning with the Euphrates and Jerusalem, then moving over Libya, Ethiopia, India, and on to Egypt, the Red Sea, Morocco, Spain, Calais, the Thames, and finally "Londones tovne" (l. 95), where the herald lands. Along the way, the herald sees three ships, each with lettering on its side. The first ship, from which a man fishes but brings up empty nets, has on one side the words "grande travayle" and on the other "nulle avayle" (ll. 62–63), underscoring the fisherman's fruitless labor. The second ship, which the herald encounters as it is unloading, has a cabin gaily painted with flowers and a slogan in French stressing the need to be thankful for whatever fortune brings. The third ship, the one closest to London's port, holds another fisherman, but this time one whose nets overflow with so many fish that "he nyst what til do" (l. 88). On the side of this ship, the mottos "grande peyne" and "grande gayne" (ll. 90–91) are painted—a pointed inversion of the first ship's testimony to profitless toil. This progression from dearth to prosperity as the herald nears London emphasizes the city's wealth, which radiates out to those near it, and sets the stage for the final set of ships the herald encounters, which are anchored on the Thames ("Hem to refresshe and to taken ayr," l. 100) and from which men, possibly paid performers or members of the Mercers' Company, descended to visit "the noble Mayr" (l. 102), bringing gifts of silk, one of the commodities in which mercers traded.[44]

In its structure, this mumming is not unlike the mumming for Richard II in 1377, when London's civic authorities rode to the palace of Kennington at night disguised as a pope, emperor, cardinals, and African or Eastern ambassadors. When they arrived, they dismounted and carried three gifts for the king into the hall—a bowl, a cup, and a ring of gold—with several smaller gifts for the queen mother and other family members. After dancing, the mummers played a dice game with loaded dice to be sure Richard would win the gifts.[45] In both the Kennington and Mercers' mummings, the performance functions as a reminder of the mutual obligations of ruler and ruled, with the mummers' gifts not only honoring the mayor or king but also underscoring his responsibility to his subjects. The giving and receiving of the gifts, including the gift of the performance itself, enacts a reciprocal relationship premised on loyal service on the part of the subordinates and beneficent paternalism on the part of the ruler. Such gift giving was well suited to the Feast of the Epiphany, when the Magi presented gifts to the infant Jesus as a sign of obeisance and humility. Epiphany was the inspiration for a number of dramatic performances, but none as far removed from liturgical sources as Lydgate's mumming. The Christian typography underlies the *Mumming for the Mercers* but, in Lydgate's hands, is turned into a thoroughly civic, urban spectacle. As Lydgate shows, the liturgical message of Epiphany could be readily appropriated within the context of a guildhall performance to reaffirm structures of authority and patterns of obligation linking mayor and merchants.[46]

As a letter in the form of a ballade, Lydgate's mumming for the Mercers brings together two registers of vernacular writing. The writing of letters in English was becoming increasingly common by the fifteenth century and would have been especially familiar to an urban audience dependent on work-related correspondence.[47] Letter writing had its own rhetorical techniques, in the form of the *ars dictaminis*, which guided persuasive epistolary writing. Although *dictamen* would have been familiar to Lydgate, it may have been less so to Shirley and to the mercers and their mayor, except indirectly through its influence on imaginative writing in Middle English.[48] Like other loose-sheet writing, the letter was usually bureaucratic in nature or related to business, and Shirley's description of Lydgate's verses as taking that form invokes a similar utilitarianism.[49] Strictly defined, a ballade was a three-stanza poem with refrain, a favorite French poetic form derived from dance music that never achieved wide popularity in Middle English. Shirley uses the term less precisely, here and elsewhere, to designate poems of rhyme-royal stanzas.[50] In describing what Lydgate produced for the mercers as simultaneously letter and ballade, Shirley may be taking pains to note the formal features of what Lydgate wrote as well as how it was conveyed to the mercers and mayor, even as he also blends familiarly pragmatic—familiar both to himself through his work as Beauchamp's secretary and to the mercers as tradesmen dependent on the exchange of information through letters—and lesser-known poetic forms of the vernacular.[51] Shirley's efforts conform to what Emily Steiner has described as the "documentary poetics" that characterized English writing in the late fourteenth and early fifteenth centuries, as poets such as Chaucer and Hoccleve drew on documentary culture "as a means of articulating the strategies and ambitions of their own literary making."[52]

Lydgate may be less indebted to documentary culture than many of his predecessors were, but it nonetheless informs his performance pieces in various ways, including the use of letters and bills in his mummings and disguisings, as I will discuss more fully in this and later chapters. It is important to note, however, that in the *Mumming for the Mercers* and elsewhere, Lydgate draws not just from the worlds of poetry and prose but also from drama, specifically the liturgical dramas that since the twelfth century had been composed for and performed on the same feasts for which Lydgate was now writing performance pieces for Londoners. Part of the process of domesticating poetry that Lydgate engaged in was to give the pan-European performances of Christian ritual a local habitation and a secular, even commercial, form. Secular performances naturally followed the church calendar, because there was no "alternative, secular reckoning of time," as Eamon Duffy notes, and thus the liturgical calendar with its public seasonal rounds of celebration and penance by default provided the rhythms of the festive year.[53] In addition to that default linkage to the liturgical calendar, Lydgate's vernacular poetry sometimes had a more pointed connection to religious ritual, drawing on occasion directly from the liturgy, as in the verse translations he made of the liturgical calendar and of devotions from the Latin primer, presumably for use by his various patrons and readers around the Bury monastery or court.

While his mummings do not translate liturgical plays in any direct fashion, they are indebted to them in a number of ways. In the case of the *Mumming for the Mercers*, the calendrical link was to Twelfth Night, or the Feast of the Epiphany, the last day of the twelve-day Christmas season. Epiphany was traditionally associated with the biblical story of the Magi, and since at least the twelfth century had been an occasion for dramatic enactments of the appearance of the star and the coming and inquiry of the three kings, both of which feature in the antiphon and response in the liturgy for Epiphany.[54] Gordon Kipling has convincingly argued that in a diffuse way not tied to a specific day of the year, royal entries borrowed the gift giving associated with Epiphany, as civic officials gave actual or symbolic gifts to the royal visitor entering the city, thus performing "a symbolic act of recognition and acclamation."[55] A similar echoing of the themes of Epiphany can be seen, even if ingeniously obliquely, in Lydgate's recasting of three visitors bearing gifts as a visit from a pursuivant who passes a trio of ships bearing symbolic mottoes and, in the final stanza, "certein estates" come to honor the mayor.

Out of its mixing of epistolary and lyric discourses and allusions drawn from biblical narrative, liturgical plays, classical mythology, and the vernacular tradition, the *Mumming for the Mercers* constructs a vernacular poetics grounded in an urban-national geography and, as Maura Nolan notes, associated with the origins of poetry ("Cyrrea" and "Parnaso") and with the practice of mumming. The mumming features an East-West axis populated by figures who, in Nolan's view, "represented the cultural capital of the aristocratic and royal elites," and it dramatizes the assimilation of the alien messenger and oriental merchants into the socioeconomic milieu of the mayor and guildsmen. The welcoming of those outsiders conveys the impression in the mumming that mercantile London is capable of absorbing potentially alien groups along with their cultural products, especially poetry.

The "famous rethorycyens" and "musycyens" the mumming invokes include Ovid, Vergil, Petrarch, and Boccaccio, and Lydgate nods toward French vision poetry in the mumming, but no English writers are mentioned. Nolan argues that this notable lack of reference to vernacular poetry throws into relief the relations between a foreign (European or classical) poetics and a native cultural practice (mumming); the omission of Chaucer, an author Lydgate is in other instances happy to claim as an inspiration, stresses an unmediated relation to a European poetic tradition and Lydgate's "own centrality to the didactic project of the text and performance" presented through a *translatio* of European culture.[56] (The other *translatio* at work in the mumming is of the liturgical material, as I noted above, with the beckoning star and the visit of the three kings bearing gifts for the Christ child transformed into Phoebus's light, the pursuivant's journey, the three traveling ships, and the merchants who come to visit London's mayor.) Whether or not he sees a distinction between a foreign poetics and a native performance, in describing Lydgate's rhyme-royal stanzas as a ballade, Shirley calls attention to the high literariness of the verses being presented to the Mercers, as well as to their foreignness.

The practice of mumming itself may be less the point of contrast with European culture than is the description of the verses as a letter. That is, the opposition is not between poetry and performance but between two forms of vernacular writing: ballade and letter. And that opposition is not really one, since as Shirley's headnote says, the ballade and the letter are one and the same: what the pursuivant brings to the mayor is a "lettre made in wyse of balade." Shirley does not explain how the ballade-letter was used in the performance, but presumably it was read aloud by the pursuivant to accompany the actions of the costumed mummers. If that is what happened during the performance, then the mayor and audience would have seen a familiar kind of vernacular writing used to convey not the pragmatic information expected from the form but poetry. With its ballade-letter, then, and the contrast between expectations raised visually by the delivery of the letter and actual contents heard aurally as its rhyme-royal verses were read aloud, the *Mumming for the Mercers* domesticates the exotic use of the vernacular represented by the ballade as a genre and by the verses' poetic form and their allusions to a European poetic tradition. The effect would have been intensified in performance given that the sudden appearance of the pursuivant "recalls the romance conventions of other courtly revels," as Clopper observes, and that the journey described in Lydgate's ballade traverses "an allegorical romance landscape," all of which occurs within the familiar setting of a hall in a London guildhall or house.[57]

The likelihood that spectators grasped those cultural references is increased by the reputation mercers had for being well educated and intellectually curious. Books were among the piece-goods mercers traded in and are mentioned in mercers' wills; apprentice mercers were expected to be able to read, write, and count and would have improved their French or Dutch during travels to the continent. The Mercers' Company owned many books, including accounts, deeds, registers, and reference books, as well as books for their chapel and even literary manuscripts (including, later in the century, copies of Lydgate's writings), and they employed Adam Pinkhurst, Chaucer's scribe, as late as 1427.[58] The mercers who watched Lydgate's mumming in 1430 would have been familiar with practical writing in English, including the writing of letters, and, through their travels to the continent, acquainted with the French language.[59] Like other literate members of the prosperous urban classes, they may also have had an awareness of French poetry, given the extent to which French culture formed part of the English literary landscape.[60]

Despite mercers' educational attainments, Shirley's extensive glosses explaining Lydgate's allusions imply that he felt—accurately or not—that his intended readers would need help assimilating the poetic and classical references in the mumming.[61] In English and Latin, his marginal notes explain that "Mars is god of batayle," "Tulius a poete and a rethorisyen of Rome," "Phebus in Aquario is als miche to seyne as thanne the sonne is in that signe," and so on. Although Shirley's intended audience for the manuscript that contained the *Mumming for the Mercers* was probably the Beauchamp household in which he had served for so many years, it is worth noting that Shirley also had connections with mercers.[62] Roger Amorigy, a mercer, was connected with "a crowd of literati," including Shirley, who lived in or near St. Bartholomew's Hospital, and John Carpenter, common clerk of the city (1417–38), was an executor of the will of the mercer Richard Whittington.[63] Those connections do not necessarily translate into the ability to catch clerical and courtly references, but they at least suggest an awareness of literary culture and its value in a mercantile milieu.

The *Mumming for the Goldsmiths*, performed less than a month later, similarly features a visit from outsiders and links poetry to civic aspirations. The mumming mixes homage, praise, veiled advice, and wishful thinking offered by the Goldsmiths to Estfeld in an evening performance on Candlemas, a festival in honor of the presentation of the infant Jesus in the temple and the purification of the Virgin Mary. Jesse, David, and the twelve tribes of Israel who figure in the mumming were traditionally associated with Candlemas, since they emphasize the lineage of Jesus. Candlemas plays were already known in the vernacular by the time Lydgate wrote his verses for the Goldsmiths, and six extant Middle English play-texts on the subject have survived.[64] In the N-Town play of the Purification, for instance, which includes a speech by Simeon that is a literal translation of the opening psalm of the mass of the feast, the liturgical song "Nunc dimittis" is sung, Jesus distributes candles, and the main characters process to the altar—all echoes of the liturgy.[65] The Digby Candlemas play includes similar elements along with a sermon spoken by Simeon that echoes Candlemas homilies in its comparison of the candle to Christ. The Digby play includes dances, which in Duffy's view show "the links between liturgical observation and the 'secular' celebratory and ludic dimensions of lay culture at the end of the Middle Ages."[66] That Lydgate's play handles the traditional material of Candlemas as loosely as it does may be because, as Nolan observes, the *Mumming for the Goldsmiths* is embedded in a particularly dense referential field: allusions to Candlemas shape the text, but they are only one among many references out of which Lydgate builds his mumming.[67] That mixing of references makes sense given the reminder offered by Amy Appleford and Nicholas Watson about "the seriousness with which privileged Londoners took their religion" and the extent to which they embraced literary works that "taught them how to be saved as people living in the world of trade and exchange."[68]

Like the oriental merchants of the *Mumming for the Mercers*, the Israelites in the *Mumming for the Goldsmiths* bring gifts to the mayor, this time not the goods that the company trades in but rather symbolic treasures "boþe hevenly and moral," having to do with, in the words of the presenter, "good gouuernuance" (ll. 19–20). Chief among these symbols of good governance is the Ark of the Covenant, which, the presenter promises, will ensure both long prosperity for the city and protection for the mayor and the citizens of the town, keeping the city perpetually "at rest" (ll. 27–28, 68, 77). As the latter claim implies, one of the values of the ark is its peacekeeping propensity, of use for settling both internal and external threats to urban order.

The ark contains three gifts for the mayor—"konnyng, grace and might"—which are designed to help him govern with "wisdome, pees and right" (ll. 81–82) and to ordain just laws about which no man will complain, along with a writ that specifies which offenses the mayor should punish and which he should overlook, as well as when he should exercise mercy.[69] As long as the ark stays with the mayor, the presenter promises, adversity will be banished and "pees and rest, welfare and vnytee" (l. 97) will reign throughout the city. The not-so-hidden message in these lines is that the mayor is expected by the Goldsmiths to exercise his office effectively and fairly, assuring the smooth running of the city and therefore the continued profitability of its mercantile communities. Disorder, unrest, and lawlessness must be cast out in order for the commercial enterprises of the city to thrive. Along with its gifts to the mayor, the mumming offers, then, a pointed reminder of his responsibilities as the chief authority of the city.

Although there is no reference to this mumming in their records, the Goldsmiths possessed the wherewithal for a "fresshe and costelé" performance such as this one. The company had a tradition of entertainments on its annual St. Dunstan's Day feast and in mayoral processions; it owned musical instruments as well as a "summer-castle" that (equipped with "virgins" throwing silver leaves) was used in the entry of Richard II in 1377 and again in 1382, and on occasion it hired minstrels and choristers from St. Paul's.[70] The Goldsmiths' pageantry was well enough known for Henry VI to refer to it in a letter of 1444–45, in which he requested a lavish display for Queen Margaret's entry.[71] The Goldsmiths were one of two guilds known to have had a hall by the end of the fourteenth century, having acquired a site for it in the parish of St. John Zachary in 1357, where they built a hall, kitchen, parlor, and other chambers.[72]

We do not know how the Goldsmiths came to commission these verses from Lydgate, but their prestige could have brought some of them into orbit with Lydgate's circle. London goldsmiths, who in 1404 numbered 102 men in the livery company (the elite group) plus another eighty out of the livery, were substantial citizens, involved in London's government and with an international reputation as skilled craftsmen.[73] As makers of luxury goods, goldsmiths had contacts with the wealthy and powerful: John Orewell, for example, who was the king's engraver, made a silver-gilt crozier for the abbot of Bury St. Edmunds in 1430, and in 1379–80, Edward III's daughter Isabella, the mayor, Lord Latimer, the Master of St. John of Clerkenwell, and others were invited to one of the Goldsmiths' feast.[74]

As he did for the verses Lydgate wrote for the Mercers, Shirley describes the *Mumming for the Goldsmiths* as a letter in the style of a ballade, once again juxtaposing two kinds of vernacular writing. As Shirley's headnote shows, those two terms are further complicated by the addition of the term *mumming* and by a use of syntax and prepositions that makes parsing the phrase difficult: "And nowe filowethe a lettre made in wyse of balade by Ledegate Daun Johan of a mommynge" (see Figure 2).[75] The sense of the first part of what Shirley is attempting to convey seems clear: what he has copied is a letter in verse that Lydgate has composed. But the second part is harder to decipher: are the following verses a ballade-like letter meant to serve as a guide for the makers of the mumming, or are they a ballade-like letter meant to be used in the mumming or some combination of both of those possibilities? Shirley's headnote does not provide an answer, and the running titles describing the verses as a disguising add further confusion, but the verses themselves offer some plausible suggestions as to what Lydgate's verses represent. No speaker is identified in those verses, but the herald named Fortune, who is described by Shirley as presenting the ballade-letter to the mayor, probably read the fourteen rhyme-royal stanzas aloud to introduce the mummers, who mimed the actions of David and the twelve tribes of Israel. Lydgate echoes his technique in the Mercers' mumming of mixing the courtly (e.g., the herald; "royal gyftes," l. 6, for the mayor, and references to Troy), the biblical (with an emphasis on lineage via the Jesse Tree, Mary, Jesus, and Samuel's anointing of David), and the mercantile (stressing good governance). He also deftly combines flattery of the mayor with an assertion of the need for humble and responsible service in office, demonstrating his ability to craft entertainments for London's wealthy and politically influential establishment that celebrate London and its values, while also subtly voicing concerns about civic government and mayoral power.[76]

Once again, Lydgate describes a series of figures who travel from afar, in this instance from Jerusalem, to "comen to þis citee" to bring the mayor "royal" gifts and "to seen and to vysyte" him (ll. 5–7). Lydgate supplements the travels of David and the Israelites with references to the sacred image of the Palladium, which was kept at the temple of Athena in Troy, joining religious and classical allusions. And once again, the sweep of the journey has the effect of making London the welcoming port for foreign travelers whose gifts will set the city perpetually at rest (ll. 76–77). Although the mumming is ostensibly

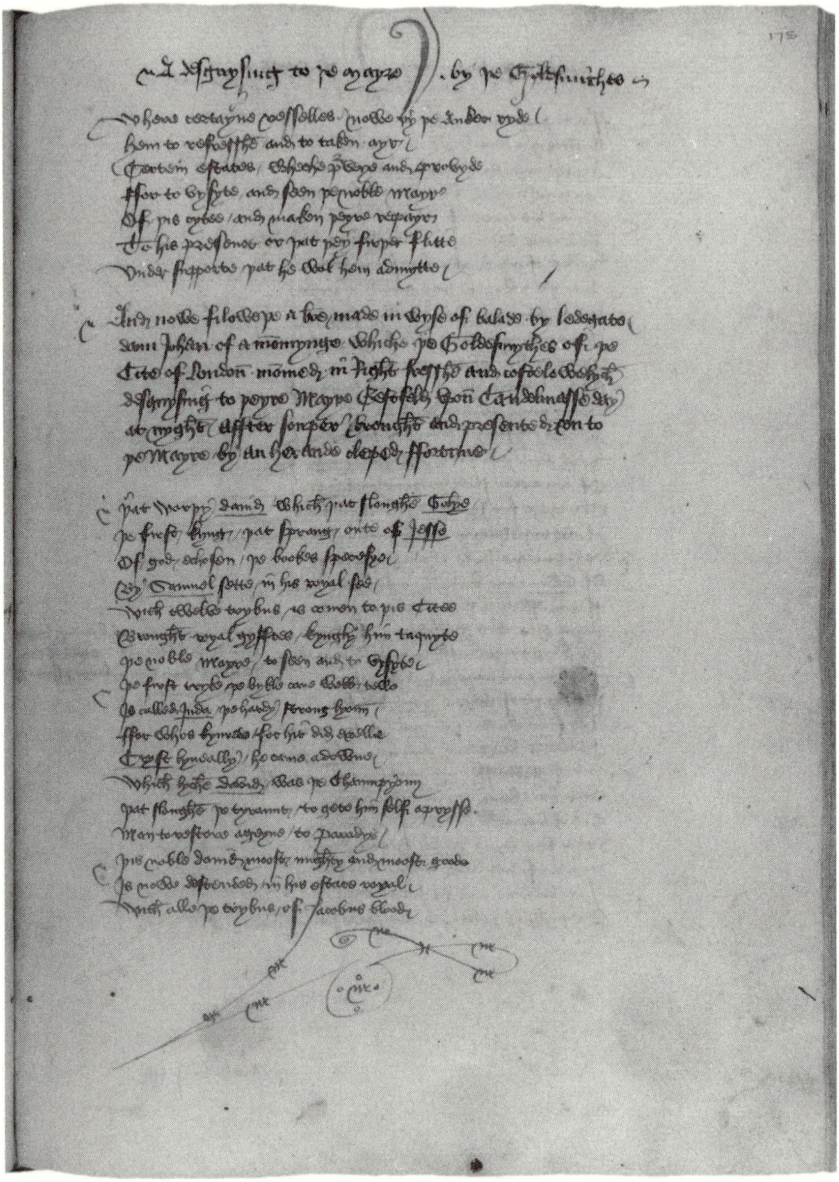

Figure 2. *Mumming for the Goldsmiths* (headnote and ll. 1–17, following last stanza of *Mumming for the Mercers*). Cambridge, Trinity College Library MS R.3.20, p. 175. By permission of the library.

being performed for the mayor, whom it directly addresses, Lydgate's verses stress a city-to-city exchange between Jerusalem (and Troy) and London, as David comes "Frome his cytee of Ihersualem" "in-to þis tovne" (ll. 22, 25). The verses refer to London a total of six times, describing it variously as "þis citee," "þis tovne," and, once, "þis noble cytee." The impression left by this linking is of London as a New Jerusalem as well as a "Nuwe Troye," as Lydgate explicitly calls it in the tenth stanza.

Complicating the opposition between practical English letters and continental poetry, the mumming introduces a third form of vernacular writing, in the form of the writ that is inside the ark brought by the Israelites. The writ, which specifies how the mayor should "punysshe" and "spare" (l. 87), contains echoes of the biblical commandments given to Moses while also calling to mind a specific documentary practice of late medieval England. In its legal sense, a writ of the later medieval period was an official letter issued by the chancery on the king's behalf, bestowing a privilege or issuing an instruction. It was usually written on one side of a sheet of paper and delivered open and ratified with a royal seal, and after 1422 was, along with other chancery material, increasingly likely to be written in English.[77] Lydgate may be using the term more broadly to embrace any written document, but his description of the writ as a piece of writing that will "declare" and "pleynly specefye" (ll. 85–86) to the mayor how he should carry out the acts of justice associated with his office carries the instructive force of a chancery-issued writ. Lydgate's verses do not make clear whether the writ was read aloud as part of the performance or whether it was left with the mayor for private reading at a later date. Whatever its method of delivery, as a form of directive writing, the writ is more complex than simple gifts of wine or wheat, as Nolan notes, since it demands "an active and engaged response" from the mayor.[78]

With their status as short pieces of vernacular writing, Lydgate's letter and writ fit within the context of pamphleteering that saw bills, broadsides, pamphlets, and poems circulating throughout London in the late fourteenth and fifteenth centuries. Bills and libels were posted on the doors of Westminster or St. Paul's, Lollard tracts were disseminated widely, the 1381 rebels wrote pseudonymous letters, and pamphleting campaigns were waged by political rivals.[79] Clementine Oliver has argued that these short, often polemical, texts "are urban artefacts formed by the intersection of parliament and the clerkly culture of those civil servants who lived and worked in the city of London in the late fourteenth century."[80] Lydgate meshes neatly with none of those contexts, and yet, as Joel Fredell has pointed out, he, too, participated in the pamphleting culture. Fredell argues that many of the first pamphlets in Middle English were in fact poems, and broadsides and court lyrics were both called "bills" and circulated on single sheets "as contending voices in the same material form." As Fredell notes, Lydgate was "clearly aware of the many possible media outlets for his poetry" and in writing a number of his short poems of the 1420s translated his aureate style into a new discursive field.[81]

As a poetic letter that was publicly performed, the mumming harnesses a vernacular literary cosmopolitanism to the display of power, even as its content—and especially the "wrytt withinn" (l. 85)—urges the need to wield authority with moderation. Like the *Mumming for the Mercers* a month earlier, the *Mumming for the Goldsmiths* depicts legendary or otherwise distinguished visitors being welcomed into "þis cytee" in a way that makes mercantile London appear both inviting and worthy of foreign attention. In both mummings, the pursuivant is described as descending "dovne" when they arrive, suggesting the honor that the arrival of the mummers disguised as foreign merchants or the twelve tribes brings to the mayor. The gift of poetry supplied by Lydgate's verses can be seen as conferring a similar honor, while also affirming the cultural prominence of the guildsmen who heard and appreciated it.

Beyond the Guildhall

Although not intended for performance for one of London's companies, the *Mumming at Bishopswood* and the *Disguising at London* share some of the features and functions of the mummings for the Mercers and Goldsmiths. Their venues and audiences are more expansive, but they exhibit a similar construction of London and show the same interest in crafting a vernacular cosmopolitanism that meshes the literary with the practical.

Shirley describes the *Mumming at Bishopswood* as a "balade" in his headnote to the verses—not a letter in ballade form—made by Lydgate for a May Day dinner of London's sheriffs and their "bretherne" at Bishop's Wood, a place owned by the bishop of London.[82] Henry MacCracken calls *Bishopswood* a mumming, but Shirley does not, and, unlike most other fourteenth- and fifteenth-century mummings, including those for the Goldsmiths and Mercers, it did not take place during the Christmas season, although it does feature the visit of outsiders bearing gifts that is characteristic of the genre. No presenter is identified, but the messenger (described by Shirley as a "poursyvant") who brought the ballade may have read it aloud while silent characters impersonated Ver (Spring) and possibly Flora (although the text implies that she is not present), as well as May (if May is a figure distinct from Ver, something the text leaves unclear). The running titles at the top of the page identify the verses as "Lydegates balades sente / To þe Shreves dyner," echoing the phrasing of Shirley's headnote and again suggesting that a pursuivant delivered and perhaps spoke the lines. There may also have been a musical interlude by figures from classical mythology (i.e., Venus, Cupid, and Orpheus, at ll. 99–105). These lines may be meant merely as a poetic description, but music was apparently a part of the mumming for the Goldsmiths, as suggested by the instruction in lines 33–34 that the Levites sing. If *Bishopswood* was mimetically performed rather than simply read aloud, it would have required four performers (a presenter and three silent actors) and thus, although there is no evidence that actors were hired for the occasion, would match the size of the usual London performing company of the period.[83]

Bishopswood is undated, but Derek Pearsall places it in May 1429, arguing that it might have accompanied the mummings for the Mercers and Goldsmiths earlier that year; if Pearsall is correct, the actual date would have to be May 1430, since Estfeld was mayor from 29 October 1429 to 29 October 1430.[84] Noting that the coronation of Henry VI in London on 6 November 1429 might have raised ordinary festivities to a higher level in the next six months, Lancashire posits May Day of 1430 as a likely date for a special commission from Lydgate for the sheriffs' dinner, especially since he had provided entertainments for the coronation ceremonies.[85] A wider range of dates for the mumming cannot be ruled out, however, since the sole extant copy is in Bodleian MS Ashmole 59, which Shirley compiled in 1447–49 while resident in the close of St. Bartholomew's Hospital in London. Shirley's inclusion of *Bishopswood* in that manuscript while he did not recopy any of the mummings from Trinity MS R.3.20, which he used as a partial exemplar for MS Ashmole 59, may suggest that he did not have a copy of *Bishopswood* when he made R.3.20 in the early 1430s, either because it had not yet been performed or, more probably, because a copy had not yet been given to him.[86] Stow included the first two stanzas, derived from MS Ashmole 59, which passed through his hands, in his *Survey of London* (1598), as an example of the "great Mayings and maygames made by the gouernors and Maisters of this Citie," a remark that may be historically inaccurate given that the earliest recorded

May game in London dates to 1458 and took place in the parish of St. Nicholas Shambles.[87]

Still, it is clear that *Bishopswood* was designed to celebrate the changing seasons, which Lydgate accomplishes through a mixing of the social and the literary in a poetic presentation of springtime sweeping away winter's woes. The mumming consists of sixteen rhyme-royal stanzas that offer political and social commentary embedded within praise of the coming of spring, in the guise of Flora's daughter, Ver, who bids flowers to bloom and birds to sing, as signs that winter has fled. Ver also ushers in prosperity, peace, and unity after the adversity and troubles of winter, and the nature imagery soon develops into a social and political commentary that imagines all estates united, with each fulfilling its proper duties so that righteousness destroys the "darkness" of extortion and leads to a joyful summer.[88] While much of this commentary is a conventional reflection on the proper roles of the various estates, it may also address real contemporary concerns, especially in its references to discord and dissension. Like many of Lydgate's other poems for Londoners, *Bishopswood* speaks to the concerns and aspirations of the city's elites, particularly for order and prosperity.

Sheriffs in later medieval London were elected annually by a select group of *probi homines* from the city. Like aldermen, sheriffs were honorary officers of the city, served by a large household and their own court, perhaps the "bretherne" referred to by Shirley, including an extensive staff of civil servants and sergeants who assisted them. Their duties included guarding the counties of London and Middlesex, keeping the assizes of bread and ale, executing royal writs after showing them to the mayor and city counsel, and serving as the mayor's deputy. In addition to being civic officials charged with maintaining law and order in the city, sheriffs were royal agents, responsible for rendering account to the barons of the Exchequer for the city's financial obligations and for carrying out the king's demands for the arrest of criminals and the execution of traitors or heretics as well as for declaring royal proclamations. They also had jurisdiction over Middlesex as well as London, a dual role that Caroline Barron notes was problematic, despite the link between the city and the county. In 1385, the common council stipulated that every mayor should first serve as sheriff so as to have his "governance and bountee" tested.[89] In May 1430, the two sheriffs were a goldsmith and a merchant tailor.[90] Although the recipient of the mumming's honorific addresses—the person addressed in such phrases as "youre hye renoun" (l. 35) and "youre Hye Excellence" (l. 80)—is unnamed, it is possible that *Bishopswood* may have honored Mayor Estfeld.[91] Whoever the exact addressee, the audience of sheriffs, aldermen, and prosperous Londoners assembled for this mumming resembled the audiences for other forms of late medieval civic drama, including the "sovereigns" mentioned in many plays, terms that entered English as borrowings from a French courtly style during the reign of Richard II.[92] Lydgate's adoption of similar terms for the *Bishopswood* audience aligns his mumming with other civic performances pitched to affluent urban citizens.

What we know about that audience, including its sharing in elite literary tastes, suggests it would have been receptive to the transformational tactics of the *Mumming at Bishopswood*, with its echoes of Chaucer and French poetry.[93] Ver, for example, is a relatively uncommon personification in Middle English poetry, as Norton-Smith notes, but Chaucer uses it in *Troilus and Criseyde* (l. 157).[94] *Bishopswood* also echoes a passage from Chaucer's *House of Fame* on Orpheus's music (ll. 1201ff), draws on the *Parliament of Fowls* for the notion of spring as a season in which birds choose mates, and references the *Canterbury Tales* in a variety of ways, including in its emphasis on the social order. These and other poachings show Lydate's reliance on not just a Chaucerian but also a French poetics that Chaucer himself wrote within. As Ardis Butterfield has argued, Chaucer himself "participated in a broad literary culture . . . that was shaped and inspired by writers in French." Chaucer's poetry shows less a pattern of borrowing from the French, Butterfield notes, than evidence of a network of relationships between England and France that extended back for several hundred years, making Chaucer to a large extent "always 'already' French."[95] Whether through Chaucer or through the continuing and pervasive influence of French cultural habits or through direct contact with French texts, Lydgate created in *Bishopswood* verses that had the same "always 'already' French" feel, now being explicitly presented to London's sheriffs and their guests.[96]

While his indebtedness to French literary culture is apparent, to what degree French performances influenced Lydgate's mummings remains uncertain. In various ways, his mummings resemble court and civic performances in France, including those in which costumed courtiers performed for aristocratic audiences or *puys* and *confréries* put on plays. Some of these sorts of performances must have been familiar to Lydgate through transmission to England, and others he may have seen firsthand while he was in France in the 1420s.[97] As Nolan notes, however, none of these performances have yet been identified as direct sources for the verses of Lydgate's mummings, even if they most likely guided his assumptions about what a mumming should—or could—be.[98]

Whether its source lies in poetry or performance—or some mix of the two, as is most likely—the vernacular cosmopolitanism of *Bishopswood* relies on assimilation of a French-inflected poetics to English writing, a poetics that carried with it a sense of prestige and high status.[99] It also, and in a parallel process, adopts forms derived from other kinds of socially elevated performances. As Walter Schirmer observes, *Bishopswood* innovatively blends pantomime-type pageants such as those found in royal entries and didactic scholastic drama such as the *Pageant of Knowledge*, and Pearsall points to its learned philosophical and scientific description of spring.[100] Like the *Mumming for the Mercers*, *Bishopswood* presents its audience with a classical poetic tradition (Parnasaus, Citherra, Caliope, Orpheus) imagined as increasing the prosperity, welfare, and happiness of the mumming's audience. The ballade, classical allusions, learned references, and nod to other types of performance all serve to make the literary a vehicle for social and economic values of benefit to the assembled sheriffs, aldermen, and other prosperous Londoners. The result is what James Simpson calls "a heterogeneous collage of differently figured histories" and aesthetic forms.[101]

Bishopwood's use of a pursuivant is one example of this collage effect. Like the herald who delivers the "lettre made in wyse of balade" to the Goldsmiths, the pursuivant carries specific ceremonial connotations. A pursuivant was a messenger, an attendant on a herald, or a junior heraldic officer attached to a royal or noble household. In the twelfth century, heralds were household servants, but in later years, they developed specific roles as keepers of chivalric devices and records and as celebrators of chivalric deeds, while also playing a part in "political, diplomatic, and administrative contexts," as Katie Stevenson has noted.[102] Besides administering tournaments, heralds also made announcements and proclamations, carried letters, and served as masters-of-ceremonies; in wardrobe accounts, they are often grouped with minstrels and other performers, explaining the frequent conflation in medieval documents of heralds and minstrels. In identifying the deliverer of the ballades for the sheriff's dinner and in other mummings as a pursuivant, it may be that Shirley is using terminology and citing personages familiar to him from his time in Beauchamp's household. It is also possible, however, that these mummings featured presenters costumed in this courtly fashion. Pursuivants and heralds were increasingly coming to be used in private ceremonies, however, suggesting a slippage from courtly to other milieu.[103] The use of a pursuivant in this mumming has the effect, then, of transferring ceremonial activities traditionally associated with the king to the mayor, sheriffs, and assembled estates, an effect consistent with the relocating of royal privilege signaled by the "honorable" nature of the dinner the sheriffs attended and by the honorifics used to address the mumming's recipients.

Lydgate includes a passage in the *Troy Book* that describes what he imagines classical tragedy to have been like in performance, and while the passage has often been dismissed as a typically inaccurate medieval understanding of ancient performance practices, it may offer information about contemporary mummings, as Glynne Wickham suggests.[104] Lydgate describes a theater in which a poet stood at a pulpit and recounted ("rad or songyn" 2:862) the deeds and, specifically, the falls of famous men while visored actors came out, "Pleying by signes in the peples sight, / That the poete songon hathe on hight" (2:903–4). These performances occurred, Lydgate says, in April or May, just as springtime was beginning, a calendrical association with *Bishopswood*'s May Day setting that may imply a connection in Lydgate's mind between the ancient performance envisioned in the *Troy Book* and the 1420s one for London's sheriffs. Since no poet is mentioned in the *Mumming at Bishopswood*, the pursuivant may have read the verses aloud while costumed mummers mimed along with them, a performance mode that would have been consistent with the role of heralds and pursuivants as participants in ceremonies and as conveyors of messages.

The expansion of milieu beyond London's companies found in Lydgate's verses and in the mumming's performance venue is echoed in the manuscript into which the *Mumming at Bishopswood* was copied. Margaret Connolly argues that MS Ashmole 59 lacks a preface not because it once had one that later was lost but that, unlike Shirley's two earlier anthologies, BL MS Add. 16165 and Trinity MS R.3.20, it was "never intended for circulation in the same type of context as the preceding anthologies." Much later in date than the earlier anthologies, more serious in tone, and compiled when Shirley had left Beauchamp's service and was living in the precincts of St. Bartholomew's Hospital, MS Ashmole 59 apparently did not have as its primary audience the noble household of which he himself had once been a member.[105] Instead, the prosperous members of the clergy and laity residing in St. Bartholomew's Close seem likely to have constituted the audience for Shirley's last anthology.[106] If that was indeed the case, then *Bishopswood* was read by individuals who, like those present at its performance for the sheriffs, were part of an urban and bourgeois milieu, not a courtly one, even if, like the sheriffs, they may have had affiliations that brought them into contact with spheres beyond the civic. Those readers, like the assembled guests at the mumming, may have welcomed the themes of peace, prosperity, and social wholeness advanced in Lydgate's verses, with their insistence that "Of alle estates there shal beo oone image" (l. 50). "Troubles exylinge," Ver once again repairs what "winter hathe so fade" (ll. 72, 86), a hopeful message that urban clergy and laity may well have been happy to embrace.

While the evidence is inconclusive, it is tempting to link the *Disguising at London* with Lydgate's other mummings for the heightened ceremonial year of 1429–30. Shirley says it was made "for the gret estates of this lande, thanne being at London," which has led to the supposition that Lydgate wrote it for a gathering of parliament. Parliament met at Westminster from 22 September 1429 to 23 February 1430, although Pearsall notes that a disguising for that session would probably have mentioned the coronation of Henry VI on 6 November 1429.[107] There may, however, be oblique reference to that event, in the disguising's inclusion of Henry V among the "prynces of latter date" (l. 266) who were guided by virtue, an inclusion that would have particular force in a year in which Henry's son assumed power (the subtleties for the coronation banquet similarly made reference to Henry V). Whatever the precise date or occasion, the text makes clear that the disguising was designed for household performance (ll. 335 and 337) during the long Christmas season (l. 280) that ran from October through early January; the hope expressed in line 334 that the virtues bestowed by the disguising will last "al this yeer" may locate the performance more precisely on a day in early January.

The disguising has the feel of a "mirror for princes," recast for a broader audience and responsive to the political instability of the late 1420s.[108] It opens with the appearance of Dame Fortune, whose dangerous mutability sets the stage for the introduction of the four cardinal virtues—Dames Prudence, Righteousness, Fortitude, and Temperance—who promise to defend all who serve them. The disguising's 342 lines of rhyming couplets consist of lengthy descriptions of each of the four virtues in turn, ending with a song that banishes fickle Fortune. As with the other mummings for the Londoners in 1429–30, a central concern of the disguising is good governance, which is seen as a remedy for Fortune's dangerous instability; the gift giving associated with the mumming takes the abstract form in Lydgate's verses of gifts of virtue, which the disguising promises will reside "in this housholde" (l. 335) for the year. The disguising suggests that embracing virtue will lead to good governance and hence offers protection against misfortune. Although the disguising was apparently performed on a national, not a municipal, occasion, its values "are practical and bourgeois," as Benson notes, and its tone is optimistic, emphasizing "the sort of pragmatic, decent, and well-regulated communal behavior advocated by medieval London citizens."[109] Nolan argues that the disguising aims "to develop a notion of virtue fit for the public realm of politics, a secularized (though hardly secular) code of behavior particularly suited to the governing classes."[110] There is certainly no lack of evidence suggesting that a performance featuring the virtues would have appeal both at court and in the city, and the virtues were even visually represented in both venues: the king's bedroom at Westminster contained a painting of the virtues battling the vices, while the rebuilt Guildhall (1411–30) included statues of Fortitude, Justice, Temperance, and Discipline.[111]

Lydgate's verses contain numerous hints about the performance for which they were written and seem especially "script-like," as Kipling has noted.[112] Entrances are marked by brief stage directions, the narrator interacts with the audience and the actors (by drawing attention to the arrival of each new character, banishing Fortune, and commanding the four virtues to sing), and the text specifies several stage properties (Prudence's mirror, Righteousness's balance, Fortitude's sword). The lack of dialogue suggests that a presenter probably read the text aloud, as Fortune and the four virtues made their appearances. Although there is no indication of the actions they might have performed, Meg Twycross and Sarah Carpenter think that the four virtues may have presented the "gift" of their attributes to the presiding dignitaries.[113] The final lines of the disguising command the four protectors to sing "Some nuwe songe aboute the fuyre" (ll. 338–40), implying that the disguising ended with music.

Although described by Shirley not as a letter or a ballade but rather as a "devyse" (a plan), the *Disguising at London* is heavily indebted to a literary poetics—French, classical, and English—particularly in its allusions to and paraphrases of the *Roman de la Rose* and its use of the literary tradition of the falls of great men, including in Chaucer's "Monk's Tale."[114] Lydgate explicitly mentions the *Roman* in line 9, and his opening description of Fortune closely follows the *Roman*. Nolan argues that in this disguising, Lydgate connects Chaucer's ideas about tragedy and comedy to dramatic performance, thus producing a text that "seeks to carve out a space for literary art in public performance," although one could argue for the same carving out in the other mummings for Londoners as well.[115]

Parliament would have been a particularly appropriate venue for such a performance, given its importance as an arena for not just political debate but also public display and artistic efforts. As Matthew Giancarlo has shown, by the late fourteenth century, parliament was a social and literary, as well as a political, event.[116] As a large assembly drawing many groups of people, parliament was a forum for popular communication in the vernacular that could take a variety of forms, including ceremonies, speeches, sermons, and petitions, among others. Increasingly, this communication was in English, making parliament a prominent force behind the growing prestige of the vernacular.[117]

When Shirley copied the *Disguising at London* into Trinity MS R.3.20, along with the mummings for the Mercers and Goldsmiths, he seems to have been intent on making sure readers grasped the "moral, plesaunt, and notable" nature of the disguising that he praised with those words in his headnote. To that end, he included various marginal notes commenting on personages or references in Lydgate's verses. Next to the description of Julius Caesar in lines 67–70, he notes that "Sesar a bakars son"; he cites a chapter of Ecclesiastes on good and bad women; he adds the Latin gloss "i. providencia" at line 165, presumably to make sure that readers know that the "lady" being referred to is Providence; and he glosses Lydgate's "commune proufyte" (the usual Middle English translation of *res publica*) in line 251 as "i. republica." Shirley's copies of the performances for the Goldsmiths and, more extensively, the Mercers are similarly glossed in Latin and English to explain allusions, personages, or biblical scriptures on which Lydgate draws. Some of those glosses may have originated in his exemplars, but others appear to be his own additions. Whatever their source, the result is to make classical and other allusions accessible to the reader, an enhanced value unavailable to those who merely watched the performances. It may indeed be the case, as Nolan suggests, that Lydgate's mummings and disguisings are in part literary works "in search of educated and savvy readers," but Shirley's glosses recognize what is latent in Lydgate's verses: that such readers can be actively made as well as passively found.[118]

A city such as London, as David Harris Sacks notes, was a shifting mix of "openness to the world of commerce and industry and closeness behind protective walls."[119] Although institutions such as the guild system, the shrievalty, and even parliament helped impose an orderly grid on urban life, lines of demarcation were often unclear, with overlapping markets and levels of authority, and with people, goods, and ideas passing into and out of the city. Medieval London was both an autonomous civic polity defined by its walled borders and a territory that spilled outside those borders and that was invaded by outsiders from the king and prelates to visiting traders and members of parliament. It was a city in which civic authority was pressured by the demands of crown and church. As Lydgate's mummings and disguising for Londoners show, it was also a city eager to establish its prestige, not least through poetry and ceremony that embraced cosmopolitanism.

Textual practices do not exist within a social vacuum but are, as Simpson recognizes, "produced by, and themselves sustain, particular social and political formations."[120] Within the particular formations of fifteenth-century London, Lydgate's mummings and disguisings for guildsmen, sheriff, and members of parliament simultaneously commemorate public occasions and construct an imaginary public. That public, while made up chiefly of elites, is nonetheless broad and even at times fractured.[121] What Lydgate offers those who commissioned and watched his entertainments was the promise of making fractured publics whole. He may only uneasily use the language of common profit that characterizes the public poetry of Chaucer and his other literary forebears, but the verses he wrote for performance in and around London achieve a similar end, by aesthetic and ceremonial means.

Andrew Galloway has persuasively argued for the importance of Lydgate in the development of what scholars have termed *vernacular humanism*. A form of humanism that broadened and extended, in Galloway's words, "the power of classical interests and their social prestige," vernacular humanism joined interest in classical sources and styles with contemporary concerns, often to promote a new kind of national identity.[122] Vernacular humanism offered a way of addressing the national and local implications of ancient thought, making it available for a range of uses beyond the purely scholarly. While Galloway argues for Lydgate's deep engagement with ancient thought, in contradistinction to Nolan's reading of Lydgate's classicism as having been mediated through Chaucer, Gower, and continental writers, both views can coexist, not just for Lydgate as a writer but for his audiences, whose literary tastes may have included direct knowledge of ancient writers, as Galloway claims was the case, as well as awareness of English and continental poetry.[123]

If vernacular humanism describes one aspect of Lydgate's literary practice, then vernacular cosmopolitanism defines another. Especially in his mummings and disguisings for urban audiences and, later, readers, Lydgate was as instrumental in shaping a vernacular cosmopolitanism with London as its center as he was in carving out a melding of classical styles and ideas with contemporary historical concerns that would lay the ground for a tradition that would flourish in the sixteenth century.[124] Like his vernacular humanism,

Lydgate's vernacular cosmopolitanism allowed him to broaden and expand a style and set of themes derived from continental poets and often filtered through Chaucer. Also like vernacular humanism, vernacular cosmopolitanism is an apparent oxymoron that joins two seemingly contradictory notions and asks that we imagine that the parochial and demotic can coexist with the transnational and sophisticated.[125] Lydgate's mummings and disguising for Londoners achieve that balance, offering to their urban audiences what Benson sees as the hallmark of "civic Lydgate": poetry that gives shape to "the idea and experience of the city."[126]

CHAPTER 3

Performing Pictures

Reading and hearing were close relatives in medieval culture. Even when not composed orally, poems long and short were sung or spoken aloud to listeners, while also offering themselves for silent, private reading. As with Chaucer's invocation of an audience for the *Canterbury Tales* of everyone who "redith or herith," a good deal of medieval poetry contains traces of the expectation of differing forms of reception, as scholars have noted.[1] Reading and looking were also near kin, and the metaphor of sight was used in the later medieval period to characterize a variety of kinds of understanding, including the understanding of the poetic text.[2] A number of scholars have examined the effects of manuscript page layout on readers and on texts, as well as the overlap between the visual and the theatrical in illustrated manuscripts.[3] Fewer, however, have looked at poems that were visually displayed outside of the codex. One result has been that the variety of places in which written texts could be encountered has not been given its full due, leading to a skewed and limited picture of the readership for a text. Those earlier studies of writing outside the book, which I discuss later in this chapter along with more recent work on graffiti and the permanent and ephemeral display of writing (as posted broadsheets or as inscriptions on walls), remind us that especially before the introduction of production processes that made handwritten texts affordable for a wider range of purchasers, many readers may have encountered poetry not on the page but on a wall, whether in a church, household, or other public or private place. Tapestries depicted scenes and speeches from drama, city spectacles included painted words and images on hanging cloths or pageant structures, and murals featured written as well as drawn representations.

On more than one occasion, Lydgate turned his hand to poems intended for visual display outside a codex, including, most famously, the *Danse macabre* or *Daunce of Poulys*, commissioned by John Carpenter for painting on the walls of the Pardon Churchyard at St. Paul's Cathedral in London; some of his other verses eventually ended up being publicly displayed, such as selections from his "Quis dabit?" and *Testament* that were incorporated into the decorations for the Clopton chantry chapel at Long Melford Church in Suffolk, not far from Bury St. Edmunds. Lydgate also made two poems for Londoners—the *Legend of St. George* and *Bycorne and Chychevache*—that John Shirley links to wall paintings or hangings. All of these pictorial verses raise questions about what difference, if any, it made that a poem was read from a manuscript page or viewed on a wall hanging or listened to in a performance, and about the limits of genre labels such as poetry, painting, or play when applied to medieval cultural forms.

Like spectacles and ceremonies, which relied on visual display to communicate with audiences, wall paintings and painted or woven tapestries depended on spectatorship. But even if the experience of watching a play was in some ways homologous to that of looking at a tapestry, it could never be identical, if only because a live performance was a fleeting event, while a wall painting could be viewed again and again.[4] The verses Lydgate wrote for public visual display complicate notions of public poetry in late medieval England as well as notions of spectatorship. Meant to be read alongside visual images, these texts point to interactive and performative modes of looking that argue for an understanding of spectatorship as a far from passive engagement with the visual. Also, and more fundamentally, these texts reveal how such representational forms merged and differed, and with what results for theater and literary history.

Wall Hangings and Wall Paintings

Tapestries were among the most popular luxury goods of late medieval Europe and, in less lavish form, were part of everyday decoration and household furnishings, as attested by frequent mentions in wills of bequests of tapestry or arras bedclothes. They were also an important art form, particularly in the hundred or so years from 1350 through the end of the fifteenth century. Although tapestries had been produced in Europe earlier, large-scale production began in the fourteenth century in areas already known for weaving, most notably Paris and Arras, whose name became synonymous with woven figurative fabric. In the second half of the fourteenth century, tapestry grew more artistically and commercially important, and its use increased in the courts of Europe. Many tapestries depicted scenes from secular or religious history, often organized into a narrative. Best known among the large-scale historical tapestries of the fourteenth and early fifteenth centuries, which were probably used for civic or religious ceremonies, are the famous *Nine Worthies* wall hanging now in the Cloisters in New York; the *Battle of Roosbeek* (no longer extant) made for and celebrating the part played by Philip the Bold, Duke of Burgundy, in the defeat of Flemish rebels in 1382; and the *Jousts of St Denis* (no longer extant) commissioned by Charles VI in 1397.[5]

While the cost of woven tapestries limited their purchase to the wealthiest of patrons until the production boom of the late fifteenth century lowered prices, painted or "stained" hangings offered a less expensive textile medium for images and narratives. A will from 1429, for example, bequeaths to the "chapel of oure lady . . . a steyned clooth with the salutacion of oure lady ther to abide perpetuelly," while a reference from around 1449 comments, "Here in this steyned clooth, King Herri leieth a sege to Harflew."[6] As Charles Kightly's discussion of wall hangings in medieval York suggests, woven or painted tapestries could be a source of household ornamentation, a marker of social status, and, most pertinently for my arguments in this chapter, an opportunity for entertainment, given their predilection for depicting narrative.[7]

Woven or painted wall hangings often shared structural, affective, and aesthetic features with drama, as Laura Weigert has shown in the case of tapestries linked to the *Vengeance* mystery play, while in contrast, paintings of the same theme "depart significantly" from the play. Weigert argues, in fact, that of all the forms of visual representation from the late medieval and early modern periods, tapestry "exhibits the most numerous and striking similarities with mystery plays," to such an extent that the two media appear to have been mutually dependent.[8] Those similarities may be traced to instances of direct exchange, in which performances were created from famous tapestries scenes, or, more generally, to shared circumstances of production and reception, as the same wealthy patrons commissioned tapestries and performances. The similarities between the two media, including the resemblance of tapestry's life-size figures to live actors, often makes it hard to tell to which written accounts refer, since the language used to describe the two is frequently the same.

How people might have "read" stories on wall hangings or paintings is suggested by an episode in William Caxton's version of the romance *Blanchardyne and Eglantine* (c. 1489). Blanchardine, walking in his father's palace with his tutor, gazed at the "hangings of Tapestrie and Arras" on the wall. The romance describes how, "stedfastly pervsing the abstracts & deuises in the hangings," Blanchardine asked his tutor "what warlike seidge and slaughter of men that might be." So taken was he by his tutor's reply, which recounted the history of the war and the heroic feats performed by its participants, that Blanchardine himself aspired to the same honors with the result that he "continually practised, both in action and in reading, the imitation of those valorous warres; neither thought he any time so wel bestowed as either in reciting, reading, or conferring of those warres."[9] This conflation of looking and doing, reading and imitating, is consistent with and extends to secular contexts the well-documented emphasis within late medieval visual piety on affective experience and engaged remembering that were central aspects of lay devotion.[10]

Although tapestries and murals could offer legible texts well suited to spurring action and reflection alike, as the *Blanchardyne* example suggests, not all of them required an extra-textual commentator similar to Blanchardine's tutor to supply the missing verbal component needed to explain the visual depiction. As Eleanor Hammond has observed, it is not uncommon in surviving tapestries to see verses woven into the fabric. Citing evidence from the inventories of Charles VI of France and Henry V of England, Hammond notes frequent references to wall hangings *à personnages* that describe pictures of people accompanied by writing (often their names): one tapestry, for instance is described as including writing beneath its depictions of people, as well as their names ("ou il y a au dessoubz desdits personnages ecriptures et leur noms escripz"); another tapestry of many other people ("plusieurs autres personnages") contains "au dessoubz de elles a grans escriptures"; and yet another that contains many inscriptions ("plusieurs escripteaulx") is mentioned. More elaborately, the inventory of tapestries owned by Henry V cites what appears to be the opening phrase of the story ("estorie") on each tapestry: "Vessi amour sovient" (here follows love), "Cest ystorie fait remembraunce de noble Vierge Plesance" (this story commemorates the noble Virgin), "Vessi Dames de noble affaire" (here are women of noble deeds), and "Vessi une turnement comenser" (here a tournament begins).[11]

Firmer proof of words actually woven into wall hangings also survives. The January miniature of the *Très riches heures* depicts a banquet in an aristocratic household; on the wall behind the banqueting table hangs an expensively decorated tapestry that is perhaps an illustration of a tapestry that once belonged to Jean, Duc de Berry, and that includes written verses above scenes of battle. The six-piece Angers *Apocalypse* tapestries originally had panels below each scene with an inscription; the inscriptions, now lost, probably consisted of excerpts either from the text of Revelations or from a commentary on it. The tapestries of the *Romance of Jourdain de Blaye* (from the early fifteenth century) include inscriptions in a Picardy dialect. And a St. George tapestry described in the inventory of Thomas, duke of Gloucester, as "Une pece d'Arras d'or de St. George," is said to begin with an inscription in letters of gold and the arms of Gloucester ("comense en l'escripture des lettres d'or 'Geaus est Agles' ovec les armes de Monsr de Gloucestr").[12]

In what ways would spectators have interacted with woven or painted writing displayed alongside images? While direct evidence is elusive, the scholarship on religious visual experiences and devotional images provides some helpful answers. In a perceptive analysis of the late fourteenth-century altarpiece now known as the Despenser Retable—which was discovered in Norwich Cathedral in 1847 being used as a table—Sarah Stanbury observes that the retable has both a narrative as well as an iconic status ("in Walter Benjamin's terms," it carries "both cult and exhibition value") and that its five painted panels depicting the Passion "form a powerful linear narrative that operates in tandem and in dialogue with the fixity of its coats of arms." While the Despenser Retable does not mix words and images, the armorial banners that appear within its frame require of viewers the ability to take in two different forms of visual media. Stanbury shows how the visual dynamic of the piece, particularly the dominance of the frame with its coats of arms linked to powerful local families, engages the viewer in part by memorializing the community and can be understood through the history of lay self-representation, as the panels play out a narrative of social disruption and the restoration of order.[13] Although she does not focus specifically on viewer interaction with the altarpiece, Stanbury suggests that to "read" the retable, anyone looking at the retable would have had to negotiate between two narratives, one concerning a Passion sequence that moves from bodily disruption to containment, the other having to do with the local history inscribed in the armorial banners.[14] In this way two visual fields demand a back-and-forth form of looking in which meaning can only be derived from the interplay between the two fields.

Other studies of religious affect have shown that in late medieval meditative writings, the interactive engagement of spectator and image is especially strong, with the devotional image often seeming to become animated and to enter a charged space that includes the individual who gazes on it.[15] For Julian of Norwich and Margery Kempe alike, the sight of a religious image often triggers revelations or strong emotional responses. Passion poems and other visionary texts describe religious icons or images that literally speak to the spectator or become animated, among the most gripping being stories of the appearance of the Christ child in the host.[16] Iconographic representations of saints helped create a spiritual dialogue between saint and worshipper and were tied to acts of devotion such as vows, veneration of saints, and pilgrimages; a viewer's engagement with images was part of a larger involvement with devotional practices of various kinds.[17]

As the linking of viewing images with other acts of devotion suggests, there was considerable spilling over from sight to other sensory experiences and from looking to other forms of embodied action, a phenomenon Michael Camille recognizes when observing that "medieval pictures cannot be separated from what is a total experience of communication involving sight, sound, action and physical expression."[18] Far from being isolated as discrete forms of representation, images in the late medieval period took their place within a broader set of cultural practices revolving around the sending and receiving of expressive messages. To "read" an image was thus to do much more than merely decipher iconographic details; "reading" such visual works as fifteenth-century murals and large-scale panels in effect granted the viewer what Elina Gertsman calls "a participatory, performative function within the otherwise fixed interpretative visual and textual context."[19]

If the example of Blanchardyne suggests how images on tapestries were received, Colart de Laon, a French painter whose life spanned the late fourteenth and early fifteenth centuries, shows how they were produced and, specifically, how an artist might have shaped a career around providing visual representations on fabric for ceremonial uses. Colart is first mentioned in 1377, in the employ of Philip the Bold, Duke of Burgundy. Most of Colart's commissions appear to have been related to royal festivities and consisted primarily of painting banners and jousting implements. He was employed for the elaborate entry of Isabeau of Bavaria into Paris (1389) and prepared ceremonial trappings in connection with the marriage of John, eldest son of Duke Philip the Bold, in Cambrai. In December 1395, Colart was paid by Duke Philip's chamberlain for "grands tableaux," whose subject matter unfortunately went unmentioned. Soon thereafter, Colart executed "un tableau de bois qui fait ciel et dossier," which included images of the Virgin, St. John, and the Trinity, for a chapel endowed by Louis of Orléans in the church of the Celestines, Paris, and supplied a panel with Sts. Louis of France and Louis of Toulouse for the room of the Dauphin Charles. In 1400, he provided four large painted cartoons for tapestries ordered by the queen, and in 1406, he agreed to complete a tableau intended to be given as a gift from Jean de la Cloche to the Paris parliament.[20] While few have been as well documented, there must have been many similar artisans who made a living by supplying visual images for wall hangings and murals, many of them destined for ceremonial occasions and spectacles.

Lydgate's Visual Poetry

While Colart lets us glimpse a visual artist's involvement with pictorial poetry, Lydgate offers a nearly contemporary look at a poet's corresponding role. Although the paintings that accompanied Lydgate's verses have not survived, as far as we are aware, internal clues within the poems point to their connection with images as do Shirley's headnotes. Several of Lydgate's religious works were apparently intended to be read along with visual images, as they themselves tell us. "Cristes Passioun," for example, ends with the poet-speaker sending the poem ("Go, lytel bylle") to "Hang affore Iesu" in the hope that "folk that shal the see" will read "this compleynt" (ll. 113–16). "The Dolerous Pyte of Crystes Passioun," which begins, "erly on morwe, and toward nyght also, / First and last, looke on this ffygure" (ll. 1–2), and ends by stating that saying a Paternoster, Ave, and Creed while kneeling before this "dolorous pite" will earn pardons (l. 51–56), similarly suggests that the poem was intended to accompany a visual image (a "pite," or pietà) displayed in some public place, presumably a church. "The Image of our Lady" begins with a similar command to "Beholde and se this glorious fygure, / Whiche Sent Luke of our lady lyvynge / After her lyknes made in picture" (ll. 1–3), a picture that is later identified as resembling a painting in the church of Santa Maria de Populo in Rome. And the last stanza of "On De Profundis" claims that the verses were compiled at the request of William Curteys (abbot of Bury) so that he would be able "At his chirche to hang it on the wal" (ll. 167–68).[21]

Similarly, some of Lydgate's secular poems were also seemingly written to accompany visual representations. The "Sodein Fal of Princes" contains phrases (e.g., "Beholde þis gret prynce," "Se howe," "Se nowe," and "Lo here") that suggest it was intended for a mural or wall hanging or possibly a tableau or dumbshow in which silent performers mimed actions while a presenter recited the text.[22] In excerpted form, stanzas from the *Pageant of Knowledge*, such as the descriptions of the seven estates that appear in some versions of it, could readily have accompanied visual images. Lydgate also wrote verses to accompany the subtleties for the coronation banquet of Henry VI and verses related to a procession of Corpus Christi in London, performances I discuss in later chapters.

The enthusiasm Lydgate reveals for working at the crossroads linking image and written text played out within the context of larger debates in the fifteenth century about the validity of devotional images, with on the one side Lollard polemic against images and on the other such defenders as Reginald Pecock.[23] Lydgate's embrace of images is consistent with his preference for orthodoxy and, perhaps more interestingly—especially for a consideration of his verses that engage with nonreligious images—with his vernacular poetics, as the varied poems in which he reflects on the role of images show. Shannon Gayk has pointed out that a number of Lydgate's poems "instruct the viewer in how to read images" and that, more broadly, he fashions a literary practice that "inscribes the objects and practices of contemporary devotion within an increasingly textual culture."[24] That claim should be extended to nondevotional objects and practices as well, given the degree to which even in them for Lydgate images are assimilated to textual culture. Stories can be "shewyd in fygur" ("On the Image of Pity," l. 39), a choice of terms that connects *shewing* both in the mind's eye and in embodied form and *figurae* in the exegetical or symbolic sense and, as I argue in the case of the processional images discussed in the next chapter, the material (i.e., painted or displayed image).

It is not, however, just the mixing of word and picture that shapes many of Lydgate's picture-poems but also performance. Theorization of the relationship between medieval visual and dramatic texts has in recent years beneficially moved beyond an earlier preoccupation with identifying the ways in which one influenced the other to a consideration of art and drama as, in Martin Stevens's words, "intertextual, not causal or agentive."[25] Yet, even considered from the perspective of semiosis, not mimesis, as Stevens urges, the relationship between the two can be elusive, not least because of the scarcity of surviving evidence. Some medieval paintings, although not many, seem to depict plays being performed, including a book from twelfth-century St. Albans that contains the plays of Terence and shows gestures of characters in dialogue, figures from the plays, and classical masks in a structure that

seem to represent a classical *scena*; the miniature by Jean Fouquet of the martyrdom of St. Apollonia; and the depiction of the "Dance of the Wodewoses"
found in a manuscript of Froissart's *Chronicles*, c. 1470.[26]

A more extended interaction between art and drama can be found in the
paintings that precede the play-texts in the fifteenth-century manuscript of
seventy-two French plays once performed in Lille. They depict one or two
scenes from the following play and not a stage or a play being performed;
instead, they show scenes from biblical stories, just as the texts of the plays do.
Thus, in the Lille manuscript, "the paintings and plays have parallel functions
for readers and spectators," as Alan Knight has noted.[27] Something similar
occurs with the words and images in Lydgate's murals and wall hangings,
where there is also a pronounced association with performance, whether the
performance in question is a mumming, procession, dance, or religious ritual.
Mieke Bal's notion of the "cotext," as distinct from the "pre-text" of a work of
art, is useful in theorizing the relationship among words, images, and performance in these works. Rather than searching for a "pre-text" that would explain what the work of art derives from, analysis that focuses on the "cotext"
can elucidate the immediate literary and visual milieu of a work of art and
the meanings generated by that milieu. In the case of Lydgate's visual texts
linked to performance, performance does not simply lie in the background as
a precursor of the image-text but instead forms part of its immediate milieu
and shapes the viewer's interaction with the mural or wall hanging.[28]

The *Daunce of Poulys* and the *Testament*

The longest of Lydgate's poems for visual display was the *Danse macabre* or,
as it is named in one manuscript, the *Daunce of Poulys*, a translation into English of French verses from the (now lost) Dance of Death of 1424–25 painted
in the cemetery of the Church of the Holy Innocents in Paris. Lydgate probably made this poem when he was in Paris in 1426, at the behest of certain
"French clerks," as he says in the prologue to his poem.[29] Lydgate's verses
were designed, a headnote in one of the surviving copies of Lydgate's poem
tells us, for display in St. Paul's Cathedral.[30] In his *Survey of London*, John
Stow corroborates Shirley's claim, mentioning that around the interior of the
cloister on the north side of St. Paul's was once painted the Dance of Death,
like that in Paris, and that Lydgate's translation was made "with the picture
of Death, leading all estates painted about the Cloyster" at the request of

John Carpenter, London's common clerk. According to Stow, the whole cloister was pulled down by the duke of Somerset in 1549 to supply building material for his palace in the Strand.[31]

Dance of Death murals combing words and images could appear outdoors, as in the Cemetery of the Holy Innocents in Paris, but were more often displayed on church walls.[32] Carpenter's decision to have the *Daunce of Poulys* painted on panels hung on the inside walls of the cloister enclosing the cemetery known as the Pardon Churchyard, on the northwest side of St. Paul's Cathedral, placed the Dance of Death mural in a similarly interiorized and relatively secluded space, away from the bustle of St. Paul's cross and the city.[33] In a reading of the mural's significance for Londoners, Amy Appleford has argued that the collaboration between poet and bureaucrat on this visual-verbal display resulted in "the construction of an image of England's capital city as a diverse yet coherent association of people otherwise fragmented along numerous internal divides." Appleford's view of the St. Paul's mural as intervening in struggles over cultural dominance in the city by using the topos of the *memento mori* to insist on London's "autonomy from, and ability to hold its own against, alternate and competing sources of sociopolitical authority, namely, the church and the Crown" meshes well with what we know of Carpenter's concerns and of Lydgate's abilities to turn his hand to urban discourses. More to the point for my argument in this chapter, Appleford's recognition that, as common clerk, Carpenter's domain was the city's documentary culture (he was the creator around 1421 of the massive *Liber Albus* that attempts to organize centuries of archival material from London) and that he therefore not surprisingly believed in the power of the written word helps explain his decision to re-create the Parisian image-text of the Dance of Death in London.[34]

Because both the Paris and St. Paul's paintings were destroyed and because the fidelity to the original of later versions—such as Guyot Marchant's woodcuts in the 1485 edition of the *Danse macabre* and the damaged late fifteenth-century imitation of the St. Paul's paintings in the Guild Chapel at Stratford-on-Avon—is uncertain, we cannot know what anyone who visited the Pardon Churchyard saw. Stow suggested that the figure of Death led the procession around the walls, but that may be his own interpolation and cannot be verified by extant sources.[35] Presumably the mural was painted at eye level or slightly above, as was the case for the Dance of Death mural at Meslay-le-Grenet, c. 1500. In the Meslay-le-Grenet mural, the pictorial images of Death and the figures he leads dominate, while the written text appears in a much smaller border-like space immediately below. Gertsman argues that this positioning of the Meslay-le-Grenet mural made it "accessible to the congregation," and its prominence meant it was "the backdrop for every ceremony that took place within the church walls."[36] The Pardon Churchyard at St. Paul's held the Becket tomb, which was linked to one of London's patron saints, and was the destination of mayoral processions, thus making the *Daunce of Poulys* mural a similarly charged backdrop for civic ceremony in fifteenth-century London. By entering the Pardon Churchyard and territory that while once an open space had been ceded to ecclesiastical authority since the 1320s, the mayor and his entourage asserted "the city's claim to rights of way within the precinct walls," as Appleford has argued.[37]

Lydgate's Dance of Death verses survive in fifteen manuscripts, including Ellesmere 26.A.13, which was owned by John Shirley, and Trinity R.3.21, a London anthology linked to the Hammond scribe and thus, by association, to Shirley.[38] The manuscripts of Lydgate's verses fall into two groups: the A version fairly closely follows the French poem (but adds four women to the French version's all-male cast of characters and includes a Tregetour, or magician/entertainer, named Jon Rikelle), while the B version reorders and re-works the A version, omitting several characters and adding eight new ones, including a number of representatives of urban society such as a Sergeant in Law, Juror, Merchant, and Artificer.[39] We do not know what degree of collaboration was involved between Lydgate and Carpenter or if Carpenter suggested changes in the poem, but the B version certainly does a better job than the A version of fitting the St. Paul's setting and of drawing attention to the middling urban social groups usually only lightly sketched in the traditional version.

Even more so than in the A version, in their fragmented form, the B group verses offer a vision of society understood as what James Simpson has called "a complex set of self-contained and overlapping jurisdictions."[40] The B version also effectively translates the poem from a form designed for reading on the page to a text that would be viewed as part of a mural. The B version skips over the "Verba Translatoris" with which the A version opens (a section that emphasizes the craft of translating and writing) and begins with a stanza that in the A group is one of two stanzas designated as "Verba Auctoris." That stanza stresses the spectator's visual engagement with the images and verses about death, by keeping the phrase "Ye may seen heer," which appears in the A version as well, but changing A's "How ye schulle trace / the daunce of machabre" (l. 46) to "how ye shal trace / the daunce which that ye see" (l. 6).

Combined with the omission of the five stanzas explaining how the poem was translated, the stronger emphasis on sight in the first stanza of the B version of the poem immediately identifies a visual context within which the following verses are to be apprehended.

While the opening of the B version stresses vision, the following verses encode a broad range of sensory participation. The verses describing the exchange between Death and the various social groups preserved in the B version the address-and-response structure of the A group, as in alternate stanzas Death addresses in turn each figure, who is given a chance to reply. This alternation of voices creates the impression of a dialogue that injects an element of aurality into the visual representation; reader-viewers of the mural at St. Paul's were thus also asked to listen as Death engages each figure in a conversation. That engagement with the words and pictures painted on the cloister walls is intensified by the increased use in the B version of phrases that introduce the various figures by calling them forward, as in "Com forth maistresse" (l. 353) or "Come neer sir Sergeant" (l. 337), thus stressing motion in a way that resonated with the movement of viewers around the cloister walls. These altered phrases intensify the processional form of the mural and act as an encouragement to viewers to move along the walls of the cloister in a way that mirrored the procession of Death being described in the pictures and painted words. As Gertsman has argued, such features invited "a kinesthetic and participatory mode of viewing" that provided "a site for active spectatorship"; Seeta Chaganti has similarly asserted that in *Danse macabre* wall paintings, "human bodily movement represented one medium functioning as part of the installation's complete spectacle."[41] Those who walked the walls of the Pardon Churchyard, following the mural from beginning to end, would have been asked to become not just viewers but active participants in the ritual of the Dance of Death depicted before them.

The verses by Lydgate displayed in the Pardon Churchyard lay at the nexus of written words, visual images, and embodied action, but in some manuscripts of the B group, the concluding verses reframe this sensorily engaged and active participation as *reading*. All of the B group texts omit the "Lenvoye de translatoure" of the A group and end with heavily revised versions of two stanzas from A, plus, in some manuscripts, a final, newly added stanza. The two revised stanzas in BL MS Lansdowne 699, for example, change the A group's "3e folke that loken upon this purtrature / Beholdyng heer all the estates daunce" (633–34) to "3e folk that loken upon this scripture / Conceyveth here that al estatis daunce" (561–62), a shift that elevates "scrip-

ture" over "portaiture" and "conceiving" over "beholding." This emphasis on
language, apprehended through the act of reading and through processes of
taking in and understanding, as implied by the use of the verb *conceyveth*
(from *conceiven*) can be interpreted as an attempt to move the viewer's experience of the picture-poem away from "kinesthetic and participatory" viewing
and toward contemplation, a move that is underscored by the repeated exhortation (present, but in a more muted way, in the A group) to keep what has been
experienced through the act of viewing the mural "in remembraunce" (565)
and "in your memorye" (573). To end as the Lansdowne version of Lydgate's
poem does is to envision the legible text (the "scripture") as well as the viewable
pictures all as one combined image "seen" in and impressed upon the mind.
Sensation, imagination, and textuality all come together in this act of remembrance as the image is imprinted on the viewer's mind, a process that can be
seen even more strongly in the following example.[42]

A lengthy set of Lydgate's verses was used as wall art in another religious
setting, this one close to his abbey of Bury St. Edmunds. Sometime in the
late 1480s to 1490s, thirty-two stanzas from two of Lydgate's poems were
painted in the newly constructed chantry chapel of the Church of the Holy
Trinity in Long Melford. Six of the stanzas come from Lydgate's "Quis
dabit?" and twenty-six from his *Testament*, poems that were often associated
with each other in their manuscript contexts. In BL MS Harley 2255, which
was owned by Abbot William Curteys and the monastery at Bury St. Edmunds, the *Testament* is immediately followed by the "Quis dabit?" poem,
but it is almost certain that the verses were painted in the chantry not at
monastic behest but on the order of a member of the Clopton family, probably John Clopton (1423–96), a wealthy and politically prominent member of
the local gentry who was a generous benefactor in Melford and whose will
expresses a request to be buried in the chapel at Long Melford.[43] In her work
on East Anglian piety, Gail McMurray Gibson has charted a close relationship between John Clopton and Lydgate, one that would explain the choice
of the monk-poet's verses for the Clopton chantry chapel.[44]

While alterations have been made to the chantry chapel since the fifteenth century, traces of the original elaborate decoration remain and, along
with church inventories from 1529 and 1553, allow us to guess at "the visual
expectations" of churchgoers and play-goers in fifteenth-century East Anglia.[45] Verses from the *Testament* are painted in black script on a white ground
on a series of carved wooden plaques, one stanza per plaque, that form a scroll
that runs along three of the walls of the chantry chapel just below ceiling

height. The scroll begins in the southeast corner, where it is held in the painted image of a man's hand, and each plaque is connected to the next by a carved pattern of branches, leaves, and flowers on which the plaques rest. The "Quis dabit?" verses, which are also black on white, are painted on the girder that supports the lower ceiling and are preceded by a small painting of a hooded female figure.[46] Other decorations, including short phrases, legends, and coats of arms commemorating the Clopton family, appear throughout the chapel, showing that an elaborate "scheme of textual decoration," as J. B. Trapp puts it, was once a central part of the interior of the chapel. Such decorations, as Kathleen Kamerick has shown, proliferated in East Anglian parish churches in the fifteenth century and, in so doing, encouraged the visual participation in holy scenes that was a feature of late medieval devotion.[47]

Although the placement of the verses from Lydgate's *Testament* just below the ceiling makes them difficult to read, their function, Trapp believes, was "clearly didactic and penitential," a claim that has been more fully developed by Jennifer Floyd, who shows how the sacramental imagery linking the Host and Christ that is such a prominent feature of "the devotional poetics and doctrinal messages of the chantry chapel's entire decorative scheme" is echoed in Lydgate's verses, especially in the repeated refrain that requests the granting of "shrifte hosyl and repentance."[48] In that regard, the *Testament* verses are like many other visual displays in medieval churches that were designed for contemplation or edification, whether in solitude or during a church service. The choice of Lydgate's verses may be due to the poet's fame and may also reflect his relationship with Clopton.[49] Floyd argues that the use of Lydgate's verses in the chantry chapel would have strengthened the sense of cultural affinity between Clopton and his peers, who (unlike parishioners) would have had access to the chapel and chantry and were patrons or readers of Lydgate, an argument that reinforces Philippa Maddern's emphasis on the importance of friendship in fifteenth-century East Anglia and Gibson's assessment of the emphasis on family ties found in the East Anglian cult of St. Anne.[50]

As with the St. Paul's Dance of Death mural, the verses from Lydgate's *Testament* would have involved viewers in processes "of activity, of movement, of performativity" that Paul Binski has observed were an important part of how, beyond the visual or aural, worshippers encountered texts and images in churches.[51] Like a viewer of the *Daunce of Poulys*, a worshipper following the unfurling panels of the *Testament* around the chantry's wall would have been engaged in a mimetic and embodied mirroring of what the verses visually and textually displayed. Floyd suggests that the worshipper's movement around the chantry chapel becomes a kind of pilgrimage, in which the penitential themes of Lydgate's verses are bodily performed.[52]

The *Testament* painted in Long Melford selects from and reorders the verses found in manuscript versions of the poem, drawing especially from the last sections of the poem, which feature Christ's complaint and shaping them for their chantry setting, as Gibson has observed.[53] As was the case for the *Daunce of Poulys*, the aim appears to have been to create a version of Lydgate's poem suitable for the location and for visual display, although in this case, any cutting, reordering, or reworking would have been done not by the poet, who died in 1449, but by the person in charge of selecting the text that would be painted in the chantry chapel. The result, by whatever hand, is a shorter text and one in which stanzas have been moved around to create an effect that differs from what a reader of one of the manuscript versions would have experienced. The verses used in the chantry setting seem to have been chosen, rearranged, and reworked specifically so as to engage the viewer in the act of visualized and performed penance. The use of such injunctions as "beholde" and "beholde and see" stresses the act of looking, while repetition of the phrases "shrifte hosell and repentance" and "knelying on our kne" function as reminders of physical acts of penance.

It appears that in the chantry chapel, the verses from Lydgate's *Testament* were never accompanied by images illustrating the verses. Instead, the verses themselves become the image. Although Trapp claims that this usage of "*tituli* without pictures" was rare before the sixteenth century, Richard Marks notes that framed texts or "tables" were a feature of cathedrals and major monastic churches.[54] Gayk's suggestion that the painted verses at Long Melford can be taken as "a marker of increasing lay literacy and reliance on the textual as well as the visual for religious instruction" points to a use of writing as decoration that would become a more frequent practice in the following centuries.[55] Such instances of the imbrication of word and image, in which, as Simpson says, "the 'picture' is indistinguishable from the text itself," are precursors of the embrace of writing on walls as a form of interior decoration as well as a mnemonic and advisory aid that Juliet Fleming has analyzed and that would become a feature of early modern English domestic and public interiors.[56] Like that later enthusiasm for wall writing, the text-as-image nature of the *Testament* verses calls attention to the materiality of the written word and its visual essence; if not quite word become flesh, it is at least word become object, an object that could have the same impact on a viewer as an image might.

While the verses painted in the chantry chapel clearly had a site-specific effect, deriving their force from the sensory context of the room and from the immediacy of a viewer's experience of them, they also had a take-away aspect. During the time that a worshipper was in the church, including during sermons, text-image displays would have enhanced the message being preached and thus have served as a form of lay instruction.[57] They also had a less site-specific effect that allowed their power to extend beyond their immediate setting, particularly by earning indulgences for anyone who gazed on them or by serving as charms that could ward off sickness and death.[58] Floyd suggests that by encouraging meditative practices and stressing as they do the act of imprinting on the mind's eye ("emprynte theese thyng in your inward thought"), the *Testament* stanzas help the viewer create "internalized and portable 'copies'" of the verses on the wall.[59] In this regard, they are like the "posies" described by George Puttenham's *The Arte of English Poesie*, ephemeral but portable epigrams that are made to be carried away, although in the case of the Long Melford verses, their portability is limited to what can be stored in a viewer's mental and kinetic memory, to be triggered again at another time and place, regardless of whether the painted verses could be viewed again or even whether they continued to exist at all.[60]

The Legend of St. George

What path to destruction was taken by the wall hanging that displayed Lydgate's *Legend of St. George* and what it looked like we cannot say, since its only surviving traces are to be found in three unillustrated manuscript copies of Lydgate's verses.[61] In surviving, even without any illustrations, the verses expand our knowledge of the overlapping spheres of writing and reading, painting and viewing, and performing and spectating in fifteenth-century England. Their multimedia nature points to the ways in which late medieval textuality and visuality merged and to how picture-poems were used in secular and domestic settings.

Lydgate's precise role in creating the *Legend of St. George* is hard to pin down, but it apparently went well beyond just supplying the verses for the wall hanging. In his headnote, Shirley describes the *Legend* as the "devyse of a steyned halle of þe lyf of Saint George ymagyned by Daun Johan þe Munk of Bury Lydegate / and made with þe balades at the request / of þarmorieres of Londoun for þonour of þeyre broþerhoode and þeyre feest of Saint George."[62] It was Lydgate who authored the surviving thirty-five rhyme-royal ballades that relate the story of St. George's fight against the dragon and subsequent martyrdom, but Shirley's phrasing implies that Lydgate was more broadly responsible for coming up with the scheme (the device) for whole display, which was "ymagyned" (conceived, visualized, planned) by him. Although *devyse* had various meanings, in its technical sense, which is how Gordon Kipling argues Shirley is using it here, the word referred to the plan or design that served as a guide for artisans in producing a painting, performance, or building. Shirley describes two of Lydgate's other performance pieces as devices: the *Mumming at London*, which he refers to as "þe deuyse of a desguysing," and the *Mumming at Windsor*, called "þe devyse of a momyng." If Kipling is right, then Lydgate seems to have been charged with supplying the plan for the visual display as well as with making the verses that accompanied it, functioning as both poet and deviser for the commissioned piece.[63]

Of the wall hanging itself, only a few traces can be teased out. Despite Stow's note, written at the top of the page in Trinity MS R.3.21, which suggests that the paintings were murals, the "steyned halle" was probably a painted cloth, as Hammond thought and as Floyd has more recently argued. (Although its meaning had changed by Stow's time, causing him to confuse wall paintings with painted cloths, in Lydgate's day, *halle* could refer not only to a hall but also to a cloth hanging.)[64] Staining and painting seem to have been separate arts in the early fifteenth century, the former involving the use of pigments that penetrated the surface of the cloth.[65] Surviving wall paintings from parish churches (a more durable medium than painted textiles) offer a glimpse of how St. George could be represented in visual art of the period, which, befitting his status as patron saint of the Armorers, often included showing him in up-to-date armor.[66]

The scenes that accompanied Lydgate's verses and illustrated the legend of St. George may have been made to order or adapted from existing compositions. We know that in tapestry making—which has been more fully documented than has the making of painted cloths, in part because woven tapestries have survived in greater numbers—scenes and figures were frequently borrowed from painted or, later, print sources, which formed the basis for the full-size pattern in color that was painted on paper or cloth (called the "cartoon"), used by weavers. Designs could also be adapted from plays or tableaux, and the pageants built for royal entries and other civic spectacles are an especially useful source to consider for the Armorers' hanging, since they often incorporated placards bearing "scriptures" or verses explaining the scene being represented, which functioned similarly to the verses Lydgate supplied describing St. George's deeds. Evidence shows that the artists who designed civic pageantry also sometimes designed tapestries, as in the case of Jacquemart Pilet, who was trained in the atelier of Bauduin de Bailleul in Arras and was commissioned in 1468 by the aldermen of Arras to paint fourteen narrative scenes on paper that that would be acted out by members of the city corporations during the entry of Charles le Téméraire into the city in the following year. Pilet was later commissioned by parishioners of the church of Saint-Géry in Arras to design tapestries of the *Life of Saint Géry* based on a written account they gave him.[67]

The phrase "made with þe balades" does not make entirely clear how Lydgate's verses accompanied the "steyned halle" or where they were positioned on the cloth along with illustrations of St. George's life, but the verses may have appeared in scrolls or panels beneath the images. A late fifteenth-century tapestry called *The Hunt of the Frail Stag*, now in the collection of the Metropolitan Museum of Art, offers a suggestive analogue. Four surviving fragments of the *Hunt* tapestry depict episodes in an allegorical hunt along with verses on a scroll that describe the visual depiction. Another fragment from the same tapestry shows a male figure, who presumably represents the author of the verses that appear on the tapestry fragments and who stands next to a tablet on which is inscribed the moral of the allegory. Another tapestry depicting scenes from *The Story of the Trojan War*, also in the Metropolitan Museum of Art, similarly incorporates verses woven onto banners at the top and bottom of the panels and includes a final panel depicting what Adolpho Cavallo argues may be the poet or deviser, in the tradition of figures accompanying moralizing verses found in other Netherlandish tapestries of the period.[68] The words "þee poete first declareþe," which precede the first stanza of Lydgate's ballades on St. George, may point to the image of such a poet-figure, and Shirley describes a similar poet-figure in connection with *Bycorne and Chychevache.*

One scholar has suggested that the poet- or narrator-figures woven into tapestries might have derived from the theater; at the very least, they are evidence of the porous boundaries of various representational media and the overlapping nature of the terms used to describe them.[69] While the line "þee poete first declareþe" in the *Legend of St. George* probably points to a visually depicted poet-figure, it might also suggest that Lydgate's verses were recited, perhaps to accompany the unveiling of the wall hanging when it was first installed or on feast days related to St. George, when the wall hanging might have been used as a backdrop to the festivities and even perhaps to an enactment of the St. George story. The terminology used in this single line, which is the only remaining example of the "histories" (i.e., the instructions for the painter)—if that is what "þee poete first declareþe" is—that remains in the three manuscript copies of the St. George device, is not much help in sorting out these possibilities, since the verb *declaren* can be used to describe spoken or written words, as in the phrase "as bokes us declare" (e.g., Chaucer, *Troilus and Criseyde*, 5.799), or to signify nonverbal means of making something known, in the sense of "reveal, show, display."[70] Thus, like a similar line in *Bycorne and Chychevache*, in which the poet-figure is described as "seying" three balades, "declareþe" may point to written or painted words or to words spoken by a presenter, who may or may not have been identical with the author of the verses.[71]

A similar blurring of genre distinctions and terminology occurs in relation to the audience. The first stanza of the *Legend*, for instance, addresses a group of people ("O yee folk þat heer present be," l. 1), but are those "folk" viewers of the pictorial representation, spectators gathered for some sort of performance related to it, or simply the verbal residue of an oral tradition? Subsequent lines, however, stress the visual, inviting the audience to "haue Inspeccion" of the life of St. George, through whose story they "may beholde and see / His martirdome and his passyon" (ll. 2–4). The word "Inspeccion" implies a kind of attentive spectatorship or intent looking that involves careful perusal or scrutiny, while the phrase "may beholde and see" promises that viewers will have scenes on which to turn their gaze.[72] While these phrases are consistent with the assumption that spectators gazed at images and words on a wall hanging, they may also point to a live performance. Anne Lancashire notes that the wall hanging of St. George's life might have been accompanied by a mimed performance—perhaps one similar to that recorded in 1585 at an election feast of the Armorers and Brasiers, where an armed boy representing St. George and a lady leading a lamb accompanied by drum and flute marched around the hall and gave a speech—a suggestion that the first verses of the poem do not rule out.[73] Exhortations to "behold" and "inspect" may also point to meditative visualization of the sort that accompanied devotional reading, as in the case of the wall paintings at St. Paul's and Long Melford.

Despite its appeals to visualization, the *Legend* is full of references to reading and to the literate milieu from which it derives. Lydgate frequently alludes to his sources ("As þat myn Auctour lykeþe for to expresse," l. 18; "As the story of hym list to endyte," l. 23; "As clerkis of him wryte," l. 26; "þe story dooþe devyse," l. 211; "we fynden in his lyff," l. 218; etc.) and, more broadly, to the acts of reading and writing. Lydgate's chief source, from which he draws liberally, is the *Legenda Aurea*, which he uses in telling two interrelated stories: St. George's rescue of a king's daughter from a dragon, along with the subsequent conversion of her city, and George's encounter with the tyrant Dacian, who tortures the saint for his beliefs (George escapes all harm, destroys the pagan temple, and converts Dacian's wife, before finally being beheaded, after which Dacian is stricken and dies).[74] The poem also emphasizes exegesis and interpretation, for example, in its unpacking of the two meanings of George's name in the third stanza and in its invitation to link the story of St. George with the founding of the Order of the Garter by Edward III. The poem also tells a relatively complicated story, beginning with St. George's birth in Cappadocia, through his battle with the dragon, and his martyrdom.

Although this reliance on called-out sources, narrative complexity, and exegesis may seem to argue against the use of the poem on a wall hanging, other features of the poem suggest that it could well have accompanied painted images. At thirty-five stanzas, it is considerably shorter than the *Daunce of Poulys* and only slightly longer than the *Testament*. Moreover, various textual details signal that, as Derek Pearsall argues, Lydgate has reshaped his source material "as befits the occasion and the audience." Pearsall observes that the poem "is remarkably straightforward and free of the amplification that Lydgate generally introduced in purely literary treatments of saints' lives." The rhyme-royal stanzas are lively, full of action, and move smoothly to the saint's final prayer. The verses are also carefully calibrated stylistically—in a way that recalls the poetic sophistication Lydgate assumed London's Mercers and Goldsmiths would appreciate—as can be seen in the degree to which Lydgate's treatment of George's martyrdom contrasts with the colloquialism and violence of the version in the *South English Legendary*. The torture scene in this and the next stanzas, for instance, avoids the physical detail and appeal to emotions of the *Legendary* and, in Pearsall's words, "deflects the edge of suffering" through the use of conventional literary phrasing such as the absolute constructions of lines 174–75, which make the actions seem preordained rather than humanly planned. Similarly, the saint's prayer on behalf of those who venerate him (ll. 232–38) is a conventional motif, but its "abstraction and generality" differ from the "homely practicality" of the *South English Legendary*.[75]

Lydgate's stylistic choices and the verses' references to reading imply that the habits of literacy we tend to associate solely with words on a page could extend to other media, including wall hangings or even mimetic performance. Lydgate's reshaping of his material may show not just a willingness to write for the occasion, as Pearsall argues, but to write for multiple possible occasions. In the St. George verses, Lydgate seems to show an awareness of the presentational versatility of poetry in the period and to have envisioned that what he wrote might at various times be read silently from a page, listened to as it was read aloud, gazed at on a painted representation, or watched in performance. The scene of reading, Lydgate appears to have grasped, could be ever-changing.

The poem's treatment of time and its choice of verb tenses underscore this seeming awareness of multiple presentational modes. After the first stanza, which is grounded in the present ("O yee folk that heer present be," l. 1) and the immediate future ("Wheeche of this story shal have inspeccion," l. 2), the remainder of the poem is narrated in the past tense in a way that calls attention to the already enacted nature of the events being narrated. That sense of events past provides a counterpoint to any visual images or accompanying performance that, by virtue of their form, always fully inhabit the present. There is a constant reminder in the poem of the temporal unfolding of George's actions— this happens, then that, and later this—which creates a flow of events that lends itself to reading, hearing, or watching the life of the saint.

The broad appeal of St. George made him especially well suited as subject matter for multiple audiences and varied representational media. St. George's chivalrous protection of women, his piety, and his generosity to the poor assured him popularity among the knightly classes, and in the 1340s, Edward III dedicated his Order of the Garter to St. George (as the second stanza of Lydgate's poem mentions). By the end of the fourteenth century St. George had become the patron saint of England, and in 1415, after the English victory at Agincourt, where troops had carried the banner of St. George, Archbishop Chichele raised St. George's day (23 April) to the status of a Great Feast and ordered it to be celebrated on par with Christmas. St. George was the Armorers' patron saint, and Lydgate's verses may have been commissioned for one of their feasts in his honor, perhaps, as Floyd argues, the one that coincided with completion of construction on a new hall for their guild, in other words, perhaps on 23 April 1430, a date that would assign the poem to the period when Lydgate was energetically making other London entertainments.[76]

Like the verses Lydgate provided for entertainments for the Mercers and Goldsmiths, written possibly just a few months earlier, the *Legend* would appeal to prosperous and civic-minded, as well as aspirational, Londoners. St. George is described as "protectour and patroun" (l. 5) and as lodestar of knighthood (l. 6), a flattering reminder that the Armorers' patron tied them to the aristocracy. The second stanza adds more reminders of George's elite status, linking him to Edward III's founding of the Order of the Garter and to the tradition of twenty-four knights dressing in livery to celebrate his feast day each year, while the third stanza stresses that George's name signifies not just holiness but also knighthood and renown. The description of George as the king's daughter's "Chaumpyoun" (l. 96) is consistent with Lydgate's depiction of St. George as a model of chivalry. A "champion" was someone who engaged in battle for another's sake; the term was drawn from judicial duels or trials by battle in which, under English law, representatives (champions) of the two parties would fight to determine the case, with divine intervention assigning victory to the rightful side.[77] Lydgate also links the saint to the Virgin Mary (l. 85) and works in a reminder about the need to honor priesthood (ll. 144ff), as we might expect given his frequent defense of orthodox religion, which may have resonated with the poem's patrons.

The *Legend of St. George* was in all likelihood painted onto a wall hanging that was displayed in the Armorers' hall, and it may also have been read aloud, perhaps along with a mimed performance, on feast days. It was certainly read by at least some of those whose hands held one of the three manuscripts in which it survives. For all three modes of reception—viewed as pictures, heard as spoken poetry, read silently from the page—Lydgate's verses work at conveying the meaning of the saint's story. Because they do, they offer a reminder of the pervasiveness of late medieval genre blurring and media mixing, a blurring and mixing of which Lydgate himself seems to have been fully aware.

Bycorne and Chychevache

Much of what can be said about the *Legend* applies to *Bycorne and Chychevache* as well, despite its quite different narrative. The poem tells the satiric story of two legendary beasts: one who dines on patient men, the other on submissive women. Like the *Disguising at Hertford*, the poem is part of a misogynist tradition of complaints about unruly women and of advice on marital behavior, and in at least one instance appeared in a manuscript context (in Trinity MS R.3.19) that included the conduct poems *How the Good Wife Taught Her Daughter* and *How the Wise Man Taught His Son* that share some of its emphasis on social behavior. *Bycorne* also echoes Chaucer's "Wife of Bath's Tale" and "Clerk's Tale," with explicit references to patient Griselda and the question of sovereignty in marriage. While no direct source has been identified, Lydgate might have known French versions of the story, such as the *Dit de la Chincheface*.[78] Pearsall notes that the story of *Bycorne and Chychevache*, already widespread by Chaucer's time, became popular in murals and tapestries of the fifteenth century, the most famous example being the mural paintings in the castle of Villeneuve-Lembron in France where the verses are written on scrolls between the pictures.[79] Lydgate's poem consists of nineteen stanzas written in rhyme royal: the first three stanzas are narrated by an "ymage in poete-wyse," while the following stanzas consist of direct speech from, in turn, Bycorne, a group of husbands, a woman who is being devoured by Chychevache, and, finally, Chychevache and an old man whose wife has been eaten. Prose headings between stanzas describe what is being portrayed by the verses. Like the identity of the worthy citizen of London for whom Shirley says it was written, the poem's date is unknown, although it may plausibly be dated to the late 1420s, the period of Lydgate's other London poems.[80]

In his copy of the poem in Trinity MS R.3.20, Shirley identifies *Bycorne and Chychevache* as a "deuise of a peynted or desteyned clothe for an halle a parlour or a chaumbre / deuysed by Iohan Lidegate at þe request of a werþy citeseyn of London," suggesting that the verses were meant for a wall hanging. If Shirley is using *device* in the technical sense, then the verses he copied may represent the plan for the wall hanging, with iconographical descriptions in prose ("histories" or instructions to the painter) and verse scriptures ("reasons," which represent the words that are to be inscribed by the painter along with each image).[81] The resulting wall hanging would have had nineteen seven-line stanzas painted onto it and, if Shirley's rubrics accurately represent the instructions to the painter, seven painted images showing the following: a poet; the two beasts, one fat and the other thin; Bycorne speaking; a company of men coming toward Bycorne, speaking; a woman being devoured by Chychevache, speaking to "alle wives"; a thin, long-horned beast (i.e., Chychevache); and a husband trying to rescue his wife from Chychevache.

Presumably, the painter would have drawn the images in such as way as to accommodate the varying number of stanzas that went with each of them.

Despite the apparent clarity of Shirley's headnote, questions about the representational form the poem took are raised by the other two extant versions of Lydgate's verses, which do not identify it as intended for a painted cloth. In addition, a close look at Shirley's headnotes for the poem (which presumably are the "histories" instructing the artisan) in R.3.20 as well as Lydgate's text reveals features that point to multiple possible forms of representational display. Some scholars have argued that *Bycorne* may have been intended for dramatic presentation, perhaps as a pantomimed mumming, a claim encouraged by the running titles in Trinity MS R.3.19, which identify the text as being in the form or manner of a disguising or in the guise of a mumming, as well as by the direct speeches of the poet-like figure and the characters in the poem.[82] The use of "seying" in the first prose description and of variations on it in some of the subsequent headings may indicate that the verses were spoken aloud, but as with the *Legend*'s use of "declareþe," the word "seying" may simply refer to words painted on the cloth. Similarly, moments of direct address by the figures to an audience—"Felawes takeþe heede and yee may see," "Alle humble men, boþe you and me," "O noble wyves, beoþe wel ware / Takeþe ensaumple nowe by me," "you for to swalowe," "O cely housbandes! woo deon yee!" and the entire last stanza that speaks directly to patient husbands—could be literary conventions preserving traces of an oral tradition or could be words painted on a cloth to represent the speeches of painted figures; they also would not be out of place in a live performance.[83] That the "ymage in poete-wyse" is described as standing while all of the other figures are said to be portrayed could signal that the poet-figure served as a presenter who introduced the story, while the other characters acted their parts, although *stonde* might also refer to a painted poet-figure. The verb *portraien* had a range of meanings—including to draw, to paint, to depict, or to create a mental image or verbal description—and thus does not help decide the final form of *Bycorne*, but Pearsall believes that its use here (in contrast with the words "showeth," "kometh," and "demonstrando," which Shirley employs in the rubrics to the poems he explicitly calls mummings and disguisings) points to painted images.[84]

As with the other poems designed for visual display discussed in this chapter, the location of the *Bycorne and Chychevache* wall hanging is crucial for its potential meanings. Shirley's headnote indicates that the wall hanging was for display in "an halle a parlour or a chaumbre," a comment echoed by

John Stow in his note at the end of the copy of the poem in Trinity R.3.19, where he states that the ballades were designed "to be paynted in a parlor" (see Figure 3). A hall was an assembly or banquet room, while a parlor was a semi-private room off a hall; as its etymology suggests, a parlor was often used for conversation: one version of *Piers Plowman* complains about the newly fashionable preference of rich people to eat alone in a parlor rather than to dine collectively in a hall.[85] A chamber was a private apartment for personal use, such as a bedroom, but it could also refer to a room used for transacting business. Any of these rooms could have been found in a prosperous private residence, and thus the image-poem could have been viewed by a range of passersby in the household, including apprentices, servants, guests, and family members; if it was installed in a parlor or chamber, its chief viewers would have been the intimate members of the household, especially the husband and wife, whom the poem may most directly engage with its representation of gendered power imbalances and consumption of material goods.[86]

Shirley does not identify the piece's patron, leaving the "werthy citeseyn" for whom the wall hanging was designed unnamed, but by using that specific combination of adjective and noun, Shirley gives us solid evidence for assuming that the wall hanging was designed for a prosperous resident of London. *Worthy* had connotations both of status and moral worth, suggesting someone of standing who is also distinguished or honorable (e.g., "the seid Maire, Shiref, Baillifs and the worthimen of the Commune Counsell aforeseid"). A *citizen* was technically any freeman of a town or city, and the term was often used interchangeably with *burgess*, but it could be used more broadly to indicate any established inhabitant of a city or town (e.g., "Þe citezeins and burgeys of Caunterbury"). In a narrower sense, *citeseyn* could be used to describe members of the city government, as in phrases such as "John Brokley, late Citecein and Alderman of the Citee of London."[87] Since he elsewhere names mayors or guildsmen or sheriffs as recipients of Lydgate's poetic labors, Shirley's choice of words suggests either that he did not know the precise identity of the patron, including his guild affiliation or whether he held a public office, or that the patron was not prominent enough—or of enough interest to the readers Shirley envisioned as reading the anthology into which he copied the verses—to warrant mention by name.

Whatever the precise identity of the "werthy citeseyn," Lydgate's opening address to "prudent folkes" who are exhorted to "takeþe heed / And remembreþe, in youre lyves" (1–2) signals the expectation that he and other viewers of the *Bycorne* wall hanging will take to heart the poem's messages,

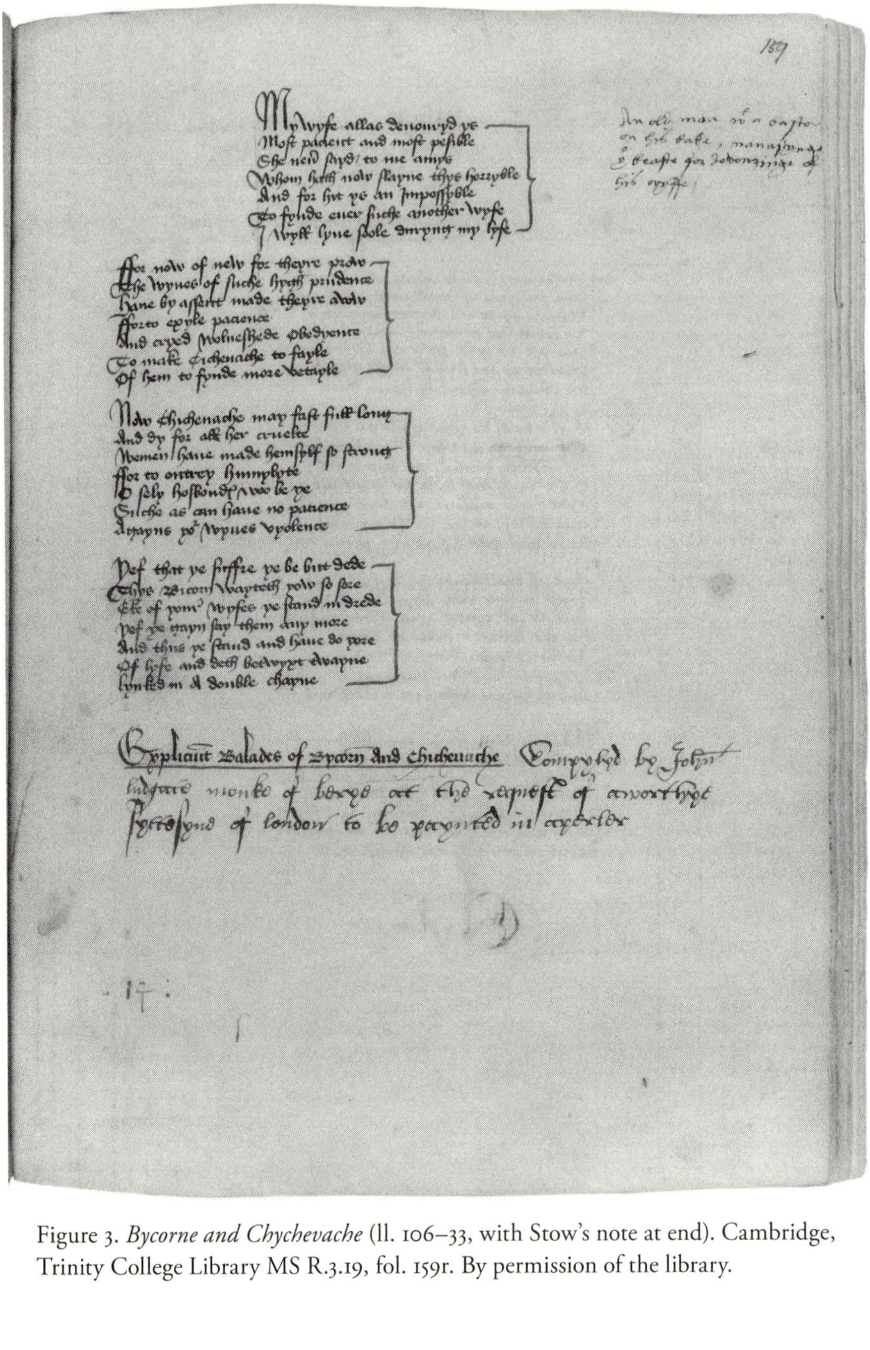

Figure 3. *Bycorne and Chychevache* (ll. 106–33, with Stow's note at end). Cambridge, Trinity College Library MS R.3.19, fol. 159r. By permission of the library.

messages that move well beyond the stock misogyny often associated with the story of the two monsters and that speak to the needs and anxieties of a London household. As Andrea Denny-Brown has shown, Lydgate's poem reshapes the misogynistic concerns found in earlier French versions by introducing an "appetitive register" that thematizes "the managing of desire and the innate mortal hunger for material (as opposed to spiritual) goods."[88] A poem about excess and dearth, a fat monster and a lean one, becomes in Lydgate's telling both a warning against avarice and an opportunity to demonstrate the dangers of imbalances within the urban household: imbalances related to the distribution of gendered power, to moderation of bodily appetites, and to acquisition of worldly goods. As a piece of writing and a visual display, *Bycorne and Chychevache* circulates within contexts that are simultaneously material, historical, and ideological, and its meanings have to be understood as varying depending on whether it was viewed by an urban household or read alongside the other chiefly poetic texts of a religious or moral nature in Trinity R.3.20 (which also included the *Legend of St. George*).[89] Yet even in its manuscript contexts, and especially in Trinity R.3.20, traces of its material presence on a "peynted or desteyned cloth" can still be detected, however faintly, waiting to activate the memory of an image or a performance once seen.

Seeing and Spectating

As objects of visual narrative that engage viewers in kinetic and even mimetic physical experiences, wall hangings overlap with other medieval performance genres. Given that overlap, the tendency of the manuscripts into which they were copied to blur genre lines and Shirley's use of multiple terms for describing Lydgate's picture-poem texts perhaps does not indicate confusion but rather reflects the determinedly mixed-media form of these texts, a form modern critical categories have had difficulty recognizing. Even though they were two-dimensional representations, such picture-poems encouraged performative looking, as I have argued, calling on viewers to activate the images and words painted on the mural or wall hanging. Performative looking of this sort was analogous to the performative reading practices that have in recent years been delineated by scholars such as Jeffrey Hamburger, who has described the *Rothschild Canticles* as a drama acted out by the reader, and Jessica Brantley, who has shown how theatrical practices informed private devotional reading.[90] In many instances, the image-text being read or viewed on a manuscript page or a wall or cloth hanging must have resembled in its combination of words and pictures the Hans Memling's Passion panel, which as Stevens has observed "does not signify an actual performance" but instead "represents the idea of a performance."[91] Paying attention to their interactive features and to the idea of performance embedded in them makes it possible to position picture-poems made for public viewing on a continuum that includes three-dimensional tableaux vivants and sculptural displays, as well as scripted plays, many of which were themselves structured as set speeches explaining visual representations.[92]

The term *pageant* usefully highlights the dilemma modern scholars face in trying to sort out the many and overlapping medieval representational forms that involved visual display. It is now often applied to the individual plays within the biblical cycles, but the use of *pageant* to refer to drama is a secondary meaning, derived from its initial use to designate something that was painted or ornamented.[93] In medieval dramatic records, the word can refer to the decorated mobile object that functioned as a stage set ("pageant wagon") or to a decorated object, such as a painted cloth, that was carried in a procession. Thomas More chose the word *pageant* to describe pictures on a painted cloth, accompanied by verses, that More in his youth devised for his father's house.[94] Although both the *OED* and *MED* seem to take their cue from the More quotation in defining *pageant* as "a scene represented on tapestry or the like," the term could be used as a synonym for picture or illustration.[95]

That range of meanings is a useful reminder of the fluid nature of representational forms in the period. Verses could be written for a wall hanging and also read aloud or mimed when the hanging was displayed. Wall hangings were themselves an integral feature of medieval performances and ceremonies, and extant records show how tapestry made its way into performances in the form of banners and hangings used to decorate halls and streets. A mid-fifteenth-century continuation of *The Brut* describes the pageants and other honors that greeted the entry of Henry V and Catherine of Valois into London in 1421 where they saw "euyry strete hongid rychely with riche clothis of gold and silke, and of velewettis and cloþis of araas, the beste that myght be gotyn."[96] Lydgate's verses for the royal entry of Henry VI in 1432 similarly recount how the king, riding to the middle of the bridge, came to a tower "arrayed with welvettes soffte, / Clothis off golde, sylke, and tapcerye, / As apperteynyth to . . . regalye" (ll. 103–5). Although we do not know what was depicted on these pieces of cloth, their images might well have amplified, supplemented, or perhaps even qualified the performances unfolding in front of them, with spoken verses, tableaux, tapestry images, and verses displayed in writing all combining to create the performance. Play-scripts themselves may have been designed to evoke a collective memory of live performance or even to invite the reader to take on various roles.[97] The mixing of so many different types of visual display suggests that narratives were purpose-built to take different forms: a long romance might have been enacted as a play and then shortened for wall decoration and truncated even more for subtleties.

Lydgate himself seems to have been particularly alert to the power of visual representation. On at least three occasions, he remarks on the impact that images had on him, especially as spurs for his writing. He tells us in the opening verses of the "Fifteen Joys and Sorrows of Mary" that he was stirred by a meditation with pictures that he happened to read in a book one night (ll. 1–35). His *Testament* recounts an earlier instance that occurred when, at fifteen years of age, he saw a crucifix "depicte upon a wall" of a cloister with the word "vide" written beside the phrase "Beholde my mekenesse, O child, and leve thy pryde" (ll. 744–46), which in old age moved him to write a "litel dite" in remembrance (ll. 750–53). And the "Debate of the Horse, Goose, and Sheep" was inspired, Lydgate says, by a scene in a wall painting he had recently seen ("a similitude / Ful craftily depeyntid vpon a wall," ll. 18–19). Besides drawing inspiration from images, Lydgate often describes his poetic making in terms drawn from the visual crafts: as Gayk points out, he often "represents his writing as painting intended to help his readers *see*."[98]

Writing in the 1440s, Lydgate's near contemporary, Reginald Pecock, saw the advantage of pictorial representation over writing in its speed of apprehension. What might take six or seven pages' worth of reading to "bringe into knowing or into remembraunce" could be quickly grasped by looking at an image or "a storie openli ther of purtreied or peintid in the wal or in a clooth." Pictorial representations, in Pecock's view, made it possible to absorb more "mater" with less labor than if a story were written. Accessibility was another advantage, for just as a man who can read, Pecock explains, can understand a long story more easily through his own reading rather than being read aloud to by someone else or listening to himself read aloud, so those who cannot read will not find someone who can read aloud to them as easily as they can find the painted walls of a church or a "clooth steyned." The clincher for Pecock was that images and paintings make a stronger impression than words and thus have much more potency, a sentiment echoed by

Lydgate's claim that images were designed so that stories might "rest with ws with dewe remembraunce."[99]

Those claims for the virtues of images offer a corrective to the dominance of the written word in our own era, which along with the unavoidable fact that written texts remain our best, and often only, source of information about medieval culture has led us to downplay the importance of other representational media within late medieval culture and to overlook their frequent intermingling. Lydgate's poems for visual display remind us that written words, the visual arts, and performances were not mutually exclusive representational forms but instead were mutually supporting. In light of the blurring of boundaries of what we now tend to think of as formally and functionally separate cultural productions, perhaps we ought to expand our understanding of what it meant to be a writer in late medieval culture, adding to our sense of the poet the notion of writer as fabricator—or weaver and painter of words—whose writerly craft could be both inspired by the visual and embodied within it.

CHAPTER 4

Performance and Gloss: The *Procession of Corpus Christi*

When John Shirley copied the verses now known as the *Procession of Corpus Christi*, he included a headnote describing them as "an ordenaunce of a precessyoun of the feste of corpus cristi made in london by daun John Lydegate."[1] Welcome though they are as an anchor for what would otherwise be a free-floating set of verses, Shirley's words are not without ambiguity. What he means by "ordenaunce" and "precessyoun" is not entirely certain, and his phrasing does not make clear whether it was the "precessyoun" that took place in London or the writing of the poem. Despite that cloudiness, what Shirley has preserved appears to be the only known example of a poetic account of a Corpus Christi procession in London. Shirley's description of the *Procession of Corpus Christi* as an "ordenaunce" positions the verses at the intersection of visual spectacle and written exegesis, of ephemeral performance (open to multiple meanings) and durable text (presenting a specific interpretation). Lydgate's verses, as this chapter argues, turn a fleeting procession of figures on Corpus Christi day, a procession that could be understood in a variety of ways by onlookers, into a poetic form that has not only the permanence of written record but also the apparent fixity of exegetical exposition. His stanzas capture not primarily the material details of the live performance they probably are based on but, more pointedly, its symbolic significance, both of which were caught up in questions about the understanding of the sacrament at a time when eucharistic belief was one of the most controversial of English theological issues. The meanings of publicly performed dramas may have been as varied as their spectators, but poetic description offered the promise of one determinate interpretation, even if that promise could not always be fulfilled once the text came into the hands of readers. What Lydgate provides in the *Procession of Corpus Christi* can be understood as a kind of gloss or reader's guide, which uses figural interpretation and the appeal of meditative devotion to instruct viewers (now readers) about how to interpret—and use—what they have seen.

Religious Performances in London

The feast of Corpus Christi, established by the Church in the early fourteenth century, commemorates the institution of the Holy Eucharist and falls on the first Thursday following Trinity Sunday (anywhere from late May to late June). Corpus Christi was widely celebrated throughout Europe with urban performances and processions, in keeping with the importance of the eucharist, especially for teaching the laity.[2] Despite the feast's popularity, London apparently never developed a citywide celebration for Corpus Christi or an elaborate set of plays associated with it, such as those mounted in York and other provincial towns in England. That might in part be because guilds and fraternities in London organized themselves around parish churches, not the cathedral of St. Paul's, and thus lacked a central point of control or consolidation that could have mounted a large-scale performance.[3] Fragmented into smaller communities centered around parishes, Londoners may have lacked the resources for or interest in banding together to produce vernacular cycle plays that, as records from York and elsewhere attest, required substantial outlays of time and money.

Another reason for the lack of city-sponsored Corpus Christi plays in London may have to do with the not entirely firm control exercised by the city's merchant oligarchy. As Sheila Lindenbaum observes, late medieval London is best seen as a cultural field or site of social practices "where discourses not only converge but are strategically deployed by interested parties competing for power, status and resources." While the years from 1400 to 1500 can be described as a period of "normative discourse" during which the city relied on clerks (such as John Carpenter, the city's common clerk from 1417–38, compiler of the *Liber Albus*, and apparent friend of Lydgate, as his commissioning of the *Daunce of Poulys* shows) and poets to craft a common history by using a totalizing and uniform discourse, such efforts were driven by anxiety on the part of the merchant corporations about their hegemony and should be seen as the product of conflict as much as consensus. Much like the Lancastrians at court, Lindenbaum argues, London's leaders felt compelled to legitimate their regime and could not rest assured of their dominance. The merchant corporations that held sway over the city in the years after 1390 may have had a monopoly on high civic office and may have presented a united front against the artisan guilds and other contenders, but such events as the rising of Londoners under John Oldcastle in 1414 could not help but raise the specter of an artisan revolt, and citizens of lesser guilds, in Lindenbaum's words, "remained capable of mounting a challenge to the merchants as late as 1444."[4]

The at least partially precarious grip on power held by London's merchants extended to their influence over the city's public culture, with Lollard bills and other forms of protest writing competing with civic-sponsored "normative discourse" and with parish affiliations exerting a centripetal pull away from craft and corporate structures.[5] In the case of the most visible forms of public culture—citywide ceremonies, festivities, and entertainments—London did not follow the pattern found in cities like York, where a civic oligarchy oversaw play cycles collectively organized by guilds for the moral good and economic profit of the whole city. Apparently not feeling the need for or not able to pull off a centrally organized ceremony, London's leaders left the entertainment needs of its citizens to private groups.[6] While the mayor and aldermen of London were to all appearances individually pious, they did not take part in a citywide Corpus Christi procession or sponsor a drama cycle associated with that feast as did the leaders of other towns.[7] Instead, London's civic entertainments tended to take the form of street pageantry devised for the entry into the city of royalty and other important visitors, an expected part of the city's relationship to the crown that, by the fifteenth century, was occurring almost every seven years.[8] Such pageantry, while no doubt requiring the assistance of many artisans, craftsmen, and performers, was planned and executed by the city government, offering small scope for participation by other groups. In other words, London's public sphere was not defined by any large-scale communal entertainment of broadly shared responsibility, to which many groups might contribute and which might be expected to express their concerns.[9]

What London did have, however, besides street pageantry, was a variety of dramatic activity related to parish churches, including boy bishop ceremonies, Palm Sunday prophets, customs such as Hocking and Maying, and pageants at Easter and Corpus Christi.[10] The fraternity at St. Botolph's Aldgate, for instance, which was dedicated to Corpus Christi, owned a vellum roll with various pageants that may have been performed on the feast.[11] All Hallows Barking owned several pageants, a term that, as Mary Erler notes, encompasses a variety of kinds of constructions ranging from pageant wagons used as platforms for cycle plays to portable pageants that could be carried to hangings or banners; records show that Barking's pageants, which the parish used in its Corpus Christi procession, were desirable enough to be sought out for rental, including by the Holy Trinity Priory, the Skinners' company, and, apparently, John Scott, who had a five-member troupe that played at court through 1509.[12]

A tantalizing potential dramatic link with Lydgate's poem can be found in the Clerkenwell/Skinners' Well plays. The area around Clerkenwell, to the northwest of the city, just beyond its walls and not far from Smithfield and the priory of St. Bartholomew, had a long association with popular gatherings and entertainments. In the late twelfth century, William FitzStephen commented on the area's popularity among students and young men, noting that wells were customary places for leisure-time activities and mentioning Clerkenwell as among the most famous. Around 1300, the prioress of St. Mary's, Clerkenwell, complained to the king about the damage caused to the priory's property by Londoners trampling fields and hedges while attending "miracles et lutes [wrestling matches]" there.[13] Janette Dillon has shown that Clerkenwell was an important site for the development of theater in London from the medieval period up through Bartholomew Fair and the Fortune playhouse, which was built by Henslowe and the Admiral's Men in 1600, and that its location outside the city walls contributed to its popularity for purposes of entertainment.[14]

Among those entertainments was a performance centered on biblical events that was apparently being performed outdoors in the late fourteenth and early fifteenth centuries at Clerkenwell/Skinner's Well. Records imply that London parish clerks were regularly performing in Clerkenwell by 1384 when a five-day "ludum valde sumptuosum" by the clerks of London is mentioned; a 1390 performance describes "a play of the Passion of our Lord and the Creation of the World;" and a 1409 performance is described as a "great play showing how God created Heaven and the Earth out of nothing and how he created Adam and on to the Day of Judgment," performed before the king, prince, and nobility, who sat on wooden scaffolding.[15] Anne Lancashire argues that these records provide evidence for the supposition that by the late fourteenth century, a religious play at Clerkenwell/Skinners' Well (apparently interchangeable names by this date) was a major annual or at least recurring spectacle that lasted several days and attracted audiences that included royalty and nobility. If there was a recurring biblical play, Lancashire notes, its development may have been influenced by the church's establishment in the early fourteenth century of the Feast of Corpus Christi. From the early fifteenth century, Clerkenwell/Skinners' Well was the site of the priory of St. John, headquarters of the Knights Hospitaller in England, a wealthy and powerful religious house, and just to the south was the priory of St. Bartholomew. Lancashire speculates that the priory of St. John may have decided "to make its mark in England in part by sponsoring" major religious plays for London and Westminster, perhaps in collaboration with the priory of St. Bartholomew. The only mention of the Clerkenwell/Skinners' Well play in the fifteenth century is in 1409, when it appears to have been a multi-day event that may have been watched by Henry IV.[16]

While civic London may have had a hand in the 1409 production, since there was a close association between St. John's Priory, which was dedicated to John the Baptist, and the Merchant Tailors (then just the Tailors), who were also closely associated with the royal court (Henry IV and Henry V were members), Lancashire suggests that the play was not organized by the city government but by parish and other clerks. Whatever the precise reasons—the financial troubles of the priory of St. John, the costs of the royal and other entries of the fifteenth century that drained resources for entertainments, or the city's nervousness about large gatherings in one place (during royal entries and processions, everyone was spread out and livery companies lined the streets in part as crowd control)—it appears that the Clerkenwell/Skinners' Well play was abandoned after 1409.[17]

According to John Stow, the Skinners, whose religious and social fraternity was dedicated to Corpus Christi, were connected with the Clerkenwell/Skinners' Well biblical play, and it is possible that their involvement turned at some point in the 1390s into their annual Corpus Christi procession.[18] In any event, after the play ended in 1409, the procession, which is first mentioned in the Skinners' 1392 Company Charter, continued, lasting into the sixteenth century.[19] The Skinners' feast-day procession began at their hall in Dungate Hill and moved through the city to St. Antholin's Church in Watling Street.[20] Stow claimed that the procession included the Skinners themselves, carrying wax torches, with more than 200 singing clerks and priests, followed by sheriffs, the mayor, aldermen, and others, all accompanied by minstrels outfitted with wings.[21] No surviving records describe tableaux or pageants, which makes it impossible to say whether or not representations of biblical figures

were part of the procession, although the model of other processions, including Sunday Prophets, suggests they might have featured either costumed
processioners or figures painted on cloth banners or portable pageants with
three-dimensional images that were carried in the procession.[22]

Lydgate's Verses and Devotional Glossing

Although Shirley's headnote does not mention a patron, Lancashire raises the
alluring possibility that the Skinners at some point asked Lydgate to record
their procession, a possibility that gains additional weight from the fact that
the Skinners' fraternity of Corpus Christi had links to royalty and nobility,
including Lydgate's patrons Henry V, Henry VI, and Humphrey, duke of
Gloucester.[23] If the Skinners did in fact make such a commission, it must
have been before the early 1430s, the completion date of Trinity MS R.3.20,
into which Shirley copied Lydgate's verses.[24]

As descriptions of an actual performance, the verses leave much to be
desired, since they omit nearly everything we might want to know about the
appearance and movement of the procession. Lydgate mentions almost nothing about the procession route, the participants, the features of the pageants,
or other "externals" of the procession and instead concentrates on "the meaning of the festival," as Walter Schirmer noted.[25] Lydgate's intent apparently
was not to create a verbal picture of what onlookers saw during the Skinners'
procession but rather to "explain the significance of the various pageants in
the procession," as Derek Pearsall has argued, or, as Andrew Cole has more
recently put it, to engage in a "poetical-theological enterprise" centering on
the meaning of the eucharist.[26]

Despite the absence of details about the physical event of the procession
that may well lie behind the verses, the idea and form of a Corpus Christi procession is essential to the poem's structure and theme. The first stanza, which
functions as a kind of introduction, declares that the poem's aim is to "magne-
fye" the "hye feste" (l. 1) being celebrated on this day, a choice of terminology
that links celebration with praise, as in the definition in the *Promptorium
Parvulorum* (1440) of *magnifien* as "make mykyl of thynge yn preysynge."[27]
The following stanzas take up one biblical or ecclesiastical figure per stanza
(Abraham, Moses, Paul, Matthew, Pope Gregory, St. Ambrose, etc.), giving a
brief description of his attributes and exhorting readers to reflect on the meaning of each figure the better to appreciate the significance of the feast day. The

"hye feste," while not explicitly named, is obviously the feast of Corpus Christi, which Lydgate calls the "Feste of festes" (l. 2) and which he vigorously defends throughout the poem.

Phrases such as "Seoþe and considereþe in youre ymaginatyf" (l. 10) and "Remembreþe eeke in youre Inwarde entente" (l. 17) are commonplaces of meditational instruction that ask readers to reflect on the meanings of what they are seeing or hearing, and they may appear to suggest that what Lydgate is writing is a meditation on the feast of Corpus Christi. Lawrence Clopper in fact thinks the verses are "a sermon, or 'process,' centered on imagined *figurae* or pictures of them," not a description of a procession.[28] Cole similarly reads the verses as a text that adopts the processional form (but does not necessarily describe an actual procession) as a way of exploring eucharistic theology beyond the orthodoxies imagined by Archbishop Arundel and others.[29] While both Clopper and Cole correctly identify an essential feature of Lydgate's verses—there is certainly something sermon- or treatise-like about them—pointing to the way they are shot through with exegetical terminology and deeply engage theological questions about the eucharist, I would like to suggest that in the *Procession of Corpus Christi*, Lydgate plays on the concept of the "figure" as a term for symbolic *and* material representation and that what he has written are verses that assume, and perhaps even require, knowledge of a real-world procession to be fully legible. We may never be able to know with certainty whether Lydgate wrote these verses for the Skinners, but the verses offer sufficient textual evidence to make a connection with an actual procession likely.

In providing an interpretation of processional figures, Lydgate was continuing the practice of genre and media mixing that I considered in the previous chapter. Shannon Gayk has argued that in his *Testament*, Lydgate juxtaposes genres, not in a way that points to what James Simpson has identified as "a problem of narrative," but instead as a kind of "poetic display and play, intended to highlight the relationships between various forms of texts."[30] What Gayk sees in Lydgate's final poem also can be found in the *Procession*, as Lydgate plays at the borderlands of genres and forms, drawing together performed and written representation in a way that is especially apt for a text focused on the eucharist, which bears a complex material and symbolic status of its own that was the basis of theological disputes over transubstantiation in the later medieval period.[31]

The mixing of symbolic and material representations and Lydgate's play with forms begins immediately in the first stanza of the *Procession*, which announces that "gracyous misteryes" that are "grounded in scripture" shall be "fette out of fygure" in "youre presence" and "declared by many unkouth signe," and the final stanza repeats that "theos figures" have been "shewed in your presence" (ll. 6–8, 217). Although Clopper warns that while "fygures" may suggest "images" to a modern reader and that Lydgate uses the term throughout his poem in the technical sense of *figurae*, Lydgate might be deliberately exploiting the ambiguity of the term as well as the slippage common in meditational texts between things seen with the physical eye and things imagined by the mind's eye. He does this elsewhere, in a poem on the *imago pietatis*, where, as Gayk has shown, a material "figure" is used to "prompt a series of figural interpretations of the Passion."[32] In the *Procession*, Lydgate's language suggests that some sort of material representation (the "figures") have been displayed ("fette out" and "shewed") before spectators (in "youre presence") in some way. Some of the stanzas contain what seem to be descriptions of the figures and their tableaux: Ecclesiastes is depicted with his castle enclosed by a red cloud, Zacharia holds a censer, and Moses has his golden horns.[33] Others stress immediacy and visible presence, through the use of the words *here* (ll. 40, 54, 105, 162) and *this* to introduce the various figures (e.g., "Þis blessed Mark, l. 129). Once Lydgate even invokes the act of looking, with an exhortation to "Beholde" (l. 81). These terms to some degree mimic the imaging techniques of late medieval meditational practice that stress the power of images, and yet Lydgate seems to be exploiting their multiple senses by deliberately conjuring up not just mental images but material presences. Even someone as healthily skeptical of too quickly assuming a text's connection to a dramatic enactment as Clopper accepts that possibility: while arguing that "shewed" need mean nothing more than "presented" or "demonstrated," he admits that "diuers likenesses" may suggest "something more tangible."[34]

While the poem draws on and seeks to spark meditative devotion, especially at the outset, subsequent stanzas suggest that Lydgate's fuller aim is to gloss the processional figures, from Adam to Thomas Aquinas, around whom the poem is structured. Lydgate is apparently not satisfied with a purely meditative register, and the poem's opening emphasis on "Inwarde entente" (l. 17) and the "ymaginatyf" (l. 10) quickly gives way to poetic discussion of the meanings of the processional figures, retelling of their background stories, and disquisition on their attributes. Thus, we learn that Abraham is an example of hospitality, that Jacob saw angels going up and down a ladder, that Mark is associated with a lion, and so on. Lydgate is glossing processional pageantry, not Scripture, yet the basic technique of medieval exegesis in which the literal is linked with its allegorical sense still holds. Each processional figure requires an explanation to reveal the symbolic meaning beneath the surface, a meaning that was authorized by modes of scriptural analysis. At the heart of each of Lydgate's glossing stanzas is an attempt to connect the processional figure to the themes of Corpus Christi, and thus the wine and bread of the sacrament, along with the allegorical association of Christ with grain and milling, make recurring appearances, with the processional figure of Jeremiah, for example, being described as carrying a chalice with "Greyne in þe middes, which to make vs dyne, / Was beete and bulted floure to make of bred."

Shirley's use of the term *ordenaunce* to describe the *Procession* suggests that in copying the poem, he was aware of the yoking of live performances and written texts that Lydgate's glossing verses depend upon. On the performance side, an "ordenaunce" could refer to preparations for various important occasions such as birth, marriage, or funeral; it could refer to acts of planning or arranging; or it could point to traditional customs and practices. On the written side, "ordenaunce" could describe the ordering of things into a pattern, including the arrangement of chapters or lines in a book. Shirley could be describing the *Procession* as a set of directions for the arrangement of a procession on Corpus Christi, in which case Lydgate's verses could be read as setting out the order of the pageants or banners in the procession and offering a brief description of each of them.[35] But like the verses Lydgate wrote describing the pageantry Londoners put on for Henry VI, which Shirley also described as "ordenaunces," the *Procession* may not be a set of instructions for the design of a performance but rather an after-the-fact account of it. In this case, the aim seems less an official commemoration than an attempt at fusing spectating and reading—and devotional activity—through the mechanisms of exegesis and instruction.

That Corpus Christi is the ceremony at the heart of the poem intensifies the impact of Lydgate's connecting of what appears to have been an actual performance with a poetic gloss on it, since the sacrament of the altar hinges on a similar yoking of things present and things imagined, of the material and the symbolic. Erler has argued that a characteristic of eucharistic procession is that it "focuses the gaze on the sacrament" and thus "acknowledges the viewer's own status as *affiliated*," hence the procession tends to be an "instrument of conservatism."[36] Lydgate's verses achieve a similar effect by focusing the reader's attention on the processional figures, which serve to affiliate the reader into a textual community organized around shared assumptions about the meanings of those figures. The effect Lydgate seems to seek is to create for the reader a powerful interpretation that is itself "an 'event' that actualizes the ethical behavior of a reader, absorbs the reader into its own ethical system, and stimulates, among other ethical acts, its own reenactment."[37]

The absorbing focus of Lydgate's verses is of course the eucharistic story from its prefigurations in Jewish history, through the Last Supper, early Christian history, and medieval theological concerns, a story that comprises, as Miri Rubin notes, "a well-wrought piece of vernacular didactic composition."[38] The poem's second line, which describes Corpus Christi as the "Feste of festes moost hevenly and devyne," introduces an extended defense of eucharistic devotion, conveyed through a series of exemplary figures whom Lydgate links to the sacrament of the eucharist and to the Passion. As Cole points out, Lydgate's history of the sacrament includes "some predictable scriptural figures," especially biblical authorities whose presence suggests that Lydgate is employing the usual allegorical pattern of prefiguration whereby Old Testament acts serve as instances of "eucharistic foreshadowing."[39] The treatment of Adam, the first figure in the poem, is emblematic of Lydgate's slanting of his figures toward eucharistic ends. Lydgate ignores most of the Genesis story to focus solely on "Adams synne" (l. 10), which provides the opportunity to move immediately to the crucified Christ, whom Lydgate envisions as an echo of the Edenic fruit hung on the tree of life, and—making the leap to the eucharist—as "oure foode" and "cheef repaste of oure redemption" (ll. 15–16). Other figures are chosen—or, as with Adam, their stories are recast—with a similar aim of creating a series of examples of the power of the eucharist. Melchizedek, the second figure in the poem, is remembered for his offering of bread and wine (drawn from Genesis 14, where he is described as bringing bread and wine to Abraham when Abraham returns from his battle with the four kings who besieged Sodom and Gomorrah) and, in his role as a type of Christ, as offering his own body and blood to his apostles when he returned "Steyned in Bosra" (l. 20), literally, "dyed red in Bosra," a reference to Isaiah 63:1–7, where God returns from battle in a blood-stained robe, a passage often interpreted as applying to the crucified Jesus. While these biblical figures are treated in a fairly conventional way, Lydgate's description of postscriptural authorities, starting with Peter Lombard, is far less orthodox, as Cole has shown. These figures offer defenses against heresy and for transubstantiation (such as the twenty-second stanza, which describes Jerome's work against heretics and contains lines that present the orthodox doctrine of transubstantiation), yet Lydgate often adopts unorthodox—or at least complicatedly orthodox—positions (such as, once again in the description of Jerome, when he "takes the contemporary issue of Christ's indivisible, fleshly body as it inheres in the host and reframes it with an . . . understanding of Christ's body as a social body").[40] Lydgate's treatment of the eucharist, especially his citation of specific figures as authorities on debates about transubstantiation, in the end offers an alternate, not thoroughly orthodox reading of the sacrament, one that, like the procession itself, affiliates believers to a particular version of the religious community.

If the Skinners requested this particular slant on the eucharist, was it because they wanted an interpretation of their procession that sided with an acceptably orthodox yet communal version of the sacrament? Cole suggests that in the *Procession*, Lydgate may be writing a sort of "urban theology" that was echoed in Corpus Christi processions and that stresses the suturing of "social divisions and hierarchies in the name of a sacrament of unity and community," a poetic position that might have appealed to the Skinners both because of their long association with Corpus Christi and because of that feast's more recent associations with disruption.[41] Lancashire speculates that the Clerkenwell/Skinners' Well plays may have ended because of nervousness about large gatherings (the priory of St. John was burned down in the 1381 revolt, although it continued to be a political force and was partly rebuilt by 1399).[42] And while the procession that appears to have replaced the plays may have seemed a more manageable alternative, an emphasis on orthodoxy might still have been desirable. As Steven Justice has shown, the 1381 uprising coincided with the feast of Corpus Christi and included aggression against the prelacy and church possessions in ways that seemed to echo the Wycliffite challenge to the sacrament of the eucharist.[43] Many chroniclers took particular note of the timing of the revolt within the period of celebration of the feast, and Margaret Aston believes that timing was both intentional and critical, pointing to the fact that during the same year, the Wycliffite challenge had come to center on the sacrament of the altar and had suggested that worship of the eucharistic host amounted to idolatry. Corpus Christi processions were in the background of the revolt, Aston reminds us, and in an inversionary form, processions shaped the movements of the rebels, as they marched on London. Processions even made their way into accounts of the revolt, such as Gower's, which sounds like a procession in the way that the author recounts the unfolding of the events in 1381.[44] Any account of the Skinners' procession that Lydgate may have written would probably not have been seen as an immediate response to the troubles of the previous century, yet a lingering sense of heretical and rebellious behavior may still have surrounded the procession and have urged the sort of poem Lydgate provided, a poem that would have accorded with the Skinners' place in the government of London and, by extension, in the city's ceremonial culture as one of the so-called Twelve Great Companies.

The extent to which Lydgate emphasizes in the *Procession* a nuanced religious orthodoxy that is presented as inclusive rather than divisive, creating a community of readers presumed to share the same values, can be seen at the level of his choice of address to readers. Most of Lydgate's other public poems and performance pieces address an audience or an individual and thus make frequent use of the second-person pronouns, with occasional reminders of the voice of the author through scattered interjections of "I."[45] Robert Meyer-Lee has observed that in devotional works, it is common for the "I" to be "generic and hence occupiable by any reader who wishes to use the poem in his or her devotions."[46] In the *Procession*, in contrast, while "youre" and "I" both make appearances, the consistent perspective is that of "us" and "oure," pronouns that address a community united by a common religiosity and that includes the poet. This use of the first-person plural works to construct an imagined religious community based on a shared understanding of eucharistic devotion, a community to whom Lydgate speaks as if he himself is also included. This communal perspective may have been part of what led Schirmer to link the poem to Lydgate's monastery of Bury St. Edmunds, but it would also have suited the occasion of commemorating the Skinners' procession and its urban setting.[47] It is worth noting in this context that unity was central to the feast and idea of Corpus Christi, and that unity may have been part of what inspired John Ball and the other rebels to seek a material as well as spiritual leveling.[48]

Lydgate's verses on the Corpus Christi procession are unusual given that in his other poems for Londoners, Lydgate rarely speaks "as if" to the entire community, as Anne Middleton argues Ricardian public poets did, and often remains distanced from the urban groups for whom he is writing. This distancing is particularly visible in Lydgate's tendency to address Londoners less intimately than he does Henry VI and Queen Catherine in the royal entertainments. Every stanza of the *Mumming at Eltham*, for instance, in which this intimacy is most pronounced, directly speaks to either Henry or his mother, liberally using "you" to create a sense of closeness between the speaker

and those addressed. Verbal intimacy of this sort has the effect of personaliz-
ing the promise of "Pees with youre lieges, plente, and gladnesse" that the
mumming promises to Henry and the increase of "ioye and gladnesse of hert"
that is the wished-for gift for Catherine. Among the London entertainments,
only the *Disguising at London* includes sustained reference to a "you" who is
being addressed ("yee may see," l. 1; "in youre presence," l. 139; "which yee
heer see," l. 213) and is additionally unusual in being one of the rare instances
in which Lydgate explicitly uses the language of "common profit" (directly
mentioned at l. 251) that Middleton views as the essential component of
Ricardian public poetry and that she notes is the usual phrase for translating
res publica or "the public."[49] While the *Disguising at London* speaks of the
"communalte" that Fortitude will establish on a ground of truth and of the
"goode comune" she will help maintain (ll. 236–39), Lydgate does not extend
that expression of a common voice to his other London entertainments, and
it is only in one of his royal mummings—the *Mumming at Windsor*—that he
includes himself in the collectivity he is imagining, referring at one point to
"oure" realm of France (l. 4).

The community constructed through Lydgate's use of pronouns lent itself not just to commemoration of a live performance but also to meditative
reading. Shirley may have copied the *Procession* for the same reasons he gathered many of Lydgate's shorter works into his anthologies: to make them
available for the circle of readers he expects will find them entertaining and
instructive and to preserve and collect them as part of Lydgate's poetic corpus. But Lydgate himself seems to have imagined that the poem would have
an afterlife beyond that of the procession it describes, an afterlife that would
harness glossing to the purposes of devotional reading. Although the poem's
stanzas concentrate on explication, Lydgate's aim of encouraging a devotional
response as the end result of his instructional glossing can be seen in the poem's repeated calls to meditate on the meaning of the biblical and ecclesiastical
figures in the procession. He urges readers to take the figures in the procession
as "token and signe" (l. 62) of the eucharist that can be inwardly and imagi-
natively re-created and calls on readers to become like spectators viewing
processional figures that are "shewed" in their "presence" (l. 217). The poem
collapses the acts of looking inward and outward, meditation and spectatorship, so that there is no functional difference in terms of affect. Both afford the
"counforte and consolacyoun" (ll. 78) that is the promise of reflection on the
eucharist, whether that reflection is triggered by public performance or private reading. As the last stanza emphasizes, remembrance is a crucial part of

the devotional process in which the act of reading works as an *aide memoire* that helps the reader call to mind previous sensory experiences, in this case the viewing of processional figures who explain and exemplify beliefs about the eucharist. Repeatedly, the verses exhort the reader to reflect on external signs and on poetic re-creation of them ("Resceiueþe hem with devoute reverence," l. 219) and to use them as spurs to internalized devotion.

The educative bent with which Lydgate approached devotional activity in the *Procession* is expanded and enriched by the series of Latin marginalia in the manuscripts that call attention to scriptural references linked to the figures. Next to the description of Abraham, for example, a marginal note from Genesis appears: "ponam bucellam Panis / Genesis xliii^e" [And I will set a morsel of bread (Genesis 18:5)]. Next to the verses describing Jacob, another note from Genesis is added: "pinguis est panis Christi / Genesis xl. ix^e" [The bread of Christ shall be fat (Genesis 49:20)]. Similar verses appear in the margins of *Henry VI's Triumphal Entry into London*, where they point to the biblical text on which the entry's various pageants were based and to the "scriptures" that appeared on those pageants. We can only speculate as to whether the marginalia in the *Procession* similarly took the form of "scriptures" that accompanied the figures in the procession, if indeed Lydgate's poem describes an actual procession, but these marginal glosses undeniably add an extra dimension to the reading experience, by situating the verses in a broader liturgical context and coupling the figures in the procession to scriptural authority.

As practiced by scholastics and clerics, glossing attempted to translate or explain passages in a text by means of comments written in the margins, between the lines, or sometimes over the text itself. To gloss was to intervene in the potential meanings of the text and to shape them in specific directions. In this regard, glossing was, in Carolyn Dinshaw's words, "a gesture of appropriation; the *glossa* undertakes to speak the text, to assert authority over it, to provide an interpretation, finally to limit or close it to the possibility of heterodox or unlimited significance."[50] Dinshaw's remarks clearly apply to the marginalia written into manuscript copies of Lydgate's *Procession*, which by linking his vernacular words to scriptural sources both pin them down and invest them with the ultimate authority, that of biblical derivation, but they also extend to the entire text of Lydgate's poem.

What is in fact unusual about the marginal glosses that appear in the manuscript copies of Lydgate's *Procession* is that they comment on a poem that is itself already a commentary on another text. "Glossatory practices in reading and writing," Nicolette Zeeman has argued, "mean that medieval thinkers are aware that things can be said in many ways and that all commentary and textual 'retelling' involves refiguration."[51] Lydgate's poetic retelling or refiguring of a Corpus Christi procession functions as a verbal gloss on a performed event. Similar glossing was sometimes directly incorporated into performances, and although Lydgate's verses stand outside a performance context, the narrative voice he adopts for his glossatory efforts bears some resemblance to expositors of doctrine in medieval plays who comment on and explain the doctrinal significance of what the spectator is watching.[52] The instructional impulse behind Lydgate's *Procession* would have fit not just the immediate context of providing a poetic gloss for the Skinners' procession, if indeed his poem comes from such a commission, but his larger and ongoing interest in expounding the meanings of religious ceremonies. A number of his religious poems take as their subject church rituals, which Lydgate undertakes to explain and, implicitly, defend, whether he is writing about the paternoster, listing the significance of the festivals of the church year, or providing commentary on the mass. Despite the tendency of glosses to restrain meanings, whether understood as marginal comments or, in the case of the *Procession*, entire texts, glossing also provides a chance for intervention and engagement with a text. As John Dagenais has argued, glossing in medieval manuscripts reveals "a textual world that is not self-sufficient, not completed, not even intended to be complete," until an individual reader intervenes and thus engages with the text in a direct way, in the present moment.[53] Lydgate's *Procession* can be seen as just such an intervention, one that assumes the performed procession that is its apparent antecedent is "not self-sufficient, not completed," but available for reshaping and reinterpretation.

One reason Lydgate may have felt the need for such an intervention may be found in attitudes toward visual representations, such as images and pageants in processions. Traditional apologists for images argued that images are useful for teaching, remembering, and arousing devotional feelings. Lydgate's *Procession* does not contradict that three-part defense but may come closer to Reginald Pecock's belief that images are useful as mnemonic devices but less functional for instruction than vernacular writings.[54] Such a view of the limited efficacy of images as tools for instruction perhaps lies behind the *Procession*'s aim of explicating the meanings of visible signs such as representations of biblical and other figures shown in processional display to "enlumyne" "al derknesse" (l. 4) as the opening stanza states. The privileging of writing as a vehicle for conveyance of the truth can be seen in the frequency with which Lydgate represents the processional figures as authorities who are authoritative precisely because they wielded the pen. Many lines emphasize learnedness and the act of writing, as Lydgate describes how Paul "wrytethe in his scripture" (l. 153), reminds that Peter Lombard is called "maystre of sentence" (l. 161), and recalls that Jerome "Wryteþe and recordeþe" (l. 170), Augustine "reherseþe in sentence" (l. 185), and Ambrose "with sugred elloquence, / Wryteþe with his penne and langage laureate" (ll. 193–94), among many other similar usages. Cole is correct in pointing out that Lydgate's reliance on a layering of theological and historical authorities is part of what gives Lydgate's position on the eucharist such complexity, but a crucial aspect of Lydgate's use of these authorities is his emphasis on their status as learned commentators and writers.[55] What those authorities have "rehearsed" in writing, Lydgate now does as well, glossing the spectacle of a procession by commenting and expounding on it.

While Lydgate may privilege written text over visual display, he by no means dismisses the latter, and the final stanza of the *Procession* seems to me to indicate the importance Lydgate places on material representational forms such as images or pageants. It seems difficult to read this stanzas in any way other than as an explicit underscoring of the physical presence of the figures he has been glossing, as he asks readers to reverently receive "þeos figures shewed in youre presence," which have been shown in "diuers liknesses" (ll. 217–18). Lydgate emphasizes the immediacy of the "figures" and "liknesses" of the biblical and ecclesiastical personages he has described in his verses, and the phrase "shewed in youre presence" seems to make clear that he is pointing to representations that readers would have seen in more than their mind's eye. If this reading is correct, then the poem has come full circle, back to the actual procession that Shirley identified as having been the impetus for Lydgate's verses. By the last stanza, the symbolic meanings of the processional figures have merged with the material forms that spectators presumably saw on painted banners or pageants carried in the Corpus Christi procession, as poetic gloss and live performance join together to create meaning for the reader. Lydgate's verses take off from, and rely upon, the physical experience of watching a procession, without which the verses' glossing would have smaller impact and make less sense. The gloss needs the performance, as a physical ground for their interpretation of the meanings and significance of what was displayed in the procession. Just as the final stanza of the *Procession* urges readers to "receive" not just the figures that have been shown in their presence but the eucharist as well, so too Lydgate brings together the sensual experience of a live procession and the instructive gloss of the poem to trigger the reader's active participation in meditative devotion on Corpus Christi.

Lydgate's gloss-on-performance poem can be viewed as an example of the process of *textualizing*, as described by Mary Carruthers, "in which the original work acquires commentary and gloss" within the context of a textual community; this is also a process of "socializing" a work of literature that involves processing and transforming words, which come through sensory gateways, into memory, thus making them one's own.[56] The poem stands as evidence of Lydgate's having made the procession his own, but did his work of textualizing have an effect within a community of readers, whether the Skinners or others? Although we have no testimony from medieval readers with which to answer that question, we can glean some clues about the readers who encountered Lydgate's verses from the manuscripts in which the *Procession* is extant. All three surviving copies of the *Procession* are linked to Shirley, who included it in the first of his anthologies, Trinity MS R.3.20. Another copy survives in BL MS Harley 2251, a miscellany derived from R.3.20 that was made by a professional London copyist after Shirley's death. The third copy of the *Procession* is in Stow's BL MS Add. 29729, for which Trinity R.3.20 was a partial exemplar.

The manuscript evidence suggests that the *Procession* circulated in the 1430s and thereafter among two groups: first, the readers linked to Beauchamp's household who may have used Trinity MS R.3.20 in the years after it was compiled and, later in the century (in the 1460s and beyond), Londoners and others who commissioned manuscripts like MS Harley 2251 that were copied in part from Shirley's manuscripts. John Vale, secretary to the draper Sir Thomas Cook, who was mayor of London in 1462–63 and a friend and associate of Shirley's brother-in-law, Avery Cornburgh, apparently was the original owner of MS Harley 2251.[57] If the Skinners ever owned a copy of the *Procession*, it has not endured, and if Lydgate kept a copy for himself, it too has vanished.[58] It is possible that some of those readers, and even Lydgate himself, may have seen the Skinners' procession, but even readers who had not would have been able to understand and respond to the verses Lydgate wrote, since the poem re-creates the shape of a live procession through an interplay of visual and verbal material and through the poem's processional form.

It may seem curious that Lydgate's poem does not survive in any official guild or city records, unlike *Henry VI's Triumphal Entry*, which was copied into a number of chronicle accounts. Perhaps accounts that may originally have contained the *Procession* have been lost or destroyed. But it may also be that the *Procession* was never entered into any official records because, unlike the *Triumphal Entry*, it is not a souvenir text. Its aim is less to preserve details of a past performance so as to increase the honor of the group that sponsored it than to offer a commentary on the performance and thus enhance meditative devotion. That difference between souvenir and instructional text can be seen in the tenses Lydgate used when writing the two poems: while the *Triumphal Entry* uses the past tense throughout, the *Procession* is cast in the present tense, creating the sense of a Corpus Christi performance that is always still happening, whenever a reader casts an eye on the poem.

Carruthers suggests that medieval literary texts were formed around "a recollecting subject, a remembered text, and a remembering audience."[59] Lydgate as glossing poet, the actual or imagined event of a Corpus Christi procession, and the readers who would have recalled such processions while absorbing Lydgate's verses formed the textual community united by those processes of writing, spectating, and reading. Whether or not Lydgate's verses were written to explicate a particular performance, they endure as a gloss on eucharistic devotion, offering a guide readers could return to again and again whenever they chose.

CHAPTER 5

Inscription and Ceremony:
The 1432 Royal Entry

On 21 February 1432, Londoners mounted a series of pageants to welcome Henry VI on his return to England after his Parisian coronation. The event was documented by John Carpenter, London's common clerk, in a Latin letter that he subsequently entered into the city's letter book. At some point soon after, Lydgate was commissioned to write a poem on the same event. That poem—in English, by a prestigious author, and with various rhetorical flourishes, including stanzas praising London—seems to have been requested to memorialize the occasion in a way that Carpenter's Latin text was incapable of doing.[1] Derek Pearsall has described Lydgate's poem as a kind of souvenir program, and Maura Nolan has called it a transformation of spectacle into poetry, both of which are apt assessments that offer an interpretive context for a consideration of performance and inscription.[2] The desire for a poetic representation of the 1432 pageantry and the turn to Lydgate as the person to undertake that literary effort reveals, among other things, an understanding of vernacular writing as a desirable adjunct to performance, as was emphasized when Lydgate's poem was subsequently copied into the city chronicles that were ushering in a new form of vernacular writing.

This chapter examines how vernacular writing intersects with ritual and ceremony in fifteenth-century England and considers the material form vernacular writing takes within public ceremonies as well as in the manuscript copies made to record those ceremonies. Inscription occurred in multiple places in and around the 1432 royal entry: in the processional route through the city followed by the king and his retinue, in the verses that were painted onto the pageants, in the accounts that reported the event, and in the manuscripts into which those accounts were copied. We usually think of unscripted performances such as processions as fleeting and of written documents such as play-texts as fixed, yet the 1432 entry shows the falsity of that opposition and suggests how performance and inscription each contains and is shaped by "the possibility of the other."[3] By looking explicitly at acts of inscription within and around the performance that greeted the young king Henry, it is possible to trace how that "possibility of the other" influenced what spectators saw and readers later read. More specifically, in the 1432 entry, quotidian (and often ephemeral) writing—such as that found in the form of short texts, signs, bills, and nonverbal signs, including the heraldic arms and blazons of aristocracy or house or shop or tavern signs that have been called "a silent language of urban people"—intersected with what might be called durable writing intended to provide an official and permanent account suitable for memorializing an event within chronicles and civic records.[4] The pageantry for Henry VI and its multiple inscriptions does not exactly pit the writing of the streets against the writing of official records but rather demonstrates how the two forms could compete and yet be dependent.

Processional Inscription

The 1432 pageants show an awareness of the tactics of ritual ceremony to craft a specific message about the city of London's relations with Henry VI, and they inscribe that message spatially and temporally onto the city through the placement of pageantry and the movement of the king's procession through the streets. After two years on the continent and having been crowned king of France, Henry VI landed at Dover and made his way to Blackheath where, on 21 February, he was met by the mayor, aldermen, and other Londoners and led past seven pageants that had been set up at various locations in the city. The pageants included a giant at London Bridge, flanked by two antelopes bearing the arms of England and France, with an inscription in Latin declaring that the giant would protect the king from foreign enemies; a tower erected in the middle of the bridge, featuring Nature, Grace, and Fortune along with maidens who presented the king with doves representing the gifts of the Holy Spirit; a tabernacle at Cornhill, with Dame Sapience and the seven sciences; at the conduit a child-king on a throne surrounded by Mercy, Truth, and Clemency; at the conduit in Cheapside, a well at which Mercy, Grace, and Pity offered wine and a paradise of fruit trees near which stood

Enoch and Elias; a castle of jasper, with a pedigree showing Henry's lineage
and a Jesse Tree; and at the conduit in St. Paul's, an image of the Trinity with
angels. When Henry reached St. Paul's, he dismounted and entered the church,
where he was greeted by the archbishop and other clerics, then continued on
to Westminster where the abbot and monks met him with the scepter of
St. Edward. On the following Saturday, the mayor and aldermen solidified
their welcome by offering the king a golden hamper filled with a thousand
pounds of gold. As best as the intentions of its planners can be deciphered
from the surviving evidence, the pageantry appears to have been designed to
convey the hopes of Londoners for their king, offer advice to him about the
qualities needed for good rule, and attempt to demonstrate London's prestige
and importance within the realm.[5]

Like other royal entries, the 1432 welcome for Henry VI inscribed social
and political relations onto the terrain of the city and made them visible.
That act of inscription was first and foremost spatial, as the processional route
marked out by the seven pageants imprinted the ritual welcome onto the
city's streets. It began with the meeting of the royal guest outside the city, at
Blackheath, by the mayor and an entourage of Londoners who escorted Henry
into the city in a gesture that combined civic deference with a reminder of
civic prestige and power.[6] After the liminal event of the crossing of London
Bridge and the viewing of its pageants, the procession followed the usual noncoronation royal entry route through the center of the city via Cornhill and
Cheapside, ending at St. Paul's, before the king moved on in postliminal fashion to Westminster.

While repetitive and routinized social movements are the stuff of ordinary daily life and thus are part of what makes up the "social order," deliberately planned and theatricalized processions featuring stops at particular spots
along the route offer ritualized and ceremonial disruptions of routine for
heightened and calculated effect. The selection of public places for the placement of pageantry in royal entry processions was both strategic (the possibility of useful symbolism adhering to a location) and pragmatic (wide streets,
location of structures useful for erecting pageantry); it was a decision organized around, in Janette Dillon's words, "'hot spots' infused with varying
intensity as a result of traditional ritualizing practices that mapped and reinforced their significance with every repetition of procession through them."[7]
The entry employed a "basic syntax" of pageant stations, as Lawrence Manley
has argued, laid out around "the same invariant landmarks" of cisterns (the
conduits in Cornhill, Cheapside, and Paul's Gate) and crosses (the cross in

Cheapside) that dotted the route.[8] This basic royal entry syntax is an aspect of what Paul Strohm has argued is "the peculiarity" of medieval space: the way it is marked by its *presignifications* and thus is "already symbolically organized by the meaning-making activities of the many generations that have traversed it."[9] The 1432 pageants, located at spots that came ready-made with past significations, both created new topographical meanings (on this occasion, the fourth pageant, at the conduit in Cornhill, emphasized justice and featured a child on a throne, dressed like a king, accompanied by Mercy, Truth, and Clemency, as well as two judges and eight sergeants-at-law) and imposed them on top of existing associations (the conduit in Cornhill had been built as a prison for nightwalkers in 1282 and in the fifteenth century still featured a timber cage used for that purpose).[10] Whether it was deliberately intended to do so by the pageant organizers or not, this palimpsest-like act of inscription, or perhaps more properly reinscription, that reused key sites in the city layered new significance designed for present purposes on top of already established spatial logics/meanings. To a spectator, the pageantry could have invoked both past and present associations with specific sites in the city.

Although the topography of medieval processional routes has often been read as creating a sense of *communitas*, royal entries involved more symbolic violence and disunity than that traditional reading recognizes.[11] At the simplest level, Henry VI's entry inscribed a linear trajectory of intrusion, containment, and ejection onto the city. The very notion of a welcome involved the latent threat of forced entry; from the moment when London's elites met their royal visitors outside the city's boundaries at Blackheath and escorted them into the city, the possibility of royal assault on the city was recoded as an invitation to come inside.[12] The bridge pageant often featured a giant with a sword, serving as a reminder of London's ability to defend itself, even if that menacing figure could be interpreted in entry pageantry as a defender of the king as well.[13] After negotiating that intrusive moment and having crossed London Bridge, the king made his way through the main thoroughfares of London, the protected guest and recipient of the pageantry's messages. After viewing the last pageant at St. Paul's, the king proceeded to ceremonies inside the church and then was taken by the mayor and citizens to Westminster; afterward, Henry went with his lords to his palace to rest, while the mayor and citizens returned to the city, a parting of the ways that ended the temporary integration of the individual (the king) with the collectivity (the citizen-spectators of London).

In its entirety, the 1432 procession was an instance of both what Henri Lefebvre describes as "spatial practice," that is, the "production and reproduction" of social space linked to "the particular locations and spatial sets characteristic of each social formation," and "representational space," by which Lefebvre means the "complex symbolisms" that create imaginative space.[14] By using the city's built spaces—its buildings, streets, and existing architectural features—as its ground, the 1432 entry traced existing social relations; by erecting purpose-built stages and scaffolding and by moving across the city in ways that did not follow ordinary paths of work or leisure, the entry created new social relations. The complex symbolisms of the representational space of the pageantry the king encountered included a specific image of royal and civic relations, an image shaped by events at hand, which included the circumstances of Henry's youth, the shakiness of the dual monarchy, and London's allegiances in struggles between the king's uncles, Bedford and Gloucester. Although the chief responsibility for the pageantry lay with the city, city and crown collaborated on the arrangements, and the imaginative space of the entry was thus to some extent the result of a collaborative agenda (the third pageant, featuring Dame Sapience, may have been requested by Gloucester, for example).[15]

Even though it was a shared enterprise between crown and city, the 1432 entry led the king on a path through the heart of the city from London Bridge to St. Paul's, along "a central civic axis" that could not help but offer a view of London's autonomy and prestige.[16] As Kathleen Ashley has pointed out, processional routes "are the clearest maps to the significant power structures within a community, since they are always deliberately designed with reference to places recognised as important."[17] The general route for royal entries into London was established early and appears to have remained much the same for centuries. That route emphasized London's "desired and expressed independence" through its focus on Cheapside, the main commercial street in the city, which was bounded by St. Thomas of Acon and St. Paul's, sites that had political and religious associations specific to London, especially those linked to Thomas à Becket, who died opposing the authority of the crown.[18]

The medieval walker was never "a free rambler," improviser, or "flâneur," Strohm claims, and no medieval perambulator could find his path less circumscribed and controlled than the royal visitor, especially one as young a Henry VI.[19] On their processional route through the city's streets, the king and his entourage followed a strenuously regulated itinerary that allowed little room for spontaneous motion. Like all royal entries, the movement of the procession was halting, involving a stop-and-go pattern of approach, arrival, pause, and departure that required the king to alter his pace to suit the topography and displays; presumably, some of the pageants, especially those that featured songs or gift giving or that were particularly elaborate, required longer stops than others. Anticipation, fulfillment, and loss were aspects of the rhythm of the procession, imposed without much choice upon the entourage makings its way through the streets. If the royal entry inscribes sovereign power on the king's body, it also forces that body to conform to the urban spaces through which it moves.

As he processed through London, Henry VI would have been met by carefully contrived imaginative representations. The purpose of the processional route the king traversed and the pageantry he viewed along the way was to impress upon him a particular understanding of his expected relations with the city, a purpose that can be seen in the pageantry's slanting of the traditional themes of royal entries. When set against earlier London entries—such as the 1392 reconciliation of Richard II, the coronation entry for Henry V in November 1413, the welcome for Henry V in November 1415 after his victorious return from Agincourt, the welcome and coronation of Catherine of Valois in February 1421, the welcome of the duke and duchess of Bedford in January 1426, or the coronation entry of Henry VI in November 1429—the pageantry for 1432 shows a departure from the typical reliance on religious themes with instead a preference for didacticism blended with motifs drawn from chivalric romance.[20] Henry's procession drew on the liturgies of Advent and Epiphany, as Gordon Kipling has shown, to construct Henry as a kind of infant savior, but the seven pageants the king encountered deviated from the usual pattern by downplaying religious imagery while adopting an instructional focus on the qualities of the ideal king.[21]

Kipling observes that the 1432 entry was chiefly interested in "creating individual epiphanies for Henry," using its seven pageants to stage for the young king manifestations of his messianic royalty.[22] The pageantry also offered admonitory models of justice, wise rule, and other attributes London's government would have found useful in the king, seeking to turn him into an ideal ruler from not just a royal but also a civic perspective. At the same time, the mere display of the king's body asserted his status and, despite his youth, his claim to lordship. His public presence as he was escorted through the city's streets signaled his authority and reminded everyone he passed of the fact of royal power over the city. Even a circumscribed and constrained royal body could transform urban space just as that space sought to transform him.[23]

In its inscription of an anticipated set of social relations onto the city, the procession revealed not just the political ties between sovereign and subjects but also the structure of civic London, at the level of both the government and artisans and laborers. As Dillon has noted, a royal entry into London was "as much a negotiation and affirmation of the values and meanings of the city as it was of the values and meanings of the court,"[24] and if there was an implicit production of internal cohesiveness in the entry of 1432, there was also an acknowledgment of disparate spaces, neighborhoods, and locales, each with its own identity and group affiliations not always in solidarity with the rest of the city. Miri Rubin argues that large-scale processions fell into two groups: those demarcating territories and those linking them.[25] Interestingly, the 1432 entry fits into both categories. That combining of linking and demarcating behavior was visibly announced at the outset of the procession, when all of the Londoners appeared wearing white, but with guilds adding their own distinctive insignia. Linking and demarcating continued as the procession crossed parishes and neighborhoods, moving through and drawing together different industrial areas of the city.[26] At the same time, by stopping to view pageants that had been erected at specific locations that had associations to local structures, the procession called attention to those spots, thus distinguishing them one from another. The pageantry seemed to have been designed with an awareness of site-specific differences and could incorporate local features or associations into an individual pageant's theme, as occurred with the use of a giant in the first pageant, at London Bridge.

Although less visibly so, as a spatial practice, the procession was also inscribed economically into London. The medieval city was a space of exchange and accumulation, as Lefebvre has argued, and that financial orientation can be seen in the mounting of the 1432 entry.[27] Entry pageantry was neither voluntary nor spontaneous but rather required as part of the city's relationship to the crown. While expensive for the city government, the royal entries provided work for artisans, laborers, and provisioners; they also attracted crowds that generated business for inns, taverns, and other purveyors of goods, so much so that the prevalence of pageants and processions in their city may explain why Londoners did not need the sorts of religious plays, with their socioeconomic benefits, put on in York, Coventry, or Chester. Occasions such as royal entries allowed London craftsmen "to display their wares" to the king, the court, and other visitors, as Caroline Barron notes, channeling money into the pockets of merchant suppliers and artisans.[28]

Besides having a spatial presence in the city, the procession for Henry was temporally inscribed as well. Royal entries as a performance form participated in a double temporal patterning, on one level emphasizing invariance, by reusing similar themes and pageant structures again and again, thus acquiring a kind of ritual timelessness that transmitted a sense of traditional ceremonial order, and on another, responding to specific historical events.[29] The timing of the 1432 entry, as with all royal entries, was determined not by a fixed date or season—as were Midsummer Watches or Corpus Christi or mayoral processions—but by the political concerns of the moment. Unlike seasonal processions, royal entries were infrequent events, even in London. Some royal entries were devised following advance warning, but most were fairly hasty arrangements in which the hosting city had to act quickly to mount the expected pageantry. Although no chronicle records its duration, the 1432 entry may have taken about half a day, like other noncoronation entries that typically took place on one day (that of 1415 lasted five hours, from 10 a.m. to 3 p.m.).[30] Coronation entries, in contrast, were two-day events in which the royal visitor was met outside the city and escorted past bridge pageantry to an overnight stay in the Tower, with the second day procession beginning at the Tower and moving to Cornhill, Cheapside, St. Paul's, and Westminster. Henry VI's coronation procession in 1429 may have unusually comprised just one day, with the Tower stay condensed to just a midday meal.[31] Use of the city's streets in the compact space of less than one day must have heightened the intensity of the 1432 procession—it was fleeting, it could be seen just once—while also marking it off from ordinary time, whether of the ritual or workaday year.[32]

Given its physical (spatial, economic, and temporal) movement through a landscape, a procession always has inscriptive force, marking out territories, drawing together disparate locations, and showing structures of authority and social connections (as well as exclusions) in a community. The movement of the king, his entourage, and the mayor and citizens as they traversed London in the 1432 entry performed real and desired relations between crown and city, stamping into the streetscape for all to see, even if only momentarily, the marks of civic and royal negotiations of power and authority.

Pageantry Inscription

While entries on the continent were primarily a form of visual art that drew on tableaux and painted images, English entry pageantry included words.[33] Although there is no hard evidence that actors in English entries delivered mimed speeches until the 1445 pageants for Margaret of Anjou, they did sing songs and the pageants used painted "scriptures" to get their meanings across.[34] The 1392 show for Richard II included a *custos*, or expositor, who traveled with the king and made formal speeches explaining each pageant, while the actors who were costumed as angels and saints sang songs and delivered gifts for the king to the *custos*.[35]

As recorded in various surviving accounts, the 1432 triumphal entry was a wordy spectacle. Speech, song, and writing were a part of the pageantry, beginning with the ritual welcome of the king at Blackheath, during which the mayor, John Welles, delivered a greeting in English, a speech that was recorded in English by Carpenter and included in Lydgate's poem, with slightly different wording. Carpenter reports that the mayor's speech in English was followed by an assembly of 120 clergy at Deptford singing Latin antiphons to the king.[36] The volubility of the 1432 entry reveals how the traditions of writing in both Latin and the vernacular intersect with ritual and ceremony while also calling attention to the way the entry's words were communicative acts shaped by specific material media—painted words, vernacular speech, Vulgate scriptures, and songs in Latin and English.

Like the procession itself, the language inscribed onto and around the pageants is a form of communication, one that operates from within a specific material medium and that intersects with the live performance of the king's movements through the city. Although a reliance on words was unusual in medieval spectacles, especially those on the continent, many art objects, such as paintings and vases, contained readable inscriptions. As Whitney Davis notes, such inscriptions would require the information on the inscription "to be 'seen' and 'read' at one and the same time" and thus such inscriptions intensify the activity of looking, by asking viewers to also become "close readers."[37] In the case of sung or spoken words accompanying visual spectacle, viewers would also be asked to become "close listeners," increasing the sensory-processing demands being made by the pageantry. Not all members of the audience would have met or even cared about such demands, and for many spectators, especially those not close enough to see or hear clearly, the words inscribed into the 1432 pageantry may have been little more than a blur or a murmur. As the convention of the *custos* shows, however, the royal visitor had help with those close reading tasks, and the 1432 entry seems even more determined than most to make its writing legible, if what Lydgate says about the "scriptures" being able to be read "with-oute a spectakle" (l. 267) is accurate.

A focus on language was apparently a consistent part of the design of the 1432 pageantry. In the first pageant, which was located at the entrance to London Bridge, the king encountered a giant with a raised sword. A giant, a champion of the city, seems to have been standard for pageants at this location; in 1415, a giant held an axe in one hand and the keys to the city in the other, and was accompanied by a giantess, the two probably representing Gog and Magog. The 1432 giant was flanked by two antelopes, one of the heraldic devices associated with the Lancastrians, and was apparently rigged for movement, as were the giants who bowed in the pageants for Catherine of Valois in 1421.[38] In 1432, this visual spectacle was accompanied by writing. On either side of the giant was a scripture, which Carpenter gives in Latin, reading "Inimicos eius induam confusione" (His enemies I will clothe with confusion [Psalms 131:18]). Lydgate renders the scripture in English and at greater length, turning it into a full stanza that translates the Vulgate phrase while elaborating on its present meaning, all couched in a style that gives the appearance of direct speech "seyde" by the giant's scripture. Since there is no mention in accounts of the 1432 royal entry of a *custos* who could explain the scripture to the king, presumably Henry was expected to be able to read and understand the Latin biblical phrases on his own. Lydgate's translation into English in his record of the royal entry registers a different audience and different ends for the poem he was commissioned to produce.

Like the welcoming giant, the second pageant underscored its visual imagery with judicious use of language. Located at the drawbridge, this pageant featured a tower out of which came three empresses—Nature, Grace, and Fortune—who gave the king gifts of various strengths and virtues, intended to ensure his long reign. They were accompanied, on the right, by seven angelic maidens dressed in white, who presented the king with seven gifts of the Holy Ghost in the guise of seven white doves and a scripture and, on the left, by seven other maidens who also presented symbolic gifts to the king and sang a roundel of welcome.[39] Visual images, including signs and tokens, as well as the objects given as gifts—a crown of glory, sword of justice, scepter of mercy, mantle of prudence, shield of faith, helmet of health, and girdle of peace, which resemble the metaphorical dressing of a knight in Caxton's *Boke of the Ordre of Chyualry* and the garbing of the king in a coronation—conveyed the pageant's meanings.[40] While surely striking and efficacious, these visual images and material objects did not stand alone, with scriptures and song being used to underscore the display.

The three Latin scriptures cited by Carpenter as accompanying the gift giving of the second pageant are hortatory as well as aspirational. The first expresses the hope that Henry will "Set out, proceed prosperously, and reign" ("Intende, prospere, procede, et regna" [Psalms 44:5]). The second asks that "God send you the spirit of wisdom, and of understanding, the spirit of counsel, and of fortitude, the spirit of knowledge, and of godliness" ("Impleat te Deus spiritu sapiencie . . ." [Isaiah 11:2]). The third echoes the *ordo* for a coronation and requests that "The Lord clothe you with the crown of glory, the sword of justice, the scepter of mercy, the mantle of prudence, the shield of faith, the helmet of health, and the girdle of peace" ("Induat te Dominus corona glorie, gladio iusticie, septro clemencie, palio prudencie, scuto fidei, galea salutis et vinculo pacis"). While deriving from biblical and liturgical sources, used in the context of the entry, these scriptures take on a distinctly instructional air, with London cast in an advisory role.[41]

According to both Carpenter and Lydgate, the second pageant's scriptures were delivered through writing, speech, and song. The first scripture was written, while the second scripture was spoken by the first set of maidens. Carpenter introduces the maidens' scripture with the words "dicentes per rescriptum," which Lydgate translates as "seyyng to him, lyke as clerkes write" (l. 180), giving an expanded version of the Latin Vulgate sentence in English. Both writers also report that the second set of maidens sang their roundel in English. Henry MacCracken believes that the version of the roundel recorded by Carpenter was the one that was actually sung, while Lydgate's is "an artistic revision" of what Henry heard.[42]

Yet, despite the reference to speech and vernacular song in the second pageant, if Carpenter is to be believed, the scriptures used in the 1432 pageantry were written and were in Latin, as his choice of the words *rescribere* and *subscribere* to describe them indicates. Lydgate in most instances changes Carpenter's account by describing actors who seem to speak the lines in English and, in so doing, may have suggested the possibilities for dramatic speeches to the devisers of the 1445 entry, who appear for the first time to have presented actors with a complete series of mimed speeches.[43] Lydgate's recasting of Carpenter's (and presumably the pageants') written Latin scriptures as English speech also of course meshes with his purposes in providing an account for the mayor written in English verse. Particularly in the form in which Carpenter presents them, the Latin scriptures linked the pageantry to another performance context, that of the liturgy. By recalling religious services, the scriptures associated the ritual procession of the king through

London's streets with the rites of the mass. Like the inscriptional characters
Marshall McLuhan has called "trapped words," the Latin mottoes Carpenter
describes as having been written on the pageants captured biblical phrases
and froze them in place.[44] At the same time, however, those "trapped" scriptures escaped their pageant entrapment through recollection of their biblical
source text as well as their enactment in liturgical services.

The pattern set up in the first two pageants was followed in the third and
fourth, which like them incorporated words to identify and explain the scene
being visually depicted. Near St. Peter's in Cornhill, the king encountered a
tabernacle built for Dame Sapience and the seven liberal sciences and their
classical practitioners. Once again, the two Latin scriptures written above
and in front of Sapience express the intended message: "Per me reges regnant
et gloriam sapiencie possidebunt" (Through me kings reign and possess the
glory of wisdom [Proverbs 8:15]), and "Et nunc reges intelligite et erudimini
qui iudicatis terram" (And now, kings, understand and receive instruction,
you who judge the earth [Psalms 2:10]). (Lydgate implies that the second of
the scriptures was written in a fashion that made it "Able to be redde with-
oute a spectakle" (l. 267) and that Sapience also said it aloud to the king in
English.) The fourth pageant was at the conduit in Cornhill and featured a
child on a throne, dressed like a king, accompanied by Mercy, Truth, and
Clemency, as well as two judges and eight sergeants-at-arms with four scriptures emphasizing equity and justice. The pageant was a representation of a
verse from Proverbs 20:28, as one of the scriptures makes clear: "Misericordia
et veritas custodiunt regem" (Mercy and Truth preserve the king). The other
scriptures for the child-king pageant are psalms that similarly stress the king's
need to rule justly. Although Lydgate does not present these scriptures as anything other than written mottoes, they speak directly to Henry, stressing law
and justice in a part of the city linked to issues of justice since Cornhill was
the area of the city in which commercial abuses were punished by the pillory.[45]
With its two judges and eight sergeants in a tableau of *Iusticia*, the fourth
pageant perhaps also alluded to the growing lawlessness of the early 1430s,
including the 1431 Lollard uprising.[46]

As the fourth pageant shows especially well, the vernacular speeches and
the Latin scriptures were involved in an exchange of meanings with the
iconography of the pageants. What was elaborated through scenery and the
gestures of costumed actors impersonating allegorical and biblical figures
was distilled into a succinct snippet of writing or oral comment. Together,
the scriptures in their written and uttered form and the tableaux with their

costumed actors created an interplay of signs that shaped the spectator's and auditor's experience of the event, offering both dilation and contraction of the pageantry's themes.

In the fifth pageant, a Wells of Paradise scene at the conduit in Cheapside depicted the water from the fountains being miraculously turned into wine and included three scriptures, two of which Lydgate treats as speeches.[47] After Mercy, Grace, and Pity drew the wine, Enoch and Elijah greeted the king. Lydgate refashions the written Latin scriptures that Carpenter describes into words spoken by Enoch and Elijah to the king. "Nichil proficiat Inimicos . . ." (The enemy shall have no advantage . . . [Psalms 88:23]) becomes an utterance by Enoch as the king rides by and "Dominus conseruet eum . . ." (The Lord preserve him . . . [Psalms 40:3]) is translated into English words spoken by Elijah. Both scriptures are appropriate for figures known as the guardians of Paradise as well as lawgivers, and they emphasize, as the visual imagery alone would be unable to do, that an earthly paradise requires law and order. Lydgate follows Carpenter in depicting the third scripture, "Haureietis aquas . . ." (Thou shalt draw waters . . . [Isaiah 12:3]) as being written at the front of the well, where it commends the curative powers of the waters.

While each individual pageant integrated imagery with scriptural mottoes to make up a legible entity, the inscriptions also developed larger meanings from their relations to one another and to the whole ritual event. Like the processional route itself, by means of which the meaning of the ceremony unfolded gradually through the ritual progress through the streets of London, the repeated use of scriptures on the pageants provided a continuity that meshed the seven pageants into a unified performance. Individual pageants communicated their own themes, which the movement of the processional route drew together, like the parts of a sentence. The syntax of the pageants that was mapped onto the ritual route of the entry was knit tighter through the repeated use of the Latin biblical mottoes painted onto the pageants. (This knitting effect is particularly notable in Carpenter's and Lydgate's written accounts, where the compactness of their texts makes the connections among the scriptures especially visible.) In addition to drawing together the pageants' themes, the mottoes also linked the unique event of the royal entry to a broader context of church ritual, grounded in biblical history. As instances of writing, the mottoes served as a compact reminder of liturgical practice; they are at once a residue of the orally performed liturgy but also a manifestation of the written scripture on which church ritual rested; the mottoes show traces of the processes of both writing and reading described by John Dagenais and are a physical remnant of biblical authority and liturgical performance harnessed for the city's welcome ceremony.[48]

The last pageant inscription viewed by Henry VI in the 1432 entry underscores, but complicates, Dagenais's claim that both oral performance and manuscript text "exist in constant dialogue with an audience."[49] After the sixth pageant at the cross in Cheapside, which featured a castle of jasper flanked by two trees but apparently no scriptures,[50] the final pageant at the conduit in St. Paul's concluded with a scripture—"Angelus eius mandavit de te" (For he hath given his angels charge over thee [Psalms 90:11])—that both Carpenter and Lydgate describe as having been written on the front of the stage on which stood the Trinity surrounded by angels. In his poem, Lydgate expands and amplifies the scripture, going well beyond Carpenter's account, turning the brief Latin motto into three stanzas of hope for the king's ability to rule wisely. Although Dagenais has in mind marginalia, interlinear comments, and glosses as examples of audience interaction with the manuscript text, Lydgate's expansion of the Latin motto on the final pageant is clearly in dialogue with Carpenter's text and, to the degree that Lydgate may have seen at least some of pageantry or have had another source to go on besides Carpenter's letter, as I will discuss in the following pages, is also perhaps in dialogue with the pageantry as well. Did the king think the thoughts expressed in Lydgate's amplification when he reached the last pageant and read that line from Psalm 90? Probably not. But it is certainly possible that Londoners, including the mayor, did and that their presumably silent interaction with the final pageant found voice, perhaps at the mayor's express request, in Lydgate's later three-stanza expansion.

We can piece together some details of the decisions that led to the inclusion of so much writing and speech in the 1432 entry from accounts from 1432, as well as the much fuller records from the 1421 entry for Catherine. Work must have started shortly after the Common Council meeting recorded on 21 January 1432 at which funding for the pageantry was secured, leaving about a month to get ready for the king's arrival. The Common Council probably asked for a general plan, which could have been supplied by Carpenter. Since the location of pageants tended to be the same from year to year, the city could then have farmed out individual pageants to groups like the bridge wardens, who would have been responsible for creating its pageant according to instructions. We know that the Fishmongers provided a ship-pageant in 1313 for the birth of Edward III and that the Goldsmiths twice provided a castle at the conduit in Cheapside in 1377 and 1382, at a cost in 1382 including minstrels of just over 35 pounds (the Grocers may have sponsored the St. John the Baptist pageant at Temple Bar on the route from St. Paul's to Westminster in 1392). The Goldsmiths' castle was built over the Great Conduit in Cheapside, the location for a pageant in 1415. That they also sponsored a pageant in 1432 is suggested by their accounts, which include a letter from Henry VI in 1444 requesting a lavish show for Margaret's entry in 1445 and mentioning their fine display on the occasion of his entry in 1432.[51] It is possible that the Grocers had a hand in the Wells of Paradise pageant at the Great Conduit in Cheapside in 1432 as well. Welles, who was mayor in 1431–32, was a grocer and had a special interest in London's water supply, including the upkeep of its conduits; the many fruit-bearing trees of the Paradise pageant also seem to echo the trade symbolism of the 1392 John the Baptist pageant that may have been sponsored by another grocer-mayor.[52]

While the writing that appeared in the 1432 entry obviously gestured toward learned, religious, and Latinate culture in its use of scriptural quotations, it also echoed secular public writing and proclamation in late medieval London. The posting of broadsides was increasingly common in London after 1377, and the 1431 uprising by Jack Sharp and his rebels adopted a sophisticated use of bills, including bills in verse.[53] Some of this public writing took the form of what Steven Justice has called "assertive literacy," a use of the written word that explicitly and defiantly positioned itself against the control of writing by elites.[54] Such bills and libels were part of the "lost literature" of medieval England or "underground writings" that offered a political alternative to the representational power of the king's presence as an embodiment of power. Topical writing of this sort, which was often associated with rebellion, could be transmitted quickly in a variety of ways—posted on windows or doors, scattered on highways, attached to city gates, or spread by word of mouth (including as popular or liturgical songs). Bills exploited written textuality to give voice to popular dissent and formed a continuum with rumor as well as with official channels of petition and complaint to the king, as Wendy Scase has noted.[55]

These protest forms of what Jennifer Summit has called "ephemeral literacy" merged with other kinds of public writing in the city, including commercial signs.[56] Michael Camille has called attention to the signage that was a feature of the medieval city of Paris, with signs designating houses, shops, and taverns contrasting with the signs of the aristocracy, such as blazons and heraldric arms, that were appearing in the city at the same time. Such signs were for urban dwellers "part of the texture and negotiation of everyday life," Camille argues, and indicated location of people and activities, as well as their position and status. The signs Camille points to were pictorial, taking the form of carved or painted images, and thus were based "not upon textual learning but another system of understood symbols and structures."[57] Yet written signs were a feature of the public space of the medieval city as well, especially by the fifteenth century. Like the graffiti found in early modern contexts that Juliet Fleming has discussed, signs containing words joined bills and pamphlets as part of the "publicness" of writing in London in Lydgate's day.[58] Writing of this sort had as its audience all passersby even as it was aimed especially at tradesmen and artisans, many of whom could read, some even in Latin, and who participated in the "middle-class" writing of the city through such activities involving pen and paper as the recording of business debts, keeping accounts of credit and real estate, and writing letters.[59]

How thoroughly practices of urban writing were etched into the social and political structures of the city can be seen in the economics that lay behind the sung and written texts that were such a distinctive part of the 1432 royal entry. The pageants required the work of a large number of craftsmen: in 1421, nearly 700 days' work was billed for the bridge pageants, and in 1432, painters were paid for 220 days, stainers for 87, and carpenters for 11.5; as Barron observes, the actual labor time and costs in 1432 may have been similar to those in 1421 but were not recorded in a way visible today.[60] Many of these craftsmen also supplied material (paint, gold and silver foil, paper, wire, cloth, fur), and there may have been men and women who made a business of hiring out pageant props, such as Agnes Edward, wife or widow of Thomas Edward, who in 1432 hired out six cushions, a cloth of gold, and two animals for 2s 6d.[61] In addition to payments to craftsmen to construct the pageants, funds also supported writers who painted the Latin scriptures on the pageants and musicians who provided the music. In 1432, eleven of the choirboys costumed as virgins in the Nature, Grace, and Fortune pageant at the drawbridge were paid 4d each, and three (presumably more experienced) earned 12d each, with the result that the choir of fourteen altogether cost 6s 8d (with a further 16d spent on their food). Barron suggests that the choirmaster may have been William Holford, who is named in the accounts along with the singers and was paid 5s. Holford was a clerk in the chapel of St. Thomas on the bridge and the son of Nicholas Holford, who was a toll-keeper on the bridge as well as one of the chapel clerks; in his 1434 will, he was described as

a "text-writer," an indication that he may have been involved in writing the
scrolls or the music or providing the overall design in 1426. The 1432 accounts
also record payment to John Steyno[ur], clerk of St. Dunstan's [in the East]
"pro factura cantus," suggesting he may have written the words for the songs
or the music or served as choirmaster, presumably for the vernacular "novum
canticum sive carmen" copied by Carpenter into his Latin account, a song
that Barron believes Carpenter probably wrote the words for, Steynour provided the music for, and boys, directed by William Holford, sang.[62] As these
records reveal, writing of the sort found in the 1432 entry was part of the
economic activity of London and partook of broader patterns of vernacular
literacy within an urban context.

Poetic Inscription

While the mottoes on the pageants emblazoned words onto a performance,
Lydgate's verses reinterpret the public event of the entry through inscription
into the cultural field of vernacular poetry. Although I have suggested that
Lydgate's verses can be understood as a kind of audience response to the 1432
entry, another useful way to think of the relation of his verses to the actual
pageantry is as what Gregory Nagy has called a *transcript*, that is, "a record of
performance, even an aid for performance, but not the equivalent of performance."[63] As a transcript, Lydgate's poem can be seen as transcribing both
the pageantry and aspects of the procession, which together made up London's welcome to Henry. Transcription, as its root words reveal, involves an
act of crossing over in which something is taken from one place and put in a
new location. While transcription usually refers to the act of writing down
spoken language or of copying words from one page or book to another, the
transcript Lydgate produced crossed not just from another written text (although it did that, using as one source Carpenter's letter) but from the performance itself, or from memories and ideas about that performance and its
meanings. The commission for the poem interrupted work on the *Fall of
Princes*, which Lydgate had been writing at Gloucester's request, and would
be quickly followed by the English version of the *vita* of St. Edmund Curteys
requested to commemorate the occasion of Henry VI's visit to Bury that
lasted from Christmas eve 1433 to 23 April 1434.[64] As a close look at the verses
reveals, the classicizing and monkish values of those two projects find their
way into the *Triumphal Entry*, where they help reshape an event that was di-

rected primarily to the king into a poem aimed at Londoners, representing it in a distinctive way not found in other written accounts of the 1432 pageantry, including Carpenter's.[65]

This transcribing that is also a recasting, or reinscription, can be seen immediately in Lydgate's narrative decisions. While Carpenter privileges what might be called documentary situatedness, carefully recording such factual information as the date and time in relation to Henry's reign and giving precise numbers for the mayor's entourage and for the clergy who greeted the king at Deptford, Lydgate eschews precision for other ends. Carpenter's "viginti-quatuor seniores" and "plures quam duodecim millia civium" go unmentioned in Lydgate, as does the exact distance of Blackheath from the city. In their place, Lydgate substitutes a vividly sketched impression of the scene that evokes the look and feel of the assembly of sheriffs, aldermen, and other citizens waiting to meet the king, in which attention to information useful for city account books gives way to poetic immediacy.

To describe Lydgate's poem in this way is not to dismiss Carpenter's version of the entry, since, as Sheila Lindenbaum has argued, he did "a great deal of creative work" when copying documents such as this one into the city's official books. That creative work involved selecting the most important documents, establishing precedents, and communicating with the city's political allies; Carpenter's recording of spectacle fit well with those aims, Lindenbaum points out, particularly in achieving the objectives of establishing a precedent (as can be seen in his starting the account of the 1432 pageantry with the words "Memorandum est" ["let it be remembered"]), especially a precedent that set limits on the city's responsibility in financing such activities. Along with Lydgate, Carpenter is interested in "forms of address and issues of representation" and uses as a model *dictamen*, the art of diplomatic letter writing in which the voices of authority are ventriloquized, which provides the source for the voices of mayor and aldermen in Carpenter's letter, who in his hands "speak as sovereigns." In London, Lindenbaum observes, "the aesthetic of civic spectacle may owe something to the work of the common clerk's office, where dictaminal practice and classical learning joined forces to serve the oligarchic elite," a connection that undergirds Carpenter's letter describing the 1432 pageantry.[66]

Just as Carpenter did in his letter, Lydgate structures his poem around the progress of the day's events, beginning with the moment when the mayor and his entourage meet the king at Blackheath, following the procession through the streets of London, and ending with the service in Westminster, after which the king rode to his palace and the mayor and citizens returned to their homes. But where Carpenter's account tends toward static description, Lydgate's is active, capturing more vividly than Carpenter does a sense of the processional movement. The result is a stronger impression of the unfolding of the day's events as they might have been experienced by participants and spectators.

A key feature of Lydgate's reinscription of the events of the 1432 royal entry is a shift in perspective from king to Londoners. In royal entries, the visitor is the focus of attention as the chief recipient of the pageantry, with citizens cast in the role of spectators. Although the royal entourage was typically small, while the citizenry turned out in large numbers, the royal entry encouraged the visiting kings or queens to enact themselves "in their role as ruler," while the much larger group of citizens crowding the streets and watching from windows and upper rooms along the route were on their side engaged in enacting themselves as subjects.[67] Carpenter's letter preserves that focus on the king, including, for instance, a passage describing the king's arrival from Eltham with his retinue of dukes, barons, and other attendants. Lydgate introduces the king only from the moment of his appearance within the city's territory, at Blackheath, and gives the impression he is alone, omitting all mention of his retinue. Lydgate also leaves out the king's stop at Deptford, where in Carpenter's account he was greeted by 120 members of the clergy singing antiphons, an omission that fits with his reversal of Carpenter's pattern of showing the Londoners passively waiting while the king arrives: in Lydgate, the Londoners are in motion as well, riding to Blackheath, forming two columns, and waiting until the mayor goes out to greet the arriving king. Lydgate's mention in the seventh stanza of the "aliens" who were part of the group assembled to greet the king—the Genoese, Florentines, Venetians, and Easterlings—reveals keen attention to the composition of the citizen groups, and his explanation of such items as the meaning of the white livery that the citizens wear conveys interest in the details of the urban social order, both of which are generally absent from Carpenter's account.

As part of this move away from a royal perspective, Lydgate goes further than Carpenter in muting the messianic theme that had played a role in Bedford's propaganda for the dual monarchy and was emphasized in the account of the 1432 pageantry found in London, Lambeth Palace Library MS 12. Both Carpenter and Lydgate may have decided to avoid an emphasis that pro-Gloucester Londoners presumably did not endorse, but Lydgate is even more cautious in his treatment of biblical imagery, as Richard Osberg has

shown.[68] Lydgate drops, for example, Carpenter's description of the pageant
of Sapience as being built on seven columns, a reference to Proverbs 9:1. In
the same pageant, Carpenter's account for the pageant of Sapience says
"Accipe coronam glorie," which seems to suggest that the pageant figures
may have offered the crown to the king, as happened in the 1392 pageants for
Richard II, while Lydgate's phrasing ("God the endewe with a crovne off
glorie") implies that the crown of glory has not yet been conferred. Many of
the Vulgate phrases shared by the Lambeth account and Carpenter are translated in Lydgate in phrasing that plays down the messianic theme. The reference to *sponsa* in the Lambeth version is not in Lydgate, and the description
of Sapience as "in vestitu deaurato circumdatam varietate" (in Carpenter and
Lambeth) in Lydgate appears as follows:

> A tabernacle Surmountyng off beaute
> Ther was ordeyned be full fressh entayle
> Richely arrayed with Ryall Apparayle.

Osberg argues that Lydgate attributes the phrase to the decoration of the
Tabernacle rather than to the raiment of Wisdom in a way that seems deliberate given the well-established iconography of Sapientia-Ecclesia as the
sponsa. Like Carpenter, Lydgate omits the "scripture" for the fourth pageant
of the child-king as "iustitiae thronus," which is included in the Lambeth
account and depicts the king's justice as theocratic and absolute, as the scripture from Psalms 88:15–16 makes clear: "Beatus populus qui scit iubilationem.
/ Domine, in lumine vultus tiu ambulabunt." Lydgate instead gives an
English translation for a "scripture" not found in Lambeth, Carpenter, or the
Latin glosses of MS Cotton Julius B.ii: "honour off kyng which I Shall expresse / With this Scripture in euery manys siht / Off Comyn Custum lovith
equyte and Riht" (ll. 298–99), a phrase that seems to stress civil, not theocratic, law and thus limits the king's prerogative.[69]

Lydgate's muting of messianic allusions can be seen most vividly in his
treatment of the Jesse Tree pageant, as Osberg observes, where he records and
responds to disapproval of that pageant, defending it on the grounds of its
closeness to St. Paul's. The Jesse Tree pageant is the only one for which no
account records a "scripture," even though the 1456 Coventry entry for Queen
Margaret included a Jesse Tree with a scripture from Isaiah (Isaiah 11:1–7
contains the Jesse Tree theme), linking Margaret to the Virgin Mary and her
son Edward to Christ.[70] Lydgate's explanation must have been aimed at

countering objections to the theocracy of paralleling Henry with Christ. The absence of messianic imagery in Lydgate's version is all the more obvious since it had been used for Richard II in 1377 and 1392 and was part of Bedford's propaganda for the dual monarchy, appearing in various places, including in Lydgate's translation of Calot's poem.[71] Factionalism in the king's council between Gloucester (with whom Londoners tended to side) and Bedford may be reflected in Lydgate's treatment of the Jesse Tree and other pageants, as Lydgate may have minimized the theocratic suggestions in the pageants in the wake of Gloucester's many changes in the king's household on 1 March 1432 (which included the removal of men without the council's approval) and his sealing up of Henry's signet under his own, which he then put in the custody of the exchequer, suggesting that Gloucester feared, in Osberg's words, "a palace revolution centered on the possibility of Henry's first personal exercise of authority." If the king's council had a part in commissioning the pageants, then the mayor may have wanted to remove himself from any signs of complicity in messianic themes and perhaps therefore asked Lydgate for his poem with its apology for the Jesse Tree. In that case, Lydgate's poem may be less about praise for London than a cover for Welles, Osberg suggests.[72]

While Osberg may be right about the mayor's need for a strong defense against messianic readings of the pageantry, it is hard not to credit Lydgate with also championing a civic perspective in the poem. As C. David Benson argues, the *Triumphal Entry* expands on the meanings of the original pageants in ways that seem strategically designed to take up the concerns of Londoners. The second pageant, featuring Nature, Fortune, and Grace, for example, has a domestic message that emphasizes the bourgeois values of comfort and prosperity, while the third and fourth pageants, of Dame Sapience and the child-king, point to the law and justice in a part of the city in which commercial abuses were punished by the pillory. The Wells of Paradise pageant stages an earthly paradise in which the commercial heart of London becomes a place of pleasure and abundance.[73] Similarly, Lydgate's stress on peace and prosperity in his verses may reflect Londoners' hope for an end to the war's drain on their finances.[74]

Whether in response to specific requests from the mayor or others, Lydgate's poem adopts the viewpoint of the thousands of Londoners who watched the display. He echoes Carpenter in envisioning the sun that emerged on the blustery day of Henry's welcome as brushing away from the citizens "alle theyre hevynesse" (l. 8) but then concentrates on the reactions of the Londoners assembled "Alle off assent" (l. 27) to greet the king. In the description of the second pageant, where Carpenter focuses just on the gifts that Nature, Grace, and Fortune give to the king ("et assurgentes in adventum Regis, ipsum praetereuntem suis donis beatis munerabant"), Lydgate broadens his interpretive scope to comment on what the three goddesses offer to everyone, noting that when the goddesses come out from their tower, all beholders are astonished at the sight of them (ll. 111–12), and noting especially that Grace "bryngeth gladnes to citees and tovns" (l. 123). Benson observes that Lydgate's view of London is that of an outsider who wrote for London but was not of it, and yet in the *Triumphal Entry*, Lydgate does an entirely credible job of imagining what must have been the prevailing civic sentiments on that occasion, even adding an entire stanza near the end of the poem giving voice to civic pride in the splendid way Henry was welcomed (ll. 447–53).[75] The numerous references to the city and to the mayor that are dotted throughout Lydgate's poem, including the compliment to Mayor Welles inserted into his description of the Wells of Paradise pageant ("O how thes welles . . . Vnto the kyng fforto done pleasaunce," ll. 342–48, not found in Carpenter), emphasize not just the labor that went into the making of the pageantry but also its importance for "alle that duelle in this citee."

Lydgate's comparison of London to other symbolically charged places underscores this adoption of a civic perspective. In the third stanza, Lydgate's likening of Henry's welcome to David's triumphal return to Jerusalem, an analogy Carpenter does not use, echoes the often-made late medieval claim that London was a new Jerusalem.[76] This praise of the city is echoed at the close of the poem when Lydgate adds three stanzas of praise to London not found in Carpenter's letter. In several manuscripts, these stanzas are prefaced by the phrase "Verba translatoris," which seems to signal that the interpolation marks a departure from the Latin original (and which incidentally implies that Lydgate was in fact translating from a source in another language).[77] Like the reference to Jerusalem, the description of London in these stanzas as a "Newe Troye" (l. 512) links the city to a storied past, specifically the legendary history of England as recounted by Geoffrey of Monmouth in his *Historia Regum Britannorum* in which Brutus, a descendant of Aeneas, with other exiles from the Trojan War came to the island of Albion and built a capital city called Trojanova or Troynovant.[78] The notion of *translatio imperii*, which styled Troy as the original of later cities, was a medieval commonplace, but in a manner similar to the invocation of Jerusalem served as a valorization of London's special status. Similarly, the description of London as the king's chamber, a phrase used by the mayor in his speech to Henry (after l. 63) that Lydgate adopts in the closing line of his stanzas of praise to London (l. 530), exalts the city while also asserting its privileged connection with the royal court.[79]

The choice of a London perspective is at one with Lydgate's use of the vernacular in the poem. Both Lydgate's paraphrasing in English of the pageant "scriptures" Carpenter gives in Latin and his tendency to make them seem like speeches delivered by the actors rather than mottoes painted on the pageants help make his description accessible and conjure up the ceremony with immediacy, as Carpenter's Latin cannot. Although Carpenter records the English speech of the mayor when he greeted the king and the song of the seven virgins who offer gifts to the king in the second pageant, he usually emphasizes that the verses were written, using *rescribere* and *subscribere*. In the case of the third pageant, Lydgate has Sapience reading her scripture aloud (signaled by use of the word *quod*, a word that indicates direct quotations). While this change may not be the transformation of Carpenter's Latin mottoes, which would have been legible to only a few, into direct address to the English people, which Nolan argues it is, it certainly turns them into words said for them.[80] Such changes exploit the performative potential of speech, giving the Latin mottoes a hortatory or even imperative force that heightens the instructional thrust of the pageantry.

In line with his vernacular reinscription of the entry, Lydgate feels free to rewrite or add to Carpenter's letter, even when doing so yielded a description less faithful to the original performance. The "novum canticum, sive carmen" that the boy-virgins sing in the second bridge pageant, for example, varies considerably from the version given by Carpenter, which was probably the one actually sung. Lydgate includes a number of other literary devices, such as the humility *topos* at lines 68–70 or again in the "Lenvoye," in which he declares his lack of eloquence to describe the pageantry adequately and which gesture toward the common medieval poetic convention of begging mercy for literary lapses, changes that situate his description of the pageantry within the context of literary writing.[81] At other moments, Lydgate expands on Carpenter's account, as in his translation of Carpenter's reference to "stallatum floribus et arboribus fructiforis" into two full stanzas; Nolan aptly describes this expansion as a "poetic set piece" that takes the reader out of the world of the pageant into the world of poetic composition that substitutes for historical reality.[82] Lydgate frequently uses interpretation as well as amplification, explaining the significance of aspects of the pageantry—for example, that the antelopes with the arms of England and France are present in the first pageant "In tokenyng that God shall ffor hym provyde" (l. 94).

The final lines of Lydgate's poem imply that Mayor Welles requested the literary services Lydgate had just rendered with his transcript of the 1432 entry, services that the city of London must have funded, although no records of payment have yet been found. In any event, it seems clear that Lydgate's poem was commissioned not just to provide a lasting record of the pageantry (Carpenter's letter would have sufficed for that) but, more important, to transcribe theatrical spectacle into vernacular poetry.[83] Moving public pageantry from the streets of London via Carpenter's Latin account, Lydgate's verses reinscribed ephemeral performance into the lasting and elevated form of poetry.

Manuscript Inscription

The assertion of Dagenais that medieval manuscripts "are not just 'physical support' for texts, nor are they simply documents or artifacts for a cultural history of the Middle Ages," but are instead texts in their own right, to be understood in terms of their materiality as well as the agendas of their compilers and readers, makes a useful point of departure for any consideration of the manuscripts into which accounts of the pageantry for Henry VI were copied.[84] Beyond Carpenter's letter and Lydgate's poem, a number of other very brief and a handful of longer descriptions of the 1432 pageantry survive, most of them in London chronicles and most probably deriving from official records, although a few seem to be eyewitness reports in part or whole.[85] Like processional pageantry, the medieval written text is marked by mobility, as Paul Zumthor's notion of *mouvance* recognized, and the various accounts of the 1432 entry have some of the fluidity and improvisational quality the pageants themselves must have had.[86] Just as the pageantry consisted of discrete tableaux linked by the processional route, thus achieving a cumulative effect, so too manuscript books could be made piecemeal, as texts came to hand, with groups of texts passed along together in gatherings or booklets and then assembled "like the items in a ring binder," as Julia Boffey has described the process.[87] The motile and variable nature of manuscript contexts means that a text's meanings inevitably are also unstable, changing in accordance with its location among other texts.

To a perhaps unexpected degree, the verbal nature of the 1432 welcome for Henry VI influences its inscription within all of these documents. As Kipling notes, there are no illustrated accounts of English entries until 1604, but pageant speeches and scriptures are carefully recorded in written accounts starting from the fourteenth century.[88] Even if they have not survived, there must have been official versions of such events that were complied and circulated by the crown or city officials: Richard Maidstone wrote his Latin verses on the 1392 reconciliation pageants for propaganda purposes, and although they are no longer extant, similar civic or royal accounts probably provided the basis for descriptions of Henry V's 1415 entry by the *Gesta Henrici Quinti* author, Adam of Usk, and others, and for descriptions of Catherine's 1421 entry by Thomas of Elmham in his *Vita et Gesta Henrici Quinti Anglorum Regis*.[89] When decisions were made, by officials or by individual witnesses, to record the events of that February day in 1432, decisions were also made about the recasting of what was a visual and, in the English version, also a verbal form into the medium of writing.

It is hardly a coincidence that wordy royal entries and vernacular accounts of them begin to swell at the same historical moment, during the reign of Henry IV, who, as John Fisher and others have shown, turned to the English language as a tool of the state.[90] The London chronicles, the source of most surviving descriptions of English royal entries, first start to be written contemporaneously with the events they describe in the reign of Henry IV, perhaps as part of the usurpation that kindled an interest in political affairs "of which these Chronicles were the outcome," as Charles Kingsford argues.[91]

While Lydgate's poem represents the fullest attempt to transform spectacle into poetry, it would be a mistake to assume that other accounts of the 1432 entry did not also seek ways of representing the pageantry in writing, including in poetic language. Chroniclers and others who recorded pageantry used various literary conventions, including shorthand references meant to evoke the event. These included catchphrases such as "ryally devised," which Mary-Rose McLaren notes invokes the sumptuousness of the display.[92] With conventions such as these, chroniclers developed a repertoire of stylistic devices that could capture live performances on the written page, in a way that would re-create some of the immediacy of an event that had occurred in many cases only a short while before the written account of it appeared, in contexts where it would be read by those who had seen the original performance.

A look at the three relatively lengthy surviving independent accounts of the 1432 pageantry reveals common strategies for capturing visual and aural performance in writing despite divergent interpretations of the pageantry. Two of the accounts are written in English and appear in chronicles. The first of these, an account found in Cambridge, Trinity College Library MS O.9.1, is a *Brut* chronicle with a London continuation from 1420 to 1447; it is an elaborate manuscript in a professional hand with occasional illumination and contains some unique, and possibly eyewitness, material.[93] Its description of the 1432 entry is preceded by a detailed account of the Paris coronation and entry, perhaps suggesting that the chronicler or his source may have witnessed it (notably, the only other chronicle that includes the Paris coronation is Cambridge, University Library MS Hh.6.9, to which MS O.9.1 is related). MS O.9.1 also includes what seems to be an eyewitness account of the punishment of Eleanor Cobham in 1440. Its account of the 1432 pageantry also appears to be from an eyewitness; the description of the pageantry is fairly detailed but omits the pageant of Sapience and the seven sciences.[94] A second, related account is in Cambridge, University Library MS Hh.6.9, also a *Brut* manuscript with London continuation from 1420, which is less elaborate than MS O.9.1 with no illumination and written in one hand. Its description of the 1432 pageantry is very close to that of MS O.9.1, with the chief difference being that it includes a description of the Sapience pageant.

A third and, of the group, the most intriguing account of the 1432 pageantry is found not in the context of a chronicle but in Lambeth Palace Library MS 12, the third volume of a late fourteenth-century copy of Tynemouth's *Historia aurea* and probably the manuscript recorded in the 1395 catalogue of the library at Durham Cathedral; a Latin description of the 1432 entry was later added at folio 255.[95] Unlike Lydgate's and Carpenter's accounts, which record the meeting at Blackheath of the king and citizens, the mayor's speech, and the reception at St. Paul's after the procession, the Lambeth narrative focuses solely on the pageantry, beginning with the description of the first pageant on London Bridge and ending with the last pageant. It differs in other ways as well, omitting a song recorded by the two other accounts and skipping phrases and lines, while citing the underlying Vulgate verses better and clearly identifying "scriptures" and pageant characters with underlining. Among other variations, the Lambeth version provides an independent pageant "scripture" not found in Lydgate or Carpenter and describes the conduit in Cheap not as Lydgate (following Carpenter) does, as "Conduyte made in Cercel wyse," but with a reference to Mount Lebanon that has biblical rather than topographical meaning.[96] Osberg argues that the Lambeth version has a different political resonance than Lydgate's and Carpenter's accounts, in that it sides with Bedford and endorses the notion of messianic kingship he advocated. Osberg suggests that this account of the 1432 entry was copied into a Benedictine manuscript from Durham Cathedral thanks to connections between Oxford and London and the court.[97]

Many of those Oxford connections were allied with Beaufort interests, which help explain the sympathies for Bedford and messianic kingship found in the Lambeth account. The Oxford provenance of the Lambeth account may suggest more sympathy with Lancastrian (Bedfordian) propaganda than in Carpenter or Lydgate's London accounts and, if the king's council played a role in commissioning the pageants, may have been requested by Mayor Welles, Osberg speculates, as protection against charges of complicity.[98]

Briefer accounts of the 1432 pageantry, a few of which are worth discussion here, can be found in several other manuscripts. In London, College of Arms MS Vincent 25(1), a manuscript of 165 folios written in more than one sixteenth-century hand, a brief description of the 1432 entry appears in an explicitly ceremonial context. The manuscript focuses on royal ceremonies, including a description of the marriage of Henry V and Catherine (fols. 97–100v), the coronation of Catherine in 1420 (fols. 101–2v), the coronation of Henry VI in 1429 (fols. 103–6), and the reception of Henry VI in 1432 (fols. 106v–7v).[99] Hatfield House Cecil Papers MS 281 is a commonplace book of 141 leaves of parchment, containing two Latin chronicles, other historical notes in English and French, the terms of the Treaty of Troyes, taxes of London, a description of the Virgin, religious notes, a moral tale, Lydgate's verses on the kings of England, and other material. On folios 32–88, there is a London chronicle whose first part (the years 1189–1437) is written in a neat professional hand.[100] Kingsford thinks the volume was made around 1440 for a London citizen, although the only clue to ownership is a "Martyn Gladell" written in a fifteenth-century hand.[101] The chronicles in both Cecil Papers 281 and Dublin, Trinity College MS 509, which it resembles, follow British Library MS Egerton 1995 closely until 1437.[102] Egerton 1995 is a commonplace book or miscellany in one hand and includes treatises, the *Siege of Rome*, various poems, statistics, other material, and a London chronicle (the so-called Gregory's Chronicle).[103] The account of the 1432 pageantry in MS Egerton 1995 is apparently indebted to Lydgate's poem but is much briefer.

As this brief and selective survey I hope shows, accounts of the 1432 pageantry appear chiefly in the context of London chronicles, official records, or, less often, in collections of ceremonial material. The London chronicle was a form of writing that burst on the literary scene in the fifteenth century and had waned by the mid-sixteenth.[104] Vernacular, secular, and communal, it in many ways echoed the royal entries and public ceremonies it often contained. That the London chronicle would be one of the most common manuscript contexts for accounts of the 1432 entry is unsurprising, given that both chronicles and royal entries reflected a mingling of the civic interests of Londoners and the ceremonial interests of the court.

With just one exception, the surviving early versions of Lydgate's poem—like these other accounts of the 1432 pageantry—share a London chronicle context. How copies of Lydgate's poem reached London chroniclers is unknown. Boffey has noted the "flimsy form" in which many of Lydgate's sources came to him, from the "lytell bille" from which he translated the Latin *Legend of St. Giles* to the French "paunflet," which was his source for his translation of "The Churl and the Bird," and his own verses linked to performance often seem to have been similarly flimsy as they moved into the hands of scribes.[105] Perhaps his poem on the 1432 entry was passed to them by Welles or perhaps they copied it from city archives.[106] McLaren observes that a number of chronicles contain poems and ballads, making Lydgate's verses unexceptional as poetry incorporated into a prose document, although it is not always clear whether they derived from oral or written sources.[107] Whatever the path of transmission, Lydgate's poem fell into the hands of writers who, as we can tell from the manuscript and textual evidence, lived in London, shared the views of the city oligarchy (which included Yorkist sympathies, approval of the duke of Gloucester, tolerance for Henry VI, disapproval of Queen Margaret, opposition to Lollards, and hatred of rebellion), and exhibited civic pride.[108] As McLaren notes, the people orchestrating the 1432 pageants were also largely the ones recording them in the London chronicles, and thus motives behind the making of the ceremony carry through into many accounts of it.[109]

The manuscripts in which Lydgate's poem describing the 1432 entry appears, which I briefly describe in the next few paragraphs, underscore Dagenais's insistence on the uniqueness of each manuscript iteration of a text, although those manuscripts are similar in significant ways. British Library MS Cotton Julius B.ii, on which MacCracken bases his edition of Lydgate's poem and which may be the earliest of the extant manuscripts, probably dating to 1435, is a volume of 102 leaves on paper and consists of a chronicle that runs from 1189 to 1432, followed on folios 89–100v by Lydgate's poem on the 1432 entry, introduced as "Ordenaunces ffor the kyng made in the Cite off London," and on folio 101 by the names of mayors and sheriffs for three subsequent years.[110] Longleat House MS Longleat 53, written on paper in one neat sixteenth-century hand, consists solely of a chronicle that begins in 1189 and ends imperfectly in the year 1432, part way through Lydgate's verses on the royal entry, whose first twenty-three stanzas appear under the heading "The ordennances made in the citie of london agaynste the comyng of the kyng ffrome his coronacion oute of ffrance." MS Longleat 53 shows an interest in clothing, ritual, and pageantry, suggesting that it was possibly written by a herald; it resembles Julius B.ii, which also ends in the year 1432, as well as Harley 3775 and British Library MS Cotton Cleopatra C.iv.[111] Cotton Cleopatra C.iv contains a chronicle of the years from 1415 to 1443 written on forty leaves of paper, now bound with other items to which it was originally unconnected.[112] The chronicle begins imperfectly in 1415 on folio 22 in the middle of a sentence and possibly ends imperfectly in the year 1443 on folio 61v; there are changes of hand in 1416 and 1420, with the third hand apparently that of a professional scribe, suggesting that the manuscript passed into a scribe's hands or the last part was commissioned.[113] Although the chronicle in Cotton Cleopatra C.iv is related to the other manuscripts discussed above, its first item is a long account of the battle of Agincourt not found elsewhere, and the item for 1416 is also unique, suggesting a degree of independence in its sources and composition.[114] Lydgate's poem is on folios 38–48v, under the rubric "Pur le Roy. Ordynaunces," and follows a description of Henry VI's French coronation. MS Harley 565 is a parchment manuscript that includes a chronicle of the years 1189 to 1443, copies of the Latin historical inscriptions on three tablets in St. Paul's Cathedral, verses on Henry V's 1415 expedition (once attributed to Lydgate), and Lydgate's poem on the 1432 entry, appearing at folios 114v–24 and ending with the colophon: "Here endith þe makyng of þe Comynge of þe kyng out of ffraunce to London, Be þe monk of Bery.—Deo Gracias."[115] In Harley 565, Lydgate's poem is written separately at the end of the volume rather than in its chronological place within the chronicle account. MS Guildhall 3313, in which Lydgate's poem appears at folios 132v–40, consists solely of a chronicle of the years 1189 to 1512. It is in a professional hand to 1438; a second hand, with a third appearing in a single quire beginning on folio 157, continues through the year 1496, with a list of mayors and aldermen and a continuation of the chronicle through 1512 followed by an index of events that occurred between 1436 and 1496. Other material has been inserted by various readers, suggesting that the chronicle was seen as "public property" that could be added to by owners or users.[116] British Library MS Cotton Nero C.xi begins as a *Brut* and becomes a London chronicle for the years 1189 to 1485, with a last continuation ending in 1558. The chronicle was one of the sources for the chronicle printed by Richard Pynson in 1516 as *The Newe Cronycles of England and of France*, which contains selected use of Lydgate's verses often altered to represent speeches, and later printed by William Rastell (in 1553) as *Fabyan's Chronycle*.[117]

The sole exception to this pattern of copying Lydgate's poem on the 1432 entry into chronicles is found in Rome, English College MS 1306. MS Rome 1306 consists of 159 unnumbered folios of paper and can be dated by watermarks to 1436–56. It contains Lydgate's *Life of Our Lady* and *Danse macabre*; Benedict Burgh's *Parvus Cato* and *Cato Major*; *The Master of Game*, a prose treatise on hunting by Edward, duke of York; ten minor poems, mostly by Lydgate; and a diatribe against Philip of Burgundy. Rossell Hope Robbins describes MS Rome 1306 as the kind of manuscript "fairly common in upperclass families."[118] Lydgate's poem on the 1432 entry appears on folios 67–74, immediately following the *Life of Our Lady*. The most striking difference between Rome 1306 and the other extant versions of Lydgate's 1432 verses is that the roundel of welcome sung in the second pageant varies from the usual text: the roundel begins on folio 70 with the first four lines of Lydgate's version, then closely follows the roundel as recorded in Carpenter's letter.

The outlier example of MS Rome 1306 underscores the importance of a London chronicle context for the preservation and dissemination of Lydgate's verses on 1432. That just one copy appears in a noncivic and nonchronicle manuscript reveals both the connectedness of Lydgate's poem to London and its importance to Londoners involved in chronicling events affecting their city. Osberg notes that if accounts of pageantry exert "more influence on the political life and thought of a nation than do the pageants themselves," then Lydgate's poem, rather than Carpenter's letter or the Lambeth manuscript account, is what established the dominant reading of the 1432 entry of Henry VI into London and "cast the mold" for later ceremonies.[119]

Despite the general mobility of medieval writing and Dagenais's reminder about the significance of codex context, the copying into chronicles of Lydgate's verses on the 1432 entry was not entirely loose and freeform. Nelson Goodman's category of "allographic" notation, which refers to the fact that a text can be inscribed in many different ways (i.e., using different fonts or styles of handwriting) and still say the same thing, suggests how even when copied into different manuscripts, Lydgate's poem retained its own textual identity.[120] The scribe and manuscript may change, yet at some level, Lydgate's poem is recognizable. More important, the codex context in which Lydgate's poem appears stays relatively stable, as it finds its way chiefly into London chronicles.

The vernacular chronicles of fifteenth-century London suggest a use of the written word not just for entertainment or for business but for recording a communal sense of identity, a new kind of literary experience shaped primarily by the middle classes.[121] Although all of the London chronicles are anonymous, the authors/owners were laypeople involved in crafts or trades or employed as clerks. That twelve of the extant fifteenth-century London chronicles are in commonplace books and that a change of hand is found in a number of the manuscripts of London chronicles, including those that record Lydgate's verses on 1432, suggest that copies of chronicles could be purchased from professional scribes working in workshops and then continued later, presumably by the owner, who was thus able to participate in the writing of history. These chronicles represent an attempt to communicate an urban identity and experience that was absorbed via a chiefly visual and oral fashion in the medium of writing; as McLaren notes, chroniclers shaped their accounts to reflect "the visual meaning of the events they recorded," using various literary devices, such as juxtaposition, contrast, and allusion. In these works, we can see writers "struggling with the transitions from an oral and visual culture to a literate one."[122]

It should not be overlooked, however, that even the vernacular prose chronicle—a most seemingly literate of forms designed for silent reading— bore traces of performance. As Joyce Coleman has shown, even as literacy and private reading expanded in the fourteenth and fifteenth centuries, histories and chronicles were commonly read aloud and in public.[123] Whether Lydgate's poem on the 1432 royal entry was ever performed aloud is not known, and it might not have suggested itself for public reading as readily as the exemplary passages about past kings and heroes that Coleman focuses on. But the possibility exists that the pageantry for Henry VI escaped the page and returned to a context of live enactment, or at least public recitation.

Whether read in private or in public, these chronicles, as McLaren has said, "record a history perceived as common by the citizens of London and commonly recorded by them"; the 1432 royal entry certainly counts as a civic event that would find its way into such accounts.[124] In commissioning a poem from Lydgate to commemorate the ephemeral events they mounted for the king, Londoners ensured that an entertainment for the king became an enduring story about the city's prestige. Representative forms, including cultural practices like royal entries as well as written productions like poetry and histories, express ideologies but never rein in their excesses, with the result that in the end, as Nolan argues, "the persistence of form achieves a kind of victory over the insistence of ideology precisely because forms contain histories."[125]

The written words inscribed within and around the pageantry that Londoners mounted for Henry VI in 1432, along with the persistence of Lydgate's poem in its various chronicle contexts, reveal the collusion of form and material medium, which together act as agents of cultural expression. At the intersection of performance and writing, the words surrounding the 1432 pageantry demonstrate an interplay between ephemeral and durable written forms, between the quotidian and the exalted. They also show not just the competition between, but the interdependence of, performance and poetry. Whether seen or heard in a performance, or read silently or aloud from a manuscript page, the various inscriptions in and around the 1432 pageantry remind us of the inescapable "possibility of the other" that made performance and the written word inseparable in the late medieval England.

CHAPTER 6

Edible Theater

The most formally odd and thoroughly material of the theatrical spectacles to which Lydgate contributed were the subtleties for the coronation banquet of Henry VI. The feast itself was a carefully designed piece of political drama in the form of ceremonies and entertainments that ushered Henry to the throne. Its stage was the hall at Westminster and its audience important members of court, city, and church, many of whom would have seen or heard the other coronation events as well. In the banquet hall at Westminster, they not only watched and listened but also consumed three subtleties, decorative confections that were served between courses and that featured three ballades written by Lydgate on themes important for the occasion. In the subtleties, spectatorship slides into feasting, visual encounters with words and images become alimentary, and writing enters not only literary and civic but also food history. The subtleties present, in short, an extreme version of the media mixing and sensory blending that characterized late medieval culture and that I have been arguing Lydgate's performance texts utilized, as the taste for performance is embodied in the act of eating.

The subtleties and the banquet came at the end of a long day of coronation events and were to all appearances designed with that larger context in mind. On 4 November 1429, Henry rode with his lords from Kingston over the London Bridge to the Tower. On the following Saturday, Henry's entourage was joined by priests, the mayor, and aldermen who rode with Henry to Westminster; en route, Henry was entertained by a "toure full of Angels" and a "mimic queen" with maidens and pages at London Bridge, the conduits in Cheapside running with wine, and a "riall castell" at the cross in Cheapside.[1] On Sunday, the 6th, Henry was crowned at Westminster, in the company of ecclesiastics and lords temporal, as well as his mother Catherine, "a grete

noumbre of ladis and gentill-wemmen rially arayed," and a surprise visitor—
the son of the king of Portugal.[2] The coronation ceremony involved elaborate
rituals of dressing and undressing, anointing, presentation of scepter and
sword, and finally the costuming of Henry as a bishop and the setting of the
crown of St. Edward on his head, all accompanied by the saying of mass. His
bishop's garments were then removed and he was dressed in royal garb and
crowned with the crown Richard II had made for himself. Afterward, Henry
was led in a retinue through the palace to the hall where he sat at his coronation banquet, surrounded by people of note, who were seated by rank. At the
first course, the king's heralds ushered in Sir Philip Dymmock, who on the
council's orders rode into the hall costumed as St. George and proclaimed
that Henry was the rightful heir to the crown of England and that he, Dymmock, was ready to defend him as his knight and champion.[3]

Presumably commissioned by a member of the royal household, perhaps
the same controller's deputy John Brice who Shirley says asked Lydgate for the
Disguising at Hertford, the three ballades Lydgate wrote to accompany the
subtleties featured scenes close to the concerns of the members of the council
and the household. The first showed Sts. Edward and Louis with Henry VI
between them, the second featured Henry VI kneeling before Emperor Sigismund and Henry V, and the third depicted the Virgin with child, holding a
crown in her hand, flanked by Sts. George and Denis presenting the king to
her. Lydgate's verses explain the meaning of each image, developing and in-
tensifying the themes of kingship that the images conveyed.

While the occasion was royal, the audience was broad and presumably
the themes of the subtleties were widely endorsed, given the degree to which
they meshed with other entertainments for the king made in the same period
but not directly sponsored by the court, such as the 1432 entry. Civic and religious leaders were present, including the mayor, aldermen, archbishops, and
other leading members of the church, including, most likely, the abbot of
Bury St. Edmunds, who was in London for parliament. Lower-ranking citizens would also have crowded in, as at Queen Catherine's coronation banquet in 1421, which according to one chronicler was "opyn to alle pepull."[4]
Parliament was in session at the time of the young king's English coronation,
and important people from around the realm, including the abbot of Bury
St. Edmunds, were in London.[5] By custom, Mayor Estfeld served at the coronation and was rewarded with the gift of a gold cup and ewer filled with gold,
while the aldermen, sheriffs, and recorder of London also assisted the butlers
and dined at a table in the hall.[6] Although we should not be too quick to

assume complete unanimity of affect, it seems likely that in their elucidation of the figures depicted by the subtleties, Lydgate's verses anticipated the interests of this larger group of spectators, touching on the concerns of Londoners as well as the court, particularly the vexed issue of the legitimacy of the dual monarchy and Henry's youth.[7] The verses stress the king's French heritage and his father's friendship with Emperor Sigismund, which as Ralph Griffiths notes was a reminder of "the Lancastrian *imperium* into which Henry VI was now entering," while also advocating a tough line against heretics and invoking various protectors for the young king, including the patron saints of England and France, all themes that would have had at least some degree of civic as well as courtly appeal.[8]

Although Lydgate's verses appear to be expanded versions of the short "reasons" that typically accompanied subtleties, they may also have been read aloud by a master of ceremonies so that everyone in the hall could hear them.[9] No impersonation or mimesis seems to have been involved, but if the verses were read aloud by a presenter, there would have been room for gesture and intonation to flesh out the purely visual display. Because feasting was a ritual that called upon its participants to play roles in a social drama, the subtleties function as a kind of play-within-a-play, a series of entr'actes in the larger entertainment provided by the banquet that distilled the feast's looser messages into a more concentrated essence.[10]

Like many of the other entertainments to which Lydgate contributed, the subtleties were occasional dramatic forms, created for one specific performance. Their ephemerality is complicated by their cookery form, however, since they were designed to be ingested—not just by ear and eye, in the usual way of performances—but by mouth. Surviving copies of the subtleties often try to recapture their alimentary context, by transmitting not just Lydgate's three ballades and a description of the scenes that the subtleties depicted but also the menu for the feast. As that impulse to re-create the act of eating suggests, the subtleties represent an outermost form of materiality in which food and theater—the taking in of a performance and the eating of a meal—are collapsed. Just as the ritual of the mass combines theatricality with ingestion of the host, so too the subtleties forced the assembled banqueters to participate at the most fundamental level in the entertainment, by eating the images and words displayed for their pleasure. Robert Epstein has argued that the subtleties represent a kind of "spectacular textuality"; even more so, they are evidence of alimentary spectacle, in which the performance is consumed by the spectator through the act of eating.[11]

Although it primarily serves to satisfy hunger and provide nourishment, much is also inherently performative about food, any kind of food. Food comes to the table loaded with meaning and emotion, and the codes around it—protocols of cooking, eating, and disposing of wastes—insert it into broader systems of cultural signification. To cook, to serve, to chew are also to perform; at this basic level of tools, materials, and procedures of food preparation and eating, *to perform is to do*. Food and performance intersect at two other junctures, as Barbara Kirshenblatt-Gimblett has argued. When we follow social rules about food—such as taboos, rituals, and stipulations of etiquette—we perform precepts about food that guide how we act; thus, *to perform is also to behave*. Tasting a dish begins with a physical and sensual response, but it also involves an exercise in judgment, as the food is evaluated for its flavor and appeal. Eating invites us to appraise, value, and assess, especially when the acts of doing and behaving around food are brought to the foreground and displayed in ways that underscore the theatrical and spectacular; at this juncture, *to perform is to show*.[12]

The subtleties for Henry's coronation operate at that third juncture; dissociated from bodily needs and the satisfaction of hunger, they bypass the nose and mouth, becoming showpieces or spectacles to be displayed and shown rather than foodstuffs intended to assuage hunger. They thus appeal to vision more than to taste or smell and move the experience of food beyond appetite and nourishment. In that enhanced form, the subtleties offer an example of the gastro-aesthetics of the ritualized banquet in which food becomes a performance medium. Both on the banquet table and in the manuscripts that later recorded them, the coronation subtleties for which Lydgate wrote verses provide a glimpse of a history of theater in relation to the senses, where food and spectacle—alimentary and visual consumption—come together.

Subtleties

What Marcia Reed calls "edible monuments" were highly theatricalized objects.[13] Although food historians are not in full agreement about their exact composition, subtleties were apparently most often food items, constructed of some sort of comestible—sugar, marzipan, or dough—and meant to be eaten after they were displayed to those present at a feast.[14] They could also apparently incorporate paper, wax, or other nonedible materials, much as a decorated wedding cake today might include edible decorations made of icing as well as a plastic effigy of the married couple. Subtleties would have had a short afterlife, being concocted for immediate consumption or, if not eaten on the spot, prone to quick decay. Subtleties were common at coronation and royal wedding banquets or other important ceremonial occasions. Accounts record subtleties at the coronation banquet of Henry IV in 1399, at the wedding of Henry IV and Joan of Navarre in 1403, at a royal feast during Henry IV's reign (featuring a "Ceruus," "homo," and "arbor"), at Windsor in 1416 when Henry V entertained Emperor Sigismund, for the coronation of Catherine of Valois in 1421, and at the banquet in Paris that followed Henry VI's French coronation in 1431.[15] Many of the subtleties mentioned in extant documents are not described, but those that are include a subtlety of "Seint-Jorge on horsebak and sleynge the dragun" and another of "a castel that the Kyng and the Qwhene comen in for to see how Seint Jorge slogh" from the privy purse accounts of Elizabeth of York in BL MS Arundel 334. A cookery book in BL MS Harley 4016 describes a subtlety that consisted of "a godhede in a son of gold glorified aboue; in the son the holy giste voluptable; Seint Thomas kneling a-for him, with þe poynt of a swerd in his hede & a Mitre there-vppon . . . in sinistra parte Johannes Baptista; et in iiij partibus, iiij Angeli incensantes."[16]

One of the fullest contemporary descriptions of subtleties is in the *Boke of Nurture* (c. 1460) of John Russell, usher and marshal to Humphrey, duke of Gloucester. Russell offers two examples of how to serve meals accompanied by subtleties. The first is of a meat dinner in which the first course is followed by a subtlety of Gabriel greeting the Virgin Mary with an Ave, the second course ends with a subtlety of an angel appearing and singing to three shepherds on a hill, and the third course concludes with subtleties of the Virgin presented by the kings of Cologne. His second example is even more elaborate: each of the subtleties that punctuated the four courses of a lavish fish dinner was accompanied by a couplet from the *Regimen Sanitatis Salernitanum* describing the properties of the humors. The subtlety following the first course represented a gallant youth, Sanguineus, standing on a cloud piping and singing to celebrate the season "Þat cleped is ver." The second subtlety depicted a red and fiery man of war called Estas (Summer), and the third showed a weary man carrying a sickle (Harvest) standing in a river tired and with no desire to dance. The fourth was a representation of Winter, with gray hair, sitting on a stone. As John Burrow notes, "as Duke Humphrey's guests worked their way through this very unpenitentiary fish banquet, they were invited to see in it the four courses of their own life's feast."[17] The appeal of subtleties, according to Russell, was:

These iiij. Soteltess devised in towse,
Wher þey byn shewed in an howse,
Hith*e* doth egret plesaunce
Wit*h* oþ*er* sight*es* of gret Nowelte
Þan han be shewed in Rialle feestes of solempnyte,
A notable cost þe ordynaunce.[18]

Although Russell locates subtleties within the rituals of the table, his focus on their visual appeal emphasizes their theatrical nature, including their resemblance to pageants staged in the streets.[19] Some subtleties depicted scenes full of action, such as those in the St. George's feast for the Emperor Sigismund in 1416.[20] The first subtlety presented to the emperor was of the Virgin Mary arming St. George and the angel putting on his spurs; the second was of St. George fighting the dragon, a spear in his hand; and the third, a castle, St. George, and the king's daughter leading a lamb into the castle gate. Others deployed their written verses or "reasons" so as to form a kind of dialogue among the figures in the subtlety. A subtlety at the coronation banquet of Catherine of Valois in 1421, for example, depicted St. Catherine with a reason in her hand: "La Roigne ma file," with the panther answering "In cest Ile," another beast answering "Of Albion," and another saying "Aves Renowne."[21] Another subtlety, which apparently included an actual dialogue of "Pastor Bonus," the bishop, St. Andrew, and possibly a presenter, was part of the "Convivium" celebrating the installation of John Morton as bishop of Ely on 29 August 1479.[22] There may have been a degree of crossover between drama and subtleties: Glynne Wickham observes that the three-dimensional figures of subtleties, like those of tableaux vivants, endowed images with greater realism than could be found in two-dimensional drawings and thus made them more useful as source material for early play-makers.[23]

The performative nature of subtleties is underscored by etymology and usage, which link those confectionary entertainments to theater's arts of disguise and deception. Definitions show that subtleties and subterfuge were not far apart in Middle English usage and reveal that edible tableaux could be understood to be ingenious contrivances as well as crafty deceptions that make a dish look like something it in actuality is not.[24] In his translation of the *Pilgrimage of Life*, Lydgate himself emphasized that closeness, using the phrase "many other soteltes" to translate the French "autre chose desguisee" and thus suggesting that the word *sotelte* could be used to describe the act of masquerade.[25] Like disguisings and other similar enactments, subtleties were entertainments that pleased and instructed by using an artfulness bordering on deception.

In their connection to disguise, subtleties were allied with other pro-cesses of courtly identity making of the sort that Susan Crane has described as being part of the performance of aristocratic selfhood in the late medieval period.[26] During the coronation feast of 1429, this crafting of the self was focused most intensely on the young king, as the visual and verbal features of the three subtleties presented a specific image of the newly crowned Henry. Henry's positioning in all three subtleties between historical figures who act as patron saints, and his kneeling posture, demonstrated both his centrality to the ceremony and his still subordinate role as a young ruler-supplicant in need of guidance and help. The third subtlety, with its depiction of Henry as Christ-child, displayed a dual image of the king's child-like helplessness and his near-divine power. The subtleties also looked beyond the king, engaging the banqueting guests as witnesses to the symbolic construction of Henry and ratifying their status as privileged participants in the royal ceremony, each with his or her own clearly marked place—which was signaled quite visibly by the seating arrangements—in the collective project of king mak-ing. Resembling the "voids" of renaissance banquets discussed by Patricia Fumerton, subtleties were heavily charged representational forms, as aristo-crats and wealthy commoners consumed objects removed from everyday sustenance, symbolic pseudo-foods that ratified their social status. Unlike the "detached subjectivity" that Fumerton argues characterized the renaissance feast, the subjectivity created by medieval banquets—with their mingling of people, courses, and sensory experiences—was intensely communal.[27] The coronation subtleties for Henry thus may have aimed to create a specific image of him as king, but they did so within a context of commensality as a highly social act.

Even though subtleties were solidly material, they were also a fairly rar-efied performance medium, requiring the resources of a well-stocked kitchen and skilled cooks, but their social reach extended beyond the aristocracy. A wealthy household in the fourteenth and fifteenth centuries would have had its own cooks, including a waferer and confectioner for making luxurious trifles; class issues were involved as cooks for the wealthy tried to get away from peasant life and tastes and to disguise nature with artifice.[28] While the promise of a cookery book from the reign of Richard II to teach the art of making potages and meats and "sotiltees for alle manere of states both h[y]e and lowe" seems exaggerated (how low could such an elaborate and expensive art go?), the book's assumption that subtleties could be part of banquets at various social levels is supported by other evidence.[29]

That social reach should remind us that meals themselves are a form of social patterning, in their way "a *res publica* or public thing," as Julia Lupton observes, "designed for common consumption in accordance with the order of courses, the rules of seating, and the seasonal rhythms of feast and fast."[30] A public thing within a public thing, the subtlety blended into one compact and spectacular package both the social and the symbolic aspects of dining, offering banqueters not only the chance to see themselves within the social whole but also to internalize key cultural hopes and desires. By first viewing and then eating the subtleties, banqueters played the roles of both spectators and participants, watching and taking part in a complicated performance in which food was at once a spectacle and a commestible. Raising foodstuff to the level of showpiece, subtleties deceive us into taking sugar and dough for miniature pageants, converting the fleeting materiality of pastries into the enduring symbolism of art, and asking us to both destroy that art by devouring it and preserve it by making it a part of ourselves.

Henry's Coronation Feast and the Three Subtleties

Although sharing the general contours of food as performance that I have been describing, the feast and subtleties for Henry VI were shaped by a historical context that gave them specific meanings that would have been available to those who planned and participated in the feast. Signaling opulence and immunity to the dearth felt elsewhere in England that year, the lavishness of the three courses at the 1429 feast suggests an exceptional degree of culinary richness that stands out from the norm of ordinary and even aristocratic consumption.[31] As Epstein observes, "the variety and the quantity of items, and the care taken to record each delicacy, give an impression of magnificent superfluity," an impression designed to display the royal virtue of "magnificence" and thus to demonstrate the extent of the king's wealth and power.[32] Like the other events of the coronation, the banquet's aims were the political ones of demonstrating the power of the monarchy and Henry VI's fitness for the crown. While not all of the dishes would have been served to all of the diners, their buffet-like display, deftly captured in manuscript descriptions of them, presented the image of a cornucopia of abundance and was a reminder of royal largesse and might.[33]

While lavish, the menu was not especially exotic, instead displaying native bounty. The three courses included the full span of meat, fish, and fowl available in fifteenth-century England, such as venison, boar, beef, mutton, capon, chicken, pike, crane, pig, swan, egret, carp, and crab, among many others. This display of the English wild and cultivated game was accompanied by various custards, puddings, jellies, and fritters, including "furmentie" and "viande royal," sweet porridge-like dishes typically served with meat; a "custade rooial," presumably a custard-like tart; "leches," thin slices of a pudding or jelly; and sweet or savory "fritours."[34] The peacock was served "enhakyll," in its plumage. Rich, grand, opulent, but familiar, the feast was thoroughly grounded in English cookery and represented an expansion of ordinary meals, not a departure from them. This was an English feast for an English coronation, an assertion of native identity that seems calculated to respond to the tensions of the dual monarchy by acknowledging the claims of the homeland.

Where the dishes departed from ordinary fare was in their decorative use of heraldic emblems and patterns, which linked the food with the occasion's political themes through the use of gold gilt, colors, geometric shapes, and animal figures found on heraldry: the "viande royal" in the first course was "plantid with lozenges of golde" (i.e., cut into saffron-dyed geometrical sections); the boarheads were in "castelles of earmed with golde" (i.e., a castle with black-and-white ermine spots with gold); the "redde lech" had white lions carved into it and the white "leches" featured a red antelope with a crown on a golden chain; the "custade rooial" had a golden leopard; the porkpie was "poudred" with leopards and fleur-de-lis; a cold bake-meat was shaped like a shield; and the fritter in the first course was molded into the shape of a sun with a fleur-de-lis in its center while in the fritter in the second course took the shape of a leopard's head with two ostrich feathers.[35] The insistently royal slant of the decorations—lions and leopards were on the coats of arms of Sts. Edward and Louis, and on Henry VI's, too, and the French lilies point to Henry's right to the French crown—turned the foodstuffs into dramatic props enlisted in support of the unifying goals of the occasion.

At some level, all subtleties were aligned with the ritual consumption of the eucharistic wafer, late medieval culture's most iconic form of symbolic eating, and given controversies surrounding eucharistic devotion in the fifteenth century, that connection was not surprisingly even stronger in the subjects chosen for the Henry VI's subtleties. Epstein argues that the 1429 coronation subtleties deliberately drew on religious associations to emphasize secular concerns, importing "embattled, orthodox religious practices into the performance of secular political ritual." Thus, while feasting on signs and symbols of dynastic polity created by the confectioner, the assembled guests participated in something akin to a political mass. Such a conflation should not be unexpected, Epstein notes, since the chief characteristic of Lancastrian culture, besides the politicizing of poetry and other representational forms, was "the unification of church and crown in a marriage of mutual self-interest and self-preservation."[36]

The joining of these shared interests can be seen in the subject matter of each of the three coronation subtleties. The first subtlety, like other Lancastrian productions of the 1420s and early 1430s, including the 1432 royal entry, attempted to assert the legitimacy of the dual monarchy. More pointedly, it echoes the "Roundel" and the "Ballade" Lydgate also wrote for the coronation in linking church and crown, England and France, through its depiction of Sts. Edward and Louis "bryngyng yn bitwene hem" Henry VI in his coat armor. According to Robert Fabyan's 1516 account, the two monarch-saints were accompanied on the subtlety by "a Scripture passynge from theym," which explained the meaning of the image, with a ballade "under the fete of the sayde sayntes."[37] The ballade consisted of Lydgate's eight lines of verse stressing that Henry VI is the "braunch borne of here blessid blode" (l. 3) and the inheritor of the fleur-de-lis, who will one day come to resemble his illustrious predecessors in wisdom as well as "in knyghthod & vertue" (l. 8).

The second subtlety took up the question of heresy and Lollard threats and showed Emperor Sigismund and Henry V, wearing the mantle of the Order of the Garter, with Henry VI kneeling before them "with this resoun."[38] In Lydgate's verses, Sigismund is styled a scourge "Ageinst miscreauntes [i.e., heretics]" (l. 9), and Henry V is depicted as a martial defender of "Cristes cause" and a cherisher of the Church under whom "Lollardes had a falle" (l. 13). The reference in these lines is to Sigismund's actions against the Hussites (Sigismund betrayed Jan Hus at the Council of Constance and authorized his execution, while also going to battle against his followers) and to Henry V's against the Oldcastle Lollard plot of 1413, both instances in which heterodox threats were suppressed. In the coronation "Ballade," Lydgate used the same figures and theme (see ll. 81–88), suggesting that suppression of heresy formed a dominant theme of the coronation. Mentioning Henry's father's friendship with Sigismund signals that the dual monarchy has imperial approval while also encouraging the young king to be a vigorous defender of orthodox religion.[39] In a collaborative production like the subtleties, it can be difficult to assign responsibility for specific details, but it appears as if the decision to emphasize defense of orthodoxy, if not Lydgate's own choice, is at least something his verses elaborate and expand on beyond the visual imagery of the subtlety, but the dangers of Lollardy was certainly a concern of the late 1420s, and Lydgate's decision to emphasize the king's role as champion of orthodoxy was by no means an eccentric one.[40] Epstein notes that at this moment, the banquet guests are eating a jellied dish with the words *Te Deum Laudamus* on it: "The significance of the words is threefold: they literally proclaim the diners' devotion to God; being Latin, in this context they take on an orthodox connotation; they are a royal motto. In consuming them, the diners use their own bodies to enact and to signify corporeally their fealty to the ideology of church-crown cooperation."[41]

The third subtlety showed the Virgin Mary with the Christ child in her lap; she held in her hand a crown, and Sts. George and Denis knelt on either side of her, presenting Henry VI, kneeling, to her "with this reason folowyng."[42] Like "A Prayer for King, Queen, and People," which was a translation of the hymn "Ab inimicis nostris defende nos christe" that Lydgate had made for the coronation and to which he added an envoy asking for God's blessing for the young king and his mother, the third subtlety adopts Christian symbols for political purposes. As Epstein remarks, the crown the Virgin holds is ambiguously positioned so that it is unclear which of the religiopolitically paired offspring she is crowning, an ambiguity that underscores J. W. McKenna's point about "the lengths to which the English royal administrators were prepared to go to advertise the dynastic claims of Henry VI."[43] Lydgate's verses for the third subtlety take the form of a short prayer to the Virgin and the two monarch-saints in which the poet beseeches them to show their "hevenly light" on him (l. 21) and affirms the youthful Henry's right to the dual monarchy.

Like other forms of Lancastrian public culture in the first decades of the fifteenth century, the three subtleties touched on the chief concerns of Lancastrian rule—the legitimacy of dynastic succession and the dual monarchy and the need to suppress heresy and support orthodox religion—making those issues the central focus of the coronation banquet. The attempt of the subtleties to fuse the interests of church and crown, interests that would presumably have been at least partially shared by the civic guests at the banquet as well, was made easier by the ways in which the ritual of coronation feasts echoed the ritual of the mass. In a discussion of the mass as ritual and as sacramental theater, Sarah Beckwith observes that "the host will not magically resolve

discord or disharmony"; instead, "its properties lie in the structures of relation that are established between the ritual participant and the ritual object."[44] Like the mass, a coronation feast employed food as a performance
medium to bind a community around shared values. The powerful latent
symbolism of the mass infused this secular feast and the subtleties that were
a part of it, harnessing religious ritual for secular political ends, even if—as
with the mass—no magical resolution could be assured. If the subtleties were
eaten, the consumption of such charged texts and images would have made
Lancastrian propaganda unusually compelling as it was literally incorporated
by the assembled guests. Even if they were only consumed visually and aurally, as they would have been if Lydgate's verses were read aloud or simply
left to be viewed by king and guests, the feasting context would have imbued
the subtleties with similarly heightened meanings.[45]

The surviving manuscripts do not make clear where on the subtleties for
Henry VI's coronation the verses by Lydgate appeared, but Fabyan's account
suggests that they could issue from the mouths of the figures, be carried in
their hands, or be written beneath the tableau.[46] In BL MS Cotton Julius B.i.,
Lydgate's verses are described as "reasons" or "scriptures," terms that were used
interchangeably to describe the verses that accompanied visual representations.
While it could broadly describe various kinds of spoken discourse, the Middle
English word *resoun* also had a more specialized meaning as a written verse or
motto, especially one engraved, embroidered, or inscribed on an object.[47]

The innovation of the 1429 subtleties comes in the expansion of these
"reasons" or typically short mottoes or banners typically found on subtleties
into full ballades, an innovation that was perhaps specially requested to enhance
the impact of the subtleties to suit the importance of the occasion. The elaborateness of Lydgate's verses suggests, in Gordon Kipling's view, "that the household
was attempting something more ambitious on this occasion. In commissioning
England's most eminent poet to provide the scriptures, they expected—and
got—not just a few phrases of emblematic scripture, but stanzas of verse."[48] It
is possible that Lydgate was responsible for the design of the subtleties (the
"device"), but someone else may have decided on the emblematic subject matter that the artisans and cooks created, and Lydgate was merely assigned the
task of writing the accompanying verses or "scriptures," thus limiting his inven-
tive freedom. The planning for the coronation apparently began in the summer
after being set in motion by the coronation of Charles VII at Rheims in July,
leaving time for the household to compose the device for the subtleties, send it
to Lydgate, and receive the scriptures in return.[49]

Although commonly ascribed to him, Lydgate's authorship of the bal-lades for the subtleties is not absolutely certain. They were not copied by Shirley and are not attributed to Lydgate in the surviving manuscripts or in Fabyan's account. That lack of attribution may arise from the nature of the sources: many are chronicles that include the verses as part of their accounts of the coronation, and chroniclers may have been unaware of Lydgate's role in creating the verses or may have been indifferent to the cachet that in some circles was attached to Lydgate's name. Despite this lack of attribution, Mac-Cracken judged that the verses were "certainly" by Lydgate on the grounds that they fit with the other poems Lydgate wrote for the coronation, a claim that has never been seriously challenged.[50]

Edible Text/Legible Text

The subtleties themselves were eaten or disassembled or rotted away soon after they were displayed, but Lydgate's three ballades—and in many cases a list of the courses at the feast and a description of the subtleties—made their way into the written record, thus preserving in the medium of words a feast in which the food was "conspicuously discursive."[51] Food appeals to the senses of smell, taste, touch, and sight, and few of those can be adequately represented through the medium of written words. In that regard, the scribal problem of recording the subtleties was not much different from difficulties involved in representing pageantry or mumming or processions on the manuscript page. None of the manuscripts containing descriptions of the subtleties for which Lydgate provided verses aspires to or attains the level of representational vivid-ness of the souvenir-like festival books and prints produced in later centuries for the elite participants at banquets and for those unable to attend.[52] As the heavily symbolic aspect of the subtleties suggests and despite their obvious materiality as items meant to be eaten, when copied into manuscripts, they inevitably came unmoored from their connection to food, as they were trans-formed from nourishment into image and text. And yet, manuscript copies of the subtleties frequently attempt to hold onto an alimentary context, striv-ing to convey something of the materiality of the subtleties as foodstuffs and as performance objects.

The textual legacy of the feast for Henry VI offers a glimpse of the gastro-aesthetics of the coronation banquet and also suggests which readers would have been interested in Lydgate's verses as textual representations of the material objects displayed and consumed at the coronation. Not all extant descriptions of the 1429 coronation banquet include the verses Lydgate was commissioned to write; some contain just the courses for the feast along with brief descriptions of the subtleties. Where Lydgate's three ballades do survive is, overwhelmingly, in the context of London chronicles. That context might seem strange, given the pronounced lack of interest in chivalry among Londoners in the fifteenth century. Perhaps Lydgate's verses for the subtleties owe their survival to a concern with royal politics that had implications for the city, or to recognition that there was money to be made in hosting tournaments and supplying the trappings of chivalry and writing down the romances that described it.[53]

There are three interrelated groups of London chronicles in which Lydgate's ballades appear. The first group includes BL MS Egerton 1995, a late fifteenth-century commonplace book or miscellany written in one hand. It contains treatises, the *Siege of Rome*, and other material in prose and verse such as model letters, recipes, medical remedies, a courtesy poem, and the chronicle known as "Gregory's Chronicle," into which Lydgate's verses on the subtleties are inserted as part of its account of the history of London.[54] Mary-Rose McLaren describes the personality of the author of the chronicle as "that of an older, class-conscious, worldly wise, philosophical man," noting that he is a fair commentator even if sympathetic to uprisings and injustices, is involved in trade (but is probably not a mercer, since he makes disparaging remarks about mercers), is critical of the king but speaks of Eleanor Cobham as "my lady of Gloucester" and is a supporter of "my good lord Montagewe," is interested in religion and in the mayoralty, and seems to have contacts outside London.[55] Given the strong interest in the gentry and aristocracy that Egerton 1995 shows, the appearance of the subtleties is not a surprise. Egerton 1995 shares some content with a group of manuscripts identified by Margaret Connolly as produced by scribes who had access to Shirley's manuscripts, although Linne Mooney cautions against assuming that Shirley's manuscripts were the exemplars for all of these copies.[56] In Egerton 1995, as in the related BL MS Cotton Vitellius A.xvi, Lydgate's ballades are not written in verse, although line breaks are indicated by capital letters and the text of the subtleties is underlined in red, setting Lydgate's poetry off from the description of the courses. BL Vitellius A.xvi contains 213 leaves of paper and is made up of three separate chronicles in different hands that are arranged as continuations of one another; the subtleties appear on folio 91.[57]

The second group of related chronicle manuscripts containing Lydgate's ballades includes London Guildhall Library MS 3313, which consists entirely of a London chronicle; to 1438 it is in a neat, professional hand, but a second hand (with a third appearing in a single quire beginning on fol. 157) continues through 1496, at which point there appears a list of mayors and aldermen, then a continuation of the chronicle through 1512 and an index of events between 1436 and 1496, with other material inserted by various readers.[58] Guildhall 3313 also includes Lydgate's verses on the 1432 royal entry and, on folio 129v, his ballades for the subtleties. Guildhall 3313 appears to be the product of a workshop or professional scribe commissioned to write up a chronicle that could later be added to by the owner.[59] The version found in BL MS Cotton Julius B.i., which MacCracken uses as the base text for his edition of Lydgate's subtleties, appears in a London chronicle whose focus is on the succession of mayors and other aspects of civic government, even though it also includes notable historical events, such as Henry VI's coronation. The manuscript shows evidence of having been carefully produced, but whether for private use or for sale or on commission is impossible to say.[60] Julius B.i. is a manuscript of 102 leaves of paper, written in one neat hand to 1436 with space left for decorated initials; at the year 1432, the page layout changes, which probably marks the point of private ownership, and there is a further change of hand at 1436.[61] Along with Lydgate's verses for the subtleties, the manuscript also includes ordinances, *La Bataille du Roy*, and some heraldic texts in a variety of hands, although the titles throughout the manuscript are all probably in the hand of the first scribe.[62] A similar manuscript with the subtleties is BL MS Cotton Vitellius F.ix., which contains a London chronicle written in the same hand on seventy leaves of paper; the chronicle begins in 1189 and ends in 1439, and up to 1431 it is identical with Julius B.i.[63]

Also part of this second group is Oxford, St. John's College MS 57, a folio of 242 leaves of paper in a hand of the first half of the fifteenth century, probably that of a professional scribe. The manuscript is made up of three originally separate booklets all in Middle English containing the *Prick of Conscience*, a fifteenth-century chronicle of London that covers the years 1189 to 1431, and Chaucer's *Parliament of Fowls*, to which is appended Henry V's Statutes and Ordinances for the army at Mantes (1419).[64] Linne Mooney and Lister Matheson have identified its scribe, whom they call "the Beryn scribe," as being the same as the copyist of the Duke of Northumberland's *Canterbury*

Tales, which contains a copy of the non-Chaucerian *Tale of Beryn*, and six other manuscripts, including five copies of the Middle English prose *Brut* and a copy of Lydgate's *Life of Our Lady*. Mooney and Matheson localize the spelling of the scribe in south-central Essex but suggest that he may have moved to London to ply his trade. They note that the text of the *Life of Our Lady* is related to Trinity MS R.3.21, which was written in a London, commercial book-producing setting and, like St. John's MS 57, was originally composed of booklets.[65] The second booklet of St. John's MS 57 contains a fifteenth-century London chronicle, listing mayors and sheriffs through 1431; while Kingsford classifies its text as one of the earliest of the London chronicles, Mooney and Matheson date the copy to the 1440s or 1450s, on paleographical grounds.[66] The text of St. John's MS 57's chronicle is close to that of Cotton Julius B.i., Vitellius F.ix, and Guildhall 3313; Lydgate's ballades for the subtleties appear on folio 221v. Mooney and Matheson note that the Beryn scribe's access to an early copy of the London chronicle suggests that he or his patron had an interest in English history. Piecing together the scant evidence, Mooney and Matheson conclude that the manuscripts copied by the Beryn scribe were owned by members of the lesser nobility and knightly classes, merchants, and civil servants, who, while geographically dispersed, appear to have relied on London scriptoria for their books.[67]

The subtleties appear in three other chronicle contexts. Dublin, Trinity College MS 509 is a miscellany of historical and theological works in English and Latin that includes a list of names of London churches, the oath of the mayor and sheriffs of London, the *Gesta Edwardi III*, a life of the Virgin Mary, a list of English and Irish saints, and the chronicle known as "Bale's Chronicle," which includes the subtleties.[68] Hatfield House MS Cecil Papers 281 is a commonplace book of 141 leaves of parchment, probably compiled as one book; it contains a variety of material, including two Latin chronicles, records of taxes of London, religious notes, a moral tale, and Lydgate's verses on the kings of England.[69] On folios 32–88, there is a London chronicle in three different hands from 1189 to 1440 with a continuation for the years 1446–50; the chronicle resembles the chronicle in Trinity College, Dublin 509, and both Cecil 281 and Dublin 509 follow Egerton 1995 closely until the year 1437.[70] Last of the three, BL MS Cotton Nero C.xi. is a heraldic miscellany containing a chronicle that begins as a *Brut* and becomes a London chronicle at 1189; it runs until 1485, with a last continuation ending in 1558. It was published as *The Newe Cronycles of England and of France* by Pynson in 1516 and was later printed as *Fabyan's Chronycle* by Rastell in 1553. The chronicle is close to St. John's 57, Vitellius F.ix, Julius B.i, and Guildhall 3313 but unusual in its style and sources.[71]

In only two instances do Lydgate's ballades for the subtleties appear in nonchronicle contexts; both of those appearances are in manuscripts whose contents emphasize matters of chivalry and statecraft. The subtleties are the second item in BL MS Lansdowne 285 (1450–75) (fols. 6v–7r) and follow immediately after a description of "The maner and forme of the Kyngis and Quenes coronacion in Englonde" (fol. 2). Lansdowne 285 may have been the "Grete Boke" copied for Sir John Paston by William Ebesham, a professional scribe, or the "Grete Boke" and Lansdowne may share a common original; in any case, it contains a number of short items related to chivalry and politics during the reign of Edward IV.[72] It also contains Lydgate's translation of the *Secreta Secretorum*, which was completed by Benedict Burgh. Lansdowne 285 is a coherently organized miscellany of mainly chivalric and heraldic writings clearly written for the landed gentry. In describing the subtleties, Lansdowne 285 lists the menu for each course, under headers written in French ("le primier cours pur la ioure del coronacion," "le seconde cours," "le trecie cours"), but does not describe the subtleties; it calls Lydgate's verses "baladis" (using English rather than French). New York Pierpont Morgan Library MS 775 is an illustrated miscellany of chivalric material written before 1461 for Sir John Astley, a Knight of the Garter who was well established at court and skilled in royal tournaments. The miscellany was dedicated to an unidentified "hye princesse" and "good ladyship," raising the possibility that it belonged to a woman.[73] In addition to Lydgate's verses for the subtleties, the manuscript contains various works on chivalry and statecraft, including a translation of Vegetius's *de Re Militari*, Christine de Pisan's *Epistle of Othea* (a tract on advice in the form of a mirror), and Lydgate's *Secreta Secretorum*.[74] G. A. Lester believes that Morgan 775 served as a model for Paston's "Grete Boke," which contains the same material with minor variations, but it is also possible that both derived from a common original that circulated among professional scribes.[75]

Although it is obvious why Lydgate's verses for the 1432 royal entry would tend to appear in the context of London chronicles, given the city's involvement in producing them, it is less apparent why his verses for the subtleties, which were presumably sponsored solely by the royal court, would too. Perhaps their occurrence in chronicles can be explained by the fact that they are linked to the important occasion of the coronation, an event of state that would have interested Londoners. Perhaps because the mayor and important

Londoners attended the 1429 banquet, they wanted to commemorate a ceremony they had seen. But the appearance of the subtleties in miscellanies of mostly chivalric and heraldic material suggests that they were also viewed as moments of royal ceremony of interest to aristocratic readers.

How did Lydgate's verses on the subtleties reach the compilers of London chronicles? They may be an example of passages of verse that occasionally appear in prose chronicles, which Julia Boffey and A. S. G. Edwards view as instances of "random access to illustrative material" or "opportunistic interpolation."[76] Epstein echoes this suggestion, arguing that given the inclusion of the ballades in a relatively high number of chronicle manuscripts, their appearance may be more "opportunistic" than "random"; they may have been deliberately circulated so that they could be included in written documents like chronicles that would ensure them a life beyond the ephemeral occasion of performance. If Epstein is right, the verses may represent authorized models of textual production and reception; like other Lancastrian texts, "they explicitly promulgate dynastic ideology and implicitly appropriate contested orthodox ritual." The copying of performance texts and their dissemination to readers, Epstein argues, "evokes rituals, performances, and displays with endless public and political ramifications" and constitutes a kind of "political communion, in which the ideology of the regime is symbolically consumed and internalized."[77]

While Epstein's point about the Lancastrian dynasty's desire to conscript the act of reading for its own purposes is well taken, the manuscript evidence suggests that the desires of Londoners were also a factor in the survival and dissemination of Lydgate's verses for the subtleties. It is true that several of the chronicles containing the subtleties date from the first half of the fifteenth century, very close to the time of the banquet itself, and thus might represent Lancastrian attempts at dispersal, but the positioning of the subtleties within the context of London chronicles suggests an urban co-opting of the originally royal performance represented by the subtleties. Since a number of the surviving London chronicles are in "commonplace books," McLaren suggests that they may have been thought of "as the common property of the citizens of London," which implies "a perception of a communal past drawn upon and recorded by those who saw themselves as its inheritors."[78] The three royal mummings Lydgate wrote survive in single copies by Shirley, his "Ballade" for the 1429 coronation appears in only a few manuscripts related to Shirley, and the "Roundel" for the same occasion appears only in BL MS Harley 7333, a non-Shirlean manuscript. Of Lydgate's coronation texts, only the "Prayer" survives in as many manuscripts as the subtleties, and its survival may reflect its frequent alteration for use by Edward IV. Perhaps the wider copying of Lydgate's verses for the subtleties reflects their status as a relatively public performance, one to which an audience broader than just the royal household would have had access.

All of the extant copies of Lydgate's verses for the 1429 coronation subtleties focus on his words, while offering little sense of the banqueting context or the spectacular nature of the subtleties themselves. No extant copy is accompanied by any visual representation of the subtleties, and the copyists made little attempt to describe what the subtleties looked like.[79] That lack of detailed description may reflect the copyists' source material, which Kipling suggests was the "device" or instructions provided to the cooks and pastry makers, telling them to create, in the case of the first course, a specific set of courses followed by a "sotelte, Seint Edward and Seint Lowes armed in cote armours bryngyng yn bitwene hem the Kyng in his cote armour with this scripture suyng" (MS Cotton Julius B.i., fol. 79), with accompanying scripture by Lydgate.[80] By a route not evident to us today, someone at court presumably made the device and scriptures for the banquet available to copyists, who then followed that information without embellishment—acting as faithful recorders of a preexisting textual record of the occasion, rather than as writers concerned with evoking that occasion for readers in all its multisensory detail.

That Lydgate is not identified as the author of the ballades for the 1429 subtleties suggests affinities between them and the other anonymous poetry that found its way into chronicles. While Lydgate's status as a poet may have been important for those who commissioned the verses from him, chroniclers seem to have cared less about authorial identity and its possible meanings than about the verses themselves. In the context of an urban environment in which public poetry often circulated anonymously, as surviving fifteenth-century political songs and ballads show, lack of attribution may have signaled an understanding of the publicly shared and collective nature of many verses.

In their ballade form, Lydgate's verses for the subtleties drew on the French lyric and represented a fashionable (and still innovative despite Chaucer's use of it) as well as sophisticated form of literary art. The eight-line stanzas of the subtleties, with their fairly complicated rhyme scheme of ababbcbc, were difficult to execute in English given its "skarsete" of rhymes, as Chaucer complained; requiring a high level of artistic expertise, the ballades fit the elaborateness of the coronation occasion.[81] Expanding the usual brief "scriptures" or "reasons" associated with pageants and subtleties into ballades has the effect of linking the three separate displays into one artistic unit and of refashioning them into an elevated poetic form. Just as the confectioner's art transformed pastry into spectacle, so the ballades turned simple "reasons" into poetry. As performances, the 1429 subtleties are evidence of the incorporation of poetry into spectacle; when copied into chronicles, the subtleties are evidence of the dominance of verbal over visual modes.

While the bookish nature of the subtleties in their manuscript contexts would seem to signal the triumph of script over performance, such an assumption is not entirely accurate. In the version of the subtleties found in MS Lansdowne 285, there are two substitutions of N for the name of Henry, in lines 11 and 20. The N presumably stands for the Latin word *nomen* and, like the similar usage in the N-Town Proclamation that gives the play its name, may signal that any name could be inserted as needed. This possible recycling of the verses for other use resembles the treatment of Lydgate's "Prayer for King, Queen, and People," which in some manuscript versions has been altered to use for Edward IV.[82] Whether such recycling actually occurred or not, the scribal alteration holds out the possibility of a reuse of Lydgate's verses in which the almost fully poeticized textual remains of the long ago 1429 banquet could come to life once again as performances. In that oscillation from edible performance to written text back to potential performance can be found a record of the intersection of performativity and textuality embodied in the edible theater of the subtleties. Even though the surviving accounts of the subtleties are less than fully satisfying at capturing the materiality of the three subtleties or the feasting context, they nonetheless offer evidence of food as a performance medium and let us glimpse how eating, watching, and reading are all aspects of theater history.

CHAPTER 7

The Queen's Dumbshows

During a Christmas season in the late 1420s, Henry and members of his household joined his mother Catherine of Valois at her castle at Hertford. In the course of the holiday festivities, if Shirley can be believed, they were entertained by a short performance by Lydgate. The *Disguising at Hertford* seems an odd choice for a young boy. Addressed to Henry and apparently requiring his participation, the disguising is a satire that dramatizes the complaint of a group of rustic men about their wives' tyranny, followed by the wives' vigorous self-defense, and then the king's decision to grant the women another year of their customary rule over men while he deliberates and further questions the parties involved. Its final statement is a warning to men to avoid marriage, which, the disguising cautions, leads to lifelong servitude and imprisonment. On two other occasions, at Eltham and again at Windsor, Lydgate's mummings formed part of the royal household's Christmas entertainments. The *Mumming at Eltham* enacts a gift-giving ceremony in which the gods of antiquity bring gifts of "Pees, vnytee, plentee and haboundaunce" (l. 58) to the young king and his mother. The *Mumming at Windsor*, performed just after Henry's coronation in London and before his departure for Paris, where he would be crowned king of France in the upcoming year, describes how France was converted in Clovis's time through St. Clotilda, emphasizing that the golden ampulla from which Clovis was anointed will soon be Henry's "by tytle of right" (l. 91).

Whatever the appropriateness of these performances for a small boy, Henry is their ostensible focus: it is his person they flatter, his behavior they try to influence, his aspirations they champion, and his political fortunes they seek to increase. Yet Henry was not their sole witness, since members of the household and guests would also have been present as spectators. More pointedly, the holiday performances may have had yet another target, I would like to suggest: Catherine, who was present at all three and is directly addressed in—and might even have commissioned—one of them. Catherine would certainly have been a more suitable recipient of these entertainments than her young son: as an adult, better able to appreciate and understand them; as a widowed queen caught in a complicated relationship with the court, more in need of their cultural and ideological work. Although Catherine's centrality to these performances may have been obscured by a tendency to view them as directed solely to Henry, Lydgate's royal disguising and mummings have, in fact, quite a lot to say about the queen as in turn victim, manipulator, and tool of Lancastrian political efforts, each of which she seems to have been on successive occasions in the 1420s. In these performances, we can not only trace Catherine's changing fortunes but also witness the workings of late medieval courtly ceremony, particularly as it attempts to grapple with the problem of what to do with the queen.

In pulling back the curtain on Lancastrian queenship, Lydgate's royal disguising and mummings more broadly encourage a reassessment of the extent of women's involvement in both performance and reading, and of their patronage of ceremonies as well as literary works. My aim in this chapter is both focused and broad. At one level, I hope to show how Lydgate's holiday entertainments for the court revise our understanding of women's involvement in medieval performances. More broadly, as the decision to borrow this chapter's title for the title of my whole book signals, I want to foreground the most striking of the many remarkable ways in which Lydgate's performance texts expand and complicate theater history and, by extension, the histories of late medieval literature and culture as well. That Lydgate wrote plays for the queen upends much of what we think we know about the place of women in the making of medieval culture and points to why it is worth paying attention to Lydgate's performance texts—with their many surprises about early drama.

Evidence for the participation of women in drama and ceremony before the modern period is limited and, where it exists, ambiguous. That scarcity and indeterminacy have led to the widely shared assumption that women played almost no role in public performances, with all parts, including those of female characters, being played by men, and with men serving in organizational and sponsoring positions, while women were relegated to the role of spectator. Although some scholars have questioned how thoroughly women were excluded from participation in dramatic performances, the consensus for the most part has long been that in late medieval England, drama was largely a male pursuit.

That consensus has been recently challenged by scholars who have drawn attention to women's participation in premodern plays as performers, characters, backstage assistants, and spectators.[1] As this scholarship reminds us, records from France show that women or girls had speaking roles in plays, including in the 1547 Passion play at Valenciennes.[2] There are also records of women's apparent involvement as performers in convent dramas, as the work of Hildegard of Bingen and Hrotsvit of Gandersheim, and, for England, evidence from Barking abbey related to fourteenth-century Easter dramas suggests.[3] Although Jeremy Goldberg has argued that women may have performed in English plays in the early fourteenth century, documentation of women performing in English cycle plays is almost nonexistent, aside from the reference to the Chester wives, whose participation was first recorded in 1499.[4] Yet even if women seldom performed in plays, they were portrayed in them, and concerns about gender are pervasive in the extant plays, unsurprisingly given that, as Theresa Colleti has observed, "A drama that commandeered the attention and the resources of many medieval people for a long period of time and that was deeply embedded in the culture's prevailing modes of social organisation, in its dominant myths, and in its ceremonial and festive life, must surely bear important relations to medieval thinking about gender."[5]

Women also influenced early drama through their backstage work and as spectators. Natasha Korda has shown that early modern plays relied on women's work, wares, and funding, bringing to light a hidden history of women's backstage labor in relation to theatrical production.[6] In an investigation of gender and the medieval cycle plays, Katie Normington has similarly pointed to the ways in which women assisted with productions by making costumes and banners, leasing their children for roles, and providing food and drink for performers.[7] Perhaps their greatest impact, even if it was the least direct, came in women's act of viewing performances; as members of the audience, women were not merely passively spectators but had the opportunity to respond actively in ways that could shape the performance, given the nature of live performance and the openings it presented for audience engagement. Spectators were integral components of medieval plays, processions, and other dramatic rituals and entertainments, whose presence and reciprocal interactions with the performers in a very real sense helped create the performance. When women formed part of the audience, as they frequently did, their presence might well have had an impact on the performance.[8]

The dramatic entertainments Lydgate wrote for the court in the 1420s do not imply that Catherine acted in them, but they do point to her influence and, if not her direct participation, then at least her engaged spectatorship. Whether or not they were commissioned by her, as at least one of them might conceivably have been, the royal disguising and mummings show an attentiveness to the queen that suggests we should revisit the supposedly settled question of women's lack of involvement in medieval performance to consider whether the archive does in fact hold more traces than hitherto recognized of women's participation both in early drama and in its inscription as literary text.

Being able to associate Lydgate with performances that engage women underscores my larger argument in this book about the usefulness of Lydgate's corpus of entertainments for broadening our understanding of the nature and function of medieval performance. What is unusual is that the texts by Lydgate associated with ephemeral holiday entertainments put on at the English court have survived, and have survived with enough information about the performance context, thanks to John Shirley's headnotes, that we can make well-informed guesses as to the dates, locations, patrons, audiences, and even likely significance of the performances. The verses Lydgate wrote for Catherine's holiday entertainments may be nearly unique in the surviving corpus of medieval plays, but that uniqueness should not lead us to mistake the lack of surviving texts for the absence of specific performance practices. It should instead encourage us to consider the possibility that any surviving texts point to a wider group of performance practices and, in the current case, to pursue the possibility that women played a greater role in premodern drama than we have assumed.

While the program of state-sponsored linguistic nationalism launched by Henry V privileged the written word as a means of legitimizing dynastic claims and consolidating political control, the Lancastrians were well aware of the persuasive power of theatricality. During Henry VI's reign, in particular, royal entries, coronation rituals, and processions were frequently used to manipulate public opinion.[9] The royal ceremonies of the 1420s and early 1430s, in J. W. McKenna's words, "indicate the extent to which certain pervasive political conceits, deliberately fostered and disseminated, permeated the trappings which surrounded the public life of Henry VI."[10] Likewise, banquets and celebrations were, as V. J. Scattergood observes, "eagerly seized

upon as opportunities for emphasizing Henry VI's claims to the thrones
of England and France."[11] Some of these ceremonies were designed around
women. On her marriage to Richard II, Isabella of Valois was met at Blackheath by the mayor and other prominent citizens and was escorted into
London; the coronation events for Henry IV's wife, Joan, included an entry
into London in 1403; Catherine herself was greeted by a coronation entry in
London in 1421; the duchess of Bedford was welcomed to London along
with her husband, the duke of Bedford, in 1426; pageantry was arranged in
London in 1445 for Margaret of Anjou's marriage to Henry VI; and there
were coronation entries for Elizabeth Woodville in 1465 and for Elizabeth of
York in 1487.[12] Gordon Kipling has argued that since royal entries were intended for men, on the rare occasions when they were put on for women, the
sponsoring bodies encountered difficulties in reshaping a masculine mode to
honor a woman, as was the case for the Coventry shows for Margaret.[13]
Lydgate's royal disguising and mummings show an easier reshaping, proving
malleable vehicles for the expression of shifting attitudes toward a queen.

The Queen's Predicament

The daughter of Charles VI of Burgundy, Catherine was betrothed to Henry
V after the English victory at Agincourt and the subsequent Treaty of Troyes,
which designated Henry and his heirs kings of France as well as England.
Married to Henry in 1421, she soon gave birth to a son and nine months later
was widowed when her husband died of dysentery while fighting in France in
1422. She was twenty-one.[14]

Embodied sign of the legitimacy of the Lancastrian claim to the dual
monarchy of England and France, Catherine was the physical link between
deceased husband and infant son. For this reason, even though she had no
direct governmental role, since Henry V's two brothers—the dukes of
Bedford and Gloucester—had been named as protectors and, along with the
council, acted as governors of England during Henry VI's minority, Catherine
was highly visible in the early years of her infant son's kingship.[15] The *Great
Chronicle of London* records that when parliament met on 13 November 1423,
Catherine rode from Windsor through London on a moving throne drawn by
white horses; on her lap she held her infant son. Still holding Henry, she was
then enthroned among the lords in parliament. Two years later, before the
opening of parliament in 1425, Catherine again entered London with Henry

VI on her lap. On this occasion, however, when they reached St. Paul's Cathedral, the duke protector and the duke of Exeter took the king from his mother and led him up the steps to the high altar where he knelt; he was then carried into the courtyard and put alone on a horse that took him to Kennington.[16]

Consistent with the pattern of late medieval queenship recently sketched by historians, Catherine's role during the early 1420s, as these examples suggest, was largely an accessory and ceremonial one.[17] Having been increasingly denied involvement in governmental affairs from the early thirteenth century on, later medieval queens were, in Paul Strohm's deft phrasing, "compensated in sumptuous but highly inflated symbolic coin." In coronation rituals, processions, and other public events, queens were showered with pomp and splendor, in recognition not of their own power but of their utility as props in elaborately orchestrated dramas designed to ratify masculine rule. At best, as Strohm shows in his discussion of Philippa of Hainault and Anne of Bohemia, queens were permitted to extend their traditional familial roles of wives and mothers to act as petitioners and intercessors before the monarch, as Anne famously did in 1392 following Richard II's "quarrel" with London. Even then, queens were relegated to the decidedly limited role of modifying royal polity rather than being permitted to establish policies of their own and were seen as intermediaries between king and subject rather than as agents capable of their own political decisions.[18]

Catherine's public appearances, while fitting these general contours, also reveal, however, that ceremonial power no matter how accessory was nonetheless still power and therefore worth contesting. When, for instance, Henry VI was taken from Catherine's lap by his male protectors, walked up the steps of St. Paul's Cathedral, and placed alone on the altar, or when he was made to ride his own horse through London, it is possible to glimpse a struggle over the extent and nature of Catherine's ceremonial roles, over the degree of her public association with the king's person, and hence over her access to political authority.

It is this same struggle to which Lydgate's three holiday entertainments bear witness and contribute, even though they take place not on the public terrain of the streets of London but within the relative privacy of the royal household, where ceremonials played a somewhat different but perhaps no less crucial part in shaping opinion than they did the city's streets. Produced by a writer who had firm ties to masculine rule but also strong allegiances to female patrons, these performances not unexpectedly manifest contradictions in their structuring of gender relations and in their attitudes toward Catherine. From the warning of the Hertford disguising through the flattery of the mumming at Eltham and, finally, to the mythologizing of the Windsor mumming, Lydgate's entertainments reveal how the queen's position was fought over and delimited within the space of the royal household as well as how it could be exploited—perhaps even by Catherine herself—for political ends. They also offer glimpses of women's involvement in performance and of their relation to literary and legal writing.

The *Disguising at Hertford*: A Cautionary Tale

Shirley's headnote to the *Disguising at Hertford* describes it as a "bille by way of supplicacion" as in a "disguysing" of the "rude vpplandisshe poeple," written for the king for a Christmas performance at Hertford "at þe request of þe Countre Roullour Brys slayne at Loviers." "Brys" has been identified as John Brice, who as the king's cofferer was the controller's immediate deputy; Brice was probably slain at Louviers in 1431, which provides a latest date for the disguising.[19] Walter Schirmer has argued that this disguising was written in 1430, which would suggest that it was performed at Christmas in 1430 or 1431, but if that was the case, then Henry was not in the audience, since at Christmas of 1430, he was in Rouen and, in 1431, in Paris.[20] A more likely date is 1427, or possibly 1426, the two Christmases in the 1420s when Henry's whereabouts cannot be established. Of the two dates, 1427 seems the likelier, given existing evidence. Records mention that heralds, clerks, and minstrels came from Abingdon to Hertford in 1427.[21] Further support comes from the fact that Catherine and her son traveled from her castle at Hertford to St. Albans and Windsor between 4 April and 23 April in 1428, suggesting that they might have spent the entire winter—from the Christmas season of 1427 on—at Hertford.[22] Derek Pearsall also notes that 1427 fits Lydgate's career better than the other dates offered for the Hertford disguising.[23] Although attempts to link the content of a literary work to specific historical moments are often misguided and frequently prone to error, the date of 1427 for performance of the *Disguising at Hertford* makes sense given several features of the disguising as well as what we know about Catherine's situation at that point in the 1420s.

In calling the Hertford disguising a "bille," Shirley links it to a specific documentary practice of the government. Submitting a bill was a legal exercise

that became a poetic device chiefly through the work of Chaucer and signaled, as Matthew Giancarlo notes, a "particular idiom of verse that was
'courtly' in both senses, amorous and political." "Submitting a bill was a
textual exercise, literally," and bills had a powerful hold on the literary imagination of the fourteenth century, with notions of "petitionary dependence,"
as noted by Burrow and others, central to the self-conception of poets and
especially so for clerkly poets like Hoccleve.[24] Bills could also advertise demands or proclamations and were authored by both authorities and dissenters,
including Lollards who issued a petition in 1410 and Jack Sharp, who revived
it in 1431.[25] Lydgate uses the device of the bill elsewhere in his writings, including in his dream vision *The Temple of Glas* (c. 1420), in which two lovers
submit a series of bills/petitions to the court of Venus. The Hertford disguising consists of a bill submitted to the king, perhaps by a presenter who speaks
on their behalf, followed by the response of the wives and the king's reply.[26]
Unlike Anne of Bohemia, who in 1382 was passed a bill by the citizens asking
for her support for the city's liberties, Catherine is not directly addressed in
the disguising.[27]

As a monk, Lydgate was not a permanent member of the royal household
and may never have visited court during the ten years after Henry V's death.
But his appointment as prior of Hatfield Regis in 1423 would have brought
him into the neighborhood of Windsor. He was also certainly with the earl of
Warwick in Paris in 1426, probably in London for the coronation of Henry
VI in 1429, and in London once again in 1432 for Henry's triumphal entry
after his return from France.[28] While there is no hard evidence putting him
at court as a visitor, he had sufficient connections, including through Gloucester, for whom he would soon begin the *Fall of Princes*, that it would have been
natural for Lydgate to have been asked to script holiday entertainments for
the court and that he would have done so as one who had a long-standing,
even if conflicted, involvement with Lancastrian concerns.[29]

One of those concerns, as expressed by the Hertford disguising, has to
do with the education of the king; another touches on marital relations and
female power. Because it enacts the ritual of subjects petitioning their sovereign to legislate on their behalf, the Hertford disguising's 254 lines of rhyming
couplets appear designed to rehearse Henry in an upcoming role, offering him
the chance to practice within a festive context the acts he will be expected to
perform in real life in the near future.[30] The Hertford disguising thus seems
to have as one goal the modeling of appropriate behavior for Henry as king.
The disguising's overt focus on Henry is consistent with this didactic goal.

It begins with a direct address to Henry ("Moost noble Prynce," l. 1), by the narrator or presenter, possibly Lydgate himself, making reference to the fact that Henry's subjects ("Youre poure lieges," l. 4) have been granted permission to enter the castle and that among them are a group of rustics ("Certeyne sweynes," l. 6) who have come to complain to Henry about "þe trouble and þe crueltee" (l. 10) that they have suffered at their wives' hands. The presenter goes on to describe the woe that marriage brings to both old and young men, introducing the husbands one by one and describing their wives' tyranny. Although the men do not speak any lines, the disguising suggests that they are not painted images as in the case of *Bycorne and Chychevache*, Lydgate's other dramatic poem on marital relations, but instead are portrayed by actors. Marginal glosses note that "i. demonstrando vj. rusticos," "demonstrando pictaciarium," "demonstrando Carnificem," and "demonstrando þe Tynker," which strongly imply the presence of actors who impersonate the characters named and described in Lydgate's verses (see Figure 4). Who those actors were is unclear. But if Wickham is right in suggesting that the Hertford performance was not a mumming but instead a disguising, as Shirley's headnote describes it—thus implying not a visitation by outsiders but a disguising by friends, and not an exchange of gifts but a debate of a moral problem—then the messages of the performance would have to be seen as having a particularly insider-ish quality to them.[31] The complaints of the rustics gain resonance from their resemblance to the social practice of peasants bringing complaints to the royal court, a practice that, as Wendy Scase has noted, was already being put to use in vernacular poetry by Lydgate's time.[32]

After describing at comic length the wives' misbehaviors and the men's sufferings, the disguising directly addresses the child-king, asking—in lines that comically invoke the language of royal pardons and patronage—that he

> graunte hem fraunchyse and also liberte,
> Sith þey beoþe fetird and bounden in maryage,
> A sauf-conduyt to sauf him frome damage.
> Eeke vnder support of youre hyeghe renoun,
> Graunt hem also a proteccyoun. (ll. 138–42)

Asserting that female tyranny has run rampant through the country ("Conquest of wyves is ronne thoroughe þis lande," l. 143), the disguising next turns to examples from the animal world to demonstrate the unnaturalness

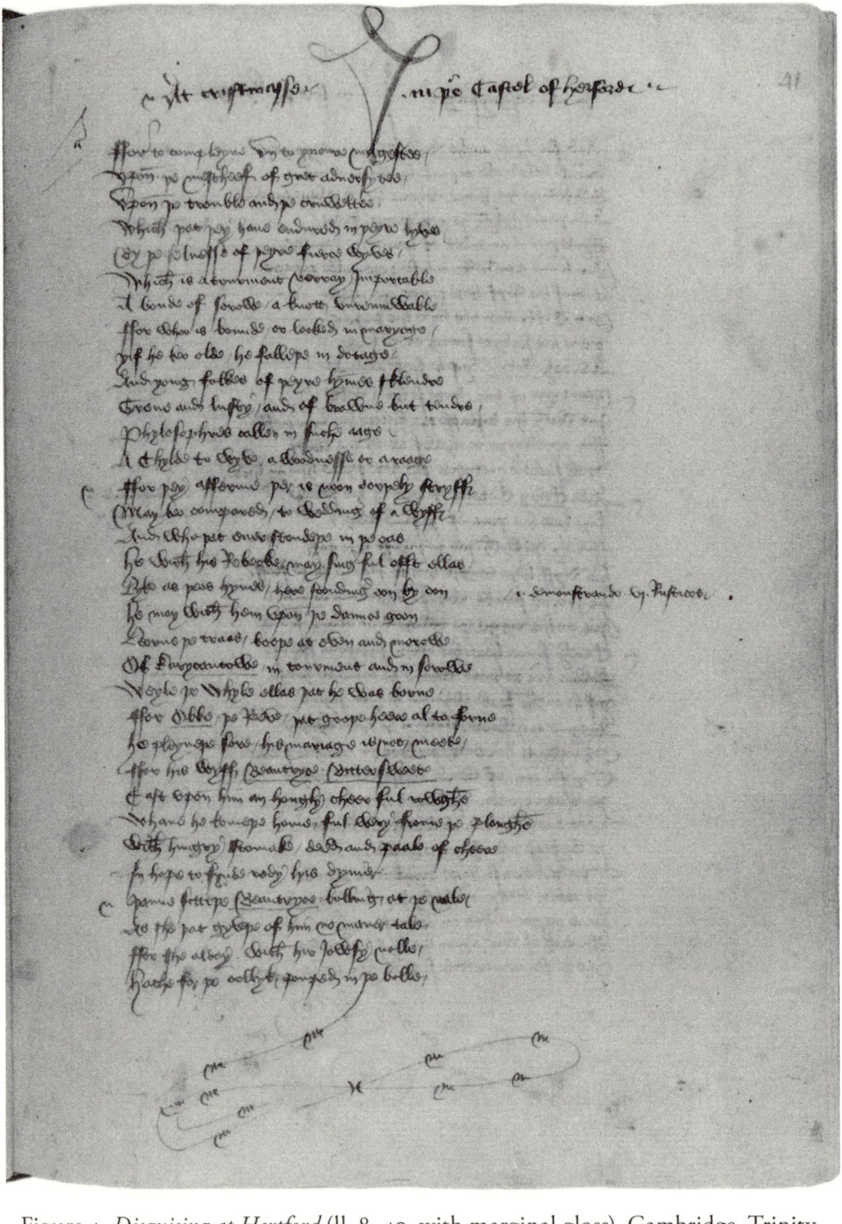

Figure 4. *Disguising at Hertford* (ll. 8–40, with marginal gloss). Cambridge, Trinity College Library MS R.3.20, p. 41. By permission of the library.

of female dominance over men, reiterating the request of the husbands that the king intercede on their behalf. The six wives, being "of oon acorde" (l. 164), are then allowed to reply, in words spoken by the presenter or perhaps by one spokeswoman. The women defend themselves by refuting their husbands' claim to mastery over them, asserting that in fact by ancient custom women traditionally rule over men. The women conclude by asking the king to take their side and to affirm those customary gender hierarchies. The disguising closes with the king's reply, conveyed via the presenter, who cautions against "þe paryll of hasty iugement" (l. 222) and advises reserving judgment until "þer beo made examynacyoun / Of oþer partye, and inquysicyoun" (ll. 225–26).[33] Taking this advice, the king rules that for the next year the women will continue their present behavior, until he discovers a reason why men should have sovereignty over their wives. The disguising ends by cautioning men to beware of the perpetual prison known as marriage, even when that prison is painted in azure or gold—an obvious allusion to the colors of the French royal arms and a sly warning to Catherine or any of her suitors.

Despite the *Disguising at Hertford*'s invocation of rituals of misrule and festive inversion in its portrayal of hen-pecked husbands and shrewish wives—an inversion intensified by the symbolic invasion of the royal household by rustics (even if those rustics are disguised household members)—its overall thrust affirms, rather than negates, a traditionally classed and gendered social structure. While the disguising seems to indulge peasants by offering them an airing of their complaints, that indulgence is at every turn constrained by the presenter who speaks for the peasant men and by the king who hands down judgment on them. Introduced primarily as comic entertainment, the peasantry is represented in entirely stereotyped ways that reinforce, rather than revise, class divisions. Plebeian culture is used in the disguising to shore up authority as an imaginary popular culture of commoners is made available to be manipulated by elites. Similarly, although the king's deferral of judgment seems to favor the wives, a normative gender order is in fact maintained. Not only do the peasant men have the first word and the boy-king the last, effectively bracketing the wives' response, but the wives' self-defense is itself part of a stock comic repertoire, drawn from a variety of sources, including the Wife of Bath, who is explicitly mentioned in the disguising. In all of these ways, the women's complaints and their desired reversal of gender hierarchies are mocked and undercut within the disguising under the guise of a return to tradition. At the same time, the young age of Henry, who is asked to adjudicate the complaint brought to him by the men, seems appropriate for the disguising's inversionary actions, recalling as it does boy-bishop ceremonies in which role reversal was the hinge on which the ritual turned.[34]

The choice of locale for the disguising's sentiments is worth noting in the context of gender relations. Even though the disguising refers to Hertford as Henry's castle (l. 3), it was in fact in Catherine's possession, the manor of Hertford having been previously held in dower by Queen Joan (it later passed to Margaret of Anjou, then to Elizabeth Woodville and Princess Mary).[35] Hertford was thus associated with queens, not kings. As a venue for this disguising, Hertford might have served as a silent reminder of Catherine's relative economic independence as well as of her control over her son, who was at Hertford as her guest. Such a reminder might in turn have given immediacy to the disguising's mixed messages about female sovereignty.

It seems fair to say that questions about female power might well have been in the air during the Christmas season of 1427, given that it would not be inaccurate to view the royal household for most of the 1420s as female dominated. Dowager queens typically lived in seclusion from the royal court and its affairs (as in all likelihood Catherine would have, too, had circumstances at the time of her husband's death been different), but given her son's infancy and Henry V's deathbed wishes, Catherine's domestic arrangements were such that until around 1427, she lived with her son and contributed funds toward his household expenses, while also maintaining her own separate residences at Leicester, Hertford, Wallingford, and Waltham to which the king sometimes traveled.[36] The effect of these arrangements was to thrust Catherine much more centrally into the king's household than would otherwise have been the case.

Besides accompanying her son on public occasions, Catherine had nearly constant access to him in private until the late 1420s, and her presence at court meant that she had a direct role in his upbringing. Additionally, many of those who served the king—many of whom were women—had ties to Catherine and served at her recommendation, enabling her to extend her influence.[37] In addition to his nurses, among them his chief nurse Joan Asteley, Henry had a governess, Alice Botiller, who had served Catherine when Henry V was alive and who was expert in "courtesy and nurture." Botiller seems to have played a large role in the household and apparently offered advice on how Henry's household funds should be spent.[38] This female milieu presented an obvious contrast with the normal state of affairs in which a king was surrounded almost exclusively by men. For a few years in the 1420s, then, the gender politics of the royal household were effectively reversed, with women occupying the most central positions nearest the king's person while men were relegated to the margins.

By Christmas of 1427, however, the date of the Hertford disguising, the circle of women surrounding Henry VI in private was being displaced by a new all-male inner group. Richard Beauchamp, the earl of Warwick, was appointed Henry's tutor on 1 June 1428, and the Oxford- and Cambridge-trained scholar John Somerset became Warwick's assistant.[39] Four knights of the body and four esquires of the body were also summoned to take up duties about Henry's person; these were in addition to the fatherless nobles who, with their *magisters*, had been invited to be resident in the king's household since 1425. As more and more men were recruited to serve him, his household, which had been small, started to grow, its cost rising from about 660 pounds per year in 1423–25 to 1,000 pounds in 1427–28 (Catherine's contribution in 1427–28 amounted to over 2,500 pounds).[40]

As her son was increasingly encircled by men, Catherine's position grew more tenuous. It is worth stressing once again the anomaly of her situation: no other queen of England had been widowed so young and remained at court (one was sent home; others were older). So long as she could play the part of maternal protector of the infant king, Catherine could be accommodated by—and made useful to—the existing structures of power without much difficulty. When she no longer fit that role, she became a more disturbing proposition, especially since if she contracted another marriage and had other children, she might endanger the paths of accession to the throne. In the mid-1420s, there were apparently rumors of her sexual involvements that played on these fears: one chronicle states that she was "unable fully to curb her carnal passions," and another suggests that she contemplated marrying Edmund Beaufort, Henry V's cousin.[41] No contemporary source remarks on her alliance with Owen Tudor, a Welshman who had been an esquire of Henry V's household, so it is unclear to what degree her affair with him was public, but by the late 1420s, she had apparently entered into a sexual relationship with him that would, by the time of her death in 1437, result in four children and become an open secret.[42] In seeming response to these rumors, a petition of the commons in parliament in 1426 interceded on Catherine's behalf, asking that hindrances to her remarriage be abolished. The petition was rejected but gave rise to a parliamentary statute introduced in 1427–28 proclaiming that anyone who married a dowager queen without the king's permission would forfeit his lands and possessions during his lifetime and that the king could give permission only after he came of age.[43]

In this context, the disguising performed at Hertford can be seen to walk a fine line between condemning and affirming female desire. Its choice of deferral as the king's response (a device reminiscent of the ending of Chaucer's *Parliament of Fowls*) is a noncommittal gesture that also offers a cautionary signal to Catherine and perhaps to potential suitors as well: go too far in the upcoming year and judgment will turn against you. If this signal reached its target, it must have seemed a pointed reversal. In 1425, Catherine had been asked to act as arbiter in Gloucester's quarrel with Bedford, and now, just two years later, she is presented with a performance in which her son is offered a similar role and she becomes the offending party whose unruly behavior must be restrained.[44] Whatever its actual (and ultimately unknowable) intent or impact, the *Disguising at Hertford* strongly suggests that women's wishes have to be denied, at least when they run up against male authority.

The *Mumming at Eltham*: The Claims of Happiness

The *Mumming at Eltham* presents an about-face: the antics of rustics that had been expressed in colloquial couplets in the Hertford disguising are now rendered in formal rhyme-royal stanzas, misogynist sentiments are now replaced by conventional homage, and the whole performance is staged in the king's, not the queen's, castle. Shirley's headnote describes the entertainment as "a balade made by daun Iohn Lidegate at Eltham in Cristmasse, for a momyng tofore þe kyng and þe Qwene." The year 1424 has been suggested as the date of the mumming, as has 1425, a year when Henry VI was known to have spent Christmas at Eltham, but 1428 is also a possibility and fits better with Lydgate's career and with the concerns expressed in the mumming.[45] Now in ruins, the king's castle of Eltham was then a fortress-like structure about two miles southeast of Greenwich often visited at Christmas by the three Henrys; its banquet hall—in which, according to Froissart, parliament sometimes met—was a suitable venue for the theatrical performances that would have formed part of the holiday entertainments during a royal visit.[46]

The *Mumming at Eltham* consists of twelve rhyme-royal stanzas introducing Bacchus, Juno, and Ceres, who preside over a gift-giving ceremony during which a group of local merchants ("marchandes þat here be," l. 5) apparently presented Henry and Catherine with wine, wheat, and oil, while the verses of the mumming were read aloud by a narrator or presenter. The first seven stanzas explain the symbolism of the gifts, with pointed reference to present political circumstances, hinting at concern over current unrest, while predicting for Henry a glorious future as a consequence of these gifts. Thus, for example, it is promised that the gift of olive oil, a symbol of peace, will help end the war of his "rebelles, " presumably the French, "wheche beon now reklesse" (l. 24) and will bring Henry acclaim throughout the two king-doms of France and England. Similarly, the mumming announces that Juno will bring Henry fame and protect him against "mescreantes in actes mar-cyal" (l. 39), while Ceres will supply provisions wherever the king rides so that he will lack for nothing. How much of this would have registered with the youthful Henry is hard to say; presumably, these sentiments would have had a greater impact on adult spectators, for whom the promise of divine protection for the king would have been a welcome prospect and the vision of Henry's glorious future a soothing balm for inevitable fears about the young king's chances for success in a precarious political situation.

After seven stanzas directed to Henry, the mumming turns its attention to Catherine. Her lineage and thus her importance as corporeal symbol of the Lancastrian claim to France is invoked as she is described as "borne of Saint Lowys blood" (l. 52). Likewise, her widowhood and her status as living legacy of Henry V are alluded to as she is offered comfort in the form of gifts designed to relieve her of sorrow—"texyle awaye al hevynesse" (l. 65)—and to increase her joy and "gladnesse of hert" year by year (l. 63). The gods also present her with peace, unity, plenty, and abundance, as well as prosperity throughout her life. She is promised "moost excellent ricchesse, / Loue of al people, grounded in stablenesse" (ll. 68–69) and "foulsomnesse, / Frome yeere to yeere in your court tabyde" (ll. 71–72); adversity is to be no menace, and care and sorrow will be forever banished.[47]

From one perspective, there is nothing unusual about the Eltham mum-ming: it is a conventional mixture of homage, praise, veiled advice, and wish-ful thinking offered by subjects to their sovereign and as such is appropriate to the holiday occasion. Nor is the treatment of Catherine at all out of the ordinary: she is addressed after her son and at less length, in a position clearly subordinate to the young king. But certain features of the mumming, and of both Lydgate's and Catherine's situations, suggest more than a secondary, accessory role for Catherine—in fact, Catherine, with Lydgate's collusion, might have been using the mumming in an attempt to strengthen her posi-tion at court.

Although there is no conclusive evidence that Lydgate wrote the *Mumming at Eltham* at Catherine's request, it would not be surprising if he had, given the frequency with which his works were commissioned by women. Like other East Anglian monks, including Osbern Bokenham and John Capgrave, Lydgate wrote not just for men but for women as well.[48] One of his patrons was Margaret, Lady Talbot, later Countess of Shrewsbury, for whom he wrote *Guy of Warwick* (Margaret claimed to be descended from the legendary Guy). Another was Isabella, third wife of the earl of Warwick, for whom he translated "The Fifteen Joyes of Oure Lady." Lydgate also provided verses for nonaristocratic women, including Lady Sibille Boys of Holm Hale in Norfolk, to whom he apparently directed the "Epistle to Sibille" and the "Treatise for Lavenders."[49] Some years before scripting the *Mumming at Eltham*, Lydgate composed a poem on the occasion of Humphrey, duke of Gloucester's marriage to Jacqueline of Hainault in 1422—the poem's theme is marital love and harmony as a microcosm for peace and national good fortune, and it recalls Henry V's marriage to Catherine as an ideal of this sort of happy political union.[50] More to the point, Lydgate had already, according to John Shirley, written a poem at "Þe commaundement of þe Quene Kateryn as in here sportes she wallkyd by the medowes that were late mowen in the monthe of Iulij." The poem, "That now is Hay some-tyme was Grase," which was apparently written in 1424, offered consolation to Catherine on the death of her husband, using the theme of mutability to emphasize the transitory nature of earthly life in contrast with celestial permanence.[51]

Whether the *Mumming at Eltham* was similarly created at the explicit request of Catherine and in order to offer her comfort, it undeniably takes special pains to address her and to include her within its ritual gift giving, extending to her the symbolic assets that could be acquired through such ceremonies. Catherine is pointedly not treated in an admonitory way in this mumming, as she might have been in the Hertford disguising, but rather is set up as an active agent who can garner its ideological rewards, rewards bestowed through its inscribed gift giving. Christmas and Easter were traditional times of royal largesse and almsgiving, often on a grand scale: Richard II, for example, is said to have distributed with his own hand four pence each to 12,040 paupers at Easter when he was staying at the palace of the archbishop of York.[52] But as the *Mumming at Eltham*'s presentation of gifts to the king and queen suggests, holiday gift giving was also often reciprocal and in this instance may have involved actual merchants, perhaps from nearby, who stepped forward during the mumming to present their gifts of wheat, wine, and oil.

As Rosemary Horrox observes, towns used the visit of any influential person as a chance to curry favor via gifts, usually of wine and foodstuffs, to the lord, his family, his affinity, and his household servants.[53] Peter Greenfield has shown how holiday entertainments in large households were tied to this system of gift giving designed to strengthen reciprocal relations. Greenfield argues that local inhabitants often came to the lord's manor to perform plays and dances at holidays, offering those performances as symbolic gifts and gestures of obeisance but also as timely reminders of the lord's duty toward them and of the mutual interdependence of sovereign and subject. Folk performances at manors were thus, in Greenfield's view, part of an intricate network of material and symbolic bonds linking lord and subjects.[54] From this perspective, the *Mumming at Eltham* can be seen as an attempt to represent and hence shape social and material relations between local townspeople (represented by the merchants who are referred to in the mumming) and the royal household, including Catherine. The *Mumming at Eltham* enhances Catherine's power by bringing her into the orbit of extramural reciprocal relations, which it accomplishes by making her a recipient of the merchants' gifts on terms nearly equal to her son.

The mumming also seems designed to strengthen internal relations between Catherine and the royal household. Although it is possible that not just the merchants bearing gifts but all performers in the Eltham mumming were locals, as Greenfield argues such performers often were, it is more likely that the performers, especially those playing the roles of the gods, were members of the household, perhaps of the chapel royal (men and boy choristers who were resident in the household). No external evidence has been discovered to show that chapel members performed in disguisings before Henry VII's reign, but Suzanne Westfall believes it is possible that they participated in Lydgate's mummings, which required large casts of men and women (presumably boys dressed as women, but see John Blacman's description of Henry VI's response to half-naked women in another Christmas entertainment).[55] In this regard, it is suggestive that two of Lydgate's poems, according to Shirley, were written specifically for the chapel royal; Richard Green has also suggested that Lydgate himself was a member of Henry V's chapel.[56] Because household revels integrated many types of entertainers and entertainments, they were less likely to use the service of itinerant players, Westfall argues, instead requiring in-house performers who would be available at the right moment and could rehearse ahead of time.[57] Chapel members would be the most convenient source of such performers. We do not know the number of chapel members in the 1420s, but the *Black Book* records that later in the century Edward IV employed thirty-seven chapel members, eight of them children.[58] Moreover, there is evidence that Henry VI's household contained semi-professional performers, such as his minstrel, Richard Geffrey, who was mentioned by name in 1424.[59] There were also London entertainers present at Eltham in 1425 and 1426; if they were in attendance in 1428, Westfall's claim about the use of in-house performers in household revels suggests that they did not perform in Lydgate's mumming, instead presenting their own entertainments.[60]

The household, as historians have shown, was the central institution of late medieval England and ranged in size from a modest ménage of just a few servants up to the king's household, which could have 500 members or more.[61] Organized "not horizontally but in depth," as E. F. Jacob reminds us, the great household was a microcosm of the various social classes; it was also, however, the privileged locale of the aristocratic community and the center of a group ethos.[62] Chris Given-Wilson has argued that a great household was less a place than a community; not confined to one specific architectural structure, it was instead a loosely united and peripatetic assemblage of individuals brought together to serve an aristocrat's person and property.[63] The aristocrat, in turn, was expected to support his or her retainers, providing food and shelter and inspiring loyalty through wages, gifts, properties, feasts, and entertainments. Joachim Bumke has emphasized the "occasional" nature of the medieval court, arguing that courtly culture manifested itself only on ceremonial occasions that were then documented in literary texts and visual images.[64] Often itinerant and moving among various locations, the "court," as Malcolm Vale has similarly argued, was essentially an event or a grand occasion and displayed itself chiefly through its rituals and ceremonies; ritual, luxury, and display in a court setting conveyed messages about power, the role of devotional religion, and appropriate forms of behavior.[65] For the aristocrat at the center of such a court and household, holiday theater was, in Westfall's words, "a means to secure the loyalty of his domestic army, a loyalty that both reflected and reinforced the patron's political and economic power."[66]

Within the privileged space of the household, the Christmas mumming at Eltham might have functioned as an example of what Wickham describes as the "theatre of direct address" projected at a particular audience and, more specifically, at a particular person in that audience.[67] Speaking to the young Henry and his mother, the actors in the *Mumming at Eltham* performed their dumbshow of gift giving, thereby reassuring Catherine of her importance to them and, by extension, to the household members asked to look on, enjoy, and tacitly endorse the mumming's sentiments. By settling Catherine in a position clearly secondary to the king, who receives eight stanzas of address compared to her four, the mumming puts her in her place, so to speak. At the same time, however, the mumming recognizes and endorses her claims to happiness, linking her prosperity explicitly with the king's. Perhaps this is merely Lydgate's kindhearted affection for a bereaved queen, but perhaps it is also an assertion of Catherine's power. Given Catherine's anomalous and tenuous situation at court, she might well have sought the strategic use of every means at her disposal, including household entertainments, to strengthen her position. In this regard, the final stanza is especially pointed, as it addresses first Henry and then his mother and links the two as joint recipients of the gifts brought by the mummers. By joining Catherine with Henry, the stanza emphasizes the importance of her role at court and in the monarchy: she is, at least in the space of the performance, on an equal footing with her son, the country's ruler, and hence is elevated to the highest symbolic status.

The *Mumming at Windsor*: The Limits of Power

If the Eltham mumming can be read as a bid for ascendancy on the part of Catherine, with the collusion of Lydgate, then the Windsor mumming signals the limits of that bid. The *Mumming at Windsor* registers Catherine's elision from any kind of equal consideration with her son, while presenting her with a new but decidedly offstage role—that of mythical supporter of the Lancastrian dynasty. Although the *Mumming at Windsor* is undated, it was almost certainly performed at Windsor Castle during the Christmas of 1429 just after the eight-year-old Henry VI had been crowned king of England and just before he was to leave for Paris to be crowned king of France.[68] The mumming was thus produced at precisely the moment when Henry was being thrust into full political power and when Catherine was being relegated to much diminished authority and greater invisibility. The mumming does not directly address Catherine, and Shirley's headnote never mentions her, but it is likely that she was present for the performance, as she had been for

her son's coronation earlier that year. In what can be seen as a strategic displacement of Catherine, the mumming dramatizes the story of St. Clotilda,
who spurred the conversion of France in Clovis's time, a story in which a
woman is portrayed as a supporter of male rule. This story merges with the
mumming's fairly obvious attempt to legitimize Henry's claim to the French
throne, presenting him as by right next in line to wear the fleur-de-lis and to
be anointed from the same ampulla as Clovis was. Not incidentally, the story
also rather deftly and once and for all solves the problem of what to do with
Catherine, by implicitly offering her a Clotilda-like role.[69]

The Windsor mumming consists of fourteen rhyme-royal stanzas spoken
by a narrator or presenter, which describe the actions and meanings of the
"story of þe flour delys" that follows.[70] As presented by Shirley, this story is
explicitly gendered male, despite the inclusion within it of Clotilda: Shirley's
headnote does not mention the queen as being present or as a recipient of the
mumming, nor do the running titles, which refer only to the legendary dynastic story of how the ampulla and fleur-de-lis "came to the kynges of Ffraunce"
(see Figure 5). Addressed to Henry, the mumming recounts how "oure" realm
of France (l. 4) was converted when Clovis was encouraged to abandon his
idols by Clotilda, whose "parfyt lyf," "stedfast hoope," and "conuersacyoun
moost contemplatyff" (ll. 23–25) led to the adoption of Christianity throughout France. The mumming is full of praise for Clotilda, "þe hooly qweene"
and "floure of wommanheed" (ll. 45–46), in whom is to be found "entier dili-
gence" and who is "devoyded of slouthe and necglygence" (ll. 60–61). "Loo
what grace dooþe in wymmen shyne," the narrator exclaims (l. 53).[71] As a result of Clotilda's actions, Clovis is given the fleur-de-lis, is baptized, and then
is anointed from an ampulla sent from Heaven by a dove; the ampulla is still
kept at Rheims, the narrator says, to anoint the kings of France, including
Henry VI, "þat nowe sitteþe here" (l. 84).

Since Henry VI's hasty coronation in 1429 was a direct response to the
fall of Orléans and the impact of Joan of Arc,[72] the woman who had so effectively rallied French forces against the English and enabled the crowning of Charles VII, the mumming's emphasis on female support of male
rulers stands as a creative reworking of actual events, turning to a legendary woman to counter the more immediate, militarized one who came to
the aid of the wrong (in Lancastrian eyes at least) male ruler. In one sense,
then, the mumming uses an imagined history to further current political
ends, employing Clotilda as Henry's counter-muse to Charles's maid of
Orléans.

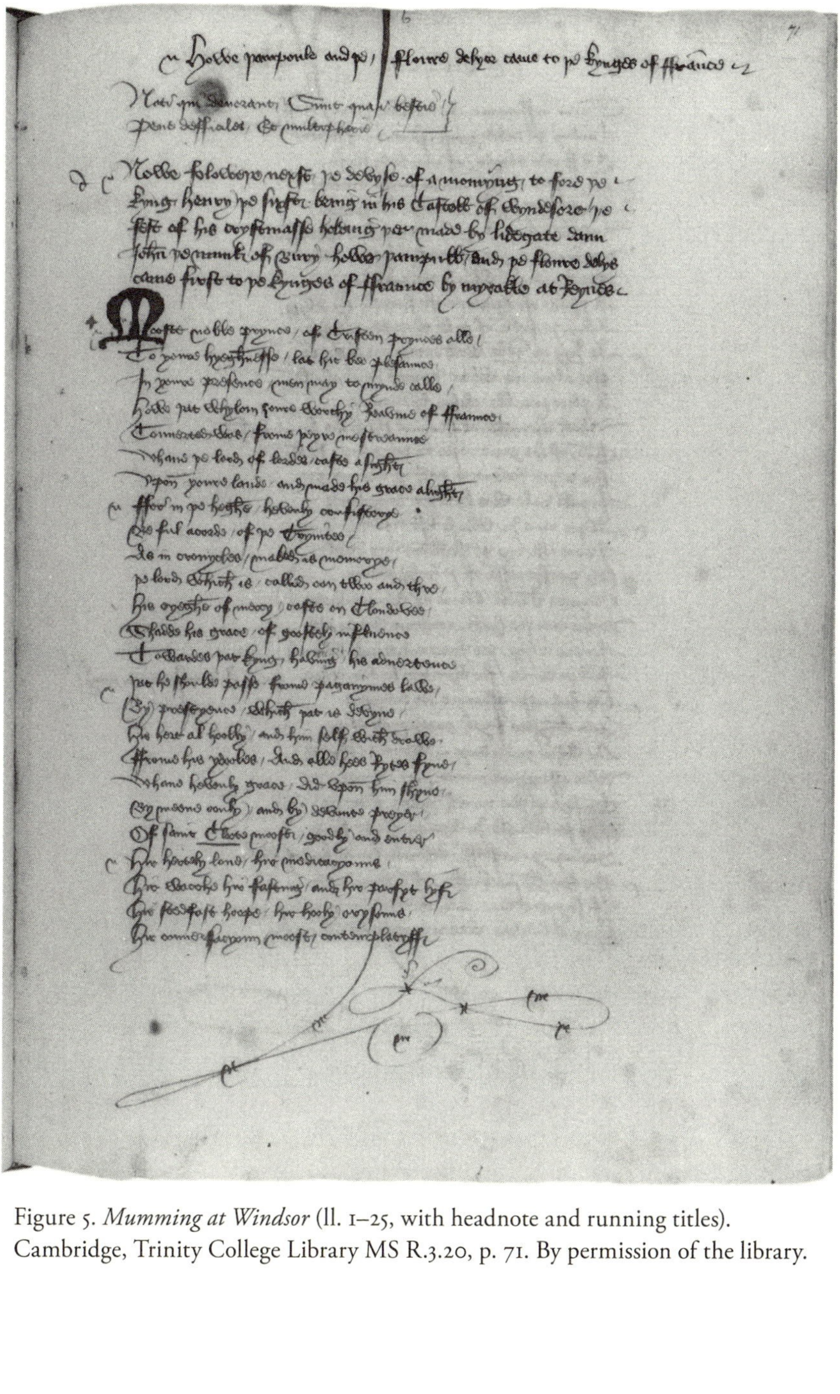
Holde pamfoule and þe / fflowre delyce came to þe kynges of ffraunce

Nowe folowepe nexst þe devyse of a mommyng to fore þe kyng henry þe sixst beinge in his Castell of wyndesore þe fest of his Crystmasse holdinge þer made by lidegate daun John þe monk of Bury howe pampull and þe floure delys came first to þe kynges of ffraunce by myrakle at Reyns.

Moste noble prynce of Cristen prynces alle
To youre hyeghnesse lat hit bee plesaunce
In youre presence men may to mynde calle
Howe þat whylom youre worthy Realme of ffraunce
Converted was from þeyre mescreaunce
Whane þe lord of lordes caste a sight
Upon youre lande and made his grace alight
ffor in þe hooly hevenly consistorye
As hit accordeþ of þe Trynitee
As in cronycles made is memorye
þe lord which is called oon and thre
his eyeghe of mercy caste on Clowdovee
Shadde his grace of gostly influence
Towardes þat kyng havinge his advertence
þat he sholde passe from paganysmes lawe
By þe prudence which þat is dyvyne
his herte al hooly and him self withdrawe
ffrome his erreures And also hees lyves fyne
Whane hevenly grace did upon him shyne
By meenes oonly and by devoute prayer
Of saint Clotild mooste goodly and entier
hir hooly lyf hir meditacyouns
hir wacches hir fastinge and hir parfyt lyfe
hir stedfast hope hir hooly orysouns
hir contemplacyoun mooste contemplatyffe

Figure 5. *Mumming at Windsor* (ll. 1–25, with headnote and running titles). Cambridge, Trinity College Library MS R.3.20, p. 71. By permission of the library.

Again, however, the mumming's range extends beyond Henry. Once more, Lydgate creates a performance that speaks to Catherine's situation, in this instance envisioning for her a new role in relation to her son. The mumming's emphasis on female virtue and omnipotence employed to authorize male rule comes, tellingly, at what was a crisis point in Catherine's own relations with masculine rule. In the story of Clotilda's aid to Clovis, a new narrative about Catherine's position vis-à-vis her son is constructed in which Catherine is made this time a tool, rather than victim or active agent, of Lancastrian ambitions. In this mumming, we can see Catherine being re-created as a quasi-mythic enabler of her son's kingship, her sexuality diffused into the role of a nonthreatening muse. It is not known whether Catherine accompanied her son on his coronation trip to France, although given her ties to that country, she would undoubtedly have been a valuable asset, especially since contemporary chronicles' lack of mention of her affair with Owen Tudor suggests that it was not yet widely known outside court. We do know that Catherine sat near Henry at his coronation in Westminster on 6 November 1429 and was apparently still living in his household and contributing to its expenses at least through 1430, but this intimacy appears to have ended after Henry's return from France in 1431.[73]

What the *Mumming at Windsor* demonstrates is a process of displacement and refashioning in which Catherine is removed from her position as visible supporter of the king in her own person and is replaced by the image of woman as mythic ally of male rulers. The real Catherine thus dissolves into an imaginary construct, a construct that, in all likelihood, was far more manageable than Catherine herself had proven to be over the course of the 1420s. No longer centrally important to her son's welfare now that he has been crowned king, and for that reason no longer much of a perceived threat, Catherine is repositioned in the Windsor mumming's triumphalist imagery as a legendary presence hovering on the edges of courtly culture.

Despite the indeterminacy that attaches to all cultural forms, especially those from the distant past, Lydgate's royal entertainments reveal a good bit about the queen's position within late medieval ceremonial culture and, more specifically, about Catherine's changing fortunes. Unlike the royal entries and processions that publicly represented royal power, household performances like Lydgate's holiday enactments were socially exclusive: those who participated or watched were among the privileged granted entrance to the royal hall or chamber. Their audience was not the city, the nation, or the commons but rather a coterie of elites and their affinities. Whatever ideological work royal disguisings and mummings performed, it was directed at this inner group, who would recognize their display of hierarchical sociability and forms of acquiescence to patterns of political organization. But like other rituals of conviviality, such performances exposed social tensions as well. Lydgate's holiday entertainments tackle the difficult problem of integrating an irregular individual into the group, as Catherine is accommodated in various ways within structures of masculine rule. Over the course of the 1420s, Catherine was refashioned by Lydgate from symbol of conquest and unity, to producer of a dynasty, to unattached and sexually threatening woman, to nurturing mother of an infant regent (with overtones of the Virgin and child), and finally to nonessential but symbolically useful accessory.

Performance is of course but one resource among many for the negotiation and production of social meaning, but in the still predominantly oral and public culture of medieval England, it was an especially important one. We have no way of knowing with any certainty the outcome of Lydgate's royal disguising and mummings. But they strongly suggest that the queen's accessory role within late medieval ceremonial culture was not always passively accepted or acquiesced to. Within the space of the royal household, Lydgate's dumbshows for the queen offer glimpses of the manipulation of cultural symbols and of the struggle to come to terms with Catherine's anomalous position.

As they address Catherine, the royal disguising and mummings offer evidence of her involvement in courtly entertainments. Other women at court participated in or watched performances and were at times the subjects of their own royal entries. While the evidence is sparse, enough exists to suggest that the involvement of women in dramatic enactments extended beyond the court. Women were in the audience during performances of urban cycle plays, as the famous example of Margery Kempe's attendance at the York play shows.[74] They authored plays, as witness the canoness Hrotswitha of Gandersheim (c. 935–73), the abbess Hildegard of Bingen (1089–1179), and Katherine of Sutton, abbess of the English convent at Barking from 1363 to 1376. They sponsored and helped produce plays: at Chester, the "wurshipfful Wyffys" put on an Assumption play, and the play of St. Catherine was commissioned and staged by a wealthy woman in Metz in 1468. They were paid for providing food, drink, and cloth for performances. They helped with scripts: Chester's Coopers' guild in 1574–75 paid a woman to make a performance copy of their play from a master text. They even played roles in dramas or joined in processions and tableaux. They were clearly also important as subjects of and characters in medieval plays, religious and secular.[75]

Women were also patrons and readers of literary works, commissioning poems and owning, using, and bequeathing books. Whether Catherine herself ever read the texts of the performances that were presented to her and her son is unknown, but women would presumably have been among the readers in the Beauchamp household whom Shirley envisioned as his primary readership for the anthology, Trinity MS R.3.20, into which he copied the Hertford, Eltham, and Windsor entertainments. And some of those women would surely have seen the original performances. While Lydgate crafted a "bille," "balade," and "devyse" for the court, Shirley's copies, as earlier chapters of this study have argued, transformed them into poetic texts available for private reading, including by women. In so doing, he flattened or failed to record most features of the live performance, beyond the words that were presumably spoken aloud in the course of the enactment. In entering the written archive, Lydgate's contributions to the royal entertainments shed most traces of the live performance repertoire of which they were once a part—but not all. Especially for Shirley's primary audience, the performance genre would have shaped the reading experience, helped along by Shirley's headnotes with their reminders of the original festive occasion for which the texts were written and by features of the texts themselves that would have encouraged performative reading. How long the specificity of the historical context, particularly the context surrounding Catherine, lasted beyond the occasion of the original performances we cannot say. But perhaps some readers recalled the queen's dilemmas as they read Shirley's copies and, in so doing, also remembered the resolutions offered, however tentatively, by Lydgate's royal disguising and mummings.

CHAPTER 8

On Drama's Trail

This book began with John Shirley and the evidence his copies—and especially their headnotes—provided about the essential questions related to theater history: authorship, patrons, locations, dates, media, and performance practices. It ends with verses that are exactly the opposite of what Shirley's hand gave us: these verses come with no hints about authorship, patrons, or any of the other things that would allow us to say who wrote them, on what occasion, and for what audience they were performed, if indeed they were ever performed at all. While Chapter 1 delighted in a plenitude of information, the present chapter grapples with a dearth of knowledge. By ending this book with an examination of verses not linked to Shirley, verses not even definitively associated with Lydgate, and verses for which the performance context remains murky, I extend my argument about Lydgate's importance for theater history to a larger consideration of the challenges faced by anyone who studies early theater. The scribal work of John Shirley is part of what makes Lydgate's surviving body of verses for performances so useful for scholars of premodern drama, but as this chapter will demonstrate, so too and even more fundamentally are the editorial decisions that ascribe authorship, establish and reproduce texts, and identify dates and venues. To a large degree, such interventions are what create a canon and thus make a body of texts available for readers and critics, as has been happening for medieval English drama from the sixteenth century onward.

No one disputes the importance of Cambridge, Trinity College Library MS R.3.19, a miscellany of verses and one prose piece produced in the London area between 1478 and 1483, for early English poetry.[1] Twenty-one Middle English verse texts are unique to it, and it contains eight almost unique texts whose only other surviving copies are in manuscripts written by the working partner (the so-called Hammond scribe) of the main scribe of R.3.19 or by John Stow.[2] Trinity MS R.3.19 was used by Wynkyn de Worde around 1498 and by John Stow, who owned and wrote in the manuscript in the mid-sixteenth century, drawing on it for his 1561 edition of Chaucer.[3] In addition to its significance for the Chaucer canon, R.3.19 contains valuable information about the taste for advisory literature, about political and ethical concerns, and about the metropolitan interest in courtly literature; it also includes what appears to be the rare occurrence of a courtly love poem written by a woman and thus is notable for what it says about gender and writing.[4] Even though R.3.19 is not an essential manuscript for Lydgate's poetry, it contains a number of his works, including extracts from the *Fall of Princes*, selections from his *Testament* and *Fables*, the poem "Horns Away," and a copy of *Bycorne and Chychevache*.

Although it has seldom been written about, the text in Trinity MS R.3.19 that is most crucial for the history of early drama is the first item in the first of the thirteen booklets that make up the manuscript, a unique copy of a twelve-stanza moralistic poem that has been printed by Carlton Brown and Rossell Hope Robbins as *A Mumming of the Seven Philosophers*.[5] A rubric at the top of the poem in the hand of the scribe who wrote the first booklet of the manuscript, and a number of the other booklets as well, reads *Festum Natalis Domini*; what follows are verses that appear to have been designed for performance on 25 December, to commemorate, as the first stanza notes, the "byrthe thys day" of Jesus (l. 2). The verses include what appear to be parts for nine actors (seven philosophers plus a "Nuncius" and a Christmas king) in a performance that would apparently have featured short speeches, mimed action, singing, and gift giving, if only of the intangible, advisory sort (see Figure 6).

Beginning with an opening stanza that establishes the occasion, an unnamed speaker, who is presumably the "Nuncius" of the last stanza, brings the greetings of Senek, "rewler of all wyldernesse" (l. 9) to his "brother" (l. 11), the King of Christmas, to explain the duties of the royal estate to which the Christmas king has been "so sodenly" called (l. 14) and to introduce him to "olde expert men" (l. 24) who will counsel him. In each of the following seven stanzas, a philosopher—who is unnamed except as "Primus Philosophus" in marginal rubrics—offers advice on not overreaching one's abilities, being moderate in spending, following the example of experienced men, ruling the body, obeying God, watching out for adverse fortune, being generous in old age, and making time for play and relaxation. The performance ends

with a concluding stanza spoken by the Nuncius, who advises the Christmas king to take the advice he has heard and then introduces a song by the philosophers.

It is notoriously difficult to uncover the motives that went into the making of most pre-1500 vernacular miscellanies of the "bespoke" period of manuscript production when books were produced on demand for specific owners, since such miscellanies are typically, in Ralph Hanna's words, "defiantly individual."[6] While R.3.19 shares that status, some useful clues can be teased out about its purposes and, more specifically, about the *Mumming of the Seven Philosophers*, particularly in relation to Lydgate. The mumming is unattributed and has never been linked to the Lydgate canon: when he had the manuscript in his possession, Stow added no marginal notes assigning the mumming to Lydgate, Henry MacCracken did not include it in his edition of Lydgate's minor poems, and while Rossell Hope Robbins commented that Lydgate was "especially active in writing" ceremonial entertainments, he stopped short of attributing this one to him.[7] Despite this seeming consensus, a case can be made—and will be made in this chapter—for assigning authorship to Lydgate and locating the performance venue in the court of Henry VI. In so doing, my aim is not to expand the Lydgate repertoire but instead to use the endeavor as a way of summing up this book's discussion of what Lydgate's performance pieces say about performance and writing before the age of print. As I hope to show, the *Mumming of the Seven Philosophers* crystallizes the complicated issues of authorship, representational forms, reception and transmission, manuscript contexts, and performance practices that I have addressed in this book, issues that are central to an understanding not just of Lydgate's involvement with ceremonial activities but also of early theater itself.

The Evidence for Lydgate's Authorship

Although its booklets do not contain many poems by Lydgate, the organization of Trinity MS R.3.19 hints at an interest in his works on the part of the scribe who copied the *Mumming of the Seven Philosophers*. R.3.19 is made up of thirteen booklets; although they show the hands of five fifteenth-century scribes as well as Stow, nine of them (booklets 1–4 and 6–10) were written by a single scribe (Scribe A).[8] The booklets may or may not have been bound together before the manuscript came into the possession of its first identifiable owner, George Wilmer, who matriculated from Trinity College in 1598.[9] Since the foliation of the manuscript shows that the quire of folios 154–69 is misbound and should follow folio 8, the first booklet would originally have contained the *Mumming of the Seven Philosophers*, extracts from Lydgate's *Testament* and the *Fall of Princes*, and *Bycorne and Chychevache*, along with various non-Lydgatean poems.[10] All other pieces by Lydgate in the manuscript are also in the hand of Scribe A, with the exception of a treatise on the seasons ascribed to Lydgate in a headnote (fols. 49r–52r), which is in the hand of Scribe B, and two of Lydgate's *Fables*, which Stow copied onto blank pages at the end of booklet 11 (fols. 235r–36r). From this evidence, it seems reasonable to conclude that the pieces by Lydgate that are included in R.3.19 are there thanks to the work of Scribe A.

Although Scribe A's identity remains unknown, he can be linked to other copyists of Lydgate's poetry, particularly the so-called Hammond scribe first identified by Eleanor Hammond and now credited with work on fourteen other manuscripts, who appears to have worked with Scribe A in a London scriptorium.[11] In addition to collaborating with Scribe A on Trinity MS R.3.21, a manuscript that contains works by Lydgate, the Hammond scribe was also responsible for thirteen other full or partial manuscripts or fragments, among them texts on heraldry and the duties of the earls marshal and constables of England, a medieval miscellany, documents concerning London and its guilds, the Statutes of the Realm, two copies of the *Canterbury Tales*, and two copies of the *Regement of Princes*.[12] More to the point for this chapter, the Hammond scribe worked on two Shirley-derived manuscripts, BL MS Add. 34360 and BL MS Harley 2251, which have similar contents. Linne Mooney observes that the workshop in which Scribe A and the Hammond scribe wrote must have had access "to a large and unique library of medieval English verse" that allowed them to produce manuscripts that contain the only surviving copies of so many Middle English texts. As various traces suggests, that library must have included John Shirley's manuscripts, which presumably passed to the workshop after his death in 1456.[13] The workshop was responsible for producing a unique copy of the long version of the *Pageant of Knowledge* (Trinity R.3.21), the only copies besides Shirley's (and later Stow's) of *Bycorne and Chychevache* (R.3.19 and Harley 2251), the *Procession of Corpus Christi* (Harley 2251), the *Sodein Fal of Princes* (Harley 2251), and a copy of the *Legend of St. George*.

What is especially important about Scribe A's association with the Hammond scribe is that it put him in the orbit of Shirley and therefore in the camp of a copyist who had a special interest in preserving and disseminating certain of Lydgate's poems. Anne Sutton and Livia Visser-Fuchs have identified the Hammond scribe as the stationer John Multon, who had links to John Vale.[14] Vale, owner of three or possibly four of the Hammond scribe's manuscripts, held roughly the same position as secretary and man of affairs for the draper Sir Thomas Cook (who was also Vale's father-in-law) as Shirley earlier had for the earl of Warwick. The many similarities Mooney has noted between Multon and Shirley would also apply to Scribe A and Shirley: both men wrote on paper in an age when many manuscripts were still on vellum, no manuscript of theirs is heavily decorated or illuminated, both had access to manuscripts of varied contents and sometimes to multiple exemplars of the same text, both were interested in history and had antiquarian leanings, and both had close ties to London mercantile society—Shirley through the family of his second wife and Multon through his ties to Vale and his connections to Cook.[15] All of this suggests that Scribe A, the copyist of the *Mumming of the Seven Philosophers*, was part of a group of Shirley-influenced copyists who shared a network of personal relations in and around London in the late fifteenth century.

The likely patterns of manuscript transmission also link R.3.19 to Shirley's circle of copyists and readers in London. Mooney believes that Shirley's three miscellanies as well as the Shirley-derived Harley 2251 and Add. 34360 made by Multon and Scribe A remained in circulation in the "same circle of London scribes, stationers, printers, and antiquarians with mercantile connections for a century after Shirley's death until they fell into Stow's hands, and thus both exemplars and copies survived together." These five "relatively inexpensive and undecorated paper miscellanies," Mooney argues, "owe their survival to their usefulness as exemplars for the book trade in London and their intrinsic interest to bibliophilic antiquarians in London in the century when many paper manuscripts were being discarded for the more 'modern' printed copies of the same texts."[16] It is therefore possible that the contents of these five manuscripts may have served as exemplars for some of the contents of other manuscripts produced in London in this same circle (e.g., R.3.19 and R.3.21, Lambeth Palace MS 306, Bodleian MS Fairfax 16, or BL MS Egerton 1995 or Harley 2255), as well as for Stow's own Harley 367 and Add. 29729. If Mooney is correct, then R.3.19 can also be placed in the context of these Shirlean London manuscripts.

That some of the contents of these manuscripts may have been used as exemplars can be seen in the twenty-six booklets of R.3.19 and R.3.21, which seem to have been written as separate units, for individual owners or for other purposes, as dirtied pages at the beginnings and endings of quires suggest, before eventually being bound together.[17] Because there is evidence of use by printers such as Caxton, Pynson, and de Worde, because they contain spaces for decoration and initials, and because they exist in single copies, Mooney speculates that some of the booklets of R.3.19 and R.3.21 may never have left the scriptoria in which they were made or the early print shops that acquired them but served as "shop copies" of Lydgate's and Chaucer's minor poems from which prospective buyers could choose, specifying what embellishments to add.[18] Some of the booklets may have been among the "paunflettis and bookys" that Caxton mentions having in his study and which he used as sources for his printed works.[19] Although Bradford Fletcher, relying heavily on the dating of the manuscript's foliation, makes a case for R.3.19's having been bound together with R.3.21 in their present form by about 1480, Mooney thinks that the twenty-six booklets of R.3.19 and R.3.21 remained separate well into the sixteenth century and were purchased individually by Stow from print shop stock or private owners—the tables of contents date from his ownership, and he liberally annotated both volumes with titles and authors' names; he may also have gathered the booklets together and foliated them or had his secretary do so.[20]

Before Stow, then, the first booklet of R.3.19 with its unique copy of the *Mumming of the Seven Philosophers* may have been freestanding and available for use by copyists or printers. Since the manuscript booklet was a unit of sale as well as of production, buyers could assemble anthologies tailored to their interests. If the first booklet of R.3.19 was privately owned, a likely candidate would be the mercer Roger Thorney (ca. 1450–1515), whose name appears in one booklet of R.3.21 and who provided manuscripts to Wynkyn de Worde, who printed *The Assembly of Gods* from R.3.19 in 1498. If Thorney did own R.3.19, as Fletcher suggests is possible, its next owner was probably his widow Eleanor's second husband, William Middleton, whom she married after Thorney's death in 1515 and whose name appears in three booklets of R.3.21. Although Fletcher notes that Middleton would have been the second owner, Felicity Riddy observes there is no reason to assume that Eleanor would not have used Thorney's books during his lifetime.[21] Certainly at least some of the contents of R.3.19 may have appealed to a female reader. It is possible, then, that Thorney and later his widow owned booklet 1 of R.3.19.

These fragments of manuscript evidence help us link the copyist of *Mumming of the Seven Philosophers* to the Shirley circle and to London in the later fifteenth century. They also allow us to hypothesize that the copyist had an ample library available to him but that he did not necessarily work in a commercial scriptorium since he apparently did not make multiple copies of the same text, as might be expected if he were working as a commercial copyist.[22] We can also assume that the extant booklets of R.3.19 that he wrote stayed in London, rather than being carried outside of the metropolis, where they would probably have been lost, as may have happened with other Shirlean exemplars and Shirley-derived copies.[23] We can further conjecture that Thorney may have owned some of the booklets in R.3.19. All of these pieces of information locate the *Mumming of the Seven Philosophers* in a context that would, if not specifically identify Lydgate as its author, at least tie it to copyists and owners who had a known affinity for Lydgate's writings.

The case for Lydgate's authorship of the mumming would be strengthened if we could tie it even more closely to Shirley, which encourages us to ask, did Scribe A use a Shirley exemplar for the *Mumming of the Seven Philosophers*? In the absence of Shirlean introductions and spellings, Mooney urges caution about assuming derivation from Shirley's manuscripts.[24] *Seven Philosophers* lacks an introduction or headnote, but there are other examples of a Shirley copy of a Lydgate text that lacks a headnote, perhaps because, as Margaret Connolly observes, Shirley was disinclined to add information about which he was not confident.[25] It is also possible that there once was a headnote, but it was lost or not copied by Scribe A; the version of *Bycorne and Chychevache* copied into R.3.19 by Scribe A also lacks a headnote, even though we know that a Shirlean headnote exists, since it appears on the version of the poem that Shirley copied into R.3.20. Moreover, like the *Mumming of the Seven Philosophers*, the version of *Bycorne and Chychevache* copied into R.3.19 by Scribe A is not attributed to Lydgate, although Stow later added both marginal notes and an attribution to rectify Scribe A's omission. Similarly, the selections from the *Fall of Princes* and the *Testament* that also appear in booklet 1 were not attributed to Lydgate, although their authorship is undisputed. Lack of a headnote, then, doesn't rule out the possibility of a Shirlean exemplar.

If Scribe A used a Shirley-derived exemplar for the *Mumming of the Seven Philosophers*, then we would expect to find traces of Shirley's characteristic spellings and use of language. Unfortunately, the linguistic evidence isn't definitive. A comparison of the forms used in the mumming with those noted in the dot maps of *A Linguistic Atlas of Late Mediaeval England* shows that the scribal dialect belongs to the Midlands area. "Shall" is always spelled with an initial *sh* (dot map 145), "though" is always spelled *though* (dot map

196), "then" is *than* (dot map 183), "them" is *hem* (dot map 40), the adverbial ending *–ly* is used consistently (dot map 608), "their" is *her* (dot map 52), the preferred usage for "are" is *be* (dot map 123), "it" is *hyt* (dot map 27), "high" is *hygh* (dot map 438), "both" is *both(e)* (dot map 368), and "not" is *nat* (dot map 276). The combination of these forms rules out the northern and southern provenances, but because they are fairly widely scattered across the Midlands, they do not help pinpoint the scribal dialect with much precision. More promising are the spellings *eny* for "any," which appears most often in the southwest Midlands (dot map 98), and the *yef* for "if," with its indication of an initial [j] sound and with a medial *e*, both of which forms predominate in the southwest Midlands area (dot maps 209 and 212), from which Shirley, if the language of his three miscellanies is any indication, came.[26] Those two spellings are the only evidence I can detect that might suggest the influence at an earlier stage of a southwest Midlands dialect, and that influence is offset by the absence of Shirley's most striking linguistic features, including the forms *beon*, *beo*, and *beope*, for which *Seven Philosophers* consistently uses *be*. As for Shirley's characteristic doublings of consonants, the poem contains some examples—*pepyll*, *counseyll*, *finissh*, *wyttes*, *mennys*, *lyberall*, *counseyll*, *ffolowe*, *ffuture*, and, most strikingly, the repeated spelling *ffor*.[27]

Given the lack of a headnote and the ambiguous evidence of Shirlean spellings and usages, derivation from a Shirley manuscript is far from conclusive. Yet the possibility of a Shirlean exemplar lurking somewhere in the background cannot be completely dismissed.

Even if the *Seven Philosophers* does not derive from a Shirlean copy, the case for Lydgate's authorship is not entirely undone. It is noteworthy that none of the poems in the thirteen booklets of R.3.19 as originally copied include authorial attributions, although attributions (some incorrect) were added later for a number of pieces.[28] Scribe A, or the exemplar from which he worked, appears in general to have been uninterested in assigning authorship and to have instead concentrated on transmitting the texts themselves. What this lack of attributions may say about copyists' and readers' tastes is a topic for another study, but certainly the implication is that Shirley's persistent concern with noting authorship is not evidenced in the booklets in R.3.19.

As for hints of Lydgate's own language and style, the evidence is mixed. In the area of word choice, there are some echoes of Lydgate's typical usages but also deviations. *Aduertyse* (ll. 59 and 80), meaning to pay attention to or consider, is one of Lydgate's favorites, but *regement* (l. 62) and *reiterate* (l. 2), the latter chiefly used in a technical or scientific sense, are not. The verses themselves are in rhyme royal, Lydgate's preferred form, and there are the echoes of Chaucer as we might expect from Lydgate (e.g., "out of old fields . . . / Cometh all these new cornes . . . ," ll. 22–23, which imitates the *Parliament of Fowls*), as well as gestures toward some of Lydgate's other poetry, including *Mesure Is Tresour* (see l. 40).

The most conclusive evidence for assigning *Seven Philosophers* to Lydgate is a note in a later hand at the top of folio 1r. The note, which reads "Poemata q[u]aedam Anglice Lidgati," postdates the fifteenth century and, like the "table of contents" that comes on an earlier folio, was probably written after the booklets had been assembled into their current form (see Figure 7).[29] One candidate for penner of that note is George Wilmer, who matriculated from Trinity College in 1598 (d. 1626) and who had the manuscript bound with his arms and donated it to Trinity College along with some thirty-seven other manuscripts. Fletcher notes that in the list of Wilmer's benefaction given in Trinity College's *Liber memorialis*, one of the volumes is described as "Opera quaedam Lidgati," "Poemata Lidgati vol. 2," or "Lidgati opera quaedam," which must refer to R.3.19.[30]

Although Scribe A didn't explicitly attribute *Seven Philosophers* to Lydgate, he seems to have thought of the mumming as forming a unit with the Lydgatean material that comes after it. The mumming is followed by ten stanzas drawn from Books III and IV of the *Fall of Princes* on the topic of chastity and good reputation for women and ends with a stanza from the Prologue to Book III that praises lords who reward and protect their servants; on folio 2r, before the *Fall* material, are eight stanzas from a love-lament ("Beauteuous braunche flour*e* of formosyte"), and another forty-two stanzas of the same lament follow the *Fall* selections. The mumming's offer of advice to princes and its emphasis on the need of rulers for good counsel "could have been culled from many sections of the *Fall*," as Nigel Mortimer notes, with the mumming warning "of the responsibilities of rule" and the material from the *Fall* being "used to examine one particular area of abuse—lust."[31] Although Mooney has shown that the intervening courtly love lyrics may well have been written by a woman and probably date from the late fourteenth century, and although the mumming ends with an "explicit" that signals its separateness as a poetic entity, Mortimer's argument about the scribe's sense of this opening material as forming a thematic unit centered on regiminal texts associated with Lydgate is nonetheless valid.[32]

Certainly, the themes and concerns of the *Mumming of the Seven Philosophers* are consistent with many of Lydgate's other didactic works. Like a

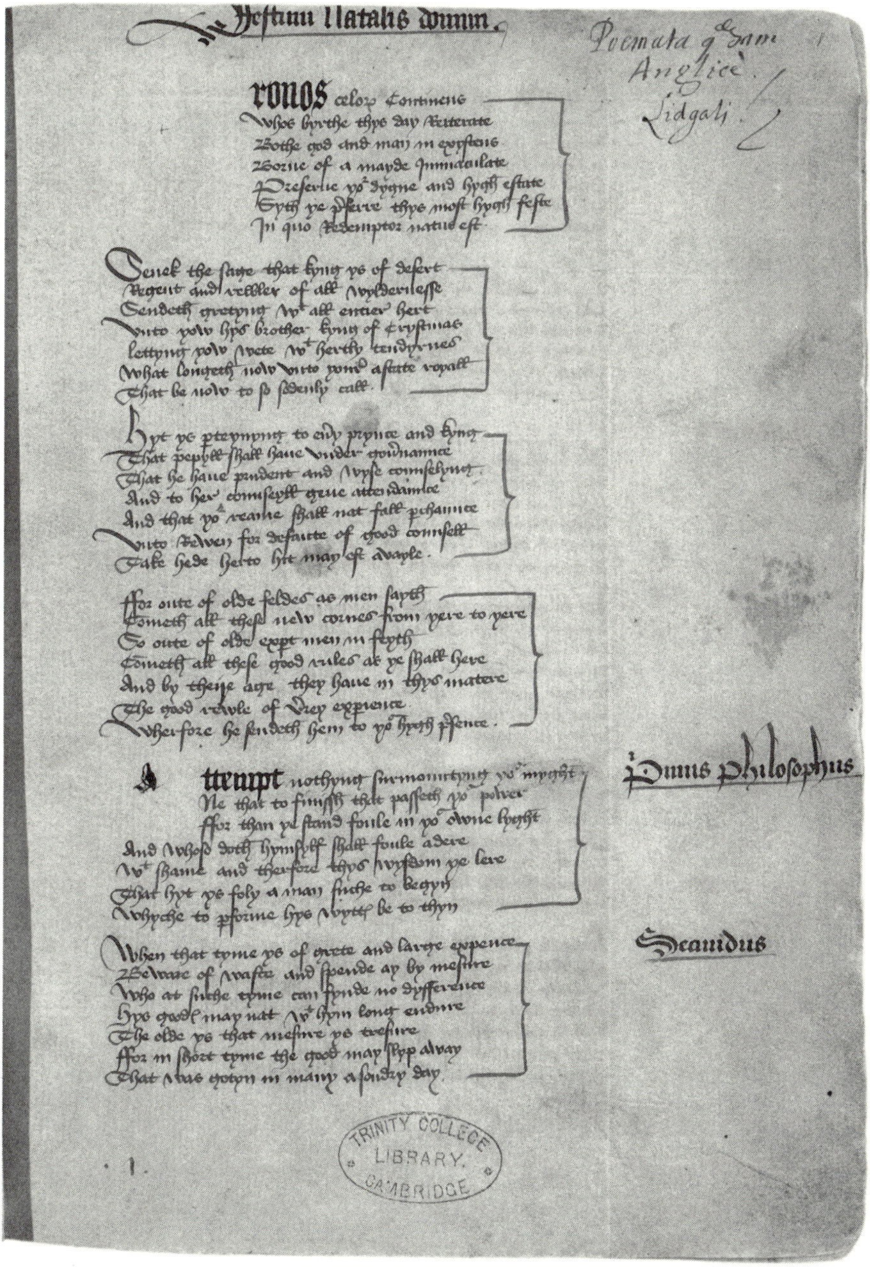

Figure 7. *A Mumming of the Seven Philosophers* (ll. 1–42, with title and note in upper corner). Cambridge, Trinity College Library MS R.3.19, fol. 1r. By permission of the library.

number of his secular poems and performance pieces, the mumming examines the nature of regnal authority, just and virtuous governance, and individual behavior. In addition to the resemblances to the *Fall of Princes* noted by Mortimer, the mumming also echoes Lydgate's "Dietary" and "Stans puer ad mensam," with their emphasis on self-governance and appropriate behavior.

The greatest resemblance, however, is to *A Pageant of Knowledge*, which is extant in numerous versions, was copied into Trinity R.3.21 by Multon, and has been ascribed to Lydgate.[33] Like the *Mumming of the Seven Philosophers*, the *Pageant* is structured around a series of sevens (and other numerical lists)—seven estates, seven "sapiencie," seven artificial and seven liberal arts, and the seven planets, as well as the twelve signs of the zodiac, the four elements, the four complexions, and the four seasons. The part of the *Pageant* that most resembles the *Mumming of the Seven Philosophers* is a section introduced by the title "Septem pagine sequntur sapiencie," a section that features one-stanza speeches by each of seven figures, including Prudence, Justice, Temperance, Discretion, Reason, Pleasance and Good Will, and Courtesy and Nurture. Both the *Mumming of the Seven Philosophers* and the *Pageant of Knowledge* draw on the tradition of the seven Greek or Roman sages who were associated with pithy maxims, epigrammatic sayings, and useful advice.[34] It would not be unlikely that the author of the *Pageant* also wrote *Seven Philosophers*.

Other echoes of Lydgate's preoccupations can be found in the *Mumming of the Seven Philosophers*, including the conceit of age advising youth, a wellworn convention of advisory literature that Lydgate uses elsewhere and that is here adapted to the common pattern of Lydgate's mummings in which a presenter ushers in figures who bring gifts both tangible and intangible to honor—and also guide—the mumming's recipient. This conceit is especially well suited to a seasonal performance linked to the ringing out of the old year and the passing on of its accumulated wisdom to the new. In *Seven Philosophers*, "olde expert men" are imagined as being like old fields that bring forth new corn as they proffer "good rules" to the new sovereign (ll. 24–25) and share the experience they have gained thanks to their advanced age (ll. 26–27).

The figure of "Senek the sage," who sends his greetings to the Christmas king, refers to both the Middle English word for an old man and the Roman author Seneca, who was often cited as a source of authoritative wisdom. The invocation of Seneca may be attributable to the influence of Chaucer, who in the *Canterbury Tales* refers to Seneca (as "clerk," "philosopher," "sage," or simply "Senek") more often than to any other philosopher but Solomon.[35] Not surprisingly, Lydgate refers to Seneca in a number of his works, including in the *Disguising at London* in his description of Prudence.[36] With its echoes of the desert fathers, the depiction of Senek in *Seven Philosophers* as ruler of the desert and the wilderness blends age and wisdom.

Convincing or not as this accumulated evidence about Lydgate's possible authorship may be, there is no doubt that, as Foucault has argued, knowing who wrote the *Mumming of the Seven Philosophers* matters for literary and theatrical scholarship.[37] The ability to anchor a text, to join it to an author's body of work, to give it a place within the themes and concerns of that author: all of these, as we know, are among the outcomes of assigning a text to a specific author, and those outcomes have interpretive significance. The consolidating power of the author function, with its capacity for finding a wayward piece of writing a home and for making it part of a larger body of work that can give it meaning within a specific discursive community and cultural context, is one of the most important meaning-making endeavors in literary history. As Foucault observes, the author function is "a characteristic of the mode of existence, circulation, and functioning of certain discourses within a society"; to attribute a text to a specific writer is thus to connect it to those same discourses, which are responsible for both creating the author function and, as a consequence, tying a literary work to a social and historical context.[38] The persistence with which scholars of medieval literature and drama seek to locate authors for anonymous works recognizes that fact and attests to the interpretive gains that come with knowing who wrote what and thus being able to position a text within the milieu within which an author moved.

Authorship is of course a problematic issue for medieval writing in general and for plays in particular. With only infrequent exceptions (Hildegard of Bingen, Jean Bodel, Adam de la Halle), most medieval dramas cannot be linked to a known writer, and most are presumed to have been produced through a collaborative process, whether under the control of the church or in a more diffuse and secular way out of existing literary, dramatic, and religious material. Yet, while collaboration was certainly a feature of most medieval performances, as it continues to be now, the anonymous nature of most surviving medieval play-scripts may have more to do with notions of textuality that devalued authorship, with the ephemerality of many performance texts, and with the loss or destruction of records than with the communal quality of early plays: we may, in other words, sometimes be too quick to assume that a medieval play cannot be assigned an author because it never had one. Although anonymity has by no means inevitably consigned individual plays to obscurity, as witness the well-known *Croxton Play of the Sacrament*, lack of a known author has often been a limit point for interpretation, even as scholars have turned to studies of dialect, textual allusions and historical references, and similar details as stand-ins that might locate a play geographically and temporally and allow educated guesses as to its performance venues. The search for authors of medieval plays, or for the scribes who copied them into manuscripts, might be worth the effort, given the potential interpretive rewards.

Locating the Performance

Even without confirmation of Lydgate's authorship, it is possible to make a number of guesses about the *Mumming of the Seven Philosophers* by examining its text. While the giver of the mumming is imagined as a wise old ruler, its recipient is the presumably young "kyng of Christmas," who has "so sodenly" been called to his new "astate royall" (ll. 13–14). Once again, the seasonal setting implies that the Christmas king, taking up his reign as the new year begins, is being advised by the visiting philosophers whose wisdom he is urged to allow to "grow vp in [his] age" (l. 81). He is associated with both princes and kings (l. 15) and addressed as "your hyghnes" (l. 84) and is also implicitly linked to Christ the king through the opening stanza, with its echoes of the advent Magnificat antiphon, *Qui celorum continues thronos*.[39] Sandra Billington notes that the Christian justification for midwinter customs of inversion was Christ's humble birth, "which was celebrated as the ultimate and Pauline example of the lowest in society as 'kyng of chrystmas' . . . the seasonal dethronement of kings at Christmas was a reminder to those in power of their relation to Christ and of the limitations of their human authority."[40] Since it is not uncommon to find associations of the king of England with Christ the king and since, as Gordon Kipling has shown, advent imagery frequently appears in royal entries, we are perhaps justified in wondering about the identity of the Christmas king who is this mumming's recipient, particularly the possibility that he may be not a play-king but a real ruler.[41]

At first glance, *Seven Philosophers* appears to resemble winter "mock king" festivities in which an individual was chosen as a temporary ruler, whether as a *rex stultorum* or king of fools in the church at New Year or a *rex fabarum* (king of the bean) in royal courts at Twelfth Night, customs that flourished in France and seem to have taken root in England by the late thirteenth century; Christmas kings are relatively well documented on the continent, while records of their appearance are scant for England until the sixteenth century.[42] The earliest known date of something like a Christmas king in England is 1277, when a king of the minstrels was chosen at the court of Edward I, and the practice continued in various fashions at court, at Oxford (and eventually Cambridge), and at the inns of court for a number of decades.[43] Evidence from London shows that Christmas kings and princes were a feature of Christmas celebrations at the Inns of Court, and a description from around 1500 describes how he was chosen by the clerks, sat at the high bench, chose officers, and then presided over entertainments and rituals.[44] The comment that the Christmas king of *Seven Philosophers* has been "so sodenly" (l. 14) called to the throne might be taken to suggest a seasonal ritual of this sort and implies that he has just recently been chosen by chance (e.g., by drawing the bean) or election.

Perhaps the best-known fifteenth-century Christmas king to be found in English records was John Gladman of the Norwich "Bachery" guild, who on Shrove Tuesday (March 5) in 1443 was "coronned as kyng of Crestemesse." Gladman rode to the priory of Norwich on a horse decorated with tinfoil, accompanied by three men carrying a crown, scepter, and sword, behind men costumed as the months of the old year, "in token that all mirths should end with the twelve months of the year," and was followed by another man impersonating Lent, who wore herring skins and was followed by a horse decked out in oyster shells, "in token that sadness and abstinence of mirth should follow and a holy time."[45] After the celebration turned into a riot against the Abbey of St. Benet's Holm, the city was fined 1,000 pounds and Gladman was arrested.[46]

Yet despite surface appearances, the *Seven Philosophers* seems only loosely connected with this tradition of rowdy rituals since it lacks the mocking and riotous qualities associated with winter kings. While some inversionary festivities included a serious imitation of the social forms being mocked—for instance, boy bishop ceremonies often began with a serious mass—they also featured a degree of mockery that is absent from this mumming.[47] Tone is of course notoriously difficult to pin down, and the verses of *Seven Philosophers* may be if not a riotous then at least a lighthearted offering of conventional advice to a mock king, who like "euery prynce and kyng" (l. 15) needs wise counsel. The joke would be in taking the mock king seriously enough to

judge him in need of counsel for his reign, and part of the fun might have
come from recognition of the gap between the sensible advice and the frivo-
lous occasion. In this reading, the advice of the seventh philosopher, to make
time for "play, recreacion, and comfort" (l. 75), might be seen as an invitation
to begin the revelry that may well have followed. It is difficult, however, to
envision these serious advisory verses as part of a Lord of Misrule game but it
is much easier to see them as consistent with Lydgate's many instances of
providing literary reminders of the demands of sovereignty and good government. For that reason, the *Seven Philosophers* perhaps makes more sense if
viewed as a seasonal entertainment aimed at offering serious advice about
rulership to a person in need of such guidance, such as members of the royal
court, a group for which Lydgate wrote other winter season entertainments.

Christmas was an important holiday for the English court in the late
medieval period. One of the three times of the year, along with Easter and
Whitsunday, when the king wore the official Crown of State, it provided an
occasion for announcing important royal decisions. It was at Christmas in
1406 that Henry IV admitted his son Henry of Monmouth to his council
and at Christmas in 1412 that he laid the plans for Henry's succession to the
throne. Since Christmas was usually the time of the next major gathering
of the court following coronations, it was also the moment when a newly
crowned monarch had the opportunity to establish the contours of his reign
and also was a tempting occasion for those who would challenge his sovereignty, as happened in 1399 during Henry IV's first Christmas after Richard
II's deposition, when supporters of Richard plotted to overthrow Henry. Although the practice is undocumented for earlier periods, a lord or abbot of
misrule appeared during most Christmases at court from 1485 to 1521 and in
1534, 1551–52, and 1552–53 as well.[48]

All of this suggests a possible occasion for the *Seven Philosophers* if it was
indeed designed to offer genuine advice to a ruler: the first Christmas following Henry VI's coronation as king of England. In the summer of 1429, the
Dauphin Charles had been crowned king of France. Even though Henry VI
was only eight years old, Charles's coronation spurred plans for Henry's
French coronation, which would have to be preceded by his crowning as king
of England, a ceremony that was performed on 6 November 1429 and for
which Lydgate supplied verses. It is fair to say that Henry had been "sodenly"
called to the throne by Charles's coronation, in a way that might have urged
the writing of a Christmas king mumming, modified to suit that sudden

event and to fit with the regiminal aims for Henry that had preoccupied his uncle, Humphrey, duke of Gloucester, in particular, and which had now taken on increased urgency. The Christmas season of 1429–30 would have offered the first occasion for Henry to appear publicly as king, and a mumming responding to his new status by offering him advice on how to rule would not have been out of place among the festivities.

Perhaps during that holiday season Henry VI watched a mumming about seven philosophers that had been written by the same East Anglian monk who had been commissioned to create other performance texts for the Lancastrian court, a mumming that played out for Henry his own situation and offered timely advice for the challenges of rulership he would soon face, including the demands that "longeth now" to his royal estate (l. 13). The advice to seek good counsel, to consult wise elders (repeated several times in the mumming), to set your sights low enough so as to be able to achieve what you set out to do, to use your time well, to govern yourself and avoid excess, to think to the future, to be generous, and to make time for play and recreation would all seem apt for Henry as he began his reign. In line with the possibility that *Seven Philosophers* may have been performed for a serious occasion is the fact that the deference in its verses seems real, not mock, especially in the final line when permission is asked for the seven philosophers to end by singing a song, "Yef to your hyghnes hit myght be plesyng" (l. 84), a line that echoes Lydgate's similarly deferential tag lines in his other royal mummings (e.g., "if ye list"). The tone of the mumming certainly seems consistent with a performance designed to offer a king pointed yet gentle advice. A Christmas king ceremony would have provided a suitable vehicle, once slightly reshaped, for presenting such advice within a festive context.

What might seem to argue against this association of the *Seven Philosophers* with the first Christmas following Henry VI's coronation is that the *Mumming at Windsor* was almost surely composed for the Christmas season of 1429–30; would the court have commissioned two entertainments from Lydgate for the same holiday? Possibly, especially if Anne Lancashire is correct in thinking that many of Lydgate's seasonal entertainments are the result of special commissions for special occasions.[49] Records suggest that Lydgate was hired at various times during the 1420s and 1430s by the court and Londoners to produce something better than the standard seasonal fare, something that could enhance and mark a special occasion. Two performance pieces by England's preeminent poet would not be unimaginable for the Christmas following such a momentous event as Henry VI's coronation, especially since the *Mumming at Windsor* that was performed during the 1430 holiday season seems to have been directed as much at Catherine as at her son.

Without further evidence documenting Christmas performances at court in the late 1420s, there is no way to be confident that Henry VI watched the *Mumming of the Seven Philosophers*. Yet the possibility that Lydgate authored the mumming and that he did so in the context of his other work as a crafter of entertainments for the court is not, I hope, idle speculation. At a minimum, associating this mumming with Lydgate should draw attention to a neglected text, one that, given the paucity of surviving Middle English play-scripts for secular performances, surely deserves the investigative energy it would receive if it were part of the poetic corpus of fifteenth-century England's best-known author.

Readers and the *Seven Philosophers*

Was it an association with Lydgate that accounted for the survival of this mumming? Possibly, but by no means definitively. As I have already noted, Trinity MS R.3.19 can be linked through its "Scribe A" with the work of the Hammond scribe, who had access to Shirley's manuscripts, which he used as source texts.[50] No evidence survives, however, to show that the *Seven Philosophers* derives from a now-lost copy by Shirley, even if the parts of the manuscript copied by Scribe A were the product of the same metropolitan context in which a number of Lydgate's other performance pieces were copied and circulated. Beyond the connection to London provided by Scribe A, the primarily secular and courtly contents of R.3.19 also suggest sophisticated metropolitan tastes. Even if we are mindful of Mooney's warning that we should be cautious about discussing the manuscript as a whole, since it may not have been bound together until the sixteenth century, the individual booklets as much as the whole manuscript show evidence of an appeal to prosperous London readers.[51] Blank spaces have been left for initials in *Seven Philosophers*, one for the "T" in "Tronos" at the start of the verses and the other for the "A" in "Attempt" at the beginning of the first speech by the philosophers; presumably, buyers who browsed this booklet and other exemplars held in the shop where it was made would have had decoration added to suit them when they purchased copies. The likely purchasers and readers of the first booklet of R.3.19, and indeed of the whole manuscript, would have been prosperous members of London's mercantile class; these readers wanted their books in English and were interested in compendia of various kinds of knowledge, even of the dull sort Fletcher views the verses in R.3.19 as being.[52]

One explanation for the survival of *Seven Philosophers* is that its themes allowed it to move beyond its immediate courtly context because they spoke to prosperous Londoners, just as Lydgate's other performance texts did. Manuscript evidence suggests that court entertainments—indeed, most dramatic performances—up to the sixteenth century only rarely circulated as written texts after the moment of performance. Lydgate's performance pieces for the court are the exception, largely thanks to Shirley, whose recording of them appears to have been motivated by the twin aims of preserving Lydgate's shorter poetry and collecting material of potential interest to Beauchamp's household. Some of Lydgate's performance pieces did, however, survive independently of Shirley, particularly those with historical appeal that appeared in London chronicles or those with didactic import, most notably *Bycorne and Chychevache* and the *Pageant of Knowledge*. The *Mumming of the Seven Philosophers* falls into that latter group. The mumming may record a courtly ceremony, but its content is in line with the advisory literature so popular among urban readers in the fifteenth century, and it is easy to imagine how such an audience would have found it useful and enjoyable as a text that could be read outside of the festive occasion that called it into being. Riddy identifies Trinity MS R.3.19 as "part of what is beginning to look like an identifiable mercantile culture," but even if it was produced for a gentry household, the overlap of tastes and interests between wealthy merchants and the gentry would have given it appeal for both groups.[53]

We may never know with any certainty who wrote the *Mumming of the Seven Philosophers*, how it was performed, through what mechanisms it circulated, or what its purposes were. At one level, it remains a mere scrap of writing, eighty-some lines that gesture toward a performance context that can probably never be identified or recovered. Although we may long for a surer grounding of the text, its unknowability makes it a compelling example, albeit an extreme one, of the questions that surround Lydgate's other performance pieces and, indeed, most dramatic records before the sixteenth century. The most valuable lesson of the *Seven Philosophers* may be, in the end, that the archive holds bits and pieces of evidence that we can only with difficulty return to anything like the performance repertoire they once constituted, and yet not to try would be to abandon both the challenges and the pleasures of literary and theatrical history.

Although I have argued in these chapters that Lydgate deserves attention given the important information about the histories of early theater and literature he offers—information seldom available from other sources—his greatest contribution may in the end be not the answers he provides but the questions he raises. I began this book by noting the unusual circumstances surrounding Lydgate's writing of verses for and about performance. Those circumstances—a known scribe who copied and disseminated the performance pieces, an author who is not anonymous, information about patrons and venues—all make Lydgate an important focus of inquiry for scholars interested in how early English entertainments and ceremonials were commissioned, made, and put on. Lydgate seems, in short, to promise a way around the impasse that usually greets investigations into medieval drama, an impasse created by a lack of play-texts and of information about how plays came into being and were experienced and understood.

Yet, that promise is not entirely fulfilled by the traces of Lydgate's work discernible in the historical record. As I have aimed to show, even though we know a remarkable amount about Lydgate's involvement with ceremonies and entertainments in the fifteenth century, many puzzles remain. How, for instance, did the commissioning process work, who approached Lydgate for the verses he wrote for performances, and how was he compensated? Who performed or recited lines in the entertainments he crafted? Who collaborated on the productions, and did Lydgate have any contact with those artisans and performers? What reactions did audiences have? What determined which performance pieces circulated in written form after the performance was done? And so on. While I have suggested answers to some of those questions, what we know about even the relatively well-documented performances such as those in which Lydgate was involved is at best partial.

Moreover, for better or for worse and inevitably or not, all of what we know is shaped by the motives and practices of those who recorded it, including

John Shirley and the other scribes who copied Lydgate's verses, and is dimmed by the long vista separating past and present. Hans-Robert Jauss's challenge to literary theory with which I began this book rests on an awareness of the constantly shifting status of texts, as they inevitably become unmoored from their original contexts and encounter successive generations of readers (if they were lucky enough to survive that long) who reshaped not only their meanings but also their very nature, so that it becomes difficult not just to discern what original audiences and readers made of those texts but even to make out what those texts are—poems meant for silent reading, play-texts to be enacted, prologues to introduce a performance, guidelines for craftsmen and actors, or any of the range of possibilities that the forms of existing texts suggest.[1] Recognition of the extent to which texts are reshaped and reappropriated once they move beyond an original audience has led cultural critics to turn to the notions of mimicry, improvisation, revision, translation, citation, and parody to describe how new meanings develop for already existing objects, events, and texts.[2] While that turn has been invigorating in many ways, especially by refusing to view texts as static and unchanging entities or audiences and readers as passive consumers, it has not always been of use in furthering our understanding of past cultural practices, as the original-staging movement as well as other attempts to recapture original textual artifacts and performance contexts have implicitly asserted.[3]

There are of course problems inherent in any attempt at recapturing past practices. As has been pointed out, the study of medieval European culture has often taken the form of a recuperative project preoccupied with beginnings, sources, and the recovery of lost originals.[4] Sixteenth-century antiquarians set the early terms of that project as they tried to preserve in writing the remnants of a fast-disappearing recent past. It is notable that one of those antiquarians, John Stow, found it worth copying a number of Lydgate's performance pieces, thus adding them to his archive of preserved cultural moments. This tendency to treat the making of literary and theater history as an act of salvage was intensified following the medieval revival of the later eighteenth and nineteenth centuries, when medieval studies became a specialized discipline. In those centuries, scholars involved in such projects as, in England, the Early English Text Society, the Society of Antiquaries, and the Rolls Series; the Monumenta series published by the Institute for Research on the German Middle Ages in Berlin; and the Société des anciens textes français and the École des Chartes in Paris labored to locate and preserve records of medieval culture.[5] The result of this history has been a tendency to privilege the textual artifact, rather than the process of cultural creation and transmission, as the focal point of study.

Lydgate is a useful figure for bringing artifacts and processes into productive play. That we have so much textual evidence for his performance works, contradictory and confusing as that evidence may sometimes be, provides a starting point for inquiries about cultural creation and transmission. As I have tried to show, the information in Shirley's headnotes to Lydgate's performance texts and the copies he and other scribes made not only or unambiguously lead to an original performance but also represent a series of textual interventions that demonstrate how drama intersected with writing and how live enactments entered into the space of the manuscript book, where it could be to at least some degree reinvented by each reader who encountered it. Sheila Lindenbaum has noted that one of the most enduring assumptions of the study of medieval drama is that plays "become fully accessible only in the moment of performance," an assumption that has become so naturalized that scholars have often passed quickly over the materiality of the written texts within which drama has been transmitted.[6] If we are attentive to those written texts, we will see that they point in two directions: the textual artifacts of Lydgate's ceremonies and entertainments that are now the only traces of what Londoners and members of the royal household once saw and heard do not so much lead backward to the original performance as they expand outward into wider circles of cultural transmission and reception. They show us something of what the first audiences of Lydgate's performances once experienced, while also revealing quite a bit about what readers and future audiences engaged with as well. An awareness of manuscript contexts as well as the reception and transmission of play-texts, as I have argued, can lead to a better understanding of original staging practices while also helping us avoid the assumption that any performance is ever recoverable in an unmediated fashion.

As the example of Lydgate demonstrates, vernacular drama in late medieval England is intimately connected to broader cultural processes, so much so that it can be hard to say where a play ends and a poem or picture starts, where reading or gazing at images differs from watching or listening to a performance. Silent mumming slides into tableau vivant; mimetic action with dialogue blends with painted wall hanging; cookery blurs into pageantry; presentational drama merges with documentary writing. Instead of attempting to arrest the slide or sort out the mixing of genres and media, we might be better off noticing when and where and why such intermingling occurs.

Spending less time attempting to distinguish one cultural form from another and more on following the routes by which they merge might yield not just a richer appreciation of drama's location within late medieval culture but also the recognition that, as Carol Symes has argued, in theory and in practice, medieval theater and medieval public life are tantamount to the same thing and that nearly every surviving record and source has performative features.[7]

If charting the scope and nature of performance poses one problem for theater historians, determining how to locate the traces of live performances that would allow us to better understand their aesthetic and mimetic features as well as to assess their cultural impact presents another. Any attempt to find those traces involves considering the relationship of surviving evidence to the original embodied performance. The field of performance studies understands surviving evidence—the texts, documents, maps, material objects, archaeo-logical remains, and other artifacts of the original event—to constitute the "archive," while ephemeral forms of embodied practice and performed knowl-edge such as sports, ritual, spoken language, dance, and acting make up the "repertoire." That the archive is unmediated and that it is resistant to "change, corruptibility, and political manipulation" are myths, as Diana Taylor has ar-gued in a critique of that idea's use in Latin American studies.[8] Like all repre-sentations, the manmade content of the archive—whether it be a play-text, a photograph of a performance, or an eyewitness account—is always simultane-ously "a facsimile and a simulacrum, a copy and a counterfeit," as Charlotte Canning and Thomas Postlewait observe.[9] There is inevitably a gap between the archive and what it represents, a gap that poses challenges for the study of any performance that cannot be observed live.

Further complicating any attempt to trace past performances is the fact that the relationship between the archive and the repertoire is temporally complex. It is, in particular, not sequential, that is, the archive does not al-ways come chronologically after the repertoire. We can observe that lack of sequentiality in the built-in assumptions about the reuse of manuscript copies of Lydgate's performance pieces, as, for example, in the replacing of the name of the specific king for whom Lydgate designed the performance with *N* for *nomen*, which opens the text for performance in new contexts: thus, the surviving manuscript copy of a mumming may postdate one perfor-mance but predate another. As we can also see from this and other examples, the path from performance to written text is not one way. Lydgate's perfor-mance pieces occupy many positions on the back-and-forth road between archive and repertoire, whether as the "device" that precedes and guides artisans and those putting on a performance, as the text that was presented or read aloud during the performance, or as a commemorative poem or meditative recollection that relies on the memory of live performance for its effect. As scholars have noted, performance was a pervasive mode for the circulation of all sorts of visual and written texts in the medieval period, and what is today identified as a "play" does not, as Lofton Durham has observed, always have much to do with "whether or not that particular texts served as template, record, or inspiration for performance."[10]

The relationship between the archive and the repertoire is also not simply false versus true, mediated versus fully present, modern versus ancient, or hegemonic versus antihegemonic, as Taylor notes. The archive can be all of those things at once, as can the repertoire of live performances. We should beware of assuming that written documents with their agendas and biases always lie or that embodied performances speak an unmediated truth. And we should be cautious about believing that written accounts always side with the powers that be, while live enactments subvert and critique them. Both archive and repertoire can deceive, and both can convey truth. Neither has a unique claim on wisdom, and both can function as acts of transfer, "transmitting social knowledge, memory, and a sense of identity."[11]

The example of Lydgate is especially instructive for thinking about this complicated relationship between the archive and the repertoire. With their uncertainties and ambiguities, the textual artifacts of his performance pieces compel us to consider what they reveal about the performance repertoire to which they gesture. Did they precede the performance event, take place within it, and recall it afterward? How different are they from other dramatic texts from the period, and what do they suggest about the relations those texts have to the performance practices they relate to? While Lydgate and Shirley offer unusual access to possible answers, these are questions that take us away from one author and one scribe to the broader context of play-making and play-copying in the late medieval period. Lydgate may offer an exceptional example, because of the relative thoroughness with which his performance pieces are documented, but he is surely not out of sync with his century's performance and manuscript practices.

The last point I want to make is that the issues this book considers continue to be significant for cultural history. Derrida has argued that our understanding of the archive "determines the structure of archival content even in its coming into existence and in its relationship to the future"; thought precedes the archive's content both at the moment of inception and as the archive endures.[12] The archive is thus prey to perpetual rethinking that never permits it the fixity of a settled body of knowledge. Theater history is particularly attuned to that dilemma, since performance "casts in miniature the dilemma of ultimate irrecuperability endemic to historical inquiry," as Bruce Holsinger has observed; as Chaucer's Canon's Yeoman so evocatively put it, performance constantly reminds us that when it comes to answers to questions about so much of medieval culture, "We faille of that which that we wolden have."[13] If the hope of a transparent, truthful, and fully informative archive that would let us reconstruct past performances and understand their cultural workings is fool's gold, then where are we left? Not, most would agree, in despair at the obdurate nature of surviving evidence and the absolute unknowability of past performances but rather in continued pursuit of better ways of, first, tracing elusive knowledge about medieval drama and, second, interpreting it. That pursuit is an ongoing one that at its best energizes current work in medieval drama studies and that promises to continue to spur exciting inquiries into the nature, uses, and meanings of performances from the premodern past.

NOTES

INTRODUCTION

1. The making of this history has been well described by Fisher, "A Language Policy for Lancastrian England"; Knapp, *Bureaucratic Muse*, esp. 1–9; Lerer, "William Caxton"; Lindenbaum, "London Texts and Literate Practice"; and Strohm, "Chaucer's Fifteenth-Century Audience and the Narrowing of the 'Chaucer Tradition.'" Summit, *Lost Property*, 12, notes that the making of this history began as early as John Skelton, one of the first English writers "to conceive of English literature as a body of texts linked by a common national and linguistic identity" and centered on Chaucer, Gower, and Lydgate. See Coletti, *Mary Magdalene and the Drama of Saints*, esp. 6–7, for a compelling critique of this standard history through analysis of the impact of a female-centric religious and dramatic culture.

2. For a broader conception of vernacular writing that considers popular and female audiences as well as the impact of Lollardy, see Aers and Staley, *Powers of the Holy*; Somerset, *Clerical Discourse and Lay Audience*; and Watson, "The Politics of Middle English Writing," esp. 342–45.

3. For a history of the REED project along with a critique of its assumptions, see Coletti, "Reading REED"; for similar archival work in Germany, see Linke, "A Survey of Medieval Drama and Theater in Germany," esp. 39 n1; and for continental archival recovery efforts with an emphasis on France, see Symes, "The Medieval Archive and the History of Theatre."

4. The record containing the Lübeck play and its significance for early drama have been discussed by Simon, "Organizing and Staging Carnival Plays in Late Medieval Lübeck," 71–72.

5. See Enders, "Spectacle of the Scaffolding," 163.

6. Symes, "The Medieval Archive and the History of Theatre."

7. Clopper, for one, has cautioned against too readily assuming that every reference to performance in the documentary record points to a play; see his "*Miracula* and *The Tretise of Miraclis Pleyinge*."

8. Jauss, "Literary History as a Challenge to Literary Theory."

9. Hanna, "Miscellaneity and Vernacularity," in *The Whole Book*, ed. Nichols and Wenzel, 47.

10. For recent studies of the rise of the vernacular, three useful collections of essays are Kullmann, ed., *The Church and Vernacular Literature in Medieval France*; Somerset and Watson, eds., *The Vulgar Tongue*; and Salter and Wicker, eds., *Vernacularity in England and Wales, c. 1300–1550*.

11. Lerer, "The Chaucerian Critique of Medieval Theatricality."

12. Middleton, "The Idea of Public Poetry in the Reign of Richard II"; Lawton, "Dullness and the Fifteenth Century."

13. Clanchy, *From Memory to Written Record*, 285.

14. Important contributions to the field of material philology have been made by Cerquiglini, *In Praise of the Variant*; Nichols, "Why Material Philology"; and Nichols and Wenzel, eds., *The Whole Book*.

15. Brantley, *Reading in the Wilderness*; Clark and Sheingorn, "Performative Reading"; and Coleman, *Public Reading and the Reading Public in Late Medieval England and France*.

16. Coletti, *Mary Magdalene and the Drama of Saints*.

17. See, among others, Cole, *Literature and Heresy in the Age of Chaucer*, who examines the literary impact of Wyclif's ideas and argues for the centrality of Wycliffism to the English literary canon.

18. Watson, "The Politics of Middle English Writing."

19. For work on regionalism in England, see Barrett, *Against All England*, on Chester; Gibson, *The Theater of Devotion*, on East Anglia; the extensive scholarship on York, including most recently King, *The York Mystery Cycle and the Worship of the City*; and the essays in Rogerson, ed., *The York Mystery Plays*.

20. Nichols and Wenzel, eds., *The Whole Book*, 1.

21. See, for example, Coletti and Gibson, "The Tudor Origins of Medieval Drama," which discusses recent reassessments of the Chester and Towneley cycle plays.

22. For an example of work on performance as a means of dispersing and increasing access to written texts, see the essays in Vitz, Regalado, and Lawrence, eds., *Performing Medieval Narrative*.

23. The most widely used anthologies of medieval plays, Bevington's *Medieval Drama* and Walker's *Medieval Drama: An Anthology*, include no works by Lydgate; similarly, most collections of scholarly essays on medieval performance, such as Simon's *Theatre of Medieval Europe*, omit Lydgate or offer only passing mention of his dramatic writings.

24. See *MPJL*; Clopper, *Drama, Play, and Game*, 163; and Lerer, *Boethius and Dialogue*, 7, in which Lerer discusses a Lydgatean echo of Boethius's tendencies.

25. Symes, "Appearance of Early Vernacular Plays," has demonstrated how slowly scribal conventions for recording dramatic texts developed.

26. See Duffy, *Stripping of the Altars*. Revisionist readings can be found in Emmerson, "Eliding the 'Medieval,'" esp. 30–33, and White, "Reforming Mysteries' End."

27. Flanigan, "Comparative Literature and the Study of Medieval Drama," esp. 57–63, provides a thorough overview of these processes.

28. Lerer, "Chaucerian Critique of Medieval Theatricality," and Epstein, "Lydgate's Mummings and the Aristocratic Resistance to Drama."

29. On Chaucer's use of drama, see Ganim, "Drama, Theatricality and Performance," and Lindhal, *Earnest Games*.

30. Coletti, *Mary Magdalene and the Drama of Saints*, 4.

31. LaCapra, *History and Criticism*, 19–20.

32. Brantley, *Reading in the Wilderness*, esp. 1–6.

33. Nolan, *John Lydgate and the Making of Public Culture*, 71.

34. See, for example, the essays in Brown, McMillin, and Wilson, eds., *Hrotsvit of Gandersheim*, and Symes, *A Common Stage*.

35. Ebin, *John* Lydgate; Pearsall, *John Lydgate (1371–1449)*; and Renoir, *The Poetry of John Lydgate*.

36. Nolan, *John Lydgate and the Making of Public Culture*; Scanlon and Simpson, eds., *John Lydgate*; Meyer-Lee, *Poets and Power from Chaucer to Wyatt*; and Cooper and Denny-Brown, eds., *Lydgate Matters*.

37. Scanlon and Simpson, eds., *John Lydgate*, 8.

38. Cooper and Denny-Brown, eds., *Lydgate Matters*, 1–11; the quotation is from 4.

39. Sponsler, ed., *John Lydgate: Mummings and Entertainments*; my earlier essays are discussed and cited in the following chapters, when relevant to the discussion at hand.

40. Scanlon and Simpson, eds., *John Lydgate*, 8.

CHAPTER 1

1. Boffey, "Short Texts in Manuscript Anthologies," 71, notes that Lydgate's practice contrasts with that of Froissart, Machaut, and Hoccleve, "whose methods for organizing their minor poems can be partially documented."

2. For a history and critique of the REED project, see Coletti, "Reading REED"; for REED's limited impact on scholars of early modern drama, see Holland, "Theatre Without Drama."

3. Johnston has summarized these outcomes in "'All the World Was a Stage,'" esp. 118–19.

4. Bevington, "*Castles* in the Air," 106.

5. See Beadle, "York Cycle," esp. 89–91, and King, *York Mystery Cycle*, esp. 2–4, for discussion of the relation between the York Register and other information about the York pageants. Records from Coventry show cycle plays as early as 1420 but do not specify the cycle's content or how many plays it included; *Two Coventry Corpus Christi Plays*, ed. Craig, xi–xiv, put it at ten, but Clopper, *Drama, Play, and Game*, 173, counts eight, and from their contents concludes that Coventry's play was chiefly a Passion Play with some additional material. The Towneley manuscript, named for its seventeenth-century owners, appears to contain a cycle of plays from one town, which in the past was identified as Wakefield from references in the manuscript (two pageants have the name "Wakefield"

written in rubrics at the head of their texts, and there are what seem to be local allusions in some of the plays); various idiosyncrasies in the manuscript have undermined any connection to Wakefield, as Palmer, "'Towneley Plays' or 'Wakefield Cycle' Revisited," notes. The five nonidentical manuscripts of the Chester plays were copied by antiquarian scribes from the city "Regenall," apparently a city register of scripts from which plays could be chosen to put together a cycle that might vary each year; see Mills, *Recycling the Cycle*. For the late dates of the manuscripts of the biblical cycle plays, see Coletti and Gibson, "Tudor Origins of Medieval Drama."

6. In addition to these extant texts, several plays survive in miscellaneous manuscripts, including the Norwich *Grocers' Play* (two versions dated 1533 and 1565); the Brome *Abraham and Isaac* (late fifteenth century); the Croxton *Play of the Sacrament* (ca. 1461); *Dux Moraud* (ca. 1425–50), a player's part for a moral play about incest; and some fragments (including the Ashmole fragment, which may be from a play of St. Lawrence). For a discussion of the southern plays, see Coldewey, "Non-cycle Plays." The southern plays have been edited by Baker, Murphy, and Hall, *Late Medieval Religious Plays of Bodleian MSS Digby 133 and E Museo 160*; Eccles, *Macro Plays*; and Spector, *N-Town Play*, all of whom discuss ownership of the manuscripts.

7. Johnston, "What If No Texts Survived?" 3.

8. We know almost nothing about how roles were learned before the development of a fully commercial theater in London; York's records suggest that guilds in that city held the copy of their pageant, which was presumably used as a master text for the learning of parts, and other extant scripts show signs of annotation for performance, but we do not know if actors worked from written copies of plays or learned their parts aurally.

9. For Young's reliance on rubrics, see Dunn, "French Medievalists and the Saint's Play," 55.

10. Clopper, *Drama, Play, and Game*, 300–306. Baker, "When Is a Text a Play?" has also noted the problem of recognizing plays in manuscripts.

11. *DTR*, xxxiii.

12. Which of Lydgate's works were dramatic remains a matter of debate. To cite just one example, Nelson, *Medieval English Stage*, 4–5 and 173–74, regards the *Procession of Corpus Christi* as a description of a series of plays, while Clopper, *Drama, Game, and Play*, 164 n67, believes that it describes a series of literary *figurae* "presented" for the reader.

13. Kastan, *Shakespeare and the Book*, 2.

14. Symes, "Appearance of Early Vernacular Plays," 778.

15. Brantley, *Reading in the Wilderness*.

16. See Coletti and Gibson, "Tudor Origins of Medieval Drama," for a concise summary of these findings and their implications for theater history.

17. The quotation is from Mills, "'The Towneley Plays' or 'The Towneley Cycle'?" 95. See also Happé, *The Towneley Cycle*, 88; Palmer, "'Towneley Plays' or 'Wakefield Cycle,'" esp. 325–28; Parkes, cited in Palmer, "Recycling 'The Wakefield Cycle,'" 96; Lumi-

ansky and Mills, *The Chester Mystery Cycle*; and Clopper, "The History and Development of the Chester Cycle."

18. Shirley did, however, copy Lydgate's "Ballade" and "Roundel" for the 1429 coronation in Trinity MS R.3.20, raising the question of why he omitted the subtleties. The 1432 entry was written too late for inclusion in R.3.20 and may not have been of interest to Shirley by the time he was compiling Bodleian MS Ashmole 59 in the late 1440s.

19. The former interpretation rests on an entry in the rental of St. Bartholomew's Hospital, compiled in 1456, which states that Shirley rented a large tenement in the middle of the courtyard with four shops; see Doyle, "More Light on John Shirley," 96.

20. Connolly, *John Shirley*, 193.

21. For a list of the contents of the three manuscripts, see Connolly, *John Shirley*, 30–31, 70–74, and 146–49.

22. A point made by Connolly, *John Shirley*, 33.

23. See Pearsall, *John Lydgate*, 160–71, for Lydgate's ties to Beauchamp.

24. See Connolly, *John Shirley*, 84–85.

25. Mooney, "Chaucer's Scribe," 121.

26. For Pinkhurst's work, see Mooney, "Chaucer's Scribe"; the sole surviving manuscript copy of "Chaucers Wordes unto Adam his owne Scriveyn" was made by Shirley, in Trinity MS R.3.20. Edwards, "Lydgate Manuscripts," 17, describes the most prolific of the scribes copying Lydgate's works in the region of Bury St. Edmunds as "a co-ordinating scribe capable of drawing upon the services of a number of proficient artists and decorators to adorn his work." We do not know how Shirley came to be the copyist for some of Lydgate's works, although Greenberg, "John Shirley and the English Book Trade," 375, speculates that some of the poet's work was sent to London to be copied and published by Shirley.

27. During the period in the late 1420s and early 1430s, when Lydgate was writing most of his performance pieces, Shirley appears to have settled in or near London but to have maintained contact with Beauchamp's household; see Connolly, *John Shirley*, 52–53.

28. Kipling, "Lydgate: The Poet as Deviser," esp. 75–76.

29. Clopper, *Drama, Play, and Game*, 165.

30. See Burrow, *Gestures and Looks*, esp. 182–83, for the problem of reproducing the aural and visual in writing in the medieval period and beyond.

31. In addition to the seminal work on sound in Smith, *Acoustic World of Early Modern England*, see the essays in McInnis and Hirsch, eds., *Embodying Shakespeare*, for a good overview of recent work on the experiential aspects of early drama.

32. Lindenbaum, "Drama as Textual Practice," 386, 388.

33. For "making" applied to mummings, see "þe Duk of Surrey, þe Duk of Excestre . . . & oþir moo of hir afinite, were accorded to make a mummyng vnto þe King . . . and þere þay cast to sle þe King yn hir revelyng" (*The Brut*, ed. Brie, 2:360, l. 32) and "certayne personys, called Lollers . . . hadde caste to have made a mommynge at Eltham, and undyr coloure of the mommynge to have dystryte the kyng and Hooly Chyrche" (*Historical Collections*, ed. Gairdner, 108).

34. *MED, devisen* v. 4(a): "To design or plan (sth.)" and (5): "To form (sth.), fashion, shape, or construct; compose (a letter, poem, etc.); portray (sth.)." *Device* is used in the following century to describe the speeches written by George Peele for pageants carried before the Lord Mayors of London in 1585 and 1591; see Peele, *Device of the Pageant Borne Before Woolstone Dixi* and *Descensus Astraeae*. "The Knight's Tale," *Riverside Chaucer*, l. 1901.

35. See "A Ballade, of Her That Hath All Virtues," "whiche þat Lydegate wrote at þe request of a squyer," and "That Now Is Hay Some-tyme Was Grase," "a balade which Iohn Lydgate the Monke of Bery wrott & made at þe commaundement of þe Quene Kateryne," *MPJL*, 2:379–81 and 2:809–13.

36. Shirley sometimes fails to make that distinction: Lydgate's translation of "So As the Crabbe Goth Forward," for example, which is preceded by the French original, is described by Shirley as having been "made in our englishe langage" by Lydgate, and another translated poem, "Gaude Virgo Mater Christi," is described as "þe translacyoune . . . made by" Lydgate; *MPJL*, 2:464–67 and 1:288–89.

37. Middleton, "Chaucer's 'New Men,'" 32.

38. Patterson, "'What Man Artow?'" 119.

39. *MPJL*, 2:649–51 and 1:290–91.

40. Stern, *Documents of Performance*, esp. 1–3.

41. Kipling, "Lydgate: The Poet as Deviser," 92.

42. Cerquiglini, *In Praise of the Variant*, 34.

43. See Doyle, "More Light," 93–101, and "English Books," 176–78; Boffey and Thompson, "Anthologies and Miscellanies," 284–87; and Edwards, "Lydgate Manuscripts," 19–21. One example of Shirley's interaction with the texts he is copying can be seen in the *Mumming at Windsor*, when Shirley responds to a misogynist comment of Lydgate's with the mocking question: "A daun Iohan, est y vray?"

44. See Seymour, *Catalogue of Chaucer Manuscripts*, 40.

45. For a detailed discussion of the contents of Trinity MS R.3.20, see Connolly, *John Shirley*, 69–101. The manuscript was probably produced in 1430–32 and consists of twenty-four gatherings and 373 pages (it was paginated, not foliated) that were once part of a larger collection, the other parts of which can be found in London, Sion College MS Arc.L.40.2/E.44 (now at Lambeth Palace) and in London, British Library, MS Harley 78, fols. 80r–83v. It contains a mix of English and French poetry, some Latin, and a few recipes, prayers, and instructional material.

46. Connolly and Plumley, "Crossing the Channel," 314.

47. Connolly and Plumley, "Crossing the Channel," 322.

48. Boffey, *Manuscripts of English Courtly Love Lyrics*, 66, believes Shirley used a written exemplar for at least one of the French songs in Trinity MS R.3.20, but Connolly and Plumley, "Crossing the Channel," 321–23, argue that the existence of these French lyrics in the song repertoire of the period "should not be overlooked" (323).

49. Symes, "Appearance of Early Vernacular Plays," 778.

50. For instance, the *Courtois d'Arras*, which modern scholars call a play, has no dramatic apparatus (stage directions or character designations) in its four extant manu-

scripts and circulated as a lai or fabliau (see Symes, "Appearance of Early Vernacular Plays," 782). *Dame Sirith* (ca. 1300) was never identified as part of the canon of English drama but perhaps should be. See also the Anglo-Norman *vita* of St. Catherine preserved in Manchester, John Rylands Library MS French 6 (ca. 1250), which has some speech tags but is a narrated text; Clopper, *Drama, Play, and Game*, 305, calls it a *ludus*, not a play, but its status seems ambiguous.

51. Although the reliability Shirley's information has been questioned, Pearsall, *John Lydgate*, 77, believes that "where he can be checked," Shirley "is very accurate in his attributions."

52. Clanchy, *From Memory to Written Record*, 268.

53. Lerer, "Chaucerian Critique."

54. See *Commonplace Book of Robert Reynes*, ed. Louis.

55. Other copyists did the same thing, for instance the fifteenth-century scribe who copied the verses from Queen Margaret's entry into London into a copy of Gower's *Confessio Amantis*, thus converting spectacle into literature; see Kipling, "London Pageants," 11.

56. Mooney, "John Shirley's Heirs," 197. Also see her "Scribes and Booklets."

57. For this and other information about Vale and Cook, see Sutton and Visser-Fuchs, "Provenance." Among the goods confiscated from Cook after his arrest were many tapestries, including a splendid one of the Siege of Jerusalem, which Cook had once declined to sell to Lord Rivers's wife, the duchess of Bedford, and which had cost Cook 8,000 pounds; see Sutton and Visser-Fuchs, "Provenance," 90.

58. Stubbes, "Clare Priory," 23.

59. Sutton and Visser-Fuchs, "Provenance," 104.

60. Ibid., 111–12. Mooney, "John Shirley's Heirs," 190 n19, notes that the activities of Shirley and Vale can be compared to those of another secretary and man of affairs of this period, William Worcester, "who like these two men kept up his antiquarian and scribal activities after the death of his patron, Sir John Fastolf."

61. Cerquiglini, *In Praise of the Variant*, 21.

62. Ibid., 26.

CHAPTER 2

1. For recent readings of Lydgate as a London writer, see Benson, "Civic Lydgate"; Sponsler, "Alien Nation"; and Strohm, "Sovereignty and Sewage."

2. The mummings and disguising are extant in a single manuscript, Trinity MS R.3.20, printed in *MPJL*, 2:695–701, with commentary 1:201–3. For the dating of the manuscript, see Connolly, *John Shirley*, 77–80; for Estfeld's mayoralty and the dates of the mummings, see Lancashire, *London Civic Theatre*, 121, and Schirmer, *John Lydgate*, 91.

3. In the *Disguising at London*, the gift giving associated with mumming takes the abstract form of gifts of virtue, which will reside "in this housholde" (l. 335) for the year. Although the disguising was apparently intended for a national, not a municipal, occasion,

its values according to Benson "are practical and bourgeois," emphasizing "the sort of pragmatic, decent, and well-regulated communal behavior advocated by medieval London citizens"; see Benson, "Civic Lydgate," 160.

4. Watson, "Politics of Middle English Writing," 331, 333.

5. Ibid., 337.

6. See Scanlon and Simpson, eds., *John Lydgate*, 7–8; Scanlon and Simpson point to the "conflicting constraints" of the three Lancastrian monarchs (Henry IV, Henry V, and Henry VI) within and for whose reigns Lydgate wrote, as well as the three centers of cultural power he crossed (London, Paris, and Bury), noting that his ornate style seems to have been in response to the Lollard use of a plain form of Middle English. Norton-Smith, *John Lydgate: Poems*, 195 n1, suggests that Lydgate may have become interested in an ornate liturgical English style through the influence of Edmund Lacy, dean of the Royal Chapel at Windsor from 1414–17 and bishop of Exeter from 1420.

7. Stanbury, "Vernacular Nostalgia," 96.

8. Norton-Smith, *John Lydgate: Poems*, 194.

9. Middleton, "The Idea of Public Poetry in the Reign of Richard II," esp. 94–95; Nolan, *John Lydgate and the Making of Public Culture*, 3–5; quotations on 3 and 5.

10. Benson, "Civic Lydgate," 154, 163.

11. For a seminal use of reader-response notions of the successive audiences to interpret medieval texts, see Strohm, "Chaucer's Fifteenth-Century Audience and the Narrowing of the 'Chaucer Tradition.' "

12. For Chaucer's inability to imagine London, see Wallace, "Chaucer and the Absent City."

13. Anderson, *Imagined Communities*, esp. 48. Since Anderson's larger project is to explain the rise and spread of nationalism, he locates the emergence of imagined national communities in the late eighteenth century, but the notion of imagined communities less directly linked to modern nationalism has become widespread in the thirty years since his book was published and can be usefully applied to earlier historical periods.

14. For representative views, see Lindenbaum, "London Texts and Literate Practice," 295, who views London as disunited and lacking a unified voice; Hanna, *London Literature*, xvii, envisions it as "a resistant and fragmented locality."

15. Bolton, *Alien Communities in London in the Fifteenth Century*, examines and reassesses the surviving evidence, charting the nationalities of London's aliens, their occupations and places of residence, and their proportion of the population, which Bolton judges to have been at least 6 percent of the likely population of 50,000 in the late fifteenth century (1–40; estimate of percentage on 8).

16. See Reddaway and Walker, *Early History of the Goldsmiths' Company*, 107.

17. Thrupp, "Aliens in and Around London," 120. Also see the discussion of alien merchants in London, and the overseas trade, in Barron, *London in the Later Middle Ages*, 14–16, 84–117; Barron notes that not until the sixteenth century did the privileges accorded to alien merchants by royal policy "cease to be an issue between the city and the Crown" (16).

18. Jacob, *Fifteenth Century*, 357. Edward III actively encouraged alien merchants, sending emissaries to Flanders to entice Flemish weavers to England and subsequently protecting aliens against the hostilities of native clothworkers; see McKisack, *Fourteenth Century*, 367–68.

19. For these terms, see Thrupp, *Merchant Class*, 2–3.

20. Bolton, *Alien Communities*, 39, notes that violence against aliens coincided both with trade recessions, as in 1468, and with moments of national and political crisis, as in 1381.

21. Justice, *Writing and Rebellion*, 72–73.

22. See Thrupp, "A Survey of the Alien Population of England in 1440"; quotation on 264.

23. *RP*, 3:578b.

24. The privileges enjoyed by Italians in the wool trade, with agents riding around the Cotswolds competing with English buyers for the best crop, was a source of insular hostility, in part responsible for the riots of the mid-1450s, which caused many Italians to leave London for Southampton and Winchester; see Jacob, *Fifteenth Century*, 352–55.

25. For a discussion of the stoning, which is described in the contemporary *Brut*, see Griffiths, "Breton Spy," 222–23.

26. McKisack, *Fourteenth Century*, 359, 378.

27. Worshipful Company of Goldsmiths, Minute Book A, 165 and 155, respectively, cited in Reddaway and Walker, *Early History of the Goldsmiths' Company*, 108–9, 123–24. Bolton, *Alien Communities*, observes that complaints against aliens often centered on the claim that they were a community apart and that they did not intermarry, ran a closed shop by employing only other aliens, and deprived Englishmen of jobs (35).

28. Reddaway and Walker, *Early History of the Goldsmiths' Company*, 122, 107–8.

29. See Campbell, "English Goldsmiths in the Fifteenth Century," 44.

30. See Minute Book A, 201–20 and 190, respectively, cited in Reddaway and Walker, *Early History of the Goldsmiths' Company*, 138, 148.

31. "Henry VI's Triumphal Entry into London," l. 46.

32. The wager is described in Herbert, *History of the Twelve Great Livery Companies*, 2:197.

33. Barron, *London*, 192; for the location of Bishopswood in Stepney, see Stow, *Survey*, 99.

34. See Rosser, *Medieval Westminster*.

35. Stow, *Survey*, 99–100.

36. On gifts in aristocratic culture, see Rosenthal, *Purchase of Paradise*. For a reading of the mummings for the Mercers and Goldsmiths as literary and performative examples of the interlocking and at times competing discourses of colony, empire, and nation within Lancastrian England, see Sponsler, "Alien Nation."

37. Wickham, *Early English Stages*, 3:48–49.

38. See Sutton, *Mercery of London*, and Keene, introduction to Imray, *Mercers' Hall*, 1–13. In the fifteenth century, the Mercers were a mixed company of shopkeepers and merchants, who by the reign of Henry VI had become dealers in silks and velvets; see Herbert, *History of the Twelve Great Livery Companies*, 1:233–34.

39. *Chronicles of London*, ed. Kingsford, 312 and note to 146, l. 13.

40. As noted by Coleman, "Coronation Plate," 49.

41. Barron, *London*, 144.

42. For the payments, see Lancashire, *London Civic Theatre*, 42, and for mercers' interest in the *puy*, see Imray, *Mercers' Hall*, 12, 438 n29.

43. Welsford, *Court Masque*, 55.

44. The image of London as a fitting end point to this majestic grand tour and as a refreshing place where visiting merchants can take the air meshes interestingly with Lydgate's view in his *Troy Book* of what Strohm aptly calls the "purified" city with its "holsom eyr" and fresh breezes (*Troy Book*, 2:668–79); see Strohm, "Sovereignty and Sewage," esp. 59–60.

45. See the discussion of the mumming for Richard II in Wickham, *Early English Stages*, 3:49.

46. For the social and political uses of Epiphany performances, see Greenfield, "Festive Drama at Christmas," 36.

47. The shift to the vernacular in English letters has been described by Kingsford, *Prejudice and Promise*, 22–47.

48. See Lawton, "Gaytryge's Sermon," for the influence of the *ars dictaminis* on the style of Middle English vernacular writing. Steiner, *Documentary Culture*, 57, notes that *dictamen* studies in England had less influence than on the continent and tended to be practically minded, yet were still linked to poetry and literary activity.

49. Deansley, "Vernacular Books in England," has shown that writing bound as books was likely to be pious, while writing on loose sheets was likely to be bureaucratic or for business purposes.

50. See Cohen, *Ballade*, 226–27.

51. As Fisher notes, most people encountered not belletristic but bureaucratic writing; see his "Chancery and the Emergence of Standard Written English," 894.

52. Steiner, *Documentary Culture*, 48.

53. Duffy, *Stripping of the Altars*, 41.

54. See Kretzmann, *Liturgical Element in the Earliest Forms of the Medieval Drama*, 53–59, for early liturgical plays on Epiphany, including Magi and Stella plays.

55. Kipling, *Enter the King*, 118.

56. The quotations in this and the preceding paragraph are from Nolan, *John Lydgate*, 102–4.

57. Clopper, *Drama, Play, and Game*, 161.

58. See Sutton, *Mercery of London*, 164–73, for mercers' education and book-owning habits. On Pinkhurst's work for the mercers, see Mooney, "Chaucer's Scribe," 119. See Meale, "*Libelle of Englyshe Polycye*," 187–88, for a discussion of manuscripts owned by mercers, and 192–98, for a discussion of guild dramas.

59. By the late fourteenth century, a number of mercers were heavily involved in overseas trade, and the Mercers' Company records show that they traveled around the Low Countries, particularly in search of cloth to buy; see Sutton, *Mercery of London*, 157.

60. See Butterfield, "Chaucer's French Inheritance," 27.

61. A point made by Benson, "Civic Lydgate," 161.

62. Connolly, *John Shirley*, 181–82.

63. Sutton, *Mercery of London*, 162–65. Carpenter compiled the *Liber Albus* of the city's laws, customs, and usages; was lay brother of the convent of the Charterhouse of London and of the fraternity of the sixty priests of London; and associated with poets and the mayor.

64. Besides the N-Town play, the extant Middle English Purification plays are as follows: Chester Play 11, lines 176–718 of the Coventry Weavers' Pageant, York Play 17, Towneley Play 17, and the Digby Candlemas Play. David and the twelve tribes of Israel were traditional and expected themes for Candelmas ceremonies; see Sponsler, "Alien Nation," 235.

65. See Rastall, *Minstrels Playing*, 106, for a discussion of the "Nunc dimittis" song.

66. Duffy, *Stripping of the Altars*, 22.

67. Nolan, "Performance of the Literary," 185.

68. Appleford and Watson, "Merchant Religion in Fifteenth-Century London," 204, 205.

69. Clopper, *Drama, Play, and Game*, 162, notes that these gifts are linked to ideals of proper civic governance; Benson, "Civic Lydgate," 163, adds that their focus is especially on justice.

70. See "Calendar of Dramatic Records," ed. Robertson and Gordon, 139; Lancashire, *London Civic Theatre*, 45–46; and Osberg, "Goldsmiths' 'Chastell.'" Herbert, *History of the Twelve Great Livery Companies*, 2:234–39, notes that the Goldsmiths' hall was on Foster Lane and lists expenses and menus in the fourteenth and fifteenth centuries for feasts on St. Dunstan's day (the company's principal election feast).

71. See *Wardens' Accounts*, ed. Jefferson, 178, 196, 532–34.

72. Unwin, *Gilds*, 178.

73. See Reddaway and Walker, *Early History of the Goldsmiths' Company*, 79, 139.

74. For Orewell's crozier, see Barron, *London*, 72; for Isabella's visit, see *Wardens' Accounts*, ed. Jefferson, 186–91.

75. In the headnote that he included in his copy of the mumming in BL MS Add. 29729, Stow dropped the phrase "in wyse of balade," referring to the verses simply as "a lettar made by Iohn lidgat," perhaps suggesting that the distinction between vernacular forms that mattered to Shirley no longer carried weight in the sixteenth century. Reflecting similar linguistic drift, Stow also changed Shirley's "mommed in right fresshe and costele welych desguysing" to "shewyd."

76. See Benson, "Civic Lydgate," 164. The mumming differs from the one Lydgate wrote for the Mercers in using its biblical material to place the mayor in his proper

relation both to God and to the goldsmiths; see Nolan, *John Lydgate*, 96–97, whose reading stresses the mumming's emphasis on the need of the powerful for humility.

77. For the growing use of English by the chancery, see Richardson, "Henry V, the English Chancery, and Chancery English," 727.

78. Nolan, *John Lydgate*, 89.

79. For bills and libels, see Scase, " 'Strange and Wonderful Bills' "; for the 1381 rebels, see Justice, *Writing and Rebellion*, esp. 29; and for Lollard texts, see Hudson, *Premature Reformation*.

80. Oliver, *Parliament and Political Pamphleteering*, 194.

81. Fredell, " 'Go litel quaier' "; quotations on 53 and 60.

82. See *DTR*, "An Index of Playing Places and Buildings to 1558," no. 90, for Bishop's Wood.

83. Lancashire, *London Civic Theatre*, 120, 262 n27.

84. Pearsall, *John Lydgate (1371–1449)*, 51.

85. Lancashire, *London Civic Theatre*, 121–22.

86. See Connolly, *John Shirley*, 152.

87. Stow, *Survey*, 99; for the 1458 date of the first London May Game, see Clopper, *Drama, Play, and Game*, 160 n57.

88. See Wickham, *Early English Stages*, 3:50, and Ebin, *John Lydgate*, 87.

89. For the information about sheriffs in this paragraph, I am indebted to Barron, *London*, 161–62; quotation on 147, citing the *Liber Albus*, 399.

90. Lancashire, *London Civic Theatre*, 276 n32.

91. Compare the *Mumming for the Goldsmiths*, in which the mayor is addressed as "youre hyeghnesse" (l. 75). If the honorifics in *Bishopswood* were directed toward the two sheriffs, Lydgate's use of the singular is puzzling.

92. See, for example, the "sovereigns" addressed in the Banns to the Croxton *Play of the Scarament* (l. 8), the "sovereigns that sit" in *Mankind* (l. 29), and the "Sofreynes and frendys" addressed by Contemplacio in N-Town Play 29 (l. 1). Butterfield, "Chaucer's French Inheritance," 22, notes that like the French kings Jean II and Charles V, Richard demanded more elaborate forms of address such as "your majesty" and "your highness" drawn from the discourse of *courtoisie*.

93. Horrox, "Urban Gentry in the Fifteenth Century," has argued for a shared culture linking urban and landed gentry, while Doyle, "English Books in and out of Court," has shown that courtly and urban readers had similar tastes.

94. Norton-Smith, *John Lydgate*, 124.

95. Butterfield, "Chaucer's French Inheritance," 21, 34. The influence of French poetry on Chaucer has been assessed by a number of scholars, from Muscatine's 1957 study (*Chaucer and the French Tradition*) to more recent work such as Wimsatt, *Chaucer and His French Contemporaries*.

96. For an analogous example, see Mortimer, *John Lydgate's Fall of Princes*, 37–44, who describes how Lydgate adapts Laurent de Premierfait's translation of Boccaccio's *De casibus* to an English context, particularly through a reshaping of nationalist sentiments.

97. Lydgate was in France in the mid-1420s, although exactly when and for what reason is unknown; see Mortimer, *John Lydgate's Fall of Princes*, 44 n93. For performances by French courtiers, see Crane, *Performance of Self*, 155–65; for one example of drama associated with a *confrérie* and *puy* in Arras, see Symes, *Common Stage*, 216–27, who notes that some of the procedures of the London *puy*, documented by Andrew Horn, who was city chamberlain from 1320 to 1328, may derive from those of the Arras *confrérie* (220). Sutton, "The *Tumbling Bear* and Its Patrons," suggests that the London *puy* may have had links to mercers.

98. Nolan, *John Lydgate*, 114 n54.

99. For a concise yet example-filled discussion of the connections between French and English court culture in the late Middle Ages, see Wilkins, "Music and Poetry at Court," esp. 210–3.

100. Schirmer, *John Lydgate*, 104, and Pearsall, *John Lydgate*, 186.

101. Nolan, *John Lydgate*, 21; Simpson, *Oxford English Literary History*, 55.

102. See Stevenson, ed., *Herald in Late Medieval Europe*, 3; and Wagner, *Heralds and Heraldry in the Middle Ages*.

103. For a discussion of the role of heralds and pursuivants in private ceremonies, see Warnicke, "Henry VIII's Greeting of Anne of Cleves," 570–72. Kipling, *Enter the King*, 175 n126, notes that in the royal entry of Henry VI into Paris in 1432, a herald represented the city of Paris.

104. Wickham, *Early English Stages*, 1:192–95.

105. Connolly, *John Shirley*, 194–95; quotation on 195.

106. Greenberg notes that the annual Bartholomew's fair (22–25 August), in existence since Henry II, may have sold books; see "John Shirley and the English Book Trade," 376.

107. Pearsall, *John Lydgate (1371–1449)*, 47 n65. Schirmer, *John Lydgate*, 186, believes the disguising may have been written for the parliament that opened at Westminster on 13 October 1427. There is also a chance it was not associated with any parliamentary meeting; see Lancashire, *London Civic Theatre*, 122–23 n33.

108. Watts, *Henry VI*, 23, notes that the four cardinal virtues were conventionally urged on late medieval kings and took precedence over the "theological" virtues of Faith, Hope, and Charity, since they were seen as more socially useful. Scanlon's description of the tradition of the king as the moral center of the realm in the "mirror for princes" genre helps explain Lydgate's use of that genre in a performance for "gret estates" concerned with the young Henry VI's ability to rule; see Scanlon, *Narrative, Authority and Power*.

109. Benson, "Civic Lydgate," 160.

110. Nolan, *John Lydgate*, 143.

111. See Binski, *Painted Chamber*, 41–43, and Barron, *Medieval Guildhall*, 27 and plates 9a, 9b, and 10.

112. Kipling, "Lydgate: The Poet as Deviser," 143.

113. Twycross and Carpenter, *Masks and Masking*, 158, n39.

114. Kipling, "Lydgate: The Poet as Deviser," 98.

115. Nolan, *John Lydgate*; quotations on 130 and 134.

116. Giancarlo, *Parliament and Literature*, esp. 14.

117. The earliest surviving petition in English for which the date is known is the "Mercers' Petition" of 1388, delivered during the Merciless Parliament; see Giancarlo, *Parliament and Literature*, 73–74.

118. Nolan, *John Lydgate*, 3. Nuttall, *Creation of Lancastrian Kingship*, notes the emergence of "close-knit communities of royal household staff, bureaucracies and political representatives" (121), many of whom would have watched the same ceremonies and performances and who were "documented readers" of vernacular poetry in the Lancastrian period (123).

119. Sacks, *Widening Gate*, 4.

120. Simpson, "The Other Book of Troy," 401.

121. Nolan, *John Lydgate*, 3–4, makes the quite different argument that instead of notions of "common profit," Lydgate attempts to assert the sovereignty of the king.

122. See Galloway, "John Lydgate and the Origins of Vernacular Humanism," 445–47; quotation on 445. Galloway's reassessment of Lydgate's engagement with his classical sources builds on Renoir, *Poetry of John Lydgate*, 1967, who viewed Lydgate as a transitional figure bridging the "medieval" and the "humanist" (44) and, more recently, Meyer-Lee, *Poets and Power from Chaucer to Wyatt*, who argues that Lydgate adopted the vocation of humanist inherited from Petrarch.

123. See the discussion of sources for *Serpent of Division*, in Nolan, *John Lydgate*, esp. 37, e.g., "Lydgate relies on medieval rather than classical texts."

124. The latter point is made by Galloway, "John Lydgate and the Origins of Vernacular Humanism," 446.

125. For this definition and further discussion of the term as it is used in cultural studies and anthropology, see Werbner, "Vernacular Cosmopolitanism," 496.

126. Benson, "Civic Lydgate," 148.

CHAPTER 3

1. Chaucer, *A Treatise on the Astrolabe*, in *Riverside Chaucer*, ed. Benson, 662, l. 42. For varied forms of reception of poetry, see Coleman, *Public Reading*, among others, and for the importance of sound to Middle English verse, see Coleman, "Aurality," in *Middle English*, ed. Strohm.

2. For the fourteenth-century development of optical and semantic ideas, see Tachau, *Vision*, esp. 16–20, where she discusses Bacon's understanding of how words, as opposed to images, signify; for the centrality of visual experience to late medieval culture, see Stanbury, "Regimes of the Visual," esp. 266–68.

3. See Brantley, *Reading in the Wilderness*; Clark and Sheingorn, "Performative Reading"; Gertsman, "Pleyinge and Peyntynge"; and, for a study that emphasizes the reciprocity between art and drama, Stevens, "Intertextuality of Medieval Art and Drama."

4. See Sheingorn, "Visual Language of Drama," for the importance of visual features of plays for audiences, and Weigert, "'Theatricality,'" esp. 225, for the homology between the viewing experience of those two representational forms.

5. For the history of medieval tapestry, see d'Hulst, *Flemish Tapestries*; Jubinal, *Recherches sur l'usage et l'origine des tapisseries*; and Lestocquoy, *Deux siècles de l'histoire de la tapisserie*.

6. Both examples are cited in the *MED*, steinen v. 3(a).

7. Kightly, "'Hangings About the Hall.'" Also see Sponsler, "Texts and Textiles," for a discussion of wall hangings and Lydgate's tapestry poems.

8. As an example of the former, Weigert, "'Theatricality,'" 226, cites the municipal authorities of the Burgundian city of Nevers, who paid two of its members to travel to nearby Moulins to study the tapestry of the Nine Worthies in the collection of the count of Bourbon; upon their return, they organized a performance on the same theme.

9. Caxton, *Blanchardyn and Eglantine*, 14.

10. The work on devotional images and late medieval spirituality is extensive. For a sampling of the most important work, see Belting, *The Image and Its Public in the Middle Ages*; Camille, *The Gothic Idol*; and Hamburger, "The Visual and the Visionary."

11. These examples are cited by Hammond, "Two Tapestry Poems by Lydgate," 22, although it is impossible to know whether these phrases formed part of the tapestries themselves or were scribal descriptions of the scenes in each tapestry.

12. For the inventory of Gloucester's goods, which were seized from his Essex castle of Pleshy in 1397, see Dillon and Hope, "Inventory of the Goods and Chattels." The inventory lists fifteen items under the heading "Draps de Arras"; their subjects include scenes from romances and histories, such as the battle of Gawain and Lancelot, the siege of Jerusalem, the story of St. George, and Judith and Holofernes, as well as religious scenes such as the nativities of Jesus and Mary.

13. Stanbury, *Visual Object of Desire*, 79–80.

14. Ibid., 94.

15. For a useful discussion of the functions of the medieval devotional image that engages the views of art historians such as Erwin Panofsky and Sixten Ringbom, see Belting, *Image and Its Public*, 41–64.

16. Rubin, *Corpus Christi*, esp. 135–36.

17. For a discussion of interactions among images and acts of devotion, see the essays in Cornelison and Montgomery, eds., *Images, Relics, and Devotional Practices*. In a related study focused on art and drama, Collins, *The N-Town Plays and Medieval Picture Cycles*, compares the iconography of medieval picture Bibles and the N-Town plays. Focusing on East Anglian drama, Scherb has discussed the overlap between devotional images and vernacular plays; see his *Staging Faith*, esp. 41–65.

18. Camille, "Seeing and Reading," 43.

19. Gertsman, "Visual Space," 32.

20. "Colart de Laon."

21. The poems have been printed in *MPJL*, 1:216–21 ("Cristes Passioun"), 1:250–52 ("The Dolerous Pyte of Crystes Passioun"), 1:290–91 ("The Image of our Lady"), and 1:77–84 ("On De Profundis").

22. *MPJL*, 2:660–61.

23. Owst, *Literature and Pulpit*, 136–48, provides an overview of preachers' debates for and against images; for Pecock's defense of images, see his *Repressor*.

24. Gayk, *Image, Text, and Religious Reform*, 84.

25. Stevens, "The Intertextuality of Late Medieval Art and Drama," 318.

26. The St. Albans manuscript is now Bodleian Library MS Auct.F.2.13; see Clifford Davidson, *Illustrations of the Stage and Acting in England to 1580*, 50–56, for a discussion of it. Whether the St. Apollonia miniature represents a play or not has been debated; see the exchange between Graham Runnalls and Gordon Kipling in *Medieval English Theatre* (1997) over the relation of Fouquet's painting to drama. The "Dance of the Wodewoses" has been recently discussed by Crane, *Performance of Self*, 155–59. Collins, *The N-Town Plays and Medieval Picture Cycles*, examines some of the shared iconography linking plays and medieval art.

27. Knight, "Manuscript Painting and Play Production," 196.

28. Bal, *Reading Rembrandt*, 189, notes that the work of art traditionally is assumed to have three sets of relationships: "one with the cotext or the literary and artistic environment, one with the historical context that frames it, and one with the preceding artistic tradition, the pre-text."

29. For Lydgate's travels to Paris, see Pearsall, *John Lydgate*, 166–69.

30. See Trinity MS R.3.21, fol. 278v.

31. Stow, *Survey of London*, 1:327.

32. See Gertsman, "Visual Space," 2–5, for illustrations of some of these murals.

33. For the Pardon Churchyard, see Barron and Rousseau, "Cathedral, City and State," 35–36.

34. Appleford, "The Dance of Death in London"; quotations on 287 and 295. Barron and Rousseau, "Cathedral, City and State," 36, noting that there is no direct evidence for why Carpenter made this benefaction and that his will does not show any particular affinity for St. Paul's, conjecture that he may have commissioned the paintings in his capacity as executor of the will of Richard Whittington (d. 1423); they further observe that the whole commission "seems to have included a strong civic element" and suggest that the paintings may even have depicted features of the city's landscape (36).

35. See Marchant, *La Danse macabre*; for the mural at Stratford, see Puddephat, "The Mural Paintings of the Dance of Death." The source for Stow's claim may have been the headnote to the version of Lydgate's verses in Trinity R.3.21, a manuscript associated with John Shirley (see Warren, *Dance of Death*, xxiii n2). An inventory of 1529 from the church at Long Melford mentions "three long cloths hanging before the Rood Loft stained or painted with 'the dawnce of Powlis' [*elsewhere called the daunce of Paule*]"; see Parker, *The History of Long Melford*, 86. Gibson, "Long Melford Church, Suffolk, 105,

interprets "Powlis" as "pole" and links the cloths to pole dances associated with parish May Day festivities, but Floyd, "Writing on the Wall," 117, connects them to Lydgate's Dance of Death verses.

36. Gerstman, "Visual Space," 4. Gertsman's essay includes photographs of the mural that clearly show the dominance of the pictorial image over the written text.

37. See Appleford, "Dance of Death," 304.

38. See Connolly, *John Shirley*, 104 and 180–81.

39. Warren, ed., *Dance of Death*, xxiv–xxxi, identifies twelve manuscripts of the poem, a list that is expanded by Seymour, "Some Lydgate Manuscripts," 22–24. Appleford argues that the A version was probably made soon after 1426 for a courtly audience (as suggested by the inclusion of the figure of the Tregetour), while the B version represents Lydgate's revision for St. Paul's, "seemingly with a powerful London civic audience in mind" ("Dance of Death," 295).

40. Simpson, *Oxford English Literary History*, 54.

41. Gertsman, "Visual Space," 24, 30; Chaganti,*"Danse macabre* and the Virtual Churchyard," 15.

42. For a discussion of the use of visual terms to describe the inner images produced by imaginative literature and the attendant anxieties about "textual reification," see Zeeman, "The Idol of the Text," esp. 43–44, and 62.

43. For Clopton's biography and his building efforts related to the Long Melford church, see Parker, *The History of Long Melford*, 43–33. For the verses painted in the chantry chapel, see Trapp, "Verses by Lydgate at Long Melford," 2.

44. See Gibson, *Theater of Devotion*, esp. 87, where Gibson notes that "it would not be surprising" if the Cloptons "owned a manuscript of Lydgate's devotional poems." Although it does not discuss Lydgate's verses, Gibson's early article, "Long Melford Church, Suffolk," considers other visual imagery, including alabasters and stained glass, in the Long Melford church.

45. For a detailed description of the chantry chapel, see Floyd, "Writing on the Wall," 44–51. Gibson, "Long Melford Church, Suffolk," 105–6, discusses the inventories; quotation on 105.

46. Trapp identifies the figure as Mary Magdalene, not the Virgin Mary, but Gibson corrects him; see "Bury St. Edmunds, Lydgate, and the *N-Town Cycle*," 81 n145.

47. Trapp, "Verses," 4; Kamerick, *Popular Piety and Art in the Late Middle Ages*, 162–69.

48. Trapp, "Verses," 4; Floyd, "Writing on the Wall," 50.

49. Trapp, "Verses," 5.

50. Floyd, "Writing on the Wall," 120–21; Maddern, "'Best Trusted Friends'"; Gibson, *Theater of Devotion*, 83.

51. Binski, "The English Parish Church and Its Art in the Later Middle Ages," 19.

52. Floyd, "Writing on the Wall," 101.

53. Gibson, *Theater*, 87. See *MPJL*, 1: 329–62, for the version from BL Harley 218, collated with other manuscripts. Trapp, "Verses," 5–11, matches the Long Melford stanzas to those printed by MacCracken in *MPJL* 1:329–62.

54. Trapp, "Verses," 5; Marks, "Picturing Word and Text in the Late Medieval Parish Church," 167.

55. Gayk, *Image, Text, and Religious Reform*, 119. Gayk believes that images may have originally accompanied the text, but no surviving evidence allows us to know for certain.

56. Simpson, "The Rule of Medieval Imagination," 21. For writing on early modern walls, see the discussion of graffiti and the conflation of word and image in its use in Fleming, *Graffiti and the Writing Arts of Early Modern England*, esp. 60–62.

57. See Marks, "Picturing Word and Text," 183–87, for a discussion of the visual and verbal representations in churches and their role in instruction of the laity.

58. For a discussion of the connection of images to indulgences and charms, see Kamerick, *Popular Piety and Art*, 169–80.

59. Floyd, "Writing on the Wall," 99.

60. See the discussion of Puttenham's notion of "posy" in Fleming, *Graffiti*, esp. 19. Wall writing was among the least durable of textual forms, susceptible to erasure, removal, or whitewashing; see Fleming, *Graffiti*, 75–76.

61. Shirley's Trinity MS R.3.20, with his headnote; Trinity MS R.3.21; and Bodleian MS 2527 (Bodley 626).

62. For the texts of *Legend of St. George* and *Bycorne and Chychevache*, see *MPJL*, 1:145–54 and 2:433–38.

63. Kipling, "Lydgate: The Poet as Deviser," esp. 81–84.

64. Hammond, "Two Tapestry Poems," 21–22; Floyd, "St. George and the 'Steyned Halle,'" argues that *halle* referred exclusively to wall hangings in the early fifteen century, but contemporary sources suggest it could also mean a room.

65. See *OED, stained*, ppl. a.3, and the discussion in Engleworth, *History of the Painter-Stainers Company*, 46–47. The *MED* also gives as one meaning of the verb *steinen* "to ornament (fabric, a garment, etc.) with an embroidered, stenciled, or woven design or pictorial representation; also, stencil or embroider (a figure on fabric)," making it possible that Shirley's headnote could be describing either a painted or a woven cloth.

66. Marshall, *Medieval Wall Painting*, points out that armor styles reflect current trends in other parish church paintings of George: the fourteenth-century George at Little Kimble in Buckinghamshire sports fourteenth-century chain mail while the fifteenth-century George at Hornton in Oxfordshire wears the full plate that became popular in this later period.

67. Cavallo, *Medieval Tapestries*, 33–35.

68. *The Hunt of the Frail Stag*, Southern Netherlands, 1495–1510, and "Scenes from *The Story of the Trojan War*," Southern Netherlands, 1470–90; discussed in Cavallo, *Medieval Tapestries*, 347–58 and 229–49, respectively. The poet-figure is reproduced on 354; Cavallo endorses the current view that it functions as an epilogue at the end of the tapestry-poem, although he notes that when the fragments were first exhibited in 1904, it was treated as the first, rather than the last, panel in the series (350).

69. See Cavallo, *Medieval Tapestries*, 234. Clark and Sheingorn, "Performative Reading," esp. 133–41, point to the speaking images next to the first lines of speech in illustrated play manuscripts.

70. *MED, declaren* v. 4.

71. Any evidence that Lydgate might have been the presenter as well as the poet and deviser is purely circumstantial and not conclusive. Lydgate's abbot kept a townhouse in London, he composed at least one of his works in the city, and he had ties to influential citizens, but none of that implies he was the presenter.

72. The poem's other direct reference to vision, which comes in the phrase "whoso list to looke" (l. 32) is an ambiguous formulation that may refer to looking at the visual images of his life or to looking at a written narrative of his life, or may simply be a handy phrase to fit the meter.

73. Lancashire, *London Civic Theatre*, 124.

74. For Lydgate's use of the *Legenda Aurea*, see Schirmer, *John Lydgate*, 157 n1. Lydgate's immediate source could have been either the Latin *Legenda* or Jean de Vignay's close fourteenth-century translation, the *Légende Dorée*.

75. Pearsall, *John Lydgate*; the quotations are from 181, 277, and 278, respectively. Lydgate's *Legenda*-based version also differs from the story found in Mirk's *Festial*.

76. For the battle of Agincourt and the carrying of the banner of St. George, see *A Chronicle of London*, ed. Nicolas and Tyrrell, 228. Floyd, "St. George," 144. The poem is undated but Pearsall assigns it to what he describes as Lydgate's London period (1427–29), during which he wrote verses for various individuals and groups in London.

77. *MED, champioun* n. 2(a).

78. Printed by Jubinal, *Mystères*, 1:390.

79. Pearsall, *John Lydgate*, 179–80; also see the discussion of various prints and tavern signs featuring the two monsters, including the wall painting of "Le dit de la chiche face" and "Le dit dela fame" (his companion-beast) at Villeneuve-Lembron, in Jones, "Monsters of Misogyny," 205–8.

80. Pearsall favors a date of 1427–29 for *Bycorne*; see *John Lydgate (1371–1449)*, 31.

81. Kipling, "Lydgate: The Poet as Deviser," 82; also see Hammond, "Two Tapestry Poems," 21, who believes that Shirley is working from an exemplar that Lydgate had made for the artisans who would create the hanging or performance.

82. See Schirmer, *John Lydgate*, 98–100, and Wickham, *Early English Stages*, 1:191 and 1:205. Only Shirley's Trinity MS R.3.20 contains a headnote identifying the verses as intended for a wall hanging. BL MS Harley 2251 omits the headnote, and Trinity MS R.3.19 omits the headnote as well as the seven headings (or "histories") before stanzas but includes running titles across the top of the page, describing the poem as "þe couronne [a mistranscription by MacCracken of "fourome"] of disguysinges contrived by Daun Iohan Lidegate. þe maner of straunge desguysinges, þe gyse of a mummynge" (*MPJL* 2:433–38).

83. The impression that the text points to some sort of performance was shared by its first editor, Isaac Reed, who added the version found in BL MS Harley 2251 to his 1780 edition of Joseph Dodsley's *Old Plays*; it was also included on a list made c. 1820 of

pre-1700 plays reputedly owned by John Warburton (1682–1759) that were destroyed by his cook; see Folger Library MS W.a.234 and the discussion of the destruction of the manuscripts in Freehafer, "John Warburton's Lost Plays."

84. Pearsall, *John Lydgate*, 179–80 and 191 n34. Goulding, "Picture-Poems of John Lydgate," notes that *Bycorne and Chychevache* resembles the verses of Henri Baude, who a few years later kept on hand "Dictz moraulx," ready-made inscriptions to accompany possible tapestries or wall paintings; in each case, a provision is made for someone who expounds the morality (41–42).

85. *Vision of William Concerning Piers the Plowman*, ed. Skeat.

86. Denny-Brown, "Lydgate's Golden Cows," 35.

87. *MED, worthi* adj. 3(e); *MED, citesein* n. 1.

88. Denny-Brown, "Lydgate's Golden Cows," 35.

89. *Bycorne and Chychevache* is the second-to-last item in quire 14 of Trinity R.3.20 and comes just before Lydgate's "A Wicked Tong will Seye Amis" (see Connolly, *John Shirley*, 70–74); it also appears in Trinity R.3.19 and Harley 2251. The *Legend of St. George* is the last of three items in quire 28 of Trinity R.3.20 and follows immediately after the *Mumming at Windsor* (once again, see Connolly, *John Shirley*, 70–74); it is also found in Trinity R.3.21 and Bodleian 2527.

90. Hamburger, *The Rothschild Canticles*; and Brantley, *Reading in the Wilderness*.

91. Stevens, "The Intertextuality of Late Medieval Art and Drama," 328.

92. For the overlap of forms, see Wickham, *Early English Stages*, 3:125, and Schirmer, *John Lydgate*, 100.

93. Clopper, *Drama, Play, and Game*, 130.

94. "Mayster Thomas More in his youth deuysed in hys fathers house in London, a goodly hangyng of fyne paynted clothe, with nyne pageauntes, and verses ouer euery one of those *pageauntes*." See Edwards, "Middle English *Pageant* 'Picture'?" quoting from More, *Workes*, ed. Wilson.

95. For example, a scribe's note in Cambridge, St. John's College MS 208 (H.5), refers to "vi payentis iic. Champis, vi, iii.c. paragraffis v." in a usage that points to the six illustrations that appear in the manuscript. See Edwards, "Middle English *Pageant* 'Picture'?" 25–26.

96. *The Brut*, ed. Brie, 2:426.

97. For this argument, see Clark and Sheingorn, "Performative Reading."

98. Gayk, *Image, Text, and Religious Reform*, 84.

99. Pecock, *Repressor*, 1:212–13. Lydgate, "On the Image of Pity," *MPJL* 1:298–99, l. 19.

CHAPTER 4

1. See *MPJL*, 1:35–43.

2. For Corpus Christi processions and plays, see Rubin, *Corpus Christi*; for a discussion showing the development of Corpus Christi as an expression of urban and social ideologies, see James, "Ritual, Drama and Social Body."

3. See Barron, "The Parish Fraternities of Medieval London," 25.

4. Lindenbaum, "London Texts and Literate Practice"; the quotations are from 285 and 293, respectively.

5. Barron, "Parish Fraternities," 34, notes that parish guilds were separate from craft guilds and were basically communal chantries that were mainly middle class and artisanal (few members of Great Companies joined parish fraternities) and were markedly female; they were also "expressions of parish, neighbourly solidarity" that, if bequests can be taken as evidence, were more important than any other civic ties.

6. See Lancashire, *London Civic Theatre*, 39–40.

7. Barron, *London*, 2. The closest London seems to have come to public drama of the sort found in provincial cities was the London *puy* of ca. 1300, a social and religious society devoted to the Virgin Mary and to musical composition and performance in her honor and with membership drawn from royalty, nobility, clergy, and urban elites, evidence of which is preserved in the *Liber Custumarum*; see Sutton, "Merchants, Music and Social Harmony."

8. While expensive, such pageantry must have provided work for artisans, laborers, and provisioners and attracted crowds that generated business for inns, taverns, and other purveyors of goods, so much so that the prevalence of pageants and processions may explain why Londoners did not need the sorts of play festivals put on in York, Coventry, or Chester; see Barron, *London*, 22.

9. Clopper, *Drama, Play, and Game*, 161, argues that the king's dominance over London is a factor in the kinds of drama it developed.

10. For the range of parish dramatic activities, see Erler, *Ecclesiastical London*, xxiii–xxxiv, and for a concise overview, Clopper, *Drama, Play, and Game*, 160–61.

11. Rubin, *Corpus Christi*, 238, citing the *Fraternity Register*, 56. Records of payments from various London parishes in the fifteenth century for canopy, fringes, flags, garlands, banners, torches, pack-thread, and so on offer further evidence for processions or performances on Corpus Christi day; see Blair, "Note on the Relation of the Corpus Christi Procession to the Corpus Christi Pageant," 88–89.

12. Erler, *Ecclesiastical London*, xxxii–xxxiii. Erler notes that Scott may have intended to use the Barking pageants in performances by his own troupe.

13. FitzStephen, *Descriptio nobilissimae*, 27; the complaints of the prioress are cited in *DTR*, no. 543.

14. Dillon, "Clerkenwell and Smithfield as a Neglected Home of London Theater."

15. *DTR*, nos. 544, 546, and 538.

16. The "pleye at Skynners Welle, whiche endured Wednesday, Thorsday, Fryday, and on Soneday it was ended" is mentioned in the chronicle found in BL MS Harley 565, fol. 68v, published as *A Chronicle of London*, ed. Nicolas and Tyrrell, 91, and in the chronicle in BL MS Julius B.i., where it is referred to as "Clerkenwelle." See the detailed discussion of evidence for the play and its possible sponsorship in Lancashire, *London Civic Theatre*, 54–62. I find Lancashire's arguments persuasive, but for a more skeptical reading of the evidence, see Clopper's "London and the Problem of the Clerkenwell Plays," which argues against a cycle and in favor of the Clerkenwell play as "probably

some sort of parish fund-raiser held in conjunction with the fair of St. Bartholomew's Priory, just one of the sights among the usual games" (300).

17. See Lancashire, *London Civic Theatre*, 57–70, for these hypotheses about the play's disappearance.

18. Lancashire, *London Civic Theatre*, 59–60, believes Stow's assertion is correct and that the Skinners' procession developed out of their involvement in the Clerkenwell play. *The Great Chronicle* (see Guildhall MS 3313, fol. 72r) claims that the Skinners organized "a grete play" for Corpus Christi that was said to have lasted from Wednesday to Friday with further celebrations on Sunday.

19. The procession is mentioned every year until 1540–41; Lancashire, *London Civic Theatre*, 277 n43.

20. Unwin, *Gilds*, 125.

21. Stow, *Survey*, 1:230–31.

22. See Erler, "Palm Sunday Prophets," esp. 64–70, for a discussion of costumes, hangings, and labels used in Palm Sunday celebrations.

23. Lancashire, *London Civic Theatre*, 124. See Lambert, *Records of the Skinners*, 54, for the fraternity's links to royal and noble persons.

24. Shirley tells us that he was working from an incomplete exemplar, saying after line 224 "Shirley kouþe fynde no more of this copye." Perhaps information about the commissioning of the poem may have been given or implied in the missing verses, as at the end of Lydgate's verses on Henry VI's triumphal entry, which conclude with praise of the mayor, demonstrating the civic impetus behind that poem.

25. Schirmer, *John Lydgate*, 175.

26. Pearsall, *John Lydgate*, 188; and Cole, *Literature and Heresy in the Age of Chaucer*, 135.

27. *Promptorium Parvulorum*, ed. Way, 2:325.

28. Clopper, *Drama, Play, and Game*, 164. Clopper believes the verses do not record an actual procession, on the grounds that none of the Corpus Christi processions for which we have documentation are "patterned on an orderly and chronologically disposed set of Old and New Testament figures (not to mention a series of Fathers and commentators)" (164–65 n67).

29. In *Literature and Heresy*, Cole argues that in the *Procession*, Lydgate "addresses the common eucharistic problems of his day" and resolves them not by taking sides but by "placing the problems in the hands of earlier authorities" (135), with the result being an alternative to the official eucharistic theologies of his day (146)—Cole even detects a whiff of Wycliffism in the verses (135).

30. Gayk, *Image, Text, and Religious Reform*, 114–15; quotation on 115. Also see Simpson, *Oxford English Literary History*, 455–56.

31. For an overview of ideas about the nature of the eucharist, including debates over Christ's physical presence in it, see Rubin, *Corpus Christi*, 12–35.

32. Gayk, *Image, Text, and Religious Reform*, 104. For meanings of the word *figure*, see the *MED*. As Gayk notes, Lydgate uses the word to mean both material representa-

tion such as statue or image (see *Troy Book* 2:1015–16) and symbolic form such as writing (see "On *De Profundis*," *MPJL* 1:79, ll. 41–42).

33. The Latin Vulgate's mistranslation of the Herbrew word *qaran* in Exodus 34:29 as "horns" rather than "rays" led to the Christian representation of Moses with a ram's horns.

34. Clopper, *Drama, Play, and Game*, 164–65.

35. This is the reading of Goulding, "Picture-Poems of John Lydgate," who believes that the directions in the *Procession of Corpus Christi* describe a procession for one of the more important London churches, possibly St. Paul's or Westminster (66 n2).

36. Erler, "Palm Sunday Prophets," 60, 78.

37. Dagenais, *The Ethics of Reading in Manuscript Culture*, 21; Dagenais is here arguing (following Judson Boyce Allen's arguments in *The Ethical Poetic of the Later Middle Ages*) for a view of all medieval literary texts not as verbal icons but as active, "ethical" agents and does not have Lydgate specifically in mind, although his claims are in my view particularly apt for the *Procession*.

38. Rubin, *Corpus Christi*, 276, and for a discussion of Lydgate's *Procession of Corpus Christi*, 229–32.

39. Cole, *Literature and Heresy*, 136.

40. Ibid., 142. Cole notes that Lydgate's solution to "the common eucharistic problems of his day" is not to take sides but to place "the problems in the hands of earlier authorities" (135), which allows him to fashion an alternative to the official eucharistic theologies of his day (146) while still retaining an orthodox position.

41. Ibid., 142, drawing on Rubin, *Corpus Christi*, 259–71, and Beckwith, *Signifying God*.

42. Lancashire, *London Civic Theatre*, 58.

43. Justice, *Writing and Rebellion*, esp. 158, describes how the rebels "transformed the feast's clerical concerns into a public language of their own" and made it part of the insurgency.

44. Aston, "Corpus Christi and Corpus Regni," esp. 7–9.

45. For a fuller discussion of this point, see Sponsler, "Lydgate and London's Public Culture," 13–33.

46. Meyer-Lee, "Lydgate's Laureate Pose," 41.

47. Schirmer, *John Lydgate*, 175, linked the procession to the London Skinners' Corpus Christi procession (the "great annual festival at which the holy sacraments were escorted through the streets by members of the furriers' guild") but without explanation asserted that the verses were commissioned by Lydgate's monastery. Schirmer's assertion may also have been inspired by knowledge of Bury's interest in Corpus Christi; Gibson, "Bury St. Edmunds," 60–61, notes that late medieval Bury had both an *interludium* and a procession of Corpus Christi.

48. Aston, "Corpus Christi and Corpus Regni," 19–20.

49. Middleton, "The Idea of Public Poetry," 96.

50. Dinshaw, *Chaucer's Sexual Poetics,* 122.

51. Zeeman, "The Idol of the Text," 44.

52. See the similar point made by Beadle, " 'Devoute Ymaginacioun,' " 7, comparing Nicholas Love's *The Mirror of the Blessed Life of Jesus Christ* to such dramatic characters as Contemplacio in the N-Town *Mary Play*.

53. Dagenais, *The Ethics of Reading*," 61.

54. See the discussion in Gayk, *Image, Text, and Religious Reform*, 164–65.

55. Cole, *Literature and Heresy*, esp. 137–40.

56. Carruthers, *The Book of Memory*, 14–15.

57. Connolly, *John Shirley*, 178–82.

58. Hammond thinks Lydgate did not retain the texts of shorter works such as the *Procession* and that they did not circulate; see "Two British Museum Manuscripts," 24.

59. Carruthers, *The Book of Memory*, 227.

CHAPTER 5

1. Although some scholars (e.g., Ebin, *John Lydgate*, 83, and Schirmer, *John Lydgate*, 139–43) have thought that Lydgate helped plan the event, it seems unlikely that he devised any of the pageants. He may have witnessed the entry, however, since he occasionally offers information not given in Carpenter's letter (e.g., the fifth pageant and the accounts of the church processions at the entry's end), although he could have acquired that information from other sources; see Kipling, *Enter the King*, 142–69, and MacCracken, "King Henry's Triumphal Entry," 95. The extant copy of Carpenter's letter is in Guildhall Letter Book K, folios 103v–4v; for a printed version, see *Munimenta Gildhallae Londoniensis*, 3:457–64. Carpenter's letter includes a closing address to a "reverende frater et amice praestantissime," which scholars take as indication that the letter was designed to assist Lydgate in crafting a different style of, but still in some sense official, commemoration. MacCracken, "King Henry's Triumphal Entry," 11, and Kipling, "Lydgate: The Poet as Deviser," 87–89, discuss Carpenter's role in providing a description for Lydgate's use. For the entering of Carpenter's letter into the London letter book, see Barron, *London*, 21.

2. Pearsall, *John Lydgate (1371–1449)*, 170; Nolan, *John Lydgate*, 235.

3. The phrase is from Chaganti, "Vestigial Signs," 50, which argues that in the poetics of the *Dream of the Rood* tradition, inscription and performance "contrast with each other to reveal a deeper interaction: each contains the possibility of the other."

4. The quotation is from Camille, "Signs of the City," 13, quoting Francesca Canadé Sautman.

5. For analyses of the themes and purposes of the entry, see Bryant, "Configurations of the Community in Late Medieval Spectacles"; Kipling, *Enter the King*, 142–69; and Nolan, *John Lydgate*, 184–255.

6. Lancashire, *London Civic Theatre*, 133, notes that with only one possible exception, no royal visitor made an entry into London from 1400 to 1500 without being ceremonially met outside the city's walls, usually at Blackheath.

7. Dillon, *The Language of Space in Court Performance*, 19.

8. Manley, *Literature and Culture in Early Modern London*, 225.

9. Strohm, *Theory and the Premodern Text*, 4.

10. Kingsford, *Chronicles of London*, 303, note to p. 106, l. 28.

11. An influential early reading of processions as engines of social wholeness can be found in James, "Ritual, Drama, and Social Body"; for a more skeptical interpretation, emphasizing dissent over consensus, see Lindenbaum, "The Smithfield Tournament of 1390."

12. Barron, "Chivalry, Pageantry and Merchant Culture," 230–31. Blackheath was the customary place at which the mayor and citizens welcomed visiting royalty.

13. Lydgate's verses do just that, styling the giant as a "sturdy champeoun," ready to protect the king against all "foreyn enmyes" (ll. 74–77).

14. Lefebvre, *The Production of Space*, 33.

15. Saygin, *Humphrey, Duke of Gloucester*, 57, argues that Gloucester asked for the pageant as part of his educative plans for the young king.

16. The phrase is Manley's in *Literature and Culture*, 237.

17. Ashley and Hüsken, eds., *Moving Subjects*, 17.

18. The quotation is from Lancashire, *London Civic Theatre*, 47; for the political and symbolic importance of the procession routes in London, see Manley, *Literature and Culture*, 225–41.

19. Strohm, *Theory and the Premodern Text*, 4.

20. For an overview of royal entries in London, see Lancashire, *London Civic Theatre*, 43–50.

21. Kipling, *Enter the King*, 143–69. The refocusing comes across in all of the extant accounts, with the exception of the Latin version in MS Lambeth 12, which stresses the messianic aspect of Henry's rule in ways absent from other accounts, as Osberg, "Jesse Tree," has demonstrated, and as I discuss later in this chapter. For the notion of Henry VI as messiah, see new coins struck in 1422 to defend the dual monarchy, which featured an angel announcing to the Virgin the coming of a savior who was Henry VI; see McKenna, "Henry VI of England and the Dual Monarchy," 145–51.

22. Kipling, *Enter the King*, 144.

23. On this point, see Evans, "The Production of Space in Chaucer's London," 52. Evans argues that the body in medieval towns was "energetic, sensual and defiant: it *takes up space*," and that "bodies also transform spaces, just as spaces transform them" and "this reciprocal effect is crucial."

24. Dillon, *The Language of Space*, 20.

25. Rubin, *Corpus Christi*, 267ff.

26. For London industries, see Barron, *London in the Later Middle Ages*, 263–65.

27. Lefebvre, *The Production of Space*, 263.

28. See Barron, *London*, 22, who also speculates that the economic benefits of royal entries made large-scale religious performances less important for Londoners.

29. See Manley, *Literature and Culture*, 222, citing Rappaport's use of *invariance* to describe a *canonical* quality of timelessness.

30. Wylie and Waugh, *Reign*, 267.

31. See Lancashire, *London Civic Theatre*, 132–34. Kipling, *Enter the King*, 143, who has argued for the liturgical and typological significance of royal entries in general, sees the 1432 entry as a dramatic "epiphany of Henry's transcendent majesty."

32. For a broad look at the rites and festivities associated with the ritual year, see Hutton, *The Rise and Fall of Merry England*; the influential article by Phythian-Adams, "Ceremony and the Citizen," was one of the first to link processions and other seasonal rituals to the social life of a town.

33. Kipling, "London Pageants," 5, notes that the continental style seemed strange to English observers, as one herald complained when witnessing the entry of Margaret of York into Sluys in 1468.

34. The scriptures were from the Vulgate but were sometimes recorded in English; Wickham, *Early English Stages*, 1:348, says "mimed direct address" characterized English civic triumph as early as 1392, but there is no definitive evidence for that claim.

35. See Kipling, "London Pageants," 25 n8.

36. MacCracken, "King Henry's Triumphal Entry," 80–81, thinks that Lydgate's improvements to the speech were made with the mayor's help. Lydgate omits the section in which Carpenter describes the song of the clergymen.

37. Davis, *A General Theory of Visual Culture*, 123–24; quotation on 124.

38. For the link to Gog and Magog, see *Chronicles of London*, ed. Kingsford, 302, note to 100, l. 4. An antelope atop a pillar and wearing a shield of the royal arms around its neck was one of the figures on the bridge in the entry of Henry V in 1415; see *Gesta Henrici Quinti*, 60–67. Lydgate's phrase, "gan manace" (l. 76), suggests that the giant moved. For the bowing giants of the 1421 entry, see *Vita Henrici Quinti*, 297–98.

39. Carpenter's letter suggests that the doves were actually released ("per emissionem septem albarum columbarum"). The 1431 Paris entry included the gift of three hearts to the king, which opened to release birds and flowers; see Wolffe, *Henry VI*, 60.

40. The account in Trinity MS 0.9.1 makes clear that Henry was given actual objects by Nature, Grace, and Fortune. For the resemblance to dressing of a knight and coronation, see McLaren, *London Chronicles*, 54. While courtly ceremony obviously dominated, the second pageant projected a civic message that emphasized bourgeois values of comfort and prosperity, as Benson, "Civic Lydgate," 156, has argued.

41. Osberg notes that Carpenter's account relies heavily on a pastiche of Vulgate verse and phrases to describe not just the pageants but even the participants (e.g., the twenty-four aldermen are described as "viginti quatuor seniores siue senatores," echoing Apocalipsis 19:4), in the tradition of "cento" passages from earlier poets woven together. Osberg, "Lambeth," 256, and for the "cento" tradition 257 n6, citing Raby, *History of Christian-Latin*, 16.

42. MacCracken, "King Henry's Triumphal Entry," 98. There is no record of who played the roles of the seven maidens and sang the roundel, but some forty years later, the boys of St. Magnus the Martyr sang for the entry of Elizabeth Woodville; see *DTR*, no. 942.

43. Kipling, "London Pageants," 6.

44. McLuhan, *Understanding the Media*, 84.

45. Benson, "Civic Lydgate," 156, notes that the castellated conduit in Cornhill was built in 1282 as a prison for night-walkers and in the fifteenth century still featured a timber cage used for that purpose, with stocks and a pillory for fraudulent bakers.

46. For this suggestion, see Griffiths, *Reign*, 144; Osberg, "Lambeth," 266.

47. The Great Conduit stood at the intersection of Poultry and Cheapside; Stow says it was built around 1285 (*Survey*, 1:17 and 1:264). Kipling, "Lydgate: The Poet as Deviser," 87, thinks that Mercy, Grace, and Pity were introduced by the pageant maker to solve the problem of a disorderly scrambling for the wine, while also adding allegorical significance and ceremony to the dispensing of wine to the king when he approached this pageant; Carpenter's letter does not include them, because he is working from the original device for the entry, which did not envision that problem.

48. Dagenais, "'That Bothersome Residue.'" Arguing against Walter Ong's claim that while "'written words are residue,'" orality "'has no such residue or deposit'" (246), Dagenais argues that the physical text is "the beginning, place of residence, and residue" of the processes of both writing and reading (255).

49. Ibid., 255–56.

50. The first tree displayed Henry's English and French ancestry (Carpenter says that these ancestors were represented "per personas vivas"), a reminder of the legitimacy of Henry's claim to the dual monarchy, while the second was a Tree of Jesse, showing the genealogy of Christ. The Jesse Tree seems to have been controversial, as Lydgate's defense of it—absent from Carpenter's account—suggests. In describing the Jesse Tree, both Carpenter and Lydgate downplay messianic themes. Carpenter writes "Iustum titulum . . . dominum nostrum Regem linealiter deuolutum," which Lydgate renders as "the degree be Iuste Successioun . . . Vnto the kyng ys now dessended dovn," while the version in Lambeth MS 12 reads "nostrum Regem linealiter stabilitum," with the use of "stabilitum" expressing in Osberg's view "more potently than 'deuolutum' ideas of affirmation and confirmation" ("Lambeth," 262). Lydgate adds a defense of the Jesse Tree, perhaps at Mayor Welles's request in response to complaints that had been raised about it; see Mac-Cracken, "King Henry's Triumphal Entry," 93, who also argues that Lydgate may have included the Jesse Tree defense because he devised the pageant himself.

51. For the letter, see *Wardens' Accounts*, ed. Jefferson, 532–34.

52. In the 1392 reconciliation entry, after leaving St. Paul's, Richard II and Anne continued toward Westminster and came to a platform at Temple Bar representing a desert with St. John the Baptist surrounded by various kinds of trees and a menagerie of strange beasts; Withington notes that the mayor that year was a grocer—William Stondon—and that the pageant mingles biblical imagery, tournament themes, and trade symbolism (Withington, *English Pageantry*, 131).

53. See Justice, *Writing and Rebellion*, 77; and for the 1431 rebellion's use of literacy, Summit, "'Stable in Study,'" 210.

54. Justice, *Writing and Rebellion*, 24.

55. See Scase, "'Strange and Wonderful Bills,'" 226–27, 238–39, and 246.

56. Summit, "'Stable in Study,'" 211.

57. Camille, "Signs of the City"; quotations on 23 and 9, respectively.

58. See Fleming, *Graffiti and the Writing Arts of Early Modern England*.

59. Clanchy, *From Memory to Written Record*, 234, notes that by the middle of the fifteenth century, London tradesmen are being described as *litteratus* (i.e., as having a minimal ability to read in Latin); for writing by merchants and artisans, see Richardson, *Middle Class Writing in Medieval London*.

60. Barron, "Pageantry on London Bridge," 96 and 94–95. Barron thinks the expenses may have been hidden elsewhere in the wardens' accounts, but it is also possible that some expenses were paid for by the city, from the money loaned by Bederendene.

61. Lancashire, *London Civic Theatre*, 199.

62. For information on Holford, see Barron, "Pageantry on London Bridge," 98.

63. Nagy, *Poetry as Performance*, 112.

64. Lydgate apparently finished the poem after the king had left Bury; see Pearsall, *John Lydgate*, 34.

65. Although Lydgate apparently works from Carpenter's letter to a fellow cleric, presumably to Lydgate himself, he offers information not in Carpenter, suggesting either he may have been present (as MacCracken, "King Henry's Triumphal Entry," 95, believes) or he is following a now-lost source distinct from Carpenter (as Ebin, *John Lydgate*, 83, assumes).

66. Lindenbaum, "Drama as Textual Practice," quotations on 388, 390, and 391, respectively.

67. Twycross, "Some Approaches to Dramatic Festivities," 7. For crowds at entries, see Wylie and Waugh, *Reign*, 267; *Gesta Henrici Quinti*, 112–13; and Lydgate, *Troy Book*, Bk. 2, ll. 4132–33: "Gret was the pres that abood to se / Of sondri folke that schove fast and croude."

68. See Kingsford, *English Historical Literature*, 88, for the bias for Gloucester found in Lydgate's version of the 1432 entry in MS Cotton Julius B.ii.; and Osberg, "Lambeth," 262, for Lydgate's reticence with biblical imagery.

69. For a discussion of these changes, see Osberg, "Lambeth," 263–67. The fourth pageant was a representation of verses from Proverbs 20:28, as Lydgate recognizes when he corrects Carpenter's misreading of *Misericordiam* (Mercy) as *Memoriam*; see Mac-Cracken's comments on this error, "King Henry's Triumphal Entry."

70. *Coventry: Records of Early English Drama*, 29–30; Osberg, "Lambeth," 264.

71. Osberg, "Lambeth," 265; for messianic propaganda, see McKenna, "Henry VI of England," 161; Wolffe, *Henry VI*, 50; and Rowe, "King Henry VI's Claim to France," 82–83.

72. Osberg, "Lambeth," 266; the quotation is from the same page.

73. Benson, "Civic Lydgate," 151–57.

74. Osberg, "Lambeth," 266; between 1428 and 1436, London loaned the king 56,776 pounds (see Griffiths, *Reign*, 58–59).

75. Benson, "Civic Lydgate," 149.

76. See Kipling, *Enter the King*, 15–16 and 143–44, for the significance of the comparison of Henry to the biblical King David and of London to Jerusalem. Andrew Horn, city chamberlain of London, described London as the "new Jerusalem" in writing of the reception of Edward II and Isabella in 1308 (*Chronicles of the Reigns of Edward I and Edward II*, ed. Stubbs, 152). Ganim, "Experience of Modernity," 86–87, notes that in medieval literature, the city "was always being filtered through the ways in which the city of God was visualized."

77. E.g., BL MSS Cotton Cleopatra C.iv, Julius B.ii, and Harley 565.

78. For a reading of Lydgate's use of the classical past in these verses, and especially his adoption of the Roman triumph as an exemplum relevant to the complexities of Lancastrian rule in the 1420s and 1430s, see Nolan, *John Lydgate*, 184–233.

79. The mayor's speech is recorded in English by Carpenter, with slightly different wording; MacCracken, "King Henry's Triumphal Entry," 80–81, suggests that Lydgate's changes, which improve the speech, were made with the help of the mayor. McLaren, *London Chronicles*, 55 n13, thinks that the description of London as the king's chamber may imply that because coronations typically took place in London, "Londoners viewed London as the heart of the land and in this way bound to the king" while also suggesting that London is the king's residence and thus more intimately his than other parts of the realm; as with the 1392 pageants for Richard II, the aim was in part for the city to win the king's favor and assert its worthiness, as Lydgate's concluding verses suggest.

80. See *MED, quthen* s.v. Nolan, *John Lydgate*, 238.

81. The envoy contains a conventional humility *topos* addressed to the mayor, asking forgiveness for the poet's efforts (his "symple makyng," l. 535); for a discussion of the fifteenth-century uses of this *topos*, see Lawton, "Dullness," 762.

82. Nolan, *John Lydgate*, 137. For Lydgate's use of the orchard, see Wickham, *Early English Stages*, 1:91.

83. Kipling, "Lydgate: The Poet as Deviser," 89, argues that Lydgate's changes did not so much alter the civic device's meanings but added to the range of meanings he found in it.

84. The quotation is from Dagenais, *The Ethics of Reading*, xvii.

85. For the sources of material found in London chronicles, including ceremonies and pageantry, see Gransden, *Historical Writing*, 232–41, and McLaren, *London Chronicles*, 41–44. The wardens' records are described in *London Bridge*, ed. Harding and Wright, esp. xxiv–xxviii. The most notable exceptions to the pattern of recording the 1432 entry in chronicles are the version found in Lambeth MS 12 and in College of Arms MS Vincent 25(1), a manuscript linked to Sir Christopher Barker (d.1550 as Garter) that includes descriptions of various ceremonies, among them the coronation of Henry VI in 1429 (fols. 103–6) and his London reception in 1432 (fols. 106v–7v); see Campbell, Steer, and Yorke, *Catalogue of Manuscripts in the College of Arms*, 1:263–65.

86. Zumthor, *Essai de poétique médiévale*, esp. 73.

87. Boffey, "Short Texts in Manuscript Anthologies," 81.

88. Kipling, "London Pageants," 5. Kipling notes a case in which the same subjects were staged in different ways on the continent and in England—the "Judgment of Paris" in the Brussels pageant for Joanna of Castile in 1496 featured a tableau of the three goddesses posed on a revolving stage, while for Anne Boleyn in London in 1533, the story took the form of a debate between the three goddesses—the records of each reflect that visual/verbal difference, with the Brussels account preserving the visual design of the pageant, while the London account preserves the script (6).

89. For a discussion of possible official accounts, see Barron, "Pageantry on London Bridge," 93. Barron, *London*, 20, believes that Londoners probably paid for Richard of Maidstone's Latin poem describing the four pageants and the king's reply to them in the reconciliation ceremonies, although it's possible that Richard II commissioned them.

90. Fisher, "Language Policy."

91. *Chronicles of London*, ed. Kingsford. In his introduction, Kingsford notes that the parliament of 1399 is the most notable event described up to that point (viii).

92. McLaren, *London Chronicles*, 57–58. Later accounts of London processions continue this practice, as in the similar use of *goodly* in early modern ceremonies.

93. Published as "Text F" in *The Brut*, 2:461–65 (collated with Cambridge MS Hh.6.9). Under the year 1419, MS O.9.1 contains a poem on Henry V's victories not found in any other manuscript except MS Hh.6.9; in MS O.9.1, the poem on Henry's victories is separated from the chronicle text, but in MS Hh.6.9, it is merged with the chronicle narrative.

94. See McLaren, *London Chronicles*, 120, for the 1415 poem, and 54, for the claim that it offers eyewitness accounts. McLaren notes that there are several examples in the London chronicles of eyewitness reports and hearsay material; *London Chronicles*, 44–45.

95. Osberg, "Lambeth," 259; also see James, *Descriptive Catalogue*, 26, and Ker, *Medieval Libraries*, 73.

96. For the conduit change, see Osberg, "Lambeth," 262.

97. Such connections included Thomas Langley, bishop of Durham, who was appointed chancellor of England on 16 November 1422, who played an important role on the council until at least 1426 and thus might have had an interest in Henry's 1432 royal entry; see Osberg, "Lambeth," 259–61.

98. Osberg, "Lambeth," 266–67.

99. For a description of the manuscript, see Campbell, Steer, and Yorke, *Catalogue of Manuscripts in the College of Arms*, 1:263–65.

100. McLaren, *London Chronicles*, 107.

101. Kingsford, "Historical Collection," 505.

102. McLaren, "Textual Transmission," 46.

103. McLaren, *London Chronicles*, 104. The London chronicle has been published as *Historical Collections*, ed. Gairdner, and is linked to BL MS Arundel 19(2) and the chronicle in BL MS Vitellius A.xvi.

104. For an account of the "quite extraordinary" beginning of vernacular chronicle writing in London, see McLaren, *London Chronicles*, 94ff.

105. Boffey, "Short Texts in Manuscript Anthologies," 71.

106. Fifteenth-century chroniclers acquired their information in various ways, including from eyewitness and oral sources, newsletters and official city records, copies of parliamentary statutes and decrees of the king's council affecting London, and material copied from city archives; see Gransden, *Historical Writing*, 238–41. McLaren, *London Chronicles*, 40–41, notes that there is little explicit evidence for the use of the city of London's letter books or other city records as sources, although enough implicit echoes exist to suggest that chronicle writers had access to city documents.

107. McLaren, *London Chronicles*, 43–44.

108. See Gransden, *Historical Writing*, 243, on the chroniclers' outlook.

109. McLaren, *London Chronicles*, 56.

110. Dagenais, *The Ethics of Reading*, xvii. MacCracken's edition of the poem is in *MPJL* 2:630–48. For the date of the manuscript, see *Chronicles of London*, ed. Kingsford, ix.

111. Fragments from the chronicle have been published in *Six Town Chronicles*, ed. Flenley; see 59–60, for the dating. For a discussion of the manuscript, see McLaren, "Textual Transmission," 67, and *London Chronicles*, 108–13. McLaren, *London Chronicles*, 110 n35, notes that we know that one other manuscript, College of Arms MS 2M6, was owned by a herald.

112. *Chronicles of London*, ed. Kingsford, ix.

113. See McLaren, "Textual Transmission," 64, who dates the chronicle manuscript to 1425–75.

114. McLaren, *London Chronicles*, 109.

115. See McLaren, "Textual Transmission," 66, for information on the manuscript.

116. McLaren, *London Chronicles*, 101. The chronicle has been published as *Great Chronicle of London*, ed. Thomas and Thornley. Guildhall 3313 appears to be the product of a workshop or professional scribe commissioned to write up the chronicle (which could later be added to). The chronicle also has what appears to be an eyewitness account of the procession of Henry VI in 1471. See Kingsford, *English Historical Literature*, 79–90, for a discussion of the relations among the various London chronicles.

117. The 1516 edition includes partial and altered versions of Lydgate's verses for the 1432 entry: it contains selected "scriptures" and verses that are recorded as speeches for the pageant characters, downplays the Jesse Tree pageant, and turns attention away from associations of king and Christ; see Osberg, "Lambeth," 267. McLaren, *London Chronicles*, 263–67, discusses the manuscript and urges caution about assuming that Fabyan was the author of the *Newe Cronycles*, as was first proposed by Rastell.

118. For discussions of the manuscript, see Klinefelter, "Newly Discovered 15th-Century English Manuscript," and "'Siege of Calais'"; as well as Robbins, "Middle English Diatribe," quotation on 135.

119. Osberg, "Lambeth," 267. Lydgate's verses were published in revised form in 1542, and this revision provided the basis for the 1547 entry into London of Edward VI (the Jesse Tree was replaced by "England," who urges Edward to follow in his father's footsteps); see Parry, "Continuity," 224, and Anglo, *Spectacle*, 285. Lydgate's verses may also have been the source of Thomas Middleton's *Triumph of Truth*; see Herbert, *History of the Twelve Great Livery Companies*, 1:92, 200, and Wickham, *Early English Stages*, 1:75, 83.

120. Dagenais, "'That Bothersome Residue,'" esp. 252, which argues for a shift from the study of "text" to "the individual, unique, concrete manuscript codex." In Goodman's scheme, allographic writing stands in contrast with the "autograph" in which the typeface or script (the "type") and the meaning (or "token") are inseparable, so that if the former changes, so does the latter; see Goodman, *Languages of Art*, 132–34.

121. McLaren, *London Chronicles*, 49.

122. See the discussion of the translation of visual spectacle into written form by McLaren, *London Chronicles*, 45–49; the quotation is on 51.

123. Coleman, "Talking of Chronicles."

124. McLaren, *London Chronicles*, 47.

125. Nolan, *John Lydgate*, 241.

CHAPTER 6

1. For the "mimic queen," see *DTR*, no. 932.

2. See the account in BL MS Egerton 650; printed in *The Brut*, 2:450–51.

3. The most detailed description of the coronation ceremony is in the so-called "Gregory's Chronicle," from BL MS Egerton 1995, printed in *Historical Collections*, ed. Gairdner, 165–68; Dymmock's role in the banquet is described on 168. For the council's writ of 4 November 1429 authorizing Dymmock's service, see *PPC* 3:6–7. In 1399, Thomas Dymmock played a similar role at the coronation feast of Henry IV; see BL MS Julius B.ii, fols. 46r–46v, in *Chronicles of London*, ed. Kingsford, 49–50.

4. For crowds at Catherine's coronation banquet, see *The Brut*, 427.

5. The abbot of Bury St. Edmunds was one of the assigned triers of petitions in the 1429 parliament (*PROME*: 1429; item 7).

6. See Letter Book K, fol. 70. Estfeld bequeathed the cup in 1445 to his grandson, John Bohun; see his will in *Calendar of Wills*, ed. Sharpe, 2:509.

7. See McKenna, "Henry VI," 157.

8. Griffiths, *Reign*, 190.

9. Lancashire makes this suggestion in *London Civic Theatre*, 125. Goulding, "Picture-Poems," notes that the MS Lansdowne 285 version of the coronation subtleties has no description of the subtleties themselves, just the verses with the title "The baladis of the same," perhaps indicating that the verses were read aloud by a master of ceremo-

nies (26, n1); a subtlety with dialogue, at Ely in 1479, offers evidence of the use of speech in such displays (cited in *DTR*, no. 642).

10. For brief mentions of a variety of subtleties and their obvious resemblance to pageantry, with which they often shared the same subjects, see Withington, *English Pageantry*, 1:82–84. Wickham, *Early English Stages*, 1:210–15, provides a concise discussion of subtleties and their overlap with other visual and dramatic forms, such as tapestries and pageants. Also see Henisch, *Fast and Feast*, 220–26.

11. See Epstein, "Eating Their Words," 371, for a discussion of the "spectacular textuality" of the subtleties.

12. Kirshenblatt-Gimblett, "Playing to the Senses," esp. 1–3.

13. Reed, "The Edible Monument."

14. Austin, *Two Fifteenth-Century Cookery-Books*, x, says that subtleties "were devices in sugar and paste, and apparently in jelly, and were, at any rate at times, made to be eaten," but Hammond, *Food and Feast*, 142, believes that "sometimes it was an ornament wholly made of sugar or 'marchpane' (marzipan) that was eaten. They were not, however, always restricted to edible materials—the cook probably used whatever was necessary to make his design." Chaucer's Parson describes in an anatomy of the sin of pride: "Pride of the table appeareth . . . ful ofte . . . in . . . swich manere bake-metès and dish-metes brennynge of wild fir and peynted and castled with papir," in *The Canterbury Tales*, *Riverside Chaucer*, ed. Benson, 301, l. 443.

15. For the 1399 subtleties, see BL MS Harley 279, fol 45; for 1403, see BL MS Harley 279, cited in Strutt, *Honda Angel-cynnan*, 2:100; for the subtlety of the stag, man, and tree, see BL MS Harley 279, fol. 48v; for 1416, see BL MS Cotton Caligula B.ii, reprinted in *A Chronicle of London*, ed. Nicolas and Tyrrell, 159; for 1421, see *A Chronicle of London*, ed. Nicolas and Tyrrell, 164; and for 1431, see Monstrelet, *Chronique*, 5:6.

16. For the St. George subtlety, see BL MS Arundel 334; for the godhead subtlety, see Austin, *Two Fifteenth-Century Cookery-Books*, 69.

17. Burrow, *Ages of Man*, 29–30.

18. See Russell, *Boke of Nurture*, ll. 690–794; the quotation is at ll. 781–86. Furnivall notes that the first word of "towse" is "neither a clear *t* nor *c*, though more like *t* than *c*. It was first written *Couse* (as if for *cou*[r]*se*, succession, which makes good sense) or *touse*, and then a *w* was put over the *u*" (*Boke of Nurture*, 53 n3). Furnivall's version is edited from BL MS Harley 4011, fols. 171ff. In the versions found in BL MS Sloane 1315 and 2027, different subtleties are given and Russell's description of the four subtleties on the four seasons is omitted (see *Boke of Nurture*, lxxiii).

19. Reed, "The Edible Monument," 143, notes that prints depicting baroque banquets "often show the elaborate arrangements of food, sugar, and ice sculptures along the tables as if they were small festival floats in a long procession."

20. *Short English Chronicle*; see *DTR*, "Doubtful Texts and Records," no. 1781. Chambers, *The Mediaeval Stage*, 1:224 and 2:132, 396–97, cites *A Chronicle of London*, ed. Nicolas and Tyrrell, to show this was a subtlety.

21. BL MS Cotton Julius B.i, in *A Chronicle of London*, ed. Nicolas and Tyrrell, 164–65 nLL.

22. *DTR*, no. 642.

23. Wickham, *Early English Stages*, 3:125.

24. See *MED*, *sotilte* n5.

25. Lydgate, *Pilgrimage*: "To thys Sect [Epicureans] yt ys endwed, With rost somwhyle, and with stewyd, To be seruyd, and metys bake, Now to ffrye, now steykes make, And many other soteltes."

26. Crane, *Performance of Self*, esp. 128–32.

27. Fumerton, *Cultural Aesthetics*, 125–26.

28. Henisch, *Fast and Feast*, 75, 101–2.

29. See, for example, *Forme of Cury*, ed. Hieatt and Butler, 20.

30. Lupton, "Thinking with Things," 76–77.

31. *The Brut* describes a dearth of wheat, beef, mutton, and other meat in 1429 lasting until Lammas and high prices for bread in London (450). For norms of food consumption, see Dyer, *Standards of Living*, 90.

32. Epstein, "Eating," 360.

33. For the serving of food at a banquet, see Tannahill, *Food in History*, 221–22.

34. For "leches" and "custade rooial," see Austin, *Two Fifteenth-Century Cookery-Books*, 134–35 and 55, and Hieatt, "Making Sense of Medieval Culinary Records," 110; and for fritters, see Scully, *Art of Cookery*, 136, and Hammond, *Food and Feast*, 136.

35. Hammond, *Food and Feast*, 137, argues that the 1429 banquet "seems to have had particularly heraldic food."

36. For the two quotations, see Epstein, "Eating," 365 and 363, respectively, and on this point more broadly, also see Kilgour, *From Communion to Cannibalism*. As Epstein points out, the beginnings of this conflation are described by McNiven, *Heresy and Politics*, while its effects are charted by Strohm, *England's Empty Throne*. Bynum, *Holy Feast and Holy Fast*, 48–49, notes that the central Christian meal was not the luxurious feast but the frugal repast of commensality, and thus there was an inherent even if submerged tension in the Lancastrian attempt to link church and crown in the coronation banquet. The subtleties also represented a carnivalesque excess that refused the ascetic disciplines of medieval Christianity and evaded regimes of dietary surveillance that were developing for the middle classes, which Lydgate himself helped promulgate in his "Dietary"; see Sponsler, "Eating Lessons."

37. Fabyan, *Newe Cronycles*. BL MS Egerton 1995 describes the verses as a "reson" (fol. 176v).

38. BL MS Julius B.i. describes Lydgate's verses as "this resoun." Fabyan says the kneeling Henry had "this balade takkyd by hym" (*Newe Cronycles*, fol. 189).

39. Griffiths, *Reign*, 190.

40. The years 1429–31 marked a period of increased concern about Lollardy. The opening sermon on the first day of parliament on 22 September 1429, which Henry VI attended, was given by the chancellor, John Kemp, archbishop of York, whose central

theme was heresy and in particular the Hussite actions in Bohemia, as well as errors and heresies at home, too.

41. Epstein, "Eating," 366; Epstein reads the banquet as ritual meal and secular mass, "a performance of secularized, politicized communion" in which the guests are both audience and performers.

42. BL MS Egerton 1995 says she held "in every honde a crowne" and does not specify that the king was kneeling (fol. 177v). Fabyan, *Newe Cronycles*, describes the figure of Henry as "beryng in hande thys balade" (fol. 189v). The subtleties at the banquet in Paris that followed Henry VI's French coronation in 1431 would also feature one of the Virgin Mary and the crowned king, another of a crowned fleur-de-lis held up by two angels, the third "une dame et ung paon," and the fourth a woman and a swan; see Monstrelet, *Chronique*, 5:6.

43. Epstein, "Eating," 374; McKenna, "Henry VI of England and the Dual Monarchy," 161. Epstein notes that while such an equation of the king with Christ might seem too blasphemous to be intentional, it has a precedent in a coin made in 1423 for the infant Henry VI on which the figures in the Annunciation image common to such coins are reversed, putting the angel Gabriel on the viewer's right and the Virgin on the left, a switch that places the angel behind the arms of England and the Virgin behind those of France in a way that McKenna argues politicizes the Annunciation, with Henry VI in the role of the infant Jesus.

44. Beckwith, *Signifying God*, 29.

45. On the eating of nobles in effigy, see Weiss, "Edible Architecture, Cannibal Architecture." Weiss describes a feast hosted by Casanova, which ended with a cake covered with the images of European nobility: "Casanova's passion for royalty was symbolically manifested in this attempt at complete devoration" (165). Lancashire, *London Civic Theatre*, 125, argues the coronation subtleties were probably read aloud, for the benefit of everyone in the hall.

46. Fabyan, *Newe Cronycles*, fols. 188v–189v.

47. *MED*, resoun, n2, 9a.

48. Kipling, "Lydgate: The Poet as Deviser," 84.

49. Ibid.; see Wolffe, *Henry VI*, 51, and Pearsall, *John Lydgate (1371–1449)*, 29, for the coronation plans.

50. *MPJL*, 1:xxviii and 2:623, although in *MPJL* MacCracken mistakenly dates the subtleties to 1432.

51. Epstein, "Eating," 367–68.

52. Reed, "The Edible Monument," 143.

53. See Barron, "Chivalry, Pageantry and Merchant Culture," for London's indifference to aristocratic chivalry and its development of its own brand of chivalric spectacle in the form of midsummer watches and "ridings" of the mayor to take his oath (225–26, 228–29).

54. See *Historical Collections*; in his introduction to the edition, Gairdner notes that the manuscript may originally have been in two volumes (1–11). The subtleties are on fols.

176v–177v, immediately after a detailed description of the coronation ceremonies that ends with the description of the costumed Dymmock offering himself as the king's champion. Although William Gregory, a member of the Skinners' Company and mayor of London in 1451–52, has usually been taken as the chronicle's author, McLaren has argued that the evidence does not support that assumption ("Textual Transmission," 59).

55. McLaren, "Textual Transmission," 59–60.

56. Connolly, *John Shirley*, chap. 8, and Mooney, "John Shirley's Heirs," 184–85. For Egerton 1995's links to other London miscellanies, see Parker, *Commonplace Book in Tudor London*.

57. The chronicle has been published as *A Chronicle of London*, ed. Nicolas and Tyrrell, and in *Chronicles of London*, ed. Kingsford.

58. Published as *Great Chronicle of London*, by Thomas and Thornley, who believed it to be a Main City Chronicle, a notion that is no longer accepted (see McLaren, "Textual Transmission," 38ff).

59. McLaren, *London Chronicles*, 101.

60. McLaren, "Textual Transmission," 60.

61. McLaren, *London Chronicles*, 102.

62. There are also four different marginal hands (McLaren, *London Chronicles*, 100); Lydgate's ballades for the subtleties appear on fols. 79–80. The years 1444–83 of the chronicle in Julius B.i. have been published in *Chronicles of London*, ed. Kingsford, with the subtleties as note TT (168–69). The chronicle ends on fol. 90; several of the subsequent leaves are blank, while others contain copies of various documents, including a list of mayors and sheriffs.

63. *Chronicles of London*, ed. Kingsford, xiii.

64. The St. John's manuscript is described by Flenley, *Six Town Chronicles*, 60–62, and Hanna, *Descriptive Catalogue*, 75–77, among others. The manuscript was at one point owned by John Davenport, a play-loving tavern keeper (Shakespeare stayed at his inn) and mayor of Oxford (d. 1621), who presented the manuscript to St. John's College (Flenley, *Six Town Chronicles*, 60).

65. Mooney and Matheson, "The Beryn Scribe," 353. On the Trinity College manuscript, see Boffey and Thompson, "Anthologies and Miscellanies," 288–90; and Mooney, "Scribes and Booklets."

66. Kingsford, *English Historical Literature*, 86–87; McLaren, *London Chronicles*, 100, notes that several chronicle manuscripts predate it; Mooney and Matheson, "The Beryn Scribe," 354. St. John's MS 57 was "compiled soon after 1430" (Lester, "*Grete Boke*," 27). McLaren, *London Chronicles*, 100, says the chronicle is in one neat hand and is probably a copy since it contains some typical copying errors.

67. Mooney and Matheson, "The Beryn Scribe," 355, 362. St. John's MS 57 appears to be the product of a workshop or of a scribe writing on commission; see McLaren, *London Chronicles*, 101.

68. See Abbott, *Catalogue of the Manuscripts in the Library of Trinity College, Dublin*, 76. Part of the chronicle has been published as *Bale's Chronicle* in Flenley, *Six Town*

Chronicles. Robert Bale wasn't recorder of London and didn't die in 1461, as Tanner thought, but Kingsford argues he was the London scrivener mentioned in several fifteenth-century Chancery Proceedings; see Kingsford, "Robert Bale, the London Chronicler," 126–28.

69. McLaren, *London Chronicles*, 107.

70. McLaren, "Textual Transmission," 46. From 1424–29, Cecil 281 agrees with Harley 565 and, from 1429–37, is "a superior version of" the text in Egerton 1995 that offers a better reading of Lydgate's three ballades (Kinsgford, "Historical Collection," 508–9).

71. See McLaren, *London Chronicles*, 100 n5.

72. Bühler, "Sir John Paston's 'Grete Booke,'" argued that Lansdowne 285 is not Paston's "grete boke" but another manuscript with very similar contents that represent an early example of "mass production" (351); the current consensus is that Lansdowne 285 is the work described in the Paston letters; see Lester, "*Grete Booke*."

73. See Bartlett, "Translation, Self-Representation, and Statecraft," and Lester, *Earliest English Translation*, 22–23.

74. See Bühler, "Sir John Paston's *Grete Booke*," 347–49, for a description of the contents of Morgan 775.

75. Lester, "*Grete Boke*," 34. But Edwards, in a review of Lester's book, finds no identifiable connection between Astley and Paston (700). Lydgate's ballades for the subtleties appear on fols 14–15 and 24.

76. Boffey and Edwards, "Middle English Verse in Chronicles," 126–27.

77. Epstein, "Eating," 368–69.

78. McLaren, "Textual Transmission," 62, 63.

79. This is to some degree unsurprising, given that in their lack of attention to the visual features of performance the subtleties resemble other dramatic texts from medieval England, which are seldom illustrated in their manuscript contexts, unlike continental dramatic manuscripts, such as the *Jour de Jugement*, which as Emmerson has observed seemed to have sought to transmit to readers "a lost theatrical performance"; see Emmerson, "Visualizing Performance," 246.

80. Kipling, "Lydgate: The Poet as Deviser." Kipling argues that this device was passed to Lydgate, with the request for suitable verses.

81. Chaucer, "The Complaint of Venus," in *Riverside Chaucer*, ed. Benson, 649, l. 80.

82. See *MPJL*, 1:215.

CHAPTER 7

1. For a brief overview of women and medieval drama, see Sponsler, "Drama."

2. See Muir, "Women on the Medieval Stage," and Davidson, "Women and the Medieval Stage."

3. For early convent drama, see Dronke, *Women Writers of the Middle Ages*, 63, and Findlay, *Playing Spaces in Early Women's Drama*, 148–54; for the Barking Easter performances, see Woolf, *The English Mystery Plays*, 19, and Young, *Drama of the Medieval Church*, 1:165. Ogden, "Women Play Women in the Liturgical Drama of the Middle Ages," has identified twenty-three music dramas dating from 1100 to 1600 that were performed by nuns.

4. Goldberg, "Craft Guilds, the Corpus Christi Play, and Civic Government," 145–47; his argument rests on the fact that mentions of men playing female roles first appear in the late fifteenth century. For the Chester wives, see *Chester: REED*, 22.

5. See Coletti, "A Feminist Approach to the Corpus Christi Cycles," 79; as well as Evans, "Body Politics: Engendering Medieval Cycle Drama" and "Feminist Re-Enactments: Gender and the Towneley *Uxor Noe*."

6. Korda, *Labors Lost*.

7. Normington, *Gender and Medieval Drama*, 41–44.

8. See ibid., 44–48, and Muir, "Eye of the Procession."

9. See Bryant, "Configurations of the Community," for a discussion of the Lancastrian spectacles of the 1420s and 1430s as forms of political propaganda.

10. McKenna, "Henry VI of England and the Dual Monarchy," 156.

11. Scattergood, *Politics and Poetry*, 74.

12. These are the known entries into London for women before 1500; see Lancashire, *London Civic Theatre*, 186–94, for a list of major royal and other entries into London from 1400 to 1558.

13. Kipling, *Enter the King*, chap. 6.

14. For Catherine's ceremonial appearances, see Strickland, *Lives of the Queens of England*, 2:146–47 (Henry V's funeral procession) and 2:148–50 (processions with her son in the early 1420s).

15. Catherine was in France visiting her parents when Henry V died near Paris and traveled back to England with his body. Meanwhile, Henry V's brother Humphrey, duke of Gloucester, and his uncle, Henry Beaufort, bishop of Winchester, were already in England and primed to take a guiding role in the upbringing of Henry VI; see Griffiths, *Reign*, 12–13.

16. Henry was present at the opening of all the early parliaments, except for the first in 1422; he led processions through London in 1425 and 1428 and again at his coronation in 1429 (see Griffiths, *Reign*, 57). For the parliaments, see *RP* 4:261, 162, 196, 316; *The Brut*, ed. Brie, 452; and the *Great Chronicle of London*, ed. Thomas and Thornley, 128, and, for the London processions, 132.

17. See Facinger, "Study of Medieval Queenship"; McCartney, "King's Mother and Royal Prerogative"; and Stafford, *Queens, Concubines, and Dowagers*.

18. Strohm, *Hochon's Arrow*, 95.

19. See Green, "Three Fifteenth-Century Notes," 14–16.

20. Schirmer, *John Lydgate*, 105; Schirmer believed Brice was killed in a skirmish at Louviers in 1430. Pearsall, *John Lydgate*, 184, and Ebin, *John Lydgate*, 89, date the Hertford disguising to 1430.

21. PRO, E28/50/22, cited in Griffiths, *Reign*, 64 n17.

22. Their visit to St. Albans is described in Amundesham, *Annales monasterii S. Albani*, 1:21. The king's itinerary has been established by Christie, *Henry VI*, 375ff.

23. Pearsall, *John Lydgate (1371–1449)*, 28.

24. Giancarlo, *Parliament and Literature*, 144–45.

25. Sharp distributed "bills" in London, Coventry, Oxford, and elsewhere and gathered a band of followers at Abingdon in his "rising" shortly before Whitsuntide in 1431; see Amundesham, *Annales monasterii S. Albani*, 1:63.

26. In *Early English Stages*, 1:204, Wickham argues that a presenter speaks on behalf of the husbands and a wife on behalf of the wives; Twycross and Carpenter, *Masks and Masking*, 160 n44, note that despite the appearance of direct speech, the wives' answer "is also a 'bill' by way of *replicatio*, which could be delivered by a representative."

27. Strohm, *Hochon's Arrow*, 107.

28. See Schirmer, *John Lydgate*, 90, for Lydgate's involvement with the court.

29. His most recent effort on their behalf had been the translation of a French poem by Lawrence Calot stressing Henry VI's descent in the line of St. Louis, commissioned by the earl of Warwick in 1426; see "The Title and Pedigree of Henry VI," *MPJL*, 2:613–22. For a discussion of the ways in which Lydgate's poetic identity was intertwined with Lancastrian monarchical identity, see Patterson, "Making Identities."

30. Under the Lancastrian kings, almost all legislation developed out of petitions presented to parliament; see Jacob, *Fifteenth Century*, 409.

31. See Wickham, *Early English Stages*, 1:197. Nolan, *John Lydgate*, argues that the real subject of Hertford is not gender or contemporary politics but genre "conceived in the broadest sense as a mode of organizing the historical" (167); thus, the lack of resolution at the end of the disguising "enacts the failure of one mode of Chaucerian discourse, the comic, to remain adequate to the representation of the present in the face of dramatic historical change" (171).

32. For the practice of peasant plaint in royal courts, see Scase, *Literature and Complaint*, 11–17, and for its use in vernacular poetry, 33–41.

33. The typical response of a king to a rejected parliamentary petition was *le roi s'avisera* ("the king would advise himself"), a polite way of saying no; see Giancarlo, *Parliament and Literature*, 161. The formel in the *Parliament of Fowls* asks for "respit for to avise me" (l. 648).

34. For boy-bishop rituals, see Hutton, *Rise and Fall of Merry England*, 8–12, and Davidson, *Festivals and Plays in Late Medieval Britain*, 5–10. Harris, *Sacred Folly*, makes the revisionary argument that the role reversal associated with the Feast of Fools was reverential, not mocking, an observation that helps explain the mingling of the carnivalesque with the serious in the Hertford disguising.

35. The castle was situated in flat, low-lying land on the south bank of the River Lea; it was apparently built after the Norman Conquest as part of a defensive ring around London. The internal arrangements of the castle shown in an Elizabethan plan of around 1582–92 in the PRO reveal main apartments grouped around a central

courtyard, with the great hall on the east. The castle seems to have been a timber-framed building, the hall an aisled building of three bays with screens and two porches at the northern end and a square oriel and a fireplace at the southern end. The great chapel was probably on the first floor of one of the wings shown projecting eastward from the building. Hertford had decayed rapidly during the fourteenth century and by 1438 was a rural manor more than a town; see the *Victoria History of the County of Hertford*, 3:502–3.

36. For Henry V's insistence that Catherine play an active role in her son's upbringing and reside in his household, see *RP*, 4:280–82, and Griffiths, *Reign*, 56. Catherine's domestic household was financed out of English lands granted as part of her dower—income from these lands appears to have been about 4,360 pounds—and presumably also from income from holdings in France, as guaranteed by the Treaty of Troyes. She also received 2,300 pounds annually from the exchequer, a sum that during the financially hard-pressed years of the 1420s might have been grudgingly given. For Catherine's income, see Griffiths, *Reign*, 56 and Crawford, "King's Burden?" 44–45.

37. Griffiths, *Reign*, 56.

38. The services of his nurses and two chamber women were so valued that in 1428, they were admitted to the confraternity of St. Albans abbey, which was patronized by the royal family; see Griffiths, *Reign*, 52.

39. Wolffe, *Henry VI*, 45–46.

40. Griffiths, *Reign*, 55–56.

41. *Incerti Scriptoris*, ed. Giles, 4:17.

42. See Crawford, "King's Burden?" 37.

43. Griffiths, "Queen Katherine of Valois and a Missing Statute of the Realm," 106–7.

44. In 1425, a quarrel between Gloucester and the duke of Burgundy quickly escalated to the point of a duel. To forestall bloodshed, the quarrel was handed over to Bedford and to the dowager queens of England (i.e., Catherine) and France for arbitration; see Jacob, *Fifteenth Century*, 226. Catherine had earlier interceded on behalf of James I of Scotland during her coronation-feast in 1421; see Strickland, *Lives*, 135–38. Did it signal a decline in Catherine's public fortunes that Lydgate dared to produce the anti-matrimonial Hertford disguising at her own residence where her son was fast becoming more guest than resident, newly absorbed as he was within his own male-centered household?

45. Schirmer, *John Lydgate*, 101, dates the *Mumming at Eltham* to 1424, as does Ebin, *John Lydgate*, 86; Pearsall, *John Lydgate (1371–1449)*, 29, prefers 1428.

46. Descriptions of Eltham palace and the plan of the great hall can be found in Hasted, *History and Topographical Survey of the County of Kent*, 1:463–68. Froissart, *Chroniques*, describes a meeting of parliament at Eltham in 1395.

47. There is some question as to whom the tenth and eleventh stanzas are addressed; they begin with the words "To Youre Hyenesse," which might seem to refer to Henry, but their content seems better geared toward Catherine, especially since the twelfth stanza, "Lenvoie," directly addresses Henry ("Prynce excellent," l. 78).

48. For the role of East Anglian women as patrons and readers, see Delany, *Impolitic Bodies*, on Bokenham's "Legend of Holy Women," commissioned by women in Suffolk; Winstead, *John Capgrave's Fifteenth Century*, on that author's patronage by women, including the Gilbert nuns at Sempringham; Gibson, *Theater of Devotion*, on East Anglian women as patrons of devotional material; and Hanna, "Some Norfolk Women and Their Books, ca. 1390–1440."

49. See Pearsall, *John Lydgate*, 71, 168–69.

50. Schirmer, *John Lydgate*, 114. Lydgate may also have been the author of a "Complaint for my Lady of Gloucester and Holland," copied by Shirley in Trinity MS R.3.20 and linked with Lydgate in a marginal note by Shirley in MS Ashmole 59 version; the poem defends Jacqueline after Gloucester's divorce of her and subsequent marriage to Eleanor Cobham, one of her ladies in waiting; see Connolly, *John Shirley*, 81–83.

51. The poem is undated, but Schirmer, *John Lydgate*, 200, conjectures it was written in 1424.

52. Given-Wilson, *Royal Household*, 69.

53. Horrox, "Urban Patronage and Patrons," 148–49.

54. Greenfield, "Festive Drama at Christmas." Since pressures on the local neighborhoods through which the household passed were considerable, especially at Christmas when there were numerous guests, with the household requiring food and drink—often paid by credit, which resulted in a good bit of local loss and animosity toward purveyors—the gift-giving rituals enacted in and by seasonal household dramas might have offered a pointed commentary on those uneasy economic relations; see Given-Wilson, *Royal Household*, 41–46.

55. Westfall, *Patrons and Performance*, 34–37. In an anecdote designed to reveal Henry's modesty, Blacman notes that once at Christmas, a certain lord mounted a dance or show featuring young women with bare breasts; Henry's reaction was to avert his eyes and leave the hall. See Blacman, *Henry the Sixth*, 8.

56. For the suggestion that Lydgate was a member of Henry V's chapel royal, see Green, *Poets and Princepleasers*, 88.

57. Westfall, *Patrons and Performance*, 34–37.

58. *Household of Edward IV*, ed. Myers, 133–36. Information on Henry VI's royal chapel comes from the *Liber Regie Capelle* written for presentation to Alfonso V of Portugal in 1449; see *Liber Regie Capelle*, ed. Ullmann, 59–60, for a discussion of the chapel's duties at feasts and on special occasions.

59. PRO, E403/681 m.3; cited in Griffiths, *Reign of King Henry VI*, 64 n17.

60. Westfall, *Patrons and Performance*, 34–37. London companies performed at Eltham at Christmas in 1425 (see PRO, E404/44/334) and again in 1426 when Henry VI was entertained by Jack Travaill's London players along with four boys, protégés of the duke of Exeter, playing interludes. The next year, the Travaill players were again at Eltham along with another company called the Jeues of Abingdon; see Wolffe, *Henry VI*, 37, 45, and Griffiths, *Reign*, 64 n17. Kipling has argued convincingly that disguisings at

the medieval English court were designed and performed by professionals, not by disguised aristocrats, the latter being an innovation of Henry VIII; until then, aristocrats were spectators and performers were drawn from the ranks of household retainers; see Kipling, "Early Tudor Disguisings," 3–8.

61. For the size of households, see Starkey, "Age of the Household," 244.

62. Jacob, *Fifteenth Century, 1399–1485,* 342. See also Morgan, "House of Policy."

63. Given-Wilson, *Royal Household,* 42.

64. Bumke, *Courtly Culture,* 4–6.

65. Vale, *The Princely Court,* 33, 165.

66. Westfall, *Patrons and Performance,* 11. In the 1420s, the lower-level members of Henry's household might have wished for more than entertainments; pages and grooms were chronically underpaid and came close to resigning en masse in May 1426; see Griffiths, *Reign,* 54.

67. Wickham, *Early English Stages,* 1:223.

68. Schirmer, *John Lydgate,* 106, suggests the mumming was composed while Lydgate was in Paris and was performed at Christmas in 1429, and Green, "Three Fifteenth-Century Notes," 15, concurs. Internal evidence supports this claim; see esp. ll. 84–88. The age at which medieval child-kings were expected to come of age remains uncertain; perhaps it was ten, as in the case of Richard II (see Watts, *Henry VI,* 120).

69. This was a gentler solution than that imposed on another superfluous queen by Henry V, who had imprisoned his father's wife Joan of Navarre on charges of witchcraft apparently in order to seize her dower to meet the expenses of an overextended government; see Watts, *Henry VI,* 326 n278.

70. Although definitive evidence is lacking, it is tempting to imagine that the "very ancient arras" described by a Swiss visitor to Windsor in 1599 as a tapestry that the "English took from the French" and that tells the story of Clotilda, Clovis, and the fleur-de-lis was hanging in the hall when Lydgate's mumming was performed; see Platter, *Travels in England in 1599,* 84–85.

71. Shirley annotates this line: "A daun Iohan, est yvray?"

72. For Joan of Arc's effects on Henry's hasty coronations, see Griffiths, *Reign,* 189.

73. See Griffiths, *Reign,* 61.

74. *Book of Margery Kempe,* ed. Meech and Allen, 23, ll. 9–10. Barry Windeatt believes Margery and her husband were returning from seeing the 1413 York plays; see *Book of Margery Kempe,* trans. Windeatt, 305 n1.

75. For these and other examples, see Davidson, "Women and the Medieval Stage"; Muir, "Women on the Medieval Stage"; and Ogden, "Women Play Women."

CHAPTER 8

1. *Manuscript Trinity R.3.19,* ed. Fletcher, xv; the manuscript is no. 599 in James, *Western Manuscripts,* 2:74.

2. Brown and Robbins, *Index*, and Robbins and Cutler, *Supplement*, list the sixteen unique texts (nos. 190.1, 267, 437, 928.5, 1172.5, 1238, 1838, 2148, 2254, 2311, 2384.8, 2588.5, 3493, 3807, 3983, and 4231). Mooney identifies another five texts not known from any other source, formerly all cited in the *Index* as 928.5, but which Mooney shows to be separate short lyrics; see Mooney, " 'A Woman's Reply.' "

3. *Manuscript Trinity R.3.19*, ed. Fletcher, xv and xxx.

4. Mortimer, *John Lydgate's Fall of Princes*, esp. 78, and Riddy, "Mother Knows Best," 80–83, discuss the manuscript's regiminal and advisory preoccupations, and Mooney, " 'A Woman's Reply,' " makes a case for female authorship of one of its poems.

5. See Brown, *Register*, no. 2448, and Brown and Robbins, *Index*, no. 3807; printed in *Secular Lyrics*, ed. Robbins, 110–13.

6. Hanna, "Miscellaneity and Vernacularity," 37.

7. Robbins, ed., *Secular Lyrics*, 267 n120.

8. See *Manuscript Trinity R.3.19*, ed. Fletcher, xv, xxvii, and xxx, and Livingston, "Sixth Hand." For the Hammond scribe, see Hammond, "Two British Museum Manuscripts," 27, and "A Scribe of Chaucer," 27–30.

9. *Manuscript Trinity R.3.19*, ed. Fletcher, xx. Fletcher, citing Greg, "Chaucer Attributions," 539–40, says that foliation in what appears to be a fifteenth-century hand suggests that the booklets had been bound together by the time of George Wilmer's ownership, who donated the manuscript to Trinity College (xx), and that the booklets were together in the present form by around 1480 (xxii). But also see Mooney, "Scribes and Booklets," 266, for a different reading of the date of the foliation, which leads her to conclude that they remained separate up to Stow's ownership.

10. For a discussion of the foliation, see *Manuscript Trinity R.3.19*, ed. Fletcher, xx–xxii.

11. Doyle argues that Trinity MS R.3.21 was produced in a "setting of John Shirley and his successors in the business of compiling manuscript miscellanies, based in a shop in St. Batholomew's Close and employing local resources, aided by a network of personal relationships"; see "An Unrecognized Piece of Piers the Ploughman's Creed," 434. Mooney discusses what is known about the scribe of R.3.21 in "A Middle English Text on the Seven Liberal Arts," 1028 n7–8, and "More Manuscripts Written by a Chaucer Scribe," 401–7.

12. See Mooney, "John Shirley's Heirs," 186–87.

13. Mooney, " 'A Woman's Reply,' " 245. Also see Connolly, *John Shirley*, 181, who argues that the main scribe of R.3.21 was probably part of "a professionally-organised secular scriptorium or workshop" in London and had access to some of Shirley's manuscripts; Hammond, "Two British Museum Manuscripts," 27; and *Manuscript Trinity R.3.19*, ed. Fletcher, xxvii.

14. See Sutton and Visser-Fuchs, "Provenance," 108–10, and for the association with Vale. In linking R.3.21 with Multon, Sutton and Visser-Fuchs follow the lead of Boffey and Thompson, "Anthologies," 287–89. Mooney, "Scribes and Booklets," 242, agrees that Multon and the Hammond scribe are one and the same.

15. Mooney, "John Shirley's Heirs," 189.

16. Ibid., 197.

17. Mooney, "Scribes and Booklets," 252.

18. Ibid., 264. Mooney endorses Hammond's view ("A Scribe of Chaucer," 28–29) that the Hammond scribe must have been a professional working in a "publishing business" in London.

19. See Caxton, Prologue to Virgil's *Eneydos*, 1.

20. *Manuscript Trinity R.3.19*, ed. Fletcher, xx–xxii. Fletcher notes that the manuscript is composed of thirteen booklets, "each separately foliated in the same fifteenth-century hand" (xx), and believes that foliation and other features of the manuscript suggest that the booklets were linked together before the end of the fifteenth century (xxii). If Stow foliated R.3.19, Mooney thinks he did it "before taking apart the first two booklets of MS R.3.19 to use individual quires for copytext and then misplaced them in the order when he came to gather them together for the bindery" ("Scribes and Booklets," 266).

21. Riddy, "Mother Knows Best," 81 n54; see *Manuscript Trinity R.3.19*, ed. Fletcher, xxix–xxx; for Thorney's life, see Bone, "Extant Manuscripts"; Bone notes that the Yorkist bent of R.3.19 may have appealed to Thorney.

22. Mooney, "John Shirley's Heirs," 189.

23. Mooney argues that the other Shirley-derived manuscripts "probably were not produced in the capital but were copied from Shirley or Shirley- derived exemplars that had been carried out of the metropolis by their owners; since they were outside the protection of metropolitan book-producing circles, they were dispersed and the exemplars not only separated from their copies but lost entirely" ("John Shirley's Heirs," 197).

24. Mooney, "John Shirley's Heirs," 184.

25. Connolly, *John Shirley*, 83.

26. Ibid., 196–203. Connolly provides a useful analysis of Shirley's dialect, based on comparison with *LALME*, and locates his origins in the area of the southwest Midlands that encompasses southwest Shropshire, north and west Worcestershire, and northeast Herefordshire.

27. *Manuscript Trinity R.3.19*, ed. Fletcher, xxvii, notes that there are, however, occasional Shirlean features elsewhere in R.3.19, including the heading to one poem (fol. 241r) and some spellings (*Hyer*, fol. 125r, l. 24; *lyef*, fol. 131r, l. 1).

28. Attributions were later added as follows: *Parliament of Fowls*, fol. 17r "by Chaucer"; "Reflections of a Prisoner," fol. 41r "Written by George Ashby prisoner in the Fleet. A.D. 1463"; *Assembly of Ladies*, fol. 55r "By Chaucer"; *Banquet of Gods and Goddesses*, fol. 68r "by Lydgate"; "Belle Dame sans Merci," fol. 98r "by Chaucer"; "Commandments of Love," fol. 109r "by Chaucer"; "Nine Ladies Worthy," fol. 110v "by Chaucer"; *Legend of Good Women*, fol. 114r "by Chaucer"; "Complaint unto Pity," fol. 151r "Geof Chaucer"; "Craft of Lovers," fol. 154v "Chaucer" with marginal note by Stow on fol. 156r "Chaucer died 1400"; a short poem, fol. 156v "Chaucer"; *Bycorne*, fol. 159r "Compyled by John Lydgate"; poems, fols 160r–161v, identified as by Chaucer; extracts from the *Fall of Princes*, fol. 171r "Translations from Bochas by Iohn Lydgate"; moral verses, fols. 205r, 205v, and 207r "Chaucer"; "Court of Love," fol. 217r "by G.Chaucer."

29. Mooney thinks that the tables of contents of R.3.19 and R.3.21 "certainly date from" Stow's ownership ("Scribes and Booklets," 266); the hand of the "Poemata" note differs from the hand of the table of contents. Greg, "Chaucer Attributions," 539, assigns the attributions and titles in R.3.19 in bold roman and copperplate hand to Beaupré Bell, who derived them from Stow's Chaucer and who entered Trinity College in 1722.

30. *Manuscript Trinity R.3.19*, ed. Fletcher, xxx.

31. Mortimer, *John Lydgate's Fall of Princes*, 224–27; quotations on 225 and 227.

32. See Mooney, " 'Woman's Reply,' " for a discussion of the courtly love verses.

33. Edited by MacCracken from the version in Trinity R.3.21; see *MPJL*, 2:724–34, and for Lydgate's authorship, *MPJL*, 1:xxiii.

34. For the tradition, see Irwin, "Seven Sages."

35. See Wilson, " 'Amonges Othere Wordes Wyse,' " 135.

36. Seneca had an important place in the curriculum of medieval schools and was considered "almost a Church Father" thanks to what was imagined to have been his correspondence with St. Paul; see Weiss, *Humanism*, 3, 132. In the "Fabula Duorum Mercatorum," Lydgate refers by name to "Senek" (l. 603) and cites Seneca's *Epistulae* (l. 611), while in the *Siege of Thebes*, pt. 3, l. 2972, he mentions "moral Senek"; in the prologue to the *Fall of Princes*, Lydgate lists prominent authors of tragedies, including "Senek in Rome."

37. For a discussion of the author and author function as a classification system, see Foucault, "What Is an Author?" Whether it also mattered to the original readers of the *Mumming of the Seven Philosophers* is a topic for another discussion, although the work of scholars on late medieval authorship would say that it did; see, for example, Minnis, *Medieval Theory of Authorship*, the seminal work on the scholastic tradition behind the ways in which vernacular writers presented themselves and were understood by readers and, more recently, the essays (and especially those that focus on codicological issues and the organization of manuscripts around a single author's work) in Partridge and Kwakkel, eds., *Author, Reader, Book: Medieval Authorship in Theory and Practice*.

38. Foucault, "What Is an Author?" 108.

39. See Frere, *Antiphonale Sarisburiense*, plate 328; Hughes, "Antiphons and Acclamations," finds a resemblance between this antiphon and coronation chants for Edward II.

40. Billington, *Mock Kings*, 93.

41. Kipling, *Enter the King*.

42. Chambers, *Mediaeval Stage*, 1:408. As Harris, *Sacred Folly*, has shown, however, much of the evidence for Christmas revels, and especially the Feast of Fools, has been misunderstood, with the result that the serious liturgical origins of the Christmas Feast of Fools ritual have been obscured.

43. See Billington, *Mock Kings*, 30–54, for a discussion of winter kings and lords of misrule. Clopper, *Drama, Play, and Game*, 61–62, argues that Christmas lords of misrule found in fifteenth-century records may have been a reformist attempt to reign in rowdiness, even if they themselves later got out of hand.

44. *Inns of Court: REED*, 1:xix–xx.

45. See Chambers, *Mediaeval Stage*, 1:261 and n4; also see *Records of the City of Norwich*, ed. Hudson and Tingey, 1:345–46. Although *DTR*, 1224, dates the masking to 5 March 1443, the exact date is uncertain, and it may well have taken place in late January, even though the document of 1443 from which the quotations come places the procession on Fastengong Tuesday, that is, Mardi Gras.

46. The record we have is the city's appeal of the fine in 1448. The connections between seasonal festivity and rebellion have been extensively examined; see Pettitt, " 'Here Comes I, Jack Straw.' "

47. For the tendency of mocking-rituals to mirror the social order they critique and to incorporate serious elements, see Lindahl, "Festive Form," esp. 551.

48. See Streitberger, *Court Revels*, 8, and Lancashire, *London Civic Theatre*, 269–70 n100.

49. Lancashire, *London Civic Theatre*, esp. 126–27, where she notes that even though the coronation-year entertainments were "unusual in their authorship and occasions" they were not "unusual in their kind, as forms of entertainment common to both court and city in the first half of the fifteenth century" (127).

50. Connolly, *John Shirley*, 181.

51. Mooney, "Scribes and Booklets," 241.

52. Ibid., 264–65. Someone, possibly Stow, later wrote a small "A" in the space left for a large initial at the start of "Attempt," perhaps to guard against the confusion that would arise if the first word of the stanza were read as "ttempt." Mooney discusses this presumed clientele in "A Middle English Treatise," 1036–37. *Manuscript Trinity R.3.19*, ed. Fletcher, xv.

53. Riddy, "Mother Knows Best," 81 and 81 n53, citing Horrox, "The Urban Gentry in the Fifteenth Century," on the latter point.

AFTERWORD

1. Jauss, "Literary History as a Challenge," esp. 8: "In the triangle of author, work and reading public the latter is no passive part, no chain of mere reactions, but even history-making energy."

2. The scholarship on this topic is by now extensive, but for early and still important studies, see Bhabha, *The Location of Culture*, for hybridity and mimicry in postcolonial contexts; Chartier, "Culture as Appropriation," for the difficulty of restricting the circulation and use of cultural objects; and De Certeau, *The Practice of Everyday Life*, especially the chapter on "Reading as Poaching," 165–76.

3. The original practices movement is particularly visible in Shakespeare studies, where a number of contemporary performance groups define themselves as original practices companies. For a discussion of original-staging practice in relation to medieval drama, see Marshall, "Modern Productions of Medieval English Plays."

4. For a discussion of the salvage impulse in anthropology, see Clifford, "Of Other Peoples"; for its influence on medieval studies, see Sponsler, "Medieval Ethnography."

5. For accounts of nineteenth-century scholarly medievalism in England, Germany, and France, see, for England, Evans, *History of the Society of Antiquaries*; for France, Keylor, *Academy and Community*; for the Monumenta and Rolls series, Knowles, *Great Historical Enterprises*; and for Germany, Reill, *German Enlightenment*.

6. Lindenbaum, "Drama as Textual Practice," 386.

7. Symes, "Toward a New History of Medieval Theatre," 3–4.

8. Taylor, *The Archive and the Repertoire*, 19.

9. Canning and Postlewait, eds., *Representing the Past*, 11.

10. For an overview of this issue that focuses on medieval liturgy, see Holsinger, "Analytical Survey 6"; the quotation is from Durham, "Reconnecting Text to Context," 41.

11. Taylor, *The Archive and the Repertoire*, 2.

12. Derrida, *Archive Fever*, 17.

13. Holsinger, "Analytical Survey 6," 274. Chaucer, "Canon's Yeoman's Tale," *Riverside Chaucer*, ed. Benson, 275, l. 998.

WORKS CITED

PRIMARY SOURCES

Adam of Usk. *Chronicon Adae de Usk. The Chronicle of Adam of Usk, 1377–1421*. Ed. and trans. Chris Given-Wilson. Oxford: Oxford University Press, 1997.

Amundesham, Johannes. *Annales monasterii S. Albani*. Ed. H. T. Riley. 2 vols. London: Longmans, 1870–71.

Arundel Cookery Recipes. In *A Collection of Ordinances and Regulations for the Government of the Royal Household*, 425–73. London, 1790.

Bevington, David, ed. *Medieval Drama*. Boston: Houghton Mifflin, 1975.

The Book of Margery Kempe. Ed. Sanford Brown Meech and Emily Hope Allen. EETS 212 o.s. Oxford: Oxford University Press, 1940. Repr. 1993.

The Book of Margery Kempe. Trans. Barry A. Windeatt. Harmondsworth: Penguin, 1985.

The Brut, or the Chronicles of England. Ed. Friedrich W. D. Brie. 2 vols. EETS o.s. 131, 136. London: Kegan Paul, Trench, Trübner, 1908.

Calendar of Letter-Books, Preserved Among the Archives of the Corporation of the City of London. Ed. R. R. Sharpe. 11 vols. London, 1899–1911.

Calendar of Wills Proved and Enrolled in the Court of Husting, London. Ed. R. R. Sharpe. 2 vols. London, 1890.

Caxton, William. *Blanchardyn and Eglantine*. Ed. Leon Kellner. EETS e.s. 58. London, 1890.

———. "Prologue to Virgil's *Eneydos*." Westminster, U.K.: Caxton, 1490.

Chaucer, Geoffrey. *Riverside Chaucer*. Ed. Larry D. Benson et al. 3d ed. Boston: Houghton Mifflin, 1987.

Chester: Records of Early English Drama. Ed. Lawrence M. Clopper. Toronto: University of Toronto Press, 1979.

A Chronicle of London from 1089 to 1483. Ed. N. H. Nicolas and E. Tyrrell. London, 1827.

Chronicles of London. Ed. Charles L. Kingsford. Oxford: Clarendon, 1905.

Chronicles of the Reigns of Edward I and Edward II: Annales Londoniensis and Annales Paulini. Ed. William Stubbs. London: Longman, 1882.

The Commonplace Book of Robert Reynes. Ed. Cameron Louis. New York: Garland, 1980.

Coventry: Records of Early English Drama. Ed. R. W. Ingram. Toronto: University of Toronto Press, 1981.

Craig, Hardin, ed. *Two Coventry Corpus Christi Plays*. 2d ed. EETS e.s. 87. Oxford: Oxford University Press, 1957.

Eccles, Mark, ed. *The Macro Plays*. EETS 262. Oxford: Oxford University Press, 1969.

Fabyan, Robert. *The Newe Cronycles of England and France*. London: Pynson, 1516.

FitzStephen, William. *Descriptio nobilissimae civitatis Londoniae*. In *Materials for the History of Thomas á Becket*, ed. J. C. Robertson and J. B. Sheppard, 3:2. 7 vols. London: Rolls Series, 1875–85.

The Forme of Cury. In *Curye on Inglysch: English Culinary Manuscripts of the Fourteenth Century*, ed. C. B. Hieatt and S. Butler. EETS s.s. 8. Oxford: Oxford University Press, 1985.

Froissart, Jean. *Chroniques*. 15 vols. Paris: Société de l'Histoire de France, 1869–92.

Gesta Henrici Quinti. Ed. F. Tayle and John S. Roskell. Oxford: Clarendon, 1975.

The Great Chronicle of London. Ed. A. H. Thomas and I. D. Thornley. London: G. W. Jones, 1938.

The Historical Collections of a Citizen of London in the Fifteenth Century. Ed. James Gairdner. Westminster, U.K.: Camden Society, 1876.

The Household of Edward IV: The Black Book and the Ordinance of 1478. Ed. A. R. Myers. Manchester: Manchester University Press, 1959.

Incerti Scriptoris Chronicon Angliae. Ed. John A. Giles. London: Nutt, 1848.

Inns of Court: Records of Early English Drama. Ed. Alan H. Nelson and John R. Elliott, Jr. 3 vols. Woodbridge, U.K.: D. S. Brewer, 2010.

Jacobus de Voragine. *Legenda Aurea. The Golden Legend: Readings on the Saints*. Trans. William Granger Ryan. 2 vols. Princeton, N.J.: Princeton University Press, 1993.

Liber Regie Capelle. Ed. Walter Ullmann. Cambridge: Henry Bradshaw Society, 1961.

London Bridge: Selected Accounts and Rentals 1381–1538. Ed. Vanessa Harding and Laura Wright. London: London Record Society, 1995.

Lydgate, John. *Lydgate's Troy Book: A.D. 1412–1420*. Ed. Henry Bergen. 4 pts. in 2 vols. EETS e.s. 97, 103, 106, 126. London: Kegan Paul, Trench, Trübner, 1906–35.

———. *The Minor Poems of John Lydgate*. 2 vols. Ed. Henry Noble MacCracken. EETS o.s. 192, e.s. 107. Oxford: Oxford University Press, 1911–34.

———. *The Pilgrimage of the Life of Man*. Ed. Frederick J. Furnivall. EETS o.s. 77, 83, 92. London: Kegan Paul, Trench, Trübner, 1899–1904.

Maidstone, Richard. *Concordia: The Reconciliation of Richard II with London*. Ed. David R. Carlson and A. G. Rigg. Kalamazoo, Mich.: Medieval Institute Publications, 2003.

Manuscript Trinity R.3.19: A Facsimile. Ed. Bradford Y. Fletcher. Norman, Okla.: Pilgrim Books, 1987.

Marchant, Guyot. *La Danse macabre: Reproduction en facsimilé de l'édition de Guy Marchant, Paris, 1486*. Paris: Editions des Quatre Chemins, 1925.

Mirk, John. *Festial. John Mirk's Festial: Edited from British Library MS Cotton Claudius A.ii*. Ed. Susan Powell. EETS o.s. 334. Oxford: Oxford University Press, 2009.

Monstrelet, Enguerrand de. *La Chronique*. Ed. Louis Douët-d'Arcq. 6 vols. Paris: Renouard, 1857–62.

More, Sir Thomas. *The Workes of Sir Thomas More*. 1557. Ed. K. J. Wilson. 2 vols. Facsimile ed. London: Scolar, 1978.

Munimenta Gildhallae Londoniensis: Liber Albus, Liber Costumarum, et Liber Horn. Ed. Henry T. Riley. 4 vols. London: Longman, 1859–62.

Mystères inédits du quinzième siècle. Ed. Achille Jubinal. 2 vols. Paris: Téchener, 1837.

Pecock, Reginald. *The Repressor of Over Much Blaming of the Clergy*. Ed. Churchill Babington. 2 vols. London: Longman, 1860.

Peele, George. *Descensus Astraeae. The Device of a Pageant, Borne Before M. William Web, Lord Mayor of the Citie of London on the Day He Took His Oath, Beeing the 29. of October. 1591*. Ann Arbor, Mich.: EEBO, 2002.

Platter, Thomas. *Travels in England in 1599*. In *The Journals of Two Travellers in Elizabethan and Early Stuart England*, ed. Peter Razell. London: Caliban Books, 1995.

Proceedings and Ordinances of the Privy Council of England. Ed. Harris Nicholas. 7 vols. London: Eyre and Spottiswoode, 1834–37.

Promptorium Parvulorum. Ed. Albert Way. 3 vols. London: Camden Society, 1843–65.

The Records of the City of Norwich. Ed. William Hudson and John C. Tingey. Norwich, U.K.: Jarrold, 1906.

Robbins, Rossell Hope, ed. *Secular Lyrics of the XIVth and XVth Centuries*. Oxford: Clarendon, 1952.

Rotuli Parliamentorum. 6 vols. London, 1767–77.

Russell, John. *The Boke of Nurture*. In *Early English Manners and Meals*, ed. Frederick J. Furnivall. EETS o.s. 32. London: Kegan Paul, Trench, Trübner, 1868.

A Short English Chronicle. In *Three Fifteenth-Century Chronicles*, ed. James Gairdner. Westminster, U.K.: Camden Society, 1880.

"'The Siege of Calais: A New Text.'" Ed. Ralph A. Klinefelter. *PMLA* 67 (1952): 888–95.

Six Town Chronicles. Ed. R. Flenley. Oxford: Clarendon, 1911.

Spector, Stephen, ed. *The N-Town Play: Cotton MS Vespasian D.8*. 2 vols. EETS s.s. 11–12. Oxford: Oxford University Press, 1991.

Sponsler, Claire, ed. *John Lydgate: Mummings and Entertainments*. Middle English Texts Series. Kalamazoo, Mich.: Medieval Institute Publications, 2010.

Stow, John. *A Survey of London*. Ed. Charles Lethbridge Kingsford. 2 vols. 1908; repr. Oxford: Clarendon, 1971.

Thomas of Elmham. *Vita et Gesta Henrici Quinti Anglorum Regis*. Ed. Thomas Hearne. Oxford, 1727.

Two Fifteenth-Century Cookery-Books, Harleian MS. 279 (ab. 1430) and Harl. MS. 4016 (ab. 1450), with Extracts from Ashmole MS. 1429, Laud MS. 533, and Douce MS. 55. Ed. Thomas Austin. EETS o.s. 91. London: Trübner, 1888.

The Victoria History of the County of Hertford. Ed. William Page. 4 vols. Westminster, U.K.: A. Constable, 1902–14.

The Vision of William Concerning Piers the Plowman. Ed. W. W. Skeat. EETS o.s. 38. Oxford: Clarendon, 1886.

Vita Henrici Quinti. Ed. Charles A. Cole. London, U.K.: Longman, 1858.

Walker, Greg, ed. *Medieval Drama: An Anthology*. Oxford: Blackwell, 2000.

Wardens' Accounts and Court Minute Books of the Goldsmiths' Mistery of London, 1334–1446. Ed. Lisa Jefferson. Woodbridge, U.K.: Boydell, 2003.

Warren, Florence, ed. *The Dance of Death, Edited from MSS. Ellesmere 26/A.13 and B.M. Lansdowne 699, Collated with the Other Extant MSS*. EETS o.s. 181. 1931; repr. Oxford: EETS, 1971.

SECONDARY SOURCES

Abbott, T. K. *Catalogue of the Manuscripts in the Library of Trinity College, Dublin*. London: Longman, Green, 1900.

Aers, David, and Lynn Staley. *The Powers of the Holy: Religion, Politics, and Gender in Late Medieval English Culture*. University Park: Pennsylvania State University Press, 1996.

Allen, Judson Boyce. *The Ethical Poetic of the Later Middle Ages: A Decorum of Convenient Distinction*. Toronto: University of Toronto Press, 1982.

Anderson, Benedict. *Imagined Communities: Reflections on the Origin and Spread of Nationalism*. London: Verso, 1983.

Anglo, Sydney. *Spectacle, Pageantry, and Early Tudor Policy*. Oxford: Clarendon, 1997.

Appleford, Amy. "The Dance of Death in London: John Carpenter, John Lydgate, and the *Daunce of Poulys*." *JMEMS* 38 (2008): 285–314.

Appleford, Amy, and Nicholas Watson. "Merchant Religion in Fifteenth-Century London: The Writings of William Litchfield." *Chaucer Review* 46 (2011): 203–22.

Ashley, Kathleen, and Wim Hüsken, ed. *Moving Subjects: Processional Performance in the Middle Ages and the Renaissance*. Amsterdam: Editions Rodopi, 2001.

Aston, Margaret. "Corpus Christi and Corpus Regni: Heresy and the Peasants' Revolt." *Past and Present* 143 (1994): 3–47.

Baker, Donald C. "When Is a Text a Play? Reflections upon What Certain Late Medieval Dramatic Texts Tell Us." In *Contexts for Early English Drama*, ed. Marianne G. Briscoe and John C. Coldewey, 20–40.

Baker, Donald C., John L. Murphy, and Louis B. Hall Jr., eds. *The Late Medieval Religious Plays of Bodleian MSS Digby 133 and E Museo 160*. EETS o.s. 283. Oxford: Oxford University Press, 1982.

Bal, Mieke. *Reading Rembrandt: Beyond the Word-Image Opposition*. Cambridge: Cambridge University Press, 1991.

Barrett, Robert W. *Against All England: Regional Identity and Cheshire Writing, 1195–1656*. Notre Dame, Ind.: University of Notre Dame Press, 2009.

Barron, Caroline M. "Chivalry, Pageantry and Merchant Culture in Medieval London." In *Heraldry, Pageantry and Social Display in Medieval England*, ed. Peter Coss and Maurice Keen, 219–41. Woodbridge, U.K.: Boydell, 2002.

———. *London in the Later Middle Ages: Government and People 1200–1500*. Oxford: Oxford University Press, 2004.

———. *The Medieval Guildhall of London*. London: Corporation of London, 1974.

———. "Pageantry on London Bridge in the Early Fifteenth Century." In *"Bring Furth the Pagants": Essays in Early English Drama Presented to Alexandra F. Johnston*, ed. David N. Klausner and Karen Sawyer Marsalek, 91–104. Toronto: University of Toronto Press, 2007.

———. "The Parish Fraternities of Medieval London." In *The Church in Pre-Reformation Society: Essays in Honour of F. R. H. Du Boulay*, ed. Caroline Barron and Christopher Harper-Bill, 13–37. Woodbridge, U.K.: Boydell, 1985.

Barron, Caroline M., and Marie-Hélène Rousseau. "Cathedral, City and State, 1300–1540." In *St. Paul's: The Cathedral Church of London, 604–2004*, ed. Derek Keene, Arthur Burns, and Andrew Saint, 33–44. New Haven, Conn.: Yale University Press, 2004.

Bartlett, Anne. "Translation, Self-Representation, and Statecraft: Lady Margaret Beaufort and Caxton's *Blanchardyn and Eglantine*." *Essays in Medieval Studies* 22 (2005): 53–66.

Beadle, Richard. *The Cambridge Companion to Medieval English Theatre*. Cambridge: Cambridge University Press, 1994.

———. " 'Devoute Ymaginacioun' and the Dramatic Sense in Love's *Mirror* and the N-Town Plays." In *Nicholas Love at Waseda: Proceedings of the International Conference, 20–22, July 1995*, ed. Shoichi Oguro, Richard Beadle, and Michael G. Sargent, 1–19. Cambridge: D. S. Brewer, 1997.

———. "The York Cycle." In *CCMET*, 85–108.

Beckwith, Sarah. *Signifying God: Social Relation and Symbolic Act in the York Corpus Christi Plays*. Chicago: University of Chicago Press, 2001.

Belting, Hans. *The Image and Its Public in the Middle Ages: Form and Function of Early Paintings of the Passion*. Trans. Mark Bartusis and Raymond Meyer. New Rochelle, N.Y.: A. D. Caratzas, 1990.

Benson, C. David. "Civic Lydgate: The Poet and London." In *John Lydgate*, ed. Larry Scanlon and James Simpson, 147–68.

Bevington, David. "*Castles* in the Air: The Morality Plays." In *The Theatre of Medieval Europe*, ed. Eckehard Simon, 97–116.

Bhabha, Homi K. *The Location of Culture*. New York: Routledge, 1994.

Billington, Sandra. *Mock Kings in Medieval Society and Renaissance Drama*. Oxford: Clarendon, 1991.

Binski, Paul. "The English Parish Church and Its Art in the Later Middle Ages: A Review of the Problem." *Studies in Iconography* 20 (1999): 1–25.

———. *Medieval Death: Ritual and Representation*. Ithaca, N.Y.: Cornell University Press, 1996.

———. *The Painted Chamber at Westminster*. London: Society of Antiquaries, 1986.

Blacman, John. *Henry the Sixth.* Ed. and trans. M. R. James. Cambridge: Cambridge University Press, 1919.

Blair, Lawrence. "A Note on the Relation of the Corpus Christi Procession to the Corpus Christi Pageant in England." *Modern Language Notes* 55 (1940): 83–95.

Boffey, Julia. *Manuscripts of English Courtly Love Lyrics in the Later Middle Ages.* Woodbridge, U.K.: D. S. Brewer, 1985.

———. "Short Texts in Manuscript Anthologies: The Minor Poems of John Lydgate in Two Fifteenth-Century Collections." In *The Whole Book*, ed. Stephen G. Nichols and Siegfried Wenzel, 69–82.

Boffey, Julia, and A. S. G. Edwards. "Middle English Verse in Chronicles." In *New Perspectives on Middle English Texts*, ed. Susan Powell and Jeremy J. Smith, 119–28. Cambridge: D. S. Brewer, 2000.

Boffey, Julia, and John J. Thompson. "Anthologies and Miscellanies: Production and Choice of Texts." In *Book Production and Publishing in Britain, 1375–1475*, ed. Jeremy Griffiths and Derek Pearsall, 279–315. Cambridge: Cambridge University Press, 1989.

Bolton, J. L., ed. *The Alien Communities of London in the Fifteenth Century: The Subsidy Rolls of 1440 and 1483–4.* Stamford, U.K.: Richard III and Yorkist History Trust in association with Paul Watkins, 1998.

Bone, Gavin. "Extant Manuscripts Printed from by W. de Worde with Notes on the Owner, Roger Thorney." *Library* 4th ser. 12 (1931–32): 284–306.

Brantley, Jessica. *Reading in the Wilderness: Private Devotion and Public Performance in Late Medieval England.* Chicago: University of Chicago Press, 2007.

Briscoe, Marianne G., and John C. Coldewey, eds. *Contexts for Early English Drama.* Bloomington: Indiana University Press, 1989.

Brown, Carlton. *A Register of Middle English Religious and Didactic Verse.* 2 vols. Oxford: Oxford University Press, 1916–20.

Brown, Carlton, and Rossell Hope Robbins. *The Index of Middle English Verse.* New York: Columbia University Press, 1943.

Brown, Phyllis, Linda A. McMillin, and Katharina Wilson, eds. *Hrotsvit of Gandersheim: Contexts, Identities, Affinities, and Performances.* Toronto: University of Toronto Press, 2004.

Brownlee, Kevin, et al. "Vernacular Literary Consciousness c. 1100–c. 1500: French, German and English Evidence." In *The Cambridge History of Literary Criticism,* vol. 2: *The Middle Ages*, ed. Alastair Minnis and Ian Johnson, 422–71. Cambridge: Cambridge University Press, 2005.

Bryant, Lawrence M. "Configurations of the Community in Late Medieval Spectacles: Paris and London During the Dual Monarchy." In *City and Spectacle in Medieval Europe*, ed. Barbara A. Hanawalt and Kathryn L. Reyerson, 3–33. Minneapolis: University of Minnesota Press, 1994.

Bühler, Curt F. "Sir John Paston's 'Grete Booke,' a Fifteenth-Century 'Best-seller.' " *Modern Language Notes* 56 (1941): 345–51.

Bumke, Joachim. *Courtly Culture: Literature and Society in the High Middle Ages*. Trans. Thomas Dunlap. Berkeley: University of California Press, 1991.

Burrow, J. A. *Ages of Man: A Study in Medieval Writing and Thought*. Oxford: Clarendon, 1986.

———. *Gestures and Looks in Medieval Narrative*. Cambridge: Cambridge University Press, 2002.

Butterfield, Ardis, ed. *Chaucer and the City*. Cambridge: D. S. Brewer, 2006.

———. "Chaucer and the Detritus of the City." In *Chaucer and the City*, ed. Ardis Butterfield, 3–22.

———. "Chaucer's French Inheritance." In *The Cambridge Companion to Chaucer*, ed. Piero Boitani and Jill Mann, 20–35. 2d ed. Cambridge: Cambridge University Press, 2003.

Bynum, Caroline Walker. *Holy Feast and Holy Fast: The Religious Significance of Food to Medieval Women*. Berkeley: University of California Press, 1987.

Camille, Michael. *The Gothic Idol: Ideology and Image-Making in Medieval Art*. Cambridge: Cambridge University Press, 1989.

———. "Seeing and Reading: Some Implication of Medieval Literacy and Illiteracy." *Art History* 8 (1985): 26–49.

———. "Signs of the City: Place, Power, and Public Fantasy in Medieval Paris." In *Medieval Practices of Space*, ed. Barbara E. Hanawalt and Michal Kobialka, 1–36. Minneapolis: University of Minnesota Press, 2000.

Campbell, Louise, Francis Steer, and Robert Yorke. *A Catalogue of Manuscripts in the College of Arms Collections*. Vol. 1. London: College of Arms, 1988.

Campbell, Marian. "English Goldsmiths in the Fifteenth Century." In *England in the Fifteenth Century*, ed. Daniel Williams, 43–52. Woodbridge, U.K.: Boydell and Brewer, 1987.

Canning, Charlotte M., and Thomas Postlewait, eds. *Representing the Past: Essays in Performance Historiography*. Iowa City: University of Iowa Press, 2010.

Carruthers, Mary. *The Book of Memory: A Study of Memory in Medieval Culture*. 2d ed. Cambridge: Cambridge University Press, 2008.

Cavallo, Adolpho Salvatore. *Medieval Tapestries in the Metropolitan Museum of Art*. New York: H. N. Abrams, 1983.

Cerquiglini, Bernard. *In Praise of the Variant: A Critical History of Philology*. Trans. Betsy Wing. Baltimore: Johns Hopkins University Press, 1999.

Chaganti, Seeta. "*Danse macabre* and the Virtual Churchyard." *Postmedieval: A Journal of Medieval Cultural Studies* 3 (2012): 7–26.

———. "Vestigial Signs: Inscription, Performance, and *The Dream of the Rood*. *PMLA* 125 (2010): 48–72.

Chambers, E. K. *The Mediaeval Stage*. 2 vols. Oxford: Oxford University Press, 1903.

Chartier, Roger. "Culture as Appropriation: Popular Cultural Uses in Early Modern France." In *Understanding Popular Culture: Europe from the Middle Ages to the Nineteenth Century*, ed. Steven Kaplan, 229–53. Berlin, N.Y.: Mouton, 1984.

Christie, Mabel E. *Henry VI*. Boston: Houghton Mifflin, 1922.

Clanchy, Michael T. *From Memory to Written Record: England 1066–1307*. 2d ed. Cambridge, Mass.: Blackwell, 1993.

Clark, Robert L. A., and Pamela Sheingorn. "Performative Reading: The Illustrated Manuscripts of Arnoul Gréban's *Mystère de la Passion*." *European Medieval Drama* 6 (2002): 129–54.

Clifford, James. "Of Other Peoples: Beyond the Salvage Principle." In *Discussions in Contemporary Culture*, ed. Hal Foster, 121–50. Seattle: Bay Press, 1988.

Clopper, Lawrence M. *Drama, Play, and Game: English Festive Culture in the Medieval and Early Modern Period*. Chicago: University of Chicago Press, 2001.

———. "The History and Development of the Chester Cycle." *Modern Philology* 75 (1978): 219–46.

———. "London and the Problem of the Clerkenwell Plays." *Comparative Drama* 34 (2000): 291–303.

———. "*Miracula* and *The Tretise of Miraclis Pleyinge*." *Speculum* 65 (1990): 878–905.

Cohen, Helen Louise. *The Ballade*. New York: Columbia University Press, 1915.

"Colart de Laon." *Grove Art Online*. http://www.groveart.com. Oxford Art Online. Oxford University Press.

Coldewey, John C. "The Non-cycle Plays and the East Anglian Tradition." In *CCMET*, 189–210.

Cole, Andrew. *Literature and Heresy in the Age of Chaucer*. Cambridge: Cambridge University Press, 2008.

Coleman, Everard Home. "Coronation Plate." *Notes & Queries* 29 (July 16, 1898): 49.

Coleman, Joyce. "Aurality." In *Middle English*, ed. Paul Strohm, 68–85.

———. *Public Reading and the Reading Public in Late Medieval England and France*. New York: Cambridge University Press, 1996.

———. "Talking of Chronicles: The Public Reading of History in Late Medieval England and France." *Cahiers de Littérature Orale* 36 (1994): 91–111.

Coletti, Theresa. "A Feminist Approach to the Corpus Christi Cycles." In *Approaches to Teaching Medieval English Drama*, ed. Richard K. Emmerson, 79–90. New York: Modern Language Association of America, 1990.

———. *Mary Magdalene and the Drama of Saints: Theater, Gender, and Religion in Late Medieval England*. Philadelphia: University of Pennsylvania Press, 2004.

———. "Reading REED: History and the Records of Early English Drama." In *Literary Practice and Social Change in Britain, 1380–1530*, ed. Lee Patterson, 248–84. Berkeley: University of California Press, 1990.

Coletti, Theresa, and Gail McMurray Gibson. "The Tudor Origins of Medieval Drama." In *A Companion to Tudor Literature*, ed. Kent Cartwright, 228–45. Malden, Mass.: Blackwell, 2010.

Collins, Patrick J. *The N-Town Plays and Medieval Picture Cycles*. Early Drama, Art, and Music Monograph Series 2. Kalamazoo, Mich.: Medieval Institute Publications, 1979.

Connolly, Margaret. *John Shirley: Book Production and the Noble Household in Fifteenth-Century England*. Aldershot: Ashgate, 1998.

Connolly, Margaret, and Yolanda Plumley. "Crossing the Channel: John Shirley and the Circulation of French Lyric Poetry in England in the Early Fifteenth Century." In *Patrons, Authors and Workshops: Books and Book Production in Paris Around 1400*, ed. Godfried Croenen and Peter Ainsworth, 311–32. Leuven: Peeters, 2006.

Cooper, Lisa, and Andrea Denny-Brown, eds. *Lydgate Matters: Poetry and Material Culture in the Fifteenth Century*. New York: Palgrave Macmillan, 2008.

Cornelison, Sally J., and Scott B. Montgomery, eds. *Images, Relics, and Devotional Practices in Medieval and Renaissance Italy*. Medieval and Renaissance Text and Studies 296. Tempe: Arizona Center for Medieval and Renaissance Studies, 2005.

Crane, Susan. *The Performance of Self: Ritual, Clothing, and Identity During the Hundred Years' War*. Philadelphia: University of Pennsylvania Press, 2002.

Crawford, Anne. "The King's Burden? The Consequences of Royal Marriage in Fifteenth-Century England." In *Patronage, the Crown and the Provinces in Later Medieval England*, ed. Ralph A. Griffiths, 33–56. Gloucester, U.K.: Alan Sutton, 1981.

Dagenais, John. *The Ethics of Reading in Manuscript Culture: Glossing the "Libro de buen amor."* Princeton, N.J.: Princeton University Press, 1994.

———. "'That Bothersome Residue': Toward a Theory of the Physical Text." In *Vox Intertexta: Orality and Textuality in the Middle Ages*, ed. A. N. Doane and Carol Braun Pasternak, 244–57. Madison: University of Wisconsin Press, 1991.

Davidson, Clifford. *Festivals and Plays in Late Medieval Britain*. Aldershot, U.K.: Ashgate, 2007.

———. *Illustrations of the Stage and Acting in England to 1580*. Kalamazoo, Mich.: Medieval Institute Publications, 1991.

———. "Women and the Medieval Stage." *Women's Studies* 11 (1984): 99–113.

Davis, Whitney. *A General Theory of Visual Culture*. Princeton, N.J.: Princeton University Press, 2011.

De Certeau, Michel. *The Practice of Everyday Life*. Trans. Steven Rendall. Berkeley: University of California Press, 1984.

Deansley, Margaret. "Vernacular Books in England in the Fourteenth and Fifteenth Centuries." *Modern Language Review* 15 (1920): 349–58.

Delany, Sheila. *Impolitic Bodies: Poetry, Saints, and Society in Fifteenth-Century England: The Work of Osbern Bokenham*. Oxford: Oxford University Press, 1998.

Denny-Brown, Andrea. "Lydgate's Golden Cows: Appetite and Avarice in *Bycorne and Chychevache*. In *Lydgate Matters: Poetry and Material Culture in the Fifteenth Century*, ed. Lisa Cooper and Andrea Denny-Brown, 35–56. New York: Palgrave Macmillan, 2008.

Derrida, Jacques. *Archive Fever: A Freudian Impression*. Trans. Eric Prenowitz. Chicago: University of Chicago Press, 1995.

d'Hulst, Roger A. *Flemish Tapestries, from the Fifteenth to the Eighteenth Century*. Trans. Frances J. Stillman. New York: Universe, 1967.

Dillon, Harold Arthur, and W. H. St. John Hope. "Inventory of the Goods and Chattels Belonging to Thomas, Duke of Gloucester." *Archaeological Journal* 54 (1897): 275–308.

Dillon, Janette. "Clerkenwell and Smithfield as a Neglected Home of London Theater." *Huntington Library Quarterly* 71 (2008): 115–35.

———. *The Language of Space in Court Performance, 1400–1625*. Cambridge: Cambridge University Press, 2010.

Dinshaw, Carolyn. *Chaucer's Sexual Poetics*. Madison: University of Wisconsin Press, 1989.

Doyle, A. I. "English Books in and out of Court from Edward III to Henry VI." In *English Court Culture in the Later Middle Ages*, ed. V. J. Scattergood and J. W. Sherborne, 163–81.

———. "More Light on John Shirley." *Medium Aevum* 30 (1961): 93–101.

———. "An Unrecognized Piece of *Piers the Ploughman's Creed* and Other Work by Its Scribe." *Speculum* 34 (1959): 428–36.

Dronke, Peter, ed. *Women Writers of the Middle Ages*. Cambridge: Cambridge University Press, 1984.

Duffy, Eamon. *The Stripping of the Altars: Traditional Religion in England c. 1400–c.1580*. New Haven, Conn.: Yale University Press, 1992.

Dunn, E. Catherine. "French Medievalists and the Saint's Play: A Problem for American Scholarship." *Mediaevalia et Humanistica* 6 (1975): 51–62.

Durham, Lofton L. "Reconnecting Text to Context: The Ontology of 'French Medieval Drama' and the Case of the *Istoire de la Destruction de Troie*." *Journal of Dramatic Theory and Criticism* 25, no. 2 (2011): 37–60.

Dyer, Christopher. *Standards of Living in the Later Middle Ages: Social Change in England, c. 1200–1520*. Cambridge: Cambridge University Press, 1989.

Ebin, Lois. *John Lydgate*. Boston: Twayne, 1985.

Edwards, A. S. G. "Lydgate Manuscripts: Some Directions for Future Research." In *Manuscripts and Readers in Fifteenth-Century England: The Literary Implications of Manuscript Study*, ed. Derek Pearsall, 15–26. Cambridge: D. S. Brewer, 1981.

———. "Middle English *Pageant* 'Picture'?" *Notes & Queries* 237 (1992): 25–26.

———. Review of Lester, *"Grete Boke."* *Speculum* 60 (1985): 699–701.

Emmerson, Richard K. "Eliding the 'Medieval': Renaissance "New Historicism" and Sixteenth-Century Drama." In *Performance of Middle English Culture*, ed. James J. Paxton, Lawrence M. Clopper, and Sylvia Tomasch, 25–41.

———. "Visualizing Performance: The Miniatures of the Besançon MS 579 *Jour du Jugement*." *Exemplaria* 11 (1999): 245–84.

Enders, Jody. "The Spectacle of the Scaffolding: Rape and the Violent Foundations of Medieval Theatre Studies." *Theatre Journal* 56 (2004): 163–81.

Engleworth, W. A. D. *The History of the Painter-Stainers Company of London*. London: Hazell, Watson, and Viney, 1950.

Epstein, Robert. "Eating Their Words: Food and Text in the Coronation Banquet of Henry VI." *JMEMS* 36 (2006): 355–77.

———. "Lydgate's Mummings and the Aristocratic Resistance to Drama." *Comparative Drama* 36 (2002): 337–58.

Erler, Mary C., ed. *Ecclesiastical London.* Records of Early English Drama. Toronto: University of Toronto Press, 2008.

———. "Palm Sunday Prophets and Processions and Eucharistic Controversy." *Renaissance Quarterly* 48 (1995): 58–81.

Evans, Joan. *A History of the Society of Antiquaries.* Oxford: Oxford University Press, 1956.

Evans, Ruth. "Body Politics: Engendering Medieval Cycle Drama." In *Feminist Readings in Middle English Literature*, ed. Ruth Evans and Lesley Johnson, 112–39. New York: Routledge, 1994.

———. "Feminist Re-Enactments: Gender and the Towneley *Uxor Noe.*" In *A Wyf Ther Was*, ed. Juliette Dor, 141–54. Liège: Université de Liège, Departement d'anglais, 1992.

———. "The Production of Space in Chaucer's London." In *Chaucer and the City*, ed. Ardis Butterfield, 41–56.

Facinger, Marion F. "A Study of Medieval Queenship: Capetian France, 987–1237." *Studies in Medieval and Renaissance History* 5 (1968): 3–47.

Findlay, Alison. *Playing Spaces in Early Women's Drama.* Cambridge: Cambridge University Press, 2006.

Fisher, John H. "Chancery and the Emergence of Standard Written English in the Fifteenth Century." *Speculum* 52 (1977): 870–99.

———. "A Language Policy for Lancastrian England." *PMLA* 107 (1992): 1168–80.

Flanigan, C. Clifford. "Comparative Literature and the Study of Medieval Drama." *Yearbook of Comparative and General Literature* 36 (1986): 56–104.

Fleming, Juliet. *Graffiti and the Writing Arts of Early Modern England.* London: Reaktion Books, 2009.

Floyd, Jennifer. "St. George and the 'Steyned Halle': Lydgate's Verses for the London Armourers." In *Lydgate Matters: Poetry and Material Culture in the Fifteenth Century*, ed. Lisa H. Cooper and Andrea Denny-Brown, 139–64.

———. "Writing on the Wall: John Lydgate's Architectural Verse." Diss., Stanford University, 2008.

———. "What Is an Author?" In *The Foucault Reader*, ed. Paul Rabinow, 101–20. New York: Pantheon, 1984.

Fredell, Joel. "'Go litel quaier': Lydgate's Pamphlet Poetry." *Journal of the Early Book Society* 9 (2006): 51–73.

Freehafer, John. "John Warburton's Lost Plays." *Studies in Bibliography* 23 (1970): 154–64.

Frere, Walter Howard, ed. *Antiphonale Sarisburiense: A Reproduction in Facsimile of a Manuscript of the Thirteenth Century.* 6 vols. London: Plainsong and Mediaeval Music Society, 1901–25.

Fumerton, Patricia. *Cultural Aesthetics: Renaissance Literature and the Practice of Social Ornament.* Chicago: University of Chicago Press, 1991.

Galloway, Andrew. "John Lydgate and the Origins of Vernacular Humanism." *Journal of English and Germanic Philology* 107 (2008): 445–71.

Ganim, John M. "Drama, Theatricality and Performance: Radicals of Presentation in the *Canterbury Tales*." In *Drama, Narrative and Poetry in the Canterbury Tales*, ed. Wendy Harding, 69–82. Toulouse: PU du Mirail, 2003.

———. "The Experience of Modernity in Late Medieval Literature: Urbanism, Experience and Rhetoric in Some Early Descriptions of London." In *Performance of Middle English Culture*, ed. James J. Paxton, Lawrence M. Clopper, and Sylvia Tomasch, 77–95.

Gayk, Shannon. *Image, Text, and Religious Reform in Fifteenth-Century England.* Cambridge: Cambridge University Press, 2010.

Gertsman, Elina. "Pleyinge and Peyntynge: Performing the Dance of Death." *Studies in Iconography* 27 (2006): 1–43.

———. "Visual Space and the Practice of Viewing: The Dance of Death at Meslay-le-Grenet." *Religion and the Arts* 9, nos. 1–2 (2005): 1–37.

Giancarlo, Matthew. *Parliament and Literature in Late Medieval England.* Cambridge: Cambridge University Press, 2007.

Gibson, Gail McMurray. "Bury St. Edmunds, Lydgate, and the *N-Town Cycle*." *Speculum* 56 (1981): 56–90.

———. "Long Melford Church, Suffolk: Some Suggestions for the Study of Visual Artifacts and Medieval Drama," *Research Opportunities in Renaissance Drama* 21 (1978): 103–15.

———. *The Theater of Devotion: East Anglian Drama and Society in the Late Middle Ages.* Chicago: University of Chicago Press, 1989.

Given-Wilson, Chris. *The Royal Household and the King's Affinity: Service, Politics and Finance in England, 1630–1413.* New Haven, Conn.: Yale University Press, 1986.

Goldberg, Jeremy. "Craft Guilds, the Corpus Christi Play, and Civic Government." In *The Government of Medieval York: Essays in Commemoration of the 1396 Royal Charter*, ed. Sarah Reese Jones, 141–63. York: Borthwick Institute of Historical Research, 1997.

Goodman, Nelson. *Languages of Art: An Approach to a Theory of Symbols.* 2d ed. Indianapolis: Hackett, 1976.

Goulding, Charles Benjamin. "Picture-Poems of John Lydgate." Ph.D. diss., Yale University, 1933.

Gransden, Antonia. *Historical Writing in England.* 2 vols. Ithaca, N.Y.: Cornell University Press, 1974–82.

Green, Richard F. "Three Fifteenth-Century Notes." *English Language Notes* 14 (1976): 14–16.

———. *Poets and Princepleasers: Literature and the English Court in the Late Middle Ages.* Toronto: University of Toronto Press, 1980.

Greenberg, Cheryl. "John Shirley and the English Book Trade." *Library* 6th ser., 4 (1982): 369–80.

Greenfield, Peter H. "Festive Drama at Christmas in Aristocratic Households." In *Festive Drama*, ed. Meg Twycross, 34–40.

Greg, W. W. "Chaucer Attributions in the MS R.3.19 in the Library of Trinity College, Cambridge." *Modern Language Review* 8 (1913): 539–40.

Griffiths, Ralph A. "A Breton Spy in London, 1425–29." In *King and Country*, 221–26.

———. *King and Country: England and Wales in the Fifteenth Century*. London: Hambledon Press, 1991.

———, ed. *Patronage, the Crown and the Provinces in Later Medieval England*. Gloucester, U.K.: Alan Sutton, 1981.

———. "Queen Katherine of Valois and a Missing Statute of the Realm." In *King and Country*, 103–13.

———. *The Reign of King Henry VI: The Exercise of Royal Authority, 1422–1461*. Berkeley: University of California Press, 1981.

Hamburger, Jeffrey. *The Rothschild Canticles: Art and Mysticism in Flanders and the Rhineland circa 1300*. New Haven, Conn.: Yale University Press, 1991.

———. "The Visual and the Visionary: The Image in Late Medieval Monastic Devotions." *Viator* 20 (1989): 161–96.

Hammond, Eleanor P. "A Scribe of Chaucer." *Modern Philology* 27 (1929–30): 27–33.

———. "Two British Museum Manuscripts." *Anglia* 28 (1905): 1–28.

———. "Two Tapestry Poems by Lydgate: The *Life of St. George* and the *Falls of Seven Princes*." *Englische Studien* 43 (1910–11): 10–26.

Hammond, P. W. *Food and Feast in Medieval England*. Gloucestershire, U.K.: Wrens Park, 1998.

Hanna, Ralph. *A Descriptive Catalogue of the Western Medieval Manuscripts of St. John's College, Oxford*. Oxford: Oxford University Press, 2002.

———. *London Literature, 1300–1380*. Cambridge: Cambridge University Press, 2005.

———. "Miscellaneity and Vernacularity: Conditions of Literary Production in Late Medieval England." In *The Whole Book*, ed. Stephen G. Nichols and Siegfried Wenzel, 37–51.

———. "Some Norfolk Women and Their Books, ca. 1390–1440." In *The Cultural Patronage of Medieval Women*, ed. June Hall McCash, 288–305. Athens: University of Georgia Press, 1996.

Happé, Peter. *The Towneley Cycle: Unity and Diversity*. Cardiff: University of Wales Press, 2007.

Harris, Max. *Sacred Folly: A New History of the Feast of Fools*. Ithaca, N.Y.: Cornell University Press, 2011.

Hasted, Edward. *The History and Topographical Survey of the County of Kent*. 12 vols. Canterbury: W. Bristow, 1797–1801. Repr., Wakefield, U.K.: EP Publishers, 1972.

Henisch, Bridget. *Fast and Feast: Food in Medieval Society*. University Park: Pennsylvania State University Press, 1976.

Herbert, William. *The History of the Twelve Great Livery Companies of London*. 2 vols. London, 1834, 1837. Repr., New York: Augustus M. Kelley, 1968.

Hieatt, Constance B. "Making Sense of Medieval Culinary Records: Much Done, but Much More to Do." In *Food and Eating in Medieval Europe*, ed. Martha Carlin and Joel T. Rosenthal, 101–16. London: Hambledon Press, 1998.

Holland, Peter. "Theatre Without Drama: Reading REED." In *From Script to Stage*, ed. Peter Holland and Stephen Orgel, 43–67. New York: Palgrave Macmillan, 2004.

Holsinger, Bruce W. "Analytical Survey 6: Medieval Literature and Cultures of Performance." *New Medieval Literatures* 6 (2003): 271–311.

Horrox, Rosemary. "The Urban Gentry in the Fifteenth Century." In *Towns and Townspeople in the Fifteenth* Century, ed. J. A. F. Thomson, 22–44. Gloucester, U.K.: Alan Sutton, 1988.

———. "Urban Patronage and Patrons in the Fifteenth Century." In *Patronage, the Crown and the Provinces in Later Medieval England*, ed. Ralph A. Griffiths, 145–66.

Hudson, Anne. *The Premature Reformation: Wycliffite Texts and Lollard History*. Oxford: Clarendon, 1988.

Hughes, Andrew. "Antiphons and Acclamations: The Politics of Music in the Coronation Ceremony of Edward II, 1308." *Journal of Musicology* 6 (1988): 150–68.

Hutton, Ronald. *The Rise and Fall of Merry England: The Ritual Year 1400–1700*. Oxford: Oxford University Press, 1994.

Imray, Jean. *The Mercers' Hall*. London: Mercers' Company, 1991.

Irwin, Bonnie D. "The Seven Sages." In *Medieval Folklore: A Guide to Myths, Legends, Beliefs, and Customs*, ed. Carl Lindahl, John McNamara, and John Lindow, 375–76. Oxford: Oxford University Press, 2002.

Jacob, E. F. *The Fifteenth Century, 1399–1485*. Oxford: Clarendon, 1961.

James, M. R. *A Descriptive Catalogue of the Manuscripts in the Library of Lambeth Palace*. Cambridge: Cambridge University Press, 1930–32.

———. *The Western Manuscripts in the Library of Trinity College, Cambridge: A Descriptive Catalogue*. Cambridge: Cambridge University Press, 1900.

James, Mervyn. "Ritual, Drama, and Social Body in the Late Medieval English Town." *Past and Present* 98 (1983): 4–29.

Jauss, Hans-Robert. "Literary History as a Challenge to Literary Theory." In *Toward an Aesthetic of Reception*, trans. Timothy Bahti, 3–45. Minneapolis: University of Minnesota Press, 1982.

Johnston, Alexandra F. " 'All the World Was a Stage': Records of Early English Drama." In *The Theatre of Medieval Europe*, ed. Eckehard Simon, 117–29.

———. "What If No Texts Survived? External Evidence for Early English Drama." In *Contexts for Early English Drama*, ed. Marianne G. Briscoe and John C. Coldewey, 1–19.

Jones, Malcolm. "Monsters of Misogyny: Bigorne and Chicheface—Suit et fin?" In *Marvels, Monsters, and Miracles: Studies in the Medieval and Early Modern Imaginations*, ed. Timothy S. Jones and David A. Springer, 203–21. Kalamazoo, Mich.: Medieval Institute Publications, 2002.

Jubinal, Achille. *Recherches sur l'usage et l'origine des tapisseries à personnages depuis l'antiquité jusqu'au XVIe siècle.* Paris: Challamel, 1840.

Justice, Steven. *Writing and Rebellion: England in 1381.* Berkeley: University of California Press, 1994.

Kamerick, Kathleen. *Popular Piety and Art in the Late Middle Ages: Image Worship and Idolatry in England, 1350–1500.* New York: Palgrave, 2002.

Kastan, David Scott. *Shakespeare and the Book.* Cambridge: Cambridge University Press, 2001.

Ker, *Medieval Libraries of Great Britain: A List of Surviving Books.* 2d ed. London: Royal Historical Society, 1964.

Keylor, William R. *Academy and Community: The Foundation of the French Historical Profession.* Cambridge, Mass.: Harvard University Press, 1975.

Kightly, Charles. " 'The Hangings About the Hall': An Overview of Textile Wall Hangings in Late Medieval York, 1394–1505." *Medieval Textiles* 28 (June 2001): 3–6.

Kilgour, Maggie. *From Communion to Cannibalism: An Anatomy of Metaphors of Incorporation.* Princeton, N.J.: Princeton University Press, 1990.

King, Pamela. *The York Mystery Cycle and the Worship of the City.* Cambridge: D. S. Brewer, 2006.

Kingsford, Charles L. *English Historical Literature in the Fifteenth Century.* Oxford: Clarendon, 1913.

———. "An Historical Collection of the Fifteenth Century." *English Historical Review* 29 (1914): 505–15.

———. *Prejudice and Promise in the XVth Century.* Oxford: Oxford University Press, 1925.

———. "Robert Bale, the London Chronicler." *English Historical Review* 31 (1916): 126–28.

Kipling, Gordon. "The Early Tudor Disguisings: New Research Opportunities." *Research Opportunities in Renaissance Drama* 17 (1974): 3–8.

———. *Enter the King: Theatre, Liturgy, and Ritual in the Medieval Civic Triumph.* Oxford: Oxford University Press, 1997.

———. "Fouquet, St Apollonia, and the Motives of the Miniaturist's Art: A Reply to Graham Runnalls." *Medieval English Theatre* 19 (1997): 101–20.

———. "The London Pageants for Margaret of Anjou: A Medieval Script Restored." *Medieval English Theatre* 4 (1982): 5–27.

———. "Lydgate: The Poet as Deviser." In *Chaucer and the Challenges of Medievalism: Studies in Honor of H. A. Kelly,* ed. Donka Minkova and Theresa Tinkle, 73–101. Hamburg: Peter Lang, 2003.

Kirshenblatt-Gimblett, Barbara. "Playing to the Senses: Food as a Performance Medium." *Performance Research* 4 (1999): 1–30.

Klinefelter, Ralph A. "A Newly Discovered 15th-Century English Manuscript." *Modern Language Quarterly* 14 (1953): 3–6.

Knapp, Ethan. *The Bureaucratic Muse: Thomas Hoccleve and the Literature of Late Medieval England*. University Park: Pennsylvania State University Press, 2001.

Knight, Alan E. "Manuscript Painting and Play Production: The Evidence from the Processional Plays of Lille." In *The Dramatic Tradition of the Middle Ages*, ed. Clifford Davidson, 195–202. New York: AMS, 2005.

Knowles, David. *Great Historical Enterprises: Problems in Monastic History*. London: Nelson, 1963.

Korda, Natasha. *Labors Lost: Women's Work and the Early Modern English Stage*. Philadelphia: University of Pennsylvania Press, 2011.

Kretzmann, Paul Edward. *The Liturgical Element in the Earliest Forms of the Medieval Drama: With Special Reference to the English and German Plays*. Minneapolis: University of Minnesota Press, 1916.

Kullmann, Dorothea, ed. *The Church and Vernacular Literature in Medieval France*. Toronto: Pontifical Institute of Medieval Studies, 2009.

LaCapra, Dominick. *History and Criticism*. Ithaca, N.Y.: Cornell University Press, 1985.

Lambert, John J. *Records of the Skinners of London Edward I to James I*. London: The Company, 1933.

Lancashire, Anne. *London Civic Theatre: City Drama and Pageantry from Roman Times to 1558*. Cambridge: Cambridge University Press, 2002.

Lancashire, Ian. *Dramatic Texts and Records of Britain: A Chronological Topography to 1558*. Toronto: University of Toronto Press, 1984.

Lawton, David A. "Dullness and the Fifteenth Century." *English Literary History* 54 (1987): 761–99.

———. "Gaytryge's Sermon, *Dictamen*, and Middle English Alliterative Verse." *Modern Philology* 76 (1979): 329–43.

Lefebvre, Henri. *The Production of Space*. Trans. Donald Nicholson-Smith. Malden, Mass.: Blackwell, 1991. *La production de l'espace*. Paris: Éditions Anthropos, 1974.

Lerer, Seth. *Boethius and Dialogue: Literary Method in the Consolation of Philosophy*. Princeton, N.J.: Princeton University Press, 1985.

———. "The Chaucerian Critique of Medieval Theatricality." In *Performance of Middle English Culture*, ed. James J. Paxton, Lawrence M. Clopper, and Sylvia Tomasch, 720–38.

———. "William Caxton." In *CHMEL*, 720–38.

Lester, Geoffrey. *The Earliest English Translation of Vegetius' De re militari, Ed. from MS Bodl. Douce 291*. Heidelberg: C. Winter, 1988.

———. *Sir John Paston's "Grete Boke": A Descriptive Catalogue, with an Introduction, of British Library Ms. Lansdowne 285*. Cambridge: D. S. Brewer, 1984.

Lestocquoy, Jean. *Deux siècles de l'histoire de la tapisserie, 1300–1500*. Arras: Commission départementale des monuments historiques du Pas-de-Calais, 1978.

Lindenbaum, Sheila. "Drama as Textual Practice." In *Middle English*, ed. Paul Strohm, 386–400.

———. "London Texts and Literate Practice." In *CHMEL*, 284–309.

———. "The Smithfield Tournament of 1390." *JMEMS* 20 (1990): 1–20.

Lindhal, Carl. *Earnest Games: Folkloric Patterns in the Canterbury Tales*. Bloomington: Indiana University Press, 1987.

———. "The Festive Form of the *Canterbury Tales*." *English Literary History* 52 (1985): 531–74.

Linke, Hansjürgen. "A Survey of Medieval Drama and Theater in Germany." *Comparative Drama* 27 (1993): 17–53.

Livingston, M. "A Sixth Hand in Cambridge, Trinity College, MS R.3.19." *Journal of the Early Book Society* 8 (2005): 229–37.

Lumiansky, R. M., and David Mills. *The Chester Mystery Cycle: Essays and Documents. With an Essay "Music in the Cycle," by Richard Rastall*. Chapel Hill: University of North Carolina Press, 1983.

Lupton, Julia. "Thinking with Things: Hannah Woolley to Hannah Arendt." *Postmedieval: A Journal of Medieval Cultural Studies* 3 (2012): 63–79.

MacCracken, Henry Noble. "King Henry's Triumphal Entry into London, Lydgate's Poem and Carpenter's Letter." *Archiv* 126 (1911): 75–102.

Maddern, Philippa. "'Best Trusted Friends': Concepts and Practices of Friendship Among Fifteenth-Century Norfolk Gentry." In *England in the Fifteenth Century: Proceedings of the 1992 Harlaxton Symposium*, ed. Nicholas Rogers, 100–117. Stamford, U.K.: P. Watkins, 1994.

Manley, Lawrence. *Literature and Culture in Early Modern London*. Cambridge: Cambridge University Press, 1995.

Marks, Richard. "Picturing Word and Text in the Late Medieval Parish Church." In *Image, Text and Church, 1380–1600: Essays for Margaret Aston*, ed. Linda Clark, Maureen Jurkowski, and Colin Richmond, 162–202. Toronto: Pontifical Institute of Medieval Studies, 2009.

Marshall, Anne. "St. George and the Dragon: Banningham, Norfolk." In *Medieval Wall Painting in the Parish Church: A Developing Catalogue*. http://www.paintedchurch.org/bannigeo.htm

Marshall, John. "Modern Productions of Medieval English Plays." In *CCMET*, 289–311.

McCartney, Elizabeth. "The King's Mother and Royal Prerogative in Early-Sixteenth-Century France." In *Medieval Queenship*, ed. John Carmi Parsons, 117–42. New York: St. Martin's, 1993.

McInnis, David, and Brett D. Hirsch, eds. *Embodying Shakespeare*. Special Issue of *Early Modern Literary Studies* 19 (2009).

McIntosh, Angus, et al. *A Linguistic Atlas of Late Mediaeval English*. 4 vols. Aberdeen: Aberdeen University Press, 1986.

McKenna, J. W. "Henry VI of England and the Dual Monarchy: Aspects of Royal Political Propaganda, 1422–1432." *Journal of the Warburg and Courtauld Institutes* 28 (1965): 145–62.

McKisack, May. *The Fourteenth Century, 1307–1399*. Oxford: Clarendon, 1959.

McLaren, Mary-Rose. *The London Chronicles of the Fifteenth Century: A Revolution in English Writing*. Cambridge: D. S. Brewer, 2002.

———. "The Textual Transmission of the London Chronicles." In *English Manuscript Studies: 1100–1700*, vol. 3, ed. Peter Beal and Jeremy Griffiths, 38–72. Toronto: University of Toronto Press, 1992.

McLuhan, Marshall. *Understanding the Media: The Extensions of Man*. Corte Madera, Calif.: Gingko, 1964.

McNiven, Peter. *Heresy and Politics in the Reign of Henry IV: The Burning of John Badby*. Woodbridge: Boydell, 1987.

Meale, Carol M. "*The Libelle of Englyshe Polycye* and Mercantile Literary Culture in Late-Medieval London." In *London and Europe in the Later Middle Ages*, ed. Julia Boffey and Pamela King, 181–227. London: Centre for Medieval and Renaissance Studies, Queen Mary and Westfield College, University of London, 1995.

Meyer-Lee, Robert J. "Lydgate's Laureate Pose." In *John Lydgate*, ed. Larry Scanlon and James Simpson, 36–60.

———. *Poets and Power from Chaucer to Wyatt*. Cambridge: Cambridge University Press, 2007.

Middleton, Anne. "Chaucer's 'New Men' and the Good of Literature in the *Canterbury Tales*." In *Literature and Society*, ed. Edward Said, 15–56. Baltimore: Johns Hopkins University Press, 1980.

———. "The Idea of Public Poetry in the Reign of Richard II." *Speculum* 53 (1978): 94–114.

Mills, David. *Recycling the Cycle: The City of Chester and Its Whitsun Plays*. Toronto: University of Toronto Press, 1998.

———. "'The Towneley Plays' or 'The Towneley Cycle'?" *Leeds Studies in English* 17 (1986): 95–104.

Minnis, Alistair. *Medieval Theory of Authorship: Scholastic Literary Attitudes in the Later Middle Ages*. 2d ed. Philadelphia: University of Pennsylvania Press, 2010.

Mooney, Linne R. "Chaucer's Scribe." *Speculum* 81 (2006): 97–138.

———. "John Shirley's Heirs." *Yearbook of English Studies* 33 (2003): 182–98.

———. "A Middle English Treatise on the Seven Liberal Arts." *Speculum* 68 (1993): 1027–52.

———. "More Manuscripts Written by a Chaucer Scribe." *Chaucer Review* 30 (1996): 401–8.

———. "Scribes and Booklets of Trinity College, Cambridge, Manuscripts R.2.19 and R.3.21." In *Middle English Poetry: Texts and Traditions: Essays in Honour of Derek Pearsall*, ed. A. J. Minnis, 241–66. York: York Medieval Press, 2001.

———. "'A Woman's Reply to her Lover' and Four Other New Courtly Love Lyrics in Cambridge, Trinity College MS R.3.19." *Medium Aevum* 67 (1998): 235–56.

Mooney, Linne R., and Lister M. Matheson. "The Beryn Scribe and his Texts: Evidence for Multiple-Copy Production of Manuscripts in Fifteenth-Century England." *Library* 7th ser., 4 (2003): 347–70.

Morgan, D. A. L. "The House of Policy: The Political Role of the Late Plantagenet Household, 1422–1485." In *The English Court: From the Wars of the Roses to the Civil War*, ed. David Starkey et al., 25–70. London: Longman, 1987.

Mortimer, Nigel. *John Lydgate's Fall of Princes: Tragedy in Its Literary and Political Contexts.* Oxford: Oxford University Press, 2005.

Muir, Edward. "Eye of the Procession: Ritual Ways of Seeing in the Renaissance." In *Ceremonial Culture in Pre-Modern Europe*, ed. Nicholas Howe, 129–54. Notre Dame, Ind.: University of Notre Dame Press, 2007.

Muir, Lynette R. "Women on the Medieval Stage: The Evidence from France." *Medieval English Theatre* 8 (1985): 107–20.

Muscatine, Charles. *Chaucer and the French Tradition: A Study in Style and Meaning.* Berkeley: University of California Press, 1957.

Nagy, Gregory. *Poetry as Performance: Homer and Beyond.* Cambridge: Cambridge University Press, 1996.

Nelson, Alan H. *The Medieval English Stage: Corpus Christi Pageants and Plays.* Chicago: University of Chicago Press, 1974.

Nichols, Stephen G. "Why Material Philology? Some Thoughts." *Zeitschrift für deutscher Philologie* 116 (1997): 1–21.

Nichols, Stephen G., and Siegfried Wenzel, eds. *The Whole Book: Cultural Perspectives on the Medieval Miscellany.* Ann Arbor: University of Michigan Press, 1996.

Nolan, Maura B. *John Lydgate and the Making of Public Culture.* Cambridge: Cambridge University Press, 2005.

———. "The Performance of the Literary: Lydgate's Mummings." In *John Lydgate*, ed. Larry Scanlon and James Simpson, 169–206.

Normington, Katie. *Gender and Medieval Drama.* Woodbridge: D. S. Brewer, 2004.

Norton-Smith, John. *John Lydgate: Poems.* Oxford: Clarendon, 1966.

Nuttal, Jenni. *The Creation of Lancastrian Kingship: Literature, Language and Politics in Late Medieval England.* Cambridge: Cambridge University Press, 2007.

Ogden, Dunbar H. "Women Play Women in the Liturgical Drama of the Middle Ages." In *Shakespearean Illuminations: Essays in Honor of Marvin Rosenberg*, ed. Jay L. Halio and Hugh Richmond, 336–60. Newark: University of Delaware Press, 1998.

Oliver, Clementine. *Parliament and Political Pamphleteering in Fourteenth-Century England.* Woodbridge: York Medieval Press, 2010.

Osberg, Richard H. "The Goldsmiths' 'Chastell' of 1377." *Theatre Survey* 27 (1986): 1–15.

———. "The Jesse Tree in the 1432 London Entry of Henry VI: Messianic Kingship and the Rule of Justice." *JMEMS* 16 (1986): 213–32.

———. "The Lambeth Palace Library Manuscript Account of Henry VI's 1432 London Entry." *Mediaeval Studies* 52 (1990): 255–67.

Owst, G. R. *Literature and Pulpit in Medieval England: A Neglected Chapter in the History of English Letters and of the English People.* 2d rev. ed. Oxford: Basil Blackwell, 1961.

Palmer, Barbara. "Recycling 'The Wakefield Cycle': The Records." *Research Opportunities in Renaissance Drama* 1 (2002): 88–130.

————. "'Towneley Plays' or 'Wakefield Cycle' Revisited." *Comparative Drama* 21 (1988): 318–48.

Parker, David R. *The Commonplace Book in Tudor London: An Examination of BL MSS Egerton 1995, Harley 2252, Lansdowne 762, and Oxford Balliol College MS 354*. New York: University Press of America, 1998.

Parker, William. *The History of Long Melford*. London: Wyman and Sons, 1873.

Parry, P. H. "On the Continuity of English Civic Pageantry: A Study of John Lydgate and the Tudor Pageant." *Forum for Modern Language Studies* 15 (1979): 222–36.

Partridge, Steven, and Erik Kwakkel, eds. *Author, Reader, Book: Medieval Authorship in Theory and Practice*. Toronto: University of Toronto Press, 2012.

Patterson, Lee. "Making Identities in Fifteenth-Century England: Henry V and John Lydgate." In *New Historical Literary Study: Essays on Reproducing Texts, Representing History*, ed. Jeffrey N. Cox and Larry J. Reynolds, 69–107. Princeton, N.J.: Princeton University Press, 1993.

————. "'What Man Artow?': Authorial Self-Definition in *The Tale of Sir Thopas* and *The Tale of Melibee*." *Studies in the Age of Chaucer* 11 (1989): 117–75.

Paxton, James J., Lawrence M. Clopper, and Sylvia Tomasch, eds. *The Performance of Middle English Culture: Essays on Chaucer and the Drama*. Cambridge: D. S. Brewer, 1998.

Pearsall, Derek. *John Lydgate*. Medieval Authors: Poets of the Later Middle Ages. London: Routledge and Kegan Paul. Repr., Charlottesville: University Press of Virginia, 1970.

————. *John Lydgate (1371–1449): A Bio-Bibliography*. English Literary Studies 71. Victoria, B.C.: University of Victoria, 1997.

Pettitt, Thomas. "'Here Comes I, Jack Straw': English Folk Drama and Social Revolt." *Folklore* 95 (1984): 3–20.

Phythian-Adams, Charles. "Ceremony and the Citizen: The Communal Year at Coventry, 1450–1550." In *Crisis and Order in English Towns, 1500–1700*, ed. Peter Clark and Paul Slack, 57–85. Toronto: University of Toronto Press, 1972.

Puddephat, Wilfrid. "The Mural Paintings of the Dance of Death in the Guild Chapel of Stratford-upon-Avon." *Birmingham Archaeological Society Transactions* 76 (1960): 29–35.

Raby, F. J. E. *A History of Christian-Latin Poetry from the Beginnings to the Close of the Middle Ages*. Oxford: Clarendon, 1927.

Rastall, Richard. *Minstrels Playing*. Vol. 2 of *Music in Early English Religious Drama*. Cambridge: D. S. Brewer, 1996–2001.

Reddaway, T. F., and Lorna E. M. Walker. *The Early History of the Goldsmiths' Company, 1327–1509, Including the Book of Ordinances 1475–83*. London: Edward Arnold, 1975.

Reed, Marcia. "The Edible Monument." In *Food in the Arts: Proceedings of the Oxford Symposium on Food and Cooking 1998*, ed. Harlan Walker, 141–50. Devon, U.K.: Prospect Books, 1999.

Reill, Peter H. *The German Enlightenment and the Rise of Historicism*. Berkeley: University of California Press, 1975.

Renoir, Alain. *The Poetry of John Lydgate*. Cambridge, Mass.: Harvard University Press, 1967.

Richardson, Malcolm. "Henry V, the English Chancery, and Chancery English." *Speculum* 55 (1980): 726–50.

———. *Middle Class Writing in Medieval London*. London: Pickering & Chatto, 2011.

Riddy, Felicity. "Mother Knows Best: Reading Social Change in a Courtesy Text." *Speculum* 71 (1996): 66–86.

Robbins, Rossell Hope. "A Middle English Diatribe Against Philip of Burgundy." *Neophilologus* 39 (1955): 131–46.

Robbins, Rossell Hope, and John L. Cutler. *Supplement to the Index of Middle English Verse*. Lexington: University of Kentucky Press, 1965.

Robertson, Jean, and D. J. Gordon, eds. "A Calendar of Dramatic Records in the Books of the Livery Companies of London, 1485–1640." *Collections III*. London: Malone Society, 1954.

Rogerson, Margaret, ed. *The York Mystery Plays: Performance in the City*. Woodbridge: York Medieval Press, 2011.

Rosenthal, Joel T. *The Purchase of Paradise: Gift Giving and the Aristocracy, 1307–1485*. London: Routledge and Kegan Paul, 1972.

Rosser, Gervase. *Medieval Westminster, 1200–1540*. Oxford: Clarendon, 1989.

Rowe, B. J. H. "King Henry VI's Claim to France in Picture and Poem." *Library* 4th ser., 13 (1932–33): 77–88.

Rubin, Miri. *Corpus Christi: The Eucharist in Late Medieval Culture*. Cambridge: Cambridge University Press, 1991.

Runnalls, Graham. "Jean Fouquet's 'Martyrdom of St Apollonia' and the Medieval French Stage." *Medieval English Theatre* 19 (1997): 81–100.

Sacks, David Harris. *The Widening Gate: Bristol and the Atlantic Economy, 1450–1700*. Berkeley: University of California Press, 1991.

Salter, Elisabeth, and Helen Wicker, eds. *Vernacularity in England and Wales, c. 1300–1550*. Turnhout, Belgium: Brepols, 2011.

Saygin, Susanne. *Humphrey, Duke of Gloucester (1390–1447) and the Italian Humanists*. Leiden: Brill, 2002.

Scanlon, Larry. *Narrative, Authority and Power: The Medieval Exemplum and the Chaucerian Tradition*. Cambridge: Cambridge University Press, 1994.

Scanlon, Larry, and James Simpson, eds. *John Lydgate: Poetry, Culture and Lancastrian England*. Notre Dame, Ind.: University of Notre Dame Press, 2006.

Scase, Wendy. *Literature and Complaint in England, 1272–1553*. Oxford: Oxford University Press, 2007.

———. "'Strange and Wonderful Bills': Bill-Casting and Political Discourse in Late Medieval England." *New Medieval Literatures* 2 (1998): 225–47.

Scattergood, V. J. *Politics and Poetry in the Fifteenth Century*. London: Blandford, 1971.

Scattergood, V. J., and J. W. Sherborne, eds. *English Court Culture in the Later Middle Ages*. New York: St. Martin's, 1983.

Scherb, Victor I. *Staging Faith: East Anglian Drama in the Later Middle Ages*. Madison, N.J.: Fairleigh Dickinson University Press, 2001.

Schirmer, Walter F. *John Lydgate: A Study in the Culture of the XVth Century*. Trans. Ann E. Keep. London: Methuen, 1961.

Scully, Terence. *The Art of Cookery in the Middle Ages*. Woodbridge, U.K.: Boydell, 1995.

Seymour, M. C. *A Catalogue of Chaucer Manuscripts*. Vol. 1, *Works Before "The Canterbury Tales."* Aldershot: Scolar, 1995.

———. "Some Lydgate Manuscripts: *Lives of Edmund and Fremund* and *Danse Macabre*." *Edinburgh Bibliographical Society Transactions* 5, no. 4 (1983–85): 10–24.

Sheingorn, Pamela. "The Visual Language of Drama: Principles of Composition." In *Contexts for Early English Drama*, ed. Marianne G. Briscoe and John C. Coldewey, 173–91.

Simon, Eckehard. "Organizing and Staging Carnival Plays in Late Medieval Lübeck: A New Look at the Archival Record." *Journal of English and Germanic Philology* 92 (1993): 57–72.

———, ed. *The Theatre of Medieval Europe*. Cambridge: Cambridge University Press, 1991.

Simpson, James. "The Other Book of Troy: Guido dell Colonne's *Historia destructionis Troiae* in Fourteenth and Fifteenth-Century England." *Speculum* 73 (1998): 397–423.

———. *The Oxford English Literary History*. Vol. 2, *1350–1547: Reform and Cultural Revolution*. Oxford: Oxford University Press, 2002.

———. "The Rule of Medieval Imagination." In *Images, Idolatry, and Iconoclasm in Late Medieval England*, ed. Jeremy Dimock, James Simpson, and Nicolette Zeeman, 4–24. Oxford: Oxford University Press, 2002.

Smith, Bruce R. *The Acoustic World of Early Modern England: Attending to the O-Factor*. Chicago: University of Chicago Press, 1999.

Somerset, Fiona. *Clerical Discourse and Lay Audience in Late Medieval England*. Cambridge: Cambridge University Press, 1998.

Somerset, Fiona, and Nicholas Watson, eds. *The Vulgar Tongue: Medieval and Postmedieval Vernacularity*. University Park: Pennsylvania State University Press, 2003.

Sponsler, Claire. "Alien Nation: London's Aliens and Lydgate's Mummings for the Mercers and Goldsmiths." In *The Post-Colonial Middle Ages*, ed. Jeffrey J. Cohen, 229–42. New York: St. Martin's, 2001.

———. "Drama." In *Women and Gender in Medieval Europe: An Encyclopedia*, ed. Margaret Schaus, 232–34. New York: Routledge, 2006.

———. "Eating Lessons: Lydgate's 'Dietary' and Consumer Conduct." In *Medieval Conduct*, ed. Kathleen Ashley and Robert L. A. Clark, 1–22. Minneapolis: University of Minnesota Press, 2001.

———. "Lydgate and London's Public Culture." In *Lydgate Matters*, ed. Lisa Cooper and Andrea Denny-Brown, 13–33.

————. "Medieval Ethnography: Fieldwork in the European Past." *Assays: Critical Approaches to Medieval and Renaissance Texts* 7 (1992): 1–30.

————. "Text and Textiles: Lydgate's Tapestry Poems." In *Medieval Fabrications*, ed. E. Jane Burns, 19–34. New York: Palgrave Macmillan, 2004.

Stafford, Pauline. *Queens, Concubines, and Dowagers: The King's Wife in the Early Middle Ages*. Athens: University of Georgia Press, 1983.

Stanbury, Sarah. "Regimes of the Visual in Premodern England: Gaze, Body, and Chaucer's *Clerk's Tale*." *New Literary History* 28 (1997): 261–89.

————. "Vernacular Nostalgia and *The Cambridge History of Medieval English Literature*." *Texas Studies in Literature and Language* 44 (2002): 92–107.

————. *The Visual Object of Desire in Late Medieval England*. Philadelphia: University of Pennsylvania Press, 2008.

Starkey, David. "The Age of the Household: Politics, Society and the Arts c. 1350–c. 1550." In *The Later Middle Ages*, ed. Stephen Medcalf, 225–90. New York: Holmes & Meier, 1981.

Steiner, Emily. *Documentary Culture and the Making of Medieval English Literature*. Cambridge: Cambridge University Press, 2003.

Stern, Tiffany. *Documents of Performance in Early Modern England*. Cambridge: Cambridge University Press, 2009.

Stevens, Martin. "The Intertextuality of Medieval Art and Drama." *New Literary History* 22 (1991): 317–37.

Stevenson, Katie, ed. *The Herald in Late Medieval Europe*. Woodbridge, U.K.: Boydell and Brewer, 2009.

Streitberger, W. R. *Court Revels, 1485–1559*. Toronto: University of Toronto Press, 1994.

Strickland, Agnes. *Lives of the Queens of England from the Norman Conquest*. 8 vols. Philadelphia: J. B. Lippincott, 1893.

Strohm, Paul. "Chaucer's Fifteenth-Century Audience and the Narrowing of the 'Chaucer Tradition.'" *Studies in the Age of Chaucer* 4 (1982): 3–32.

————. *England's Empty Throne: Usurpation and the Language of Legitimation, 1399–1422*. New Haven, Conn.: Yale University Press, 1998.

————. *Hochon's Arrow: The Social Imagination of Fourteenth-Century Texts*, 95–119. Princeton, N.J.: Princeton University Press, 1992.

————, ed. *Middle English*. Oxford Twenty-First Century Approaches to Literature. Oxford: Oxford University Press, 2007.

————. "Sovereignty and Sewage." In *Lydgate Matters: Poetry and Material Culture in the Fifteenth Century*, ed. Lisa H. Cooper and Andrea Denny-Brown, 57–70. New York: Palgrave Macmillan, 2008.

————. *Theory and the Premodern Text*. Minneapolis: University of Minnesota Press, 2000.

Strutt, Joseph. *Honda Angel-cynnan or A Compleat View of the Manners, Customs, Arms, Habits, etc. of the Inhabitants of England*. 3 vols. London, 1775–76.

Stubbes, Estelle. "Clare Priory, the London Austin Friars and Manuscripts of the *Canterbury Tales*." In *Middle English Poetry: Texts and Traditions, Essays in Honour of Derek Pearsall*, ed. A. J. Minnis, 17–26. Woodbridge, U.K.: Boydell, 2001.

Summit, Jennifer. *Lost Property: The Woman Writer and English Literary History, 1380–1589*. Chicago: University of Chicago Press, 2000.

———. " 'Stable in Study': Lydgate's *Fall of Princes* and Duke Humphrey's Library." In *John Lydgate*, ed. Larry Scanlon and James Simpson, 207–31.

Sutton, Anne F. "Merchants, Music and Social Harmony: The London Puy and Its French and London Contexts, Circa 1300." *London Journal* 17 (1992): 1–17.

———. *The Mercery of London: Trade, Goods, and People, 1130–1578*. Aldershot: Ashgate, 2005.

———. "The *Tumbling Bear* and Its Patrons: A Venue for the London Puy and Mercery." In *London and Europe in the Later Middle Ages*, ed. Julia Boffey and Pamela King, 85–110. London: Centre for Medieval and Renaissance Studies, Queen Mary and Westfield College, University of London, 1995.

Sutton, Anne F., and Livia Visser-Fuchs. "The Provenance of the Manuscript: The Lives and Archive of Sir Thomas Cook and his Man of Affairs, John Vale." In *The Politics of Fifteenth-Century England: John Vale's Book*, ed. Margaret Lucille Kekewich, et al., 73–123. Stroud, U.K.: Alan Sutton, 1995.

Symes, Carol. "The Appearance of Early Vernacular Plays: Forms, Functions, and the Future of Medieval Theater." *Speculum* 77 (2002): 778–831.

———. *A Common Stage: Theater and Public Life in Medieval Arras*. Ithaca, N.Y.: Cornell University Press, 2007.

———. "The Medieval Archive and the History of Theatre: Assessing the Written and Unwritten Evidence for Premodern Performance." *Theatre Survey* 52 (2011): 1–30.

———. "Toward a New History of Medieval Theatre: Assessing the Written and Unwritten Evidence for Indigenous Performance Practices." Paper presented at the Société Internationale pour l'étude du Théâtre Médiéval, XIIe Congrès, Lille, France, 2–7 July 2007.

Tachau, Katherine H. *Vision and Certitude in the Age of Ockham: Optics, Epistemology, and the Foundations of Semantics, 1250–1345*. Leiden: Brill, 1988.

Tannahill, Reay. *Food in History*. New York: Stein and Day, 1973.

Taylor, Diana. *The Archive and the Repertoire: Performing Cultural Memory in the Americas*. Durham, N.C.: Duke University Press, 2003.

Thrupp, Sylvia L. "Aliens in and Around London in the Fifteenth Century." In *Studies in London History Presented to P. E. Jones*, ed. A. E. J. Hollaender and W. Kellaway, 251–72. London: Hodder and Stoughton, 1969.

———. *The Merchant Class of Medieval London, 1300–1500*. Chicago: University of Chicago Press, 1948.

———. "A Survey of the Alien Population of England in 1440." *Speculum* 32 (1957): 262–73.

Trapp, J. B. "Verses by Lydgate at Long Melford." *Review of English Studies* n.s. 6 (1955): 1–11.

Twycross, Meg, ed. *Festive Drama: Papers from the Sixth Triennial Colloquium of the International Society for the Study of Medieval Theatre, Lancaster, 13–19 July, 1989*. Cambridge: D. S. Brewer, 1996.

———. "Some Approaches to Dramatic Festivities, Especially Processions." In *Festive Drama*, ed. Meg Twycross, 1–33.

Twycross, Meg, and Sarah Carpenter. *Masks and Masking in Medieval and Early Tudor England*. Burlington, Vt.: Ashgate, 2002.

Unwin, George. *The Gilds and Companies of London*. London: Methuen, 1908.

Vale, Malcolm. *The Princely Court: Medieval Courts and Culture in North-West Europe, 1270–1380*. Oxford: Oxford University Press, 2001.

Vitz, Evelyn Birge, Nancy Freeman Regalado, and Marilyn Lawrence, eds. *Performing Medieval Narrative*. Cambridge: D. S. Brewer, 2005.

Wagner, Anthony Richard. *Heralds and Heraldry in the Middle Ages*. 2d ed. Oxford: Oxford University Press, 1956.

Wallace, David, ed. *The Cambridge History of Medieval English Literature*. Cambridge: Cambridge University Press, 1999.

———. "Chaucer and the Absent City." In *Chaucer's England: Literature in Historical Context*, ed. Barbara A. Hanawalt, 59–90. Minneapolis: University of Minnesota Press, 1992.

Warnicke, Retha M. "Henry VIII's Greeting of Anne of Cleves and Early Modern Court Protocol." *Albion* 28 (1996): 565–85.

Watson, Nicholas. "The Politics of Middle English Writing." In *The Idea of the Vernacular: An Anthology of Middle English Literary Theory, 1280–1520*, ed. Jocelyn Wogan-Browne, Nicholas Watson, Andrew Taylor, and Ruth Evans, 331–52. University Park: Pennsylvania State University Press, 1999.

Watts, John L. *Henry VI and the Politics of Kingship*. Cambridge: Cambridge University Press, 1996.

Weigert, Laura. "'Theatricality' in Tapestries and Mystery Plays and Its Afterlife in Painting." *Art History* 33 (2010): 24–35.

Weiss, Allen S. "Edible Architecture, Cannibal Architecture." In *Eating Culture*, ed. Ron Scapp and Brian Seitz, 161–68. Albany: State University of New York Press, 1998.

Weiss, Roberto. *Humanism in England During the Fifteenth Century*. 2d ed. Oxford: Blackwell, 1957.

Welsford, Enid. *The Court Masque: A Study in the Relationship Between Poetry and the Revels*. Cambridge: Cambridge University Press, 1927.

Werbner, Pnina. "Vernacular Cosmopolitanism." *Theory, Culture, and Society* 23, nos. 2–3 (2006): 496–98.

Westfall, Suzanne R. *Patrons and Performance: Early Tudor Household Revels*. Oxford: Clarendon, 1990.

White, Paul Whitfield. "Reforming Mysteries' End: A New Look at Protestant Intervention in English Provincial Drama." *JMEMS* 29 (1999): 121–48.

Wickham, Glynne. *Early English Stages, 1300 to 1600*. 3 vols. London: Routledge and Kegan Paul, 1981.

Wilkins, Nigel. "Music and Poetry at Court: England and France in the Late Middle Ages." In *English Court Culture in the Later Middle Ages*, ed. V. J. Scattergood and J. W. Sherborne, 183–204.

Wilson, Grace G. "'Amonges Othere Wordes Wyse': The Medieval Seneca and the *Canterbury Tales*." *Chaucer Review* 28 (1993): 135–45.

Wimsatt, James I. *Chaucer and His French Contemporaries: Natural Music in the Fourteenth Century*. Toronto: University of Toronto Press, 1991.

Winstead, Karen. *John Capgrave's Fifteenth Century*. Philadelphia: University of Pennsylvania Press, 2007.

Withington, Robert. *English Pageantry: An Historical Outline*. 2 vols. Cambridge, Mass.: Harvard University Press, 1918.

Wolffe, Bertram. *Henry VI*. London: Methuen, 1981.

Woolf, Rosemary. *The English Mystery Plays*. Berkeley: University of California Press, 1972.

Wylie, James H., and William T. Waugh. *The Reign of Henry the Fifth*. 3 vols. Cambridge: Cambridge University Press, 1914–29.

Young, Karl. *Drama of the Medieval Church*. 2 vols. Oxford: Clarendon, 1933.

Zeeman, Nicolette. "The Idol of the Text." In *Images, Idolatry, and Iconoclasm in Late Medieval England*, ed. Jeremy Dimock, James Simpson, and Nicolette Zeeman, 43–62. Oxford: Oxford University Press, 2002.

Zumthor, Paul. *Essai de poétique médiévale*. Paris: Seuil, 1972.

INDEX

Page numbers in boldface indicate figures and images.

ACKNOWLEDGMENTS

Much of the research for this book took place at library desks, under the circles of light cast by reading room lamps. That should not be surprising, given that for the drama of a period that long predates the existence of technologies that now make it possible to capture and preserve with some degree of verisimilitude the look and sound of live performances, the chief traces of plays, ceremonies, and other entertainments are to be found in written documents, housed in archives. It is by perusing those relatively rare play-scripts, even rarer eyewitness reports, and more plentiful even if typically indirect references to performances such as household accounts, legal records, and lists of expenditures that scholarship on premodern theater gets done. Even when supplemented by the occasional visual trace of early drama in sculpture, painting, stained glass, or woven textiles, we turn to these scattered, incomplete, and often enigmatic bits of written evidence to investigate medieval performances. A queen's dumbshows are something we can now experience only through the filter of play-texts and other written documents or, less frequently, visual or material objects.

Launched in libraries, this book is an attempt to reflect on the archival record of medieval drama and to consider what that record does and does not say about the repertoire of performances that were put on in the late fourteenth and fifteenth centuries in England. John Lydgate is at this study's center, for reasons that have been made clear throughout the book, since he throws into relief the key issues involved in any such inquiry.

Work on this book has benefited from the support, direct and indirect, of a number of people and institutions. Susan Crane set it in motion with an invitation to give a talk at Rutgers University, starting me on the research that would lead to Chapter 7, and the stimulating discussion by Rutgers faculty and graduate students at my talk helped shape my thinking at an early stage. Other chapters had their impetus in other invitations, including from Stephen Orgel and Peter Holland for a symposium at the Huntington, as well as from Jeffrey Jerome Cohen, Jane Burns, Lisa Cooper, and Andrea Denny-Brown for collections of essays. The support and encouragement of Russell Peck and Derek Brewer that led to an edition of Lydgate's mummings and entertainments for the Middle English Texts Series further paved the way for the present book. Additionally, and although they may not be aware of the extent of their influence, scholars responsible for recent reassessments of Lydgate and his impact have played a large behind-the-scenes role in this book; their names appear in the endnotes and elsewhere, and at every turn, their findings have helped shape my arguments, even in those cases where I do not reach the same conclusions as they do. In its conception, this book has been enriched by the energies of two separate but sometimes overlapping fields of scholarship: performance studies and medieval studies. Delivering my preliminary findings to audiences as different as those attending the American Society for Theatre Research, on one hand, and the International Medieval Congress at Western Michigan University, on the other, has made this a better book.

I would also like to thank the enormously helpful librarians and staff at the libraries and archives I visited, particularly at Trinity College, Cambridge; the Bodleian; the British Library; and the University of Iowa. A fellowship from the National Endowment for the Humanities got this book going, and travel and research support from the Department of English and the College of Liberal Arts and Sciences at the University of Iowa kept it on track. Finally, at the University of Pennsylvania Press, I am grateful for the perceptive comments of the two anonymous readers, the backing of Ruth Karras, and the warm guidance of Jerry Singerman as well as the help of other talented members of the Press.

Parts of this book have previously appeared in "Alien Nation: London's Aliens and Lydgate's Mummings for the Mercers and Goldsmiths," in *The Post-Colonial Middle Ages*, ed. Jeffrey J. Cohen (St. Martin's, 2001), 229–42; "Drama in the Archives: Recognizing Medieval Plays," in *Redefining British Theatre History*, ed. Stephen Orgel and Peter Holland (Palgrave Macmillan, 2005), 111–30; "Lydgate and London's Public Culture," in *Lydgate Matters*, ed. Lisa Cooper and Andrea Denny-Brown (Palgrave Macmillan, 2008), 13–33; and "Text and Textiles: Lydgate's Tapestry Poems," in *Medieval Fabrications*, ed. E. Jane Burns (Palgrave Macmillan, 2004), 19–34. Permission to use these materials is gratefully acknowledged.